Early Ireland

Early Ireland

An Introduction to Irish Prehistory

Michael J. O'Kelly

Prepared for the press by

Claire O'Kelly

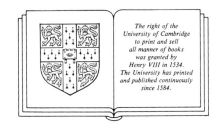

The right of the University of Cambridge to print and sell all manner of books was granted by Henry VIII in 1534. The University has printed and published continuously since 1584.

Cambridge University Press

Cambridge

New York   New Rochelle

Melbourne   Sydney

Published by the Press Syndicate of the University of Cambridge
The Pitt Building, Trumpington Street, Cambridge CB2 1RP
32 East 57th Street, New York, NY 10022, USA
10 Stamford Road, Oakleigh, Melbourne 3166, Australia

First published 1989

Printed in Great Britain
at the University Press, Cambridge

British Library cataloguing in publication data
O'Kelly, Michael J.
Early Ireland: an introduction to Irish prehistory.
1. Man, Prehistoric – Ireland
2. Ireland – Antiquities
I. Title
936.1'501   GN806.5

Library of Congress cataloguing in publication data
O'Kelly, Michael J.
Early Ireland.
Bibliography.
Includes index.
1. Man, Prehistoric – Ireland.
2. Ireland – Antiquities.
I. O'Kelly, Claire.   II. Title.
GN806.5.038 1987 936.1'5   87–10961

ISBN 0 521 33489 6 hard covers
ISBN 0 521 33687 2 paperback

Contents

8 Bronze Age burial

9 Bronze Age settlement and stone monuments

10 The Iron Age

11 Later prehistoric settlement

12 Iron Age burial

Illustrations

Bold numerals indicate photographs

vii

Preface

Professor Michael J. O'Kelly (known to his family and friends as Brian) was born in County Limerick in 1915. I first met him in the late thirties when he was a student of Seán P. Ó Ríordáin's in the Department of Archaeology at University College, Cork. When Ó Ríordáin moved in 1946 to the Chair of Archaeology in University College, Dublin, his old pupil and friend succeeded him in Cork, an appointment O'Kelly held with distinction until his retirement. He died suddenly in October 1982, the day before the Cork Historical and Archaeological Society was giving a special dinner to celebrate his retirement.

For nearly forty years Brian O'Kelly had worked in the field and in the academic world of Irish archaeology to its lasting benefit. He could never be described as an insular archaeologist. He travelled extensively outside Ireland, went to all the main international conferences, was internationally minded and saw the ancient Irish past in a wide European context. A brilliant and painstaking excavator, he worked on a wide variety of sites from the Late Stone Age to medieval times and was meticulous and prompt in publishing them. The extent and range of his interests and achievement is well reflected in his Festschrift, *Irish Antiquity*, published in 1981.

For fourteen years he excavated the great Neolithic burial mound of Newgrange in the Boyne Valley and was able to date its construction to before 3000 BC. In reviewing his *Newgrange: Archaeology, Art and Legend* (1982), Professor P. R. Giot wrote: 'O'Kelly was a man of the field, an expert excavator, an experimental archaeologist, not at all involved in pseudo-marxist, pseudo-freudian, or pseudo-structuralist interpretations. He was an archaeologist, not an ethno-archaeologist' (*Antiquity*, 57, 1983, 150).

In the preparation of his Newgrange book, as in all his work in the field and in the study, he was most ably helped by his wife Claire. They had been students together and theirs was a marriage of great happiness and scholarly co-operation. Mrs O'Kelly, an archaeologist in her own right, has made a special study of the monumental art of the Boyne tombs which is summarized in concise form in her invaluable *Illustrated Guide to Newgrange and the other Boyne Monuments* (1978).

For many years I and others had been urging Brian to write a general synthesis of Irish prehistory and he had in fact completed it in draft before his death. The manuscript has now been edited, referenced and fully updated by his wife. Claire O'Kelly has completed what Brian started, and it is a pleasure to write this prefatory note to a book which will take its place as the definitive work on Ireland in pre-Christian times for many years to come. It is a work of scholarly love and reflects the greatest credit on both.

Glyn Daniel

Acknowledgements

Since, sadly, the author of this book was unable to see it through to its final stages, acknowledgements will have to be confined to those who helped me to accomplish it in his stead. I must confess that there are very few archaeologists at present working in Ireland, as well as experts in related disciplines, to whom I did not have recourse at some stage or other, whether to read sections of the manuscript or to provide illustrations, information, advice, and so on. The list is a very long one and while I thank them with all my heart I can only single out those on whom the burden fell heaviest.

At University College, Cork, Rose Cleary, Robert Devoy, Mick Monk and Peter Woodman; at University College, Dublin, George Eogan and Barry Raftery; at University College, Galway, John Waddell; at the National Museum of Ireland, Mary Cahill; at the Office of Public Works, Dublin, Ann Lynch; at the Historical Monuments and Buildings Branch, DoE (NI), Chris Lynn; at the University of Pennsylvania, Bernard Wailes.

On what was for me the thorny question of how best to present and calibrate the radiocarbon dates I was extremely fortunate to have the expert guidance of Mike Baillie and Gordon Pearson of the Palaeoecology Centre, The Queen's University, Belfast, as well as that of Jan Lanting of the University of Groningen. In addition, Dr Pearson gave permission for the use of the Belfast 1985 radiocarbon timescale calibration curve, and Richard Warner of the Ulster Museum most kindly calibrated the radiocarbon dates used in the text.

Grateful thanks are due for permission to reproduce copyright photographs as follows (line drawings are acknowledged in the text as they occur): A. M. ApSimon 22; Cambridge University 158; Commissioners of Public Works, Ireland 48, 54, 55, 56, 123, 147; Crown Copyright (NI) 19, 72, 121, 149, 150, 162, 163, 164; G. Eogan 57, 58; Fairey Surveys of Ireland Ltd 68; H. Göransson 14; The Green Studio Ltd 38; C. T. Le Roux 51; The National Museum of Ireland 3, 17, 18, 77, 80, 84, 85, 86, 89, 91, 94, 96, 131, 139, 143, 144, 151, 169; W. O'Brien 75; B. Raftery 148; Shannon Development Authority 26, 154; L. Swan 24, 166; P. Woodman 7. Nos. 34, 42, 43, 46, 47, 50, 53, 63, 93, 99, 100, 110, 112–20, 127, 130 are by M. J. O'Kelly.

Finally I must express my gratitude to my friend, Glyn Daniel, for his constant support and help.

Claire O'Kelly

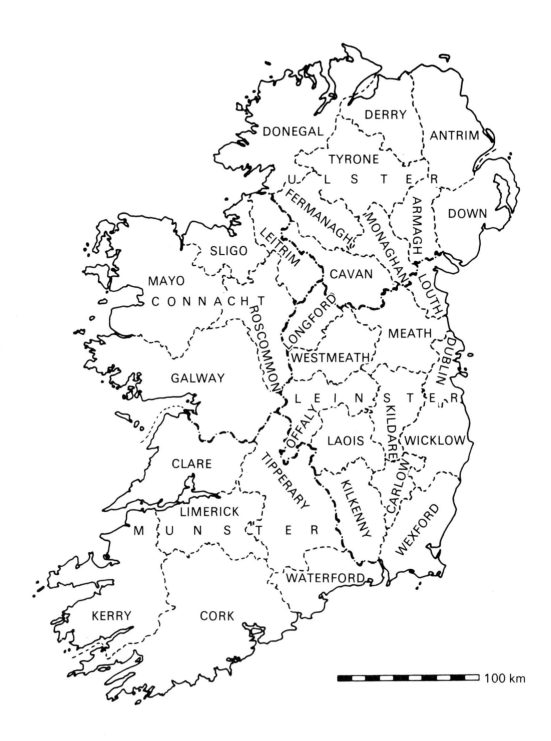

1 Map of Ireland showing provinces and counties

1

The Ice Age

The earliest part of the history of Ireland is the domain, not of the archaeologist, but of the geologist, the palaeobotanist and the palaeontologist who document respectively the structure and development of the earth's crust and the fossil remains of plants and animals contained in the various layers and deposits. Strictly speaking, the archaeologist has no function until the advent of man, but since environment is all-important to human life, it is necessary to look first at the conditions which shaped the land of Ireland before human presence was first recorded there.

In geological terms the present era is known as the Cainozoic and is divided into two periods, the Tertiary and the Quaternary. The latter consists of two epochs, the Pleistocene and the Holocene (or Recent). The Pleistocene broadly coincides with what is popularly known as the Great Ice Age. This affected the whole of northern Europe, Britain and Ireland included, and also North America, and in very general terms may be said to have begun about two million years ago or even earlier. A figure of 600,000 years ago has been proposed for the known formation of ice masses in Europe based on evidence from the land surface, and one of perhaps 250,000 years ago for the first indication of ice formation in Ireland. Man, so far as we know at present, did not inhabit Ireland until Postglacial times when the ice had melted but the presence of humans has been documented in Britain from about the middle of the Pleistocene Epoch.

The earth's history throughout the Great Ice Age was characterized by glacial and interglacial temperature oscillations. The ice advanced and retreated a number of times with varying intervals (interglacials) between. Each advance incorporated clays, muds, gravels and rocks within the moving ice and these were often transported for long distances and deposited where the ice melted. Later advances tended to destroy the deposits laid down by earlier ice so that the determination of the succession of glacial events is of great complexity. In Alpine Europe at least four major ice advances have been documented, named Güntz, Mindel, Riss and Würm, while in Northern Europe evidence has been obtained of three: Elster, Saale and Weichsel. A glacial succession has also been worked out for Britain and one for Ireland, although, as we shall see, the latter is by no means hard-and-fast. Each time the ice melted, warmth returned to the land, new vegetation spread over the ground and conditions were again favourable for animal and human life.

1

It must be realized that as the ice increased in amount over the land masses, more and more water was taken out of the seas and oceans and locked away so that sea levels were lowered and areas formerly under water became land. This is known as glacio-eustatic sea level change or movement. Shore lines were considerably altered and islands were joined to each other and to neighbouring continental land masses. As the weight of the ice on the land increased, the land was pressed down somewhat under it (glacio-isostatic movement), permitting the sea to return at least some of the way towards its old shorelines. When the ice melted, vast quantities of water were released, bringing about a rise of sea level, but the land, relieved of the weight of ice, also began to rise. The net relationship of land height to mean sea level is therefore a factor of the two effects; falling sea and sinking land as the ice increased and rising sea and rising land as the ice melted away. Efforts to establish the relationship of land height to sea level at any given time are complicated by the fact that the rising or sinking of the land was not uniform everywhere within a given area. Where the ice was especially thick and therefore very heavy, the land sank more, its surface under the ice becoming a basin-like hollow; and conversely, this area rose more, even developing a bulge, when the ice disappeared. This means that the movement in any particular place was frequently in the nature of a tilt. Another factor that must be taken into account is the possibility of tectonic activity, that is, independent movement of the earth's crust. The movements of land and sea in relation to one another have particular relevance for Ireland in the period following the retreat of the ice, the Postglacial Stage, because the earliest certain knowledge of human activity in this country dates from that time.

The various movements of the ice mass over the land surface of Ireland and over the Irish Sea have been the subject of specialized studies for more than a century, involving many disciplines. Unanimity of views is not to be expected and indeed the present-day burgeoning of new information has raised important questions about the validity of the conventional framework. The latter postulated two major ice advances in Ireland loosely corresponding to the last two advances in Britain and on the Continent. The earlier of the two was known as the Munsterian and the final one Midlandian. Evidence had also been tentatively put forward for a still earlier cold stage, the Connachtian, separated from the Munsterian in this scheme by the Gortian Warm Stage, so-called from the type-site in Co. Galway. A second and final interglacial or warm stage was postulated for the period between the Munsterian and the Midlandian Cold Stage, the latter lasting until about 10,000 years ago when the Postglacial Stage commenced.

The more recent view regards the available evidence of ice advance in Ireland as being indicative of only one major cold stage. This is based on the known stratigraphic evidence but does not dismiss the existence of ice sheets in Ireland during earlier Pleistocene time (Warren 1979; Devoy 1983). W. P. Warren

(1979, 327) asserts that on the basis of any stratigraphical approach the Gortian Warm Stage must represent, not a penultimate interglacial, but the final one, and he holds that most of the so-called Munsterian glacial deposits of the south of Ireland are in fact Midlandian in age and that only glacial deposits clearly earlier than the Gortian Warm Stage can be regarded as belonging to an earlier cold stage. These conclusions have been arrived at as a result of recent Quaternary research and studies of glacial geomorphology. For the student of archaeology, particularly of Irish archaeology, the broad general picture suffices because, as far as is known at present, there was no human presence in Ireland until the Post-glacial Stage.

In common with glaciated areas everywhere, Ireland first experienced a period of intense cold, following which ice caps developed on high peaks in Cork and Kerry in the south and south-west, in Donegal and Antrim in the north, and in Wicklow in the east. As conditions became more severe, glaciers began to move out from these areas and local glaciations developed which augmented the initial ones and coalesced with them. The eastern ice floes were joined by a great mass of ice which came thrusting down from Scotland by way of what is now the Irish Sea. The movement of this eastern ice has been traced as far west as Co. Cork. Fluctuations took place many times with ice masses forming and reducing.

During the less severe periods, animals entered Ireland and remains have been found in caves and lowland areas. One of these was the woolly mammoth, the remains of which have been found in counties Cork, Waterford and Antrim and also in Galway Bay. The reindeer, the Irish giant deer, the brown bear, the Irish hare and the spotted hyena were also present. The only known find of the latter from this country comes from Castlepook Cave in Co. Cork, excavated in the early part of this century. A mammoth bone from the same cave has been dated by radiocarbon determination (see p. 341) to 35,000 years ago (Mitchell 1976, 59).

It is believed that part of the south of Ireland remained unglaciated through-out, or certainly during the final stages of the Ice Age. This area consisted of a strip of country, or perhaps of a series of non-contiguous patches, lying between Waterford in the east and the Dingle peninsula in the west. If humans were in Ireland during the Pleistocene Epoch they should therefore be looked for here. Although it would have been too cold for humans to have survived in Ireland during the last cold period, the fact that Munster may not have been covered by ice could mean that traces of human occupation dating to the Palaeolithic or Old Stone Age may yet be found. Such sites are known in south-west Britain from just before and after the period when Britain and Ireland were last under ice.

One other effect of the glaciation, resulting from the rise and fall in relative mean sea levels, may be mentioned. This concerns a much-discussed erosion feature of the south and east coasts of Ireland. A remarkably level rock platform

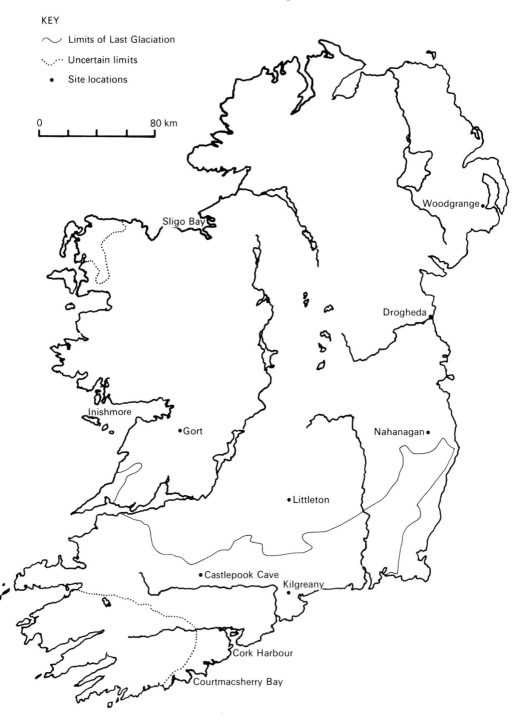

KEY

∿ Limits of Last Glaciation

⋯⋯ Uncertain limits

• Site locations

0   80 km

Woodgrange •

Sligo Bay

Drogheda •

Inishmore

• Gort

Nahanagan •

• Littleton

• Castlepook Cave

Kilgreany •

Cork Harbour

Courtmacsherry Bay

2 Limits of the last glaciation (after F. M. Synge). Glacial and postglacial sites

at about +5.2 ± 1 m Ordnance Datum (Belfast) occurs along the south coast (Devoy 1983), rising to between +9 to +20m ODB further north, the difference in present height being due to the land tilt mentioned above. It was first documented by Wright and Muff (1904). Its most notable exposure is to be seen at Courtmacsherry Bay in Co. Cork (Mitchell 1957, 33), where the top of an extensive rock outcrop has been planed off to a level surface by wave action at a time when mean sea level was higher than it is at present. At its landward end the rock is overlain by a layer of water-rolled pebbles covered by sand which in turn is covered by a great mass of boulder clay (till) deposited over it subsequently.

Palaeolithic man

The Ice Age was not a time of uniform glaciation, as has been shown, but was interspersed with less severe, and even warm, periods. Conditions at these times were suitable for plants and animals and it follows that they were also suitable for humans. Evidence of human activity in the form of assemblages of hand-axes of stone is available from Britain, dating from the penultimate interglacial in that country, that is, the Hoxnian. Its age is estimated at 200,000 to 250,000 years ago, and from then on, various Middle and Upper Palaeolithic sites have continued the story of Old Stone Age occupation in Britain. There is no evidence of this in Ireland at present.

Finds of supposed implements from a number of areas have been claimed to be of Palaeolithic date, but none of these finds is convincing and none of them is now accepted as evidence of the presence of Palaeolithic man here. We may mention a collection of objects from three sites around Sligo Bay in the north-west of Ireland – Coney Island, Rosses Point and Ballyconnell – which it was suggested showed features of the European Levallois flake-technique. The objects are from shore sites and though they are made from soft limestone, they are fresh and unrolled despite the fact that this coast is exposed to the force of the Atlantic wave action. Even if the pieces had not been accessible to the waves but had merely lain in the ground from Old Stone Age times, their surface characters would have been reduced by solution of the stone itself. They are either of recent natural origin, or if man-made, must be the result of some modern activity of fishermen or others in the area (Movius 1942, 105–14).

More serious were the claims made by E. K. Tratman (1928), leader of the Bristol Spelaeological Society's excavation in the Kilgreany cave, near Cappagh, Co. Waterford, a site which lies beyond the limit of the last ice advance. Here, 'Kilgreany B', the lower of two skeletons found in a horizon which also contained the bones of extinct fauna – Irish giant deer, for instance – was considered to be that of an Upper Palaeolithic man. At a higher level in the deposit, a female skeleton, 'Kilgreany A', had been found. When subsequently the remainder of the cave deposit was excavated by the Harvard Archaeological Expedition to Ireland, Hallam Movius (1935) showed that the whole of the deposit had suffered disturbance. Bones of domestic ox and sheep occurred in the same layers as the remains of extinct mammals; modern objects of iron, glass and pottery were associated with the bones of Late Glacial fauna; charcoal from a hearth in the same horizon as the 'Kilgreany B' skeleton was Postglacial, yielding oak, ash and hazel. Neolithic or New Stone Age pottery sherds, an amber bead probably of Bronze Age date and an Early Christian Period ornament were also found in the cave, while not a single artefact that could be considered to be of Old Stone Age date or type was found in the cave or adjacent thereto. Finally, the anthropometric data of the human skeletons do not place them within the range of known Upper Palaeolithic types. Radiocarbon dates have since confirmed that the skeletons belong to a later period, the Neolithic. The 'A' skeleton has been dated to 4580 ± 150 BP* and a slightly earlier date was obtained for the other.

In recent times G. F. Mitchell picked up a flint flake from a gravel deposit in a quarry near Drogheda, Co. Louth, on the east coast of Ireland. It was a waste piece resulting from the knapping (deliberate breaking-up) of a flint nodule. Mitchell diagnosed the gravel deposit as being of Irish Sea origin. During the glacial period when ice was moving southward from Scotland along what is now the Irish Sea, the flake was picked up with stones and gravel and was eventually washed out of the melting ice on to the Irish coast. The flake suggests that Old Stone Age hunters were at one time in what is now the basin of the Irish Sea. Palaeolithic flint experts are satisfied that the flake was struck by a technique in use in Britain during Palaeolithic times (Mitchell and Sieveking 1972). If this is indeed the case, it shows how near to Ireland Palaeolithic Man came and in fact provokes the question, why not *to* Ireland?

In 1974, a visitor to Inishmore, the largest of the islands of Aran in Galway Bay, found a small flint hand-axe amongst the stones of the *chevaux de frise* (a defence network of upright stones) that surrounds the great stone fort of Dún Aenghus. Experts accept that the axe is of Acheulian/Mousterian type, that is, Middle to Upper Palaeolithic, but its authenticity as an Irish artefact is highly suspect (Murphy 1977).

Late Glacial and Postglacial stages

About 14,000 years ago the global climate changed and the ice sheets began to retreat northwards with consequent amelioration of the previous cold conditions. Temperatures rapidly became warmer so that there was an expansion of the vegetation already present and an immigration of new species of both flora and

---

* For explanation of the convention used in quoting radiocarbon (^{14}C) dates see Appendix A. For laboratory name and sample number see Appendix D.

fauna. The first part of the Late Glacial Stage is therefore an interstadial episode in the cycle of glaciation and it was followed by a sharp return to cold conditions.

In the Postglacial Stage which commenced about 10,300 years ago the climate again began to improve and thus began the present 'warm stage' in which we now live. Mitchell (1976, 35) observes that there is no reason to think that this 'relatively genial climate of today is any more firmly established than that of previous transient "warm stages" . . . [and] will in all probability be succeeded in due course by yet another "cold stage" '.

Palaeobotanists have divided the Late Glacial and Postglacial Stages into a number of zones differentiated according to the plant pollen trapped in muds and lake beds. Pollen analysis (p. 345) enables the vegetational history of a particular area to be reconstructed and from this, temperature and other environmental conditions can be estimated. When these results are correlated with those from other areas, an overall picture of the prevailing environment can be gained. While not necessarily accurate in detail, it is adequate in very broad outline. The advent of radiocarbon dating (p. 341) has enabled the zonation to be placed within a chronological framework. The zonation scheme given below for Ireland is that of Jessen (1949), modified in the later stages by Mitchell (1951). Provided it is accepted that it is valid only within broad parameters and that only very major episodes are represented, the scheme gives a valuable vegetational, environmental and climatic record.

Pollen zones

The effect of the Late Glacial amelioration of climate can be seen in pollen Zones I and II and is documented in Ireland by a number of pollen diagrams, in particular one from Woodgrange, Co. Down; hence the name Woodgrange Interstadial or Warm Phase which has been applied to the period in question. Plant remains were scanty at first, consisting mainly of alpine-arctic types and northern grasses, some of which had probably persisted throughout part at least of the final glaciation. With the rise in temperature, this vegetation burgeoned and there was considerable immigration of new species. Sub-arctic plants, grasses, herbs and flowers such as the gentian and the mountain avens grew in open places, while stands of dwarf birch and juniper shrubs were established. There was immigration of animals also, the most notable being the Irish giant deer, formerly but erroneously known as the 'Irish Elk'. The richness of the vegetation would have provided ample sustenance for this species and also for reindeer. Remains of the giant deer have been found at some two hundred locations in Ireland (Mitchell 1969, 24), all in Zone II muds. There are some twenty records of reindeer but no other mammals have been recorded from Irish Late Glacial deposits.

About 10,500 or 11,000 years before the present (BP) a period of severe cold

Table 1 *Pollen Zones and vegetation changes in Ireland in Late and Postglacial times*

Approx. years BP	Pollen Zones	Characteristic vegetation	Archaeological periods
. . . 1500			
Sub-atlantic	VIIIb	Oak receding Development of secondary woodland Pine declines	Iron
. . . 3500			
Sub-boreal	VIIIa	Elm declines Oak rises to a maximum	Bronze
. . . 5200			
Atlantic	VII	Pine falling Mixed woodland of oak, elm and a preponderance of alder	Neolithic
. . . 7500			
Boreal	V and VI	Expansion of hazel Growth of pine, oak and elm	Mesolithic
. . . 9600			
Pre-boreal	IV	Scrub and bushes Birch, willow, poplar and juniper	
. . . 10,300			
Late glacial 14,000	I, II and III	Park tundra Alpine-arctic	

Postglacial (bracket spanning from Pre-boreal up through Sub-atlantic)

Source: after G. F. Mitchell 1965

and tundra-like conditions returned, known as the Nahanagan Stadial or Cold Phase after the site in Co. Wicklow where it was first documented. The climate must then have resembled that of northern Siberia today. Pollens of Zone III show that plants of more northern type had appeared and that woodland was reduced. Ice probably increased in mountain areas and the relative sea level, which had risen during the interstadial stage, was once again lowered. Areas of land would have been exposed off the coasts and, according to some authorities, land bridges may have existed between Ireland and Britain during this time. This is a matter of continuing controversy and some scholars hold that in all probability no firm land connections existed after about 20,000 years ago (Devoy 1983). The resolution of this question would have important implications for the immigration of humans to Ireland.

Zone IV, c. 10,300 BP, the Pre-boreal Phase, signals the beginning of the Post-glacial amelioration of climate that has continued ever since, known as the Littletonian Warm Stage after the bog site in Co. Tipperary (Mitchell 1965; 1965a) which produced one of the best early pollen sequences for vegetation changes in the Postglacial. A marked modification of the environment was observed in the pollen diagrams. Open tundra gradually gave place to woodland of birch, willow, poplar and juniper. Peat began to form in places as swamp growth increased. In Zones V and VI, *c.*9,600 BP, the Boreal Phase, birch was

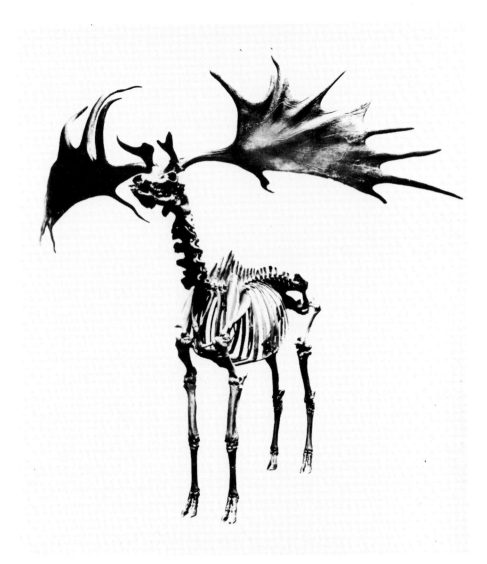

3 Giant Irish deer (*Megaceros giganteus*)

9

still present in the earlier part but hazel began to expand greatly. The lowlands and lower mountain slopes became covered in woodland and the heathlands seem to have disappeared. Pine also became prominent and while hazel continued to increase at the expense of birch, the oak and the elm made their appearance. The climate was relatively dry and not unlike that of the present day, although perhaps less stormy because forest was able to spread right down to the western coastline. Relative sea level was rising throughout this period and if land connections with Britain had previously existed, they would now have been severed. It is known that man was in Ireland at this time but whether he arrived dry-shod or in open boats is a question not yet resolved.

Towards the end of the Boreal Phase the sea had begun to invade the low-lying coasts of the North Sea and the Irish Sea and the northern coast of Ireland was also affected. This process continued during Zone VII, c. 7500 BP, the Atlantic Phase, and the maximum rate of sea level rise was attained, i.e. the Maximum Transgression. At this maximum a shore-line was formed, but subsequently the land again rose, lifting this shore-line to an average height of *c.*7.6m above present sea level in parts of the north-eastern corner of Ireland. Further south, because this land movement was part of the tilt mentioned previously (p. 2), the old shore-line was lower and nearer to that of the present day. Where the shore-line has been raised above present sea level it is known as a 'raised beach' and it is a feature of special interest in the north-east of Ireland because much of the evidence of Mesolithic or Middle Stone Age Man is associated with it. As the north-east was rising, the south may have either remained stable or else undergone some subsidence. Robert Devoy (1983) has shown that in the Cork Harbour area the sea level at *c.*8000 BP was only about 15m lower than at present. Furthermore, there are indications that in parts of west Cork and Kerry the land may have risen slightly. This improves the chances of finding Mesolithic activity in these areas. As against this, however, it has been pointed out that erosion may have had greater effect on the unconsolidated deposits of the Cork and Waterford coasts than submergence, thus providing a negative factor in regard to the finding of archaeological remains. In the course of the Atlantic Phase, the climate, though still relatively dry, is thought to have become more humid and oceanic and a temperature a few degrees higher than the present-day one was attained, the so-called 'climatic optimum' of the Postglacial Stage. The forest was by now a mixed one of oak, elm and a marked preponderance of alder. Raised peat bogs also began to form.

During the transition between the Atlantic and the Sub-boreal Phases relative sea level reached its maximum. Since the eustatic and isostatic movements were not uniform throughout Ireland, the maximum transgression has no fixed date but in general it may have occurred as early as 6000 BP along parts of the northern coast and as late as 5000 BP farther south towards Dublin Bay on the east coast. The transition phase between the zones was also marked by the sharp decline of elm (p. 33).

Towards the end of the phase, between 4000 and 1500 BP, pine virtually disappeared, allowing oak to become the dominant species with alder, hazel, holly and ivy also prominent. Through time, there was thus a decline in forest and an increase in herbaceous plants and this is generally associated with woodland clearance and agriculture. In addition, blanket bog began to invade the former woodland areas in places.

Zone VIIIb, *c.*3500 BP, the Sub-atlantic Phase, is placed by Mitchell at the point where oak begins sharply to decline and this has been linked with clearance and cultivation of the heavier soils. Throughout the whole of Zone VIII the impact of humans on the landscape and environment can be seen in the pollen record. Secondary woodland of elm and ash develops and new species of weeds appear. In archaeological terms Zone VIIIa spans the Neolithic Period and part of the Bronze Age while Zone VIIIb embraces the remainder of the Bronze Age and the whole of the Early Iron Age.

The pollen zonation outlined above is no more than a schematic system which is constantly under review and its value to the archaeologist is that it provides a framework within which the activities of humans as revealed by archaeological excavation and research can be related to the prevailing environment. Similar schemes are used in Britain and in European countries and though not comparable in many respects with the Irish zonation system, the terminology remains more or less the same.

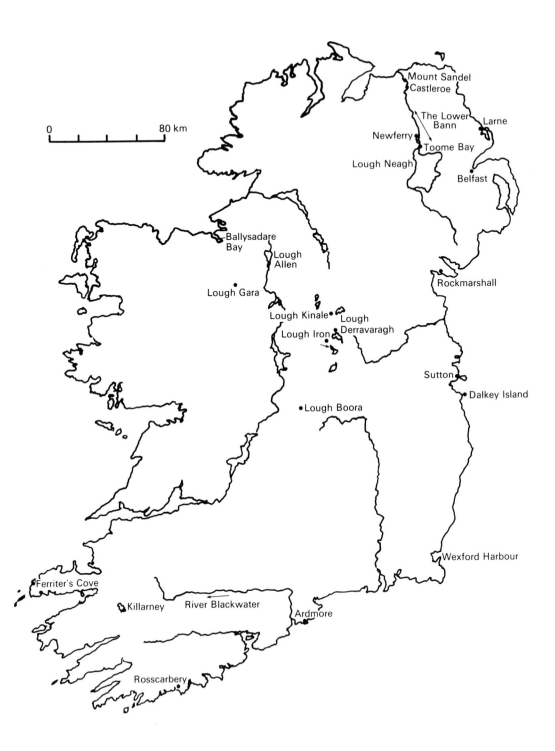

Scale: 0 — 80 km

Mount Sandel
Castleroe
The Lower Bann
Newferry
Toome Bay
Lough Neagh
Larne
Belfast
Ballysadare Bay
Lough Allen
Lough Gara
Rockmarshall
Lough Kinale
Lough Derravaragh
Lough Iron
Sutton
Dalkey Island
Lough Boora
Wexford Harbour
Ferriter's Cove
Killarney
River Blackwater
Ardmore
Rosscarbery

4 Mesolithic sites

12

2
The Mesolithic period

The Mesolithic or Middle Stone Age is the name given to the period between the Palaeolithic and the Neolithic or New Stone Age and it has special significance for Ireland because it marks the first evidence of the presence of humans. This occurred in the Boreal Phase, a time during which, as outlined previously, the land was covered by trees, in the early stages by pine and birch and later by deciduous species. At first, relative land and sea levels were lower than at present, the sea more so than the land. Large mammals such as wild cattle, roe deer and elk were absent but smaller ones such as wild pig and mountain hare were present. Fish and birds were plentiful, there were rivers and streams and lakes to be fished and there were the abundant marine resources. All in all, Ireland must have provided a very suitable habitat for humans whose way of life involved food gathering and hunting. Farming practices were unknown to the first inhabitants. Their tools would have been fabricated from stone, wood, bone, antler and possibly shell, but unless the conditions were specifically favourable to their preservation none other than the stone implements would survive. For this reason, flint is the substance which provides the chief evidence for Mesolithic activity. It is a very hard but brittle type of siliceous stone, varying in colour from grey to brown or amber, and is found in chalk deposits either as layers or as nodules. In the latter form it is plentiful in north-east Ireland where, due to erosion of the chalk, it lies on the surface as scattered nodules, particularly near cliffs and sea shores. These nodules provided the raw material for flint artefacts. Flint breaks with a conchoidal (shell-like) fracture leaving extremely sharp edges and thus its usefulness to primitive people, even without any further shaping of the broken pieces, is obvious. Various techniques were employed to produce exactly the type of tool required, but the basic objective was to cause the flint to fracture in such a way as to approximate as closely as possible to the type of tool desired. A suitable flattish surface was selected on the piece of flint and a sharp blow was directed downward on to this surface (the striking platform) so that a flake or blade became detached. The fracture property of flint is such that a swelling or bulb of percussion can be seen on the struck flake and a corresponding hollow or flake scar on the parent lump or core. The angle of the blow determined the shape and size of the flake. The blow could be delivered directly by the use of a hammerstone (direct percussion) or a piece of bone or wood could be interposed as a punch between the hammerstone and the flint (indirect per-

13

cussion). A good deal of skill and a good deal of empirical knowledge of the fracture properties of flint must have been possessed by the knappers.

Core axes were produced by striking off flakes all around the parent core so that a narrow cylinder-shaped piece of flint remained and this was rendered sharp by striking off one or two flakes transversely from one end. It could then be used as a chopping tool. Flake axes were made by striking large flakes from a prepared core so that they would have a robust straight edge. The axe was then shaped round this edge. Blades were made by striking parallel-sided flakes and these were retouched as required. In the manufacture of the implements numerous pieces were discarded. It is estimated that for every implement produced, it is probable that up to a hundred waste flakes (debitage) resulted.

According to geologists, most if not all of Ireland was once covered by a layer of chalk. It has been weathered away from all of the country except for the north-east corner where it is protected by an out-flow of the weather-resistant igneous rock, basalt. One tiny remnant of the chalk cover has been found near Killarney, Co. Kerry, and off-shore drilling has indicated its presence under the sea. Apart from the north-east, therefore, and except for the flint nodules spread by the ice and found in the boulder clay or till here and there, the rest of Ireland has no source of good flint.

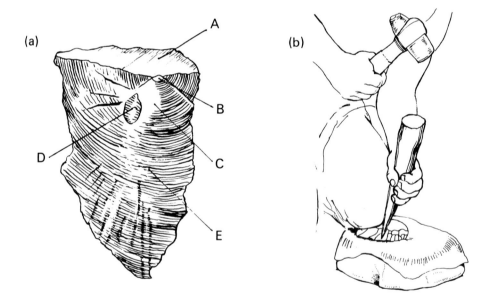

5 Flint techniques: (a) flint flake showing: A striking platform, B point of percussion, C bulb of percussion, D bulbar scar, E ripples; (b) flint flake showing indirect percussion with hammer and bone chisel or point

Until relatively recently the idea was firmly established that Mesolithic activity was confined to the north-east, partly due to its geographical proximity to Britain at this particular point but mainly because of the availability of good quality flint. For well over a hundred years, beginning about AD 1850, antiquarians and others had been building up collections of worked flints, that is, flint that had been modified by the hand of man, from the coastal raised beaches of north-eastern Ireland and from various inland sites in the neighbourhood of Lough Neagh and the valley of the Lower River Bann where the worked flint had been utilized by fishing and food-gathering communities. It was assumed that Mesolithic people were tied to the areas where flint was either readily accessible or was within a reasonable distance.

It was only natural that when the Harvard Archaeological Expedition came to Ireland in 1932 to conduct research, its study of the Mesolithic was concentrated in this area. Hallam Movius conducted excavations at five sites, four around the coast and one inland in the Lower Bann valley. The great drawback of these extremely valuable researches was that most of the material came from secondary, unstratified positions and in these circumstances it was difficult to relate any one site to another, or to obtain any visible chronological succession. Nevertheless, Movius imposed order of a kind on the enormous assemblages of flints recovered by him and he endeavoured to identify an early and a later phase of the Irish Mesolithic.

One of the sites investigated was at Larne, Co. Antrim, near the southern end of a gravel spit known as the Curran. He dug a pit 5m square and over 8m in depth and from it he recovered over 15,000 pieces of humanly worked flint. Unfortunately, very few were finished implements. It was clearly an industrial site, that is, a place where the preliminary trimming or knapping of the flint was carried out. It was the largest series hitherto obtained from an Irish Mesolithic site and because of this he used the name 'Larnian' as a general term for the whole Mesolithic culture of Ireland (Movius 1953). He postulated an Early Larnian period which, he argued, was to be found in Scotland also (because of his belief that there had been direct land connections at that time between the two shores), and a Late Larnian which developed along lines peculiar to Ireland. Until comparatively recently the chronology proposed by Movius was the generally accepted one, but post-war studies by G. F. Mitchell and P. C. Woodman among others were to extend the boundaries to which the Irish Mesolithic had hitherto been confined. With the advent of radiocarbon measurement in the 1950s, possibilities for more precise dating of material became available. In 1951 Mitchell carried out a small-scale excavation of one of the sand bars at Toome Bay on the shore of Lough Neagh in Co. Derry (Mitchell 1955). Charcoal from a hearth was radiocarbon-dated to 7680 ± 110 BP.* Some scrappy pieces of flint and some

---

* Not in calibration table. Lab. no. Y-95.

worked wood were found but in the main, the archaeological content was very small. For long this was the earliest ^{14}C date available for the Irish Mesolithic.

It is now known that people were present in Ireland at least a thousand years before that date. A distinct Early Mesolithic peculiar to Ireland has been identified which, on present evidence, lasted until about 8000 BP. The period that coincides with the Early and Late Larnian of Movius is now known as the Later Mesolithic and on present evidence dates from *c*.7500 BP to *c*.5500–5200 BP. The term 'Larnian', if it is to be used, signifies a flint industry and not a culture. It is salutary to reflect that several generations of archaeologists – and not only Irish ones – were, to put it colloquially, 'brought up on Movius' as far as the Irish Mesolithic was concerned, and yet, in little more than a decade, the changes that have taken place amount to something in the nature of a revolution. As Peter Woodman, one of the pioneers of this revolution, has written: 'A millennium or more has been added to Ireland's prehistory and, not least, mean-ingful assemblages of artifacts can now take the place of the wave-rolled flints that for so long represented almost the totality of early Irish material culture' (Woodman 1981, 132).

The 'wave-rolled flints' are a reference to the assemblages encountered in the coastal areas of the north-east during earlier investigations. In Chapter 1 some of the physical changes attendant upon the retreat of the ice were touched upon, and these had important implications for the first inhabitants, particularly in coastal areas. From about 9000 BP, sea-level was rising and continued to do so until it reached its maximum transgression on the land. Man must have been living on the extensive areas that were flooded, but if he noticed the rising sea at all at first, he would perhaps have remarked upon the way in which the full tide seemed to be coming a little farther in than before, and when storms blew up, he might have noticed that the shingle at the head of the beach was being flung a little farther inland. But it is doubtful if the people of any single generation noticed any appreciable encroachment of the sea upon the land for it was a complex and long-drawn-out affair, spread over several thousand years until eventually the point of maximum transgression was reached.

It will be appreciated that as the sea transgressed more and more upon the land, those areas that had been occupied for generations became gradually sub-merged in the water. The waves rolling inward tore up what had been the land surface and destroyed most of the evidence that would have been so valuable to present-day researchers. The postholes of the houses or the ring of stones which might have weighted down the hide covering of the tent-like huts, the layers of ash and charcoal that ordinarily would have represented the domestic hearths or cooking places, were all washed away, and with them the debris of living such as food waste in the form of animal and fish bones. Artefacts in wood, bone, antler, flint and stone, lost or dropped in or around the living quarters, were carried about by the waves and longshore currents until, in time of storm, they were flung with the shingle and sand onto the storm beach at the head of the strand. In due time this storm beach may have again been torn up and flung still further inland as the sea advanced. None except the most indestructible materials could survive such violent rolling about. It is only the flint and stone objects that have survived and these are usually of substantial size. No small artefacts such as those which characterize the Early Mesolithic survived the action of the waves. The pieces which were found in such quantities on the raised beaches were frequently found to be abraded and worn and have most of their cutting edges, arrises and identifying features rounded off. If microliths were in use during this time, they were washed away. The larger flint implements are found in numbers in the beaches formed at the point of maximum transgression of the sea, but all other kinds of evidence are lost to us.

We have already noted that gradually the land rose again so that the shoreline which had been formed at the point of maximum transgression was lifted well above the sea, in places to a height of 7.6m or more above the water in the north-east corner of Ireland. This old shoreline, or raised beach, can be identified from Wexford Harbour on the east coast, around the north coast to Sligo in the north-west. The south of Ireland suffered a submergence but present-day thinking (p. 10) does not regard it as having been as drastic or as uniform as earlier believed. Nevertheless, at times of exceptionally low tide, one can sometimes see the landward end of peat deposits which were formed before the 'tilt' of the land caused them to be submerged. These undersea peats can be seen along the south coast from Ardmore, Co. Waterford, to Rosscarbery in west Cork. The presence of submerged peats has been established at other points around the coast as well (Mitchell 1976, 64).

Who were these Mesolithic people and where did they come from in the first place? A number of answers to these questions have been offered but none is really acceptable and we must admit that we do not know who they were, where they came from or what they looked like. A badly broken male skull was found at Castle Market, Belfast, in a stratum of estuarine clay which may have formed during the later part of the Atlantic Phase, but the evidence in general is unsatisfactory. The theory that Ireland was directly colonized from the nearest land mass, Scotland, is no longer accepted unquestioningly (Woodman 1978, 208). A site at Lough Boora in Co. Offaly and the recent finds of microliths in the valley of the Blackwater in Co. Cork show that Early Mesolithic people were more widely dispersed throughout Ireland than was formerly thought.

From Woodman's study of material from a site at Mount Sandel (Upper) in Co. Derry (p. 19) it was clear that while it provided some of the earliest evidence of occupation so far discovered through excavation, it did not represent the initial colonization. He says that there is 'sufficient evidence to show that a significant, though unknown, period may have elapsed between the initial colonization and the use of the Mount Sandel site' (Woodman 1985, p. 166). The implication of this is that the antiquity of man in Ireland must be extended by a further unknown span of time but it does little to answer the perennial question regarding the method by which the earliest people entered the country, whether they came dry-shod across land connections or by boat. Present studies would seem to favour the latter and the matter is well discussed in Woodman 1981.

Because the evidence of Mesolithic man in Ireland is virtually confined to the surviving flint work, we have as yet only a meagre picture of his way of life. The soil of the north-east is acid and therefore bone does not survive unless, as was the case at Mount Sandel and Lough Boora, it was burnt and calcined from having been thrown into the domestic hearths. On the coastal sites what was not

6 Distribution map of Mesolithic sites and find spots (after P. Woodman)

destroyed by the waves was dissolved by the soil acidity. Woodman's study of the flint work has led him to say that:

> One of the most striking aspects of the Irish Mesolithic is its insularity . . . the range of equipment which at the beginning of the Mesolithic period resembles that found through the rest of Europe, gradually settles to a distinctive tradition which cannot be found elsewhere other than possibly on the neighbouring island of Man. This lack of contact in the form of new implements is the most striking aspect of the typology of the Mesolithic and would suggest rather surprisingly that there was in the Later Mesolithic no obvious contact between Ireland and even the parts of Scotland quite close at hand. (Woodman 1978, 211)

Early Mesolithic

Eight or nine sites are now known to contain Early Mesolithic assemblages. Several are present in the neighbourhood of Lough Neagh and in the Lower Bann Valley and a few are known from disturbed contexts on the north-east coast, while scatters of stone tools which could be equally early have also been found in the south of the country. Radiocarbon dates have been obtained for four sites, three in the Bann Valley and one in the centre of Ireland. These are: Mount Sandel (Upper), Mount Sandel (Lower), Castleroe and Lough Boora. An even earlier date than any of these has been obtained from a test excavation at Wood-park near Ballysadare Bay in Co. Sligo (Burenhult 1984, 64) but Woodman (1985, 169) is of the opinion that while 'this date could indicate an even earlier Mesolithic than at Mount Sandel', not only is there an insufficiency of diagnostic artefacts but there is also 'a strong possibility that the ^{14}C date came from a piece of very old wood washed up on the Littorina shoreline' (*ibid.*). Further work is needed in this neighbourhood before definite conclusions can be drawn.

The Mount Sandel area, a short distance south of Coleraine on the east side of the broad flat-floored valley of the River Bann, had long been known to the amateur flint collectors. The archaeologists had taken note of the fact that the tools found there differed from those collected in their thousands along the north-east coast, which were mostly large flint blades. Mount Sandel (Upper) is on the top of a ridge which falls steeply to the valley floor and had for long been under cultivation, hence the chance finds. These were smaller than average, consisting of tiny shaped pieces of flint (or sometimes chert) known as microliths. Small flake axes had also been found. Microliths were virtually unknown in the flint assemblages hitherto regarded as representing the Irish Mesolithic.

In 1977 Peter Woodman was given the opportunity of carrying out excavation at Mount Sandel in advance of a proposed housing development. He expected that little would emerge on account of the extensive ploughing that had taken

7 Lower River Bann near Coleraine, Co. Derry. Mount Sandel marked by arrow

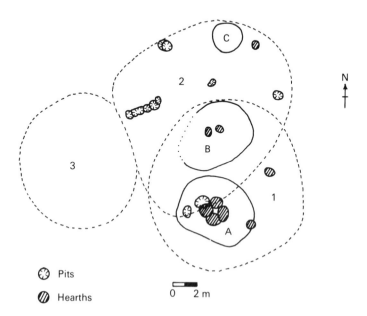

8 Mount Sandel Upper, Co. Derry, activity areas 1–3; A–C huts (after P. Woodman)

place over the years but felt, nevertheless, that at least it might be possible to find some explanation for the presence of microliths at this location in contrast to the larger-blade implements found elsewhere. The results, to say the least, were more than he had bargained for, and the excavation took ten times as long as the initial estimate (Woodman 1985).

He found that, while there had been extensive occupation of the area in Mesolithic times, it had been ploughed away over the years, but fortunately a small part had remained intact, the occupation layer being protected due to the fact that it lay in a hollow. The latter was natural but had been artificially enlarged and several roughly circular huts had been constructed within it (though not contemporaneously). Saplings had been thrust into the ground in a circle and presumably bent over and tied at the top. No internal supports were used. The huts were about 6m in diameter and each had a central hearth. Other huts had also existed but since they were not protected by being in the hollow, they had

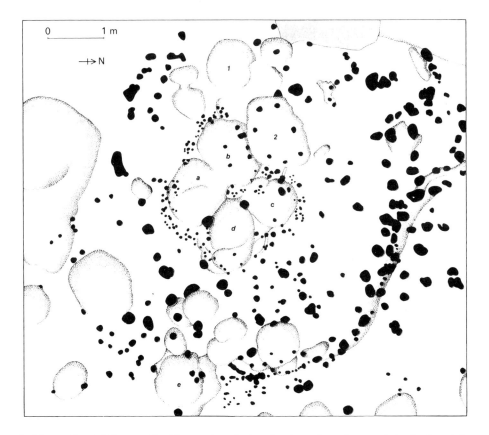

9 Mount Sandel Upper, Co. Derry: hut A showing hearths a, b, c and d; pits 1 and 2; postholes in solid black (after P. Woodman)

been ploughed away. As well as the huts, there were numerous pits, some perhaps for storage; there were also industrial areas where the flint knapping took place; and there were the remains of organic matter such as animal and fish bones, seeds and hazel-nut shells. Indications are that wild pig and hare were present, the pigs having been killed while very young. Bird bones were also present as were significant amounts of eel and salmon bones, but there was no evidence of red deer. The hazel-nut shells and charcoal provided ^{14}C dates ranging from 8960 ± 70 BP to 8440 ± 65 BP* with a concentration within the first two hundred years of this period (Woodman 1985, 148).

The flint industry is a narrow-bladed microlithic one, made from water-rolled nodules brought from elsewhere. The tiny blades whose mean length is little more than 4cm were removed from the core by controlled indirect percussion (p. 13). The cores are either single- or dual-platformed. The richest concentrations of finished implements came from the pits, which also contained burnt animal bones and nutshells. Over 200 microliths and over 1,000 blades or bladelets were found in the area of the huts. Microliths were the commonest tool and consisted of small elongated blades in the form of scalene triangles, needle-points, rods (backed bladelets probably used as knives) and micro-awls. Many of the bladelets, such as those found in clusters, were obviously part of composite implements of which the wood or bone component had not survived. A few ground stone axes were also present. Artefacts were also made from chert, a stone which resembles flint and has somewhat similar qualities. It is black in colour and breaks with a flat fracture. It is not found in the north-east but in the lime-stone country farther to the south. Woodman has suggested that perhaps its presence at Mount Sandel indicates that the occupants were in contact with other Early Mesolithic communities farther to the south.

The excavations showed that Mount Sandel was a substantial base camp which was probably occupied for most if not all of the year. A number of different ways of acquiring food were exploited such as the collection of plants, small game and bird hunting, catching of fish, storage of hazel nuts and possibly fish also. It contrasts with other Early Mesolithic sites where seasonality rather than perma-nency is suggested.

Mount Sandel (Lower) is situated on a narrow ledge about 18m above the River Bann. Extensive landslip had taken place on the precipitous bluff above the river and this had been noted in 1959. A limited excavation was carried out in that year and others in 1968 and 1973 (Collins 1983). The stratigraphy was greatly disturbed, showing a mixture of Mesolithic, Neolithic and even Beaker. The Mesolithic material was similar in many respects to that found at Mount Sandel (Upper) but axes were more numerous. Extensive flint working was

---

* Not in calibration table. Lab. nos. UB-952, UB-2008.

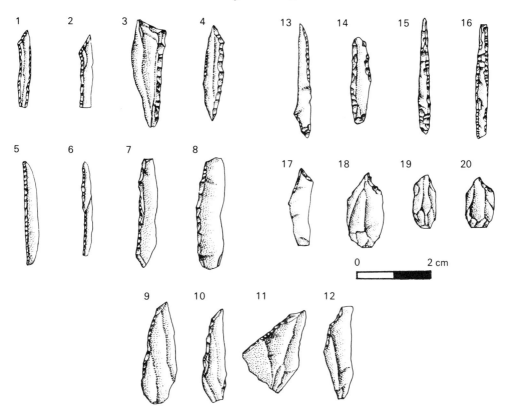

10 Flint microliths: 1–4 scalene triangles, 5–8 rods, 9–12 small knives, 13–16 possible projectiles, 17–20 waste products (after P. Woodman)

clearly carried out. A part of the site which may not have been disturbed was radiocarbon-dated to 8370 ± 200 BP.★

Castleroe (Woodman 1985) is situated on a bluff on the western bank of the River Bann. A rescue excavation exposed a small occupation site which contained archaeological material similar to that of Mount Sandel (Upper). Hazel nuts and wood charcoal provided ^{14}C dates in the first half of the eighth millennium BP.

Lough Boora is an Early Mesolithic site in the Midlands near Kilcormac in Co. Offaly and was excavated in 1977 by Michael Ryan. Vast areas in this part of the country are covered by great sheets of peat bog; wet lands that show little surface evidence of prehistoric settlement. Chance finds over the years had suggested that people were in the area in prehistoric times before the peat had

★ Not in calibration table. Lab. no. UB-532.

formed, but Early Mesolithic settlement was not suspected. Once again, more or less as in the case of Mount Sandel, the discovery came about by chance. The Midland bogs are being commercially developed to provide fuel and other products and about twenty-five years ago, as part of a general drainage scheme, the then existing Lough Boora, which was small in extent, was drained. When the surrounding peat was eventually harvested the fossil shore of the original Lough Boora, bigger than the modern one, emerged. On what had been a peninsula jutting into the water from the original shoreline, a hunting camp was found, the temporary settlement of a family group who may have occupied the area seasonally for periods of hunting, fishing and the collection of fruits and nuts; the presence in the food debris of hazel-nut shells suggests the autumn. While no evidence was found of huts like those at Mount Sandel, there were hearth sites containing the bones of young wild pig, hare and possibly also the bones of a dog. Bird bones may include those of duck, but these identifications are preliminary and must await confirmation when detailed examination has been completed.

As there is no flint in the district the local substitute, chert, was mainly used for tool-making and as at Mount Sandel (Upper), there were specific industrial areas marked by spreads of chert waste, cores and finished tools. The latter are restricted in type to microliths, of which about 200 were found and consisted of rods, needle-points and scalene triangles. In addition, there were about 350 blades, 250 cores and a small number of poorly made scrapers. The microliths, blades and cores provide close parallels for the Mount Sandel (Upper) material, as did also the ground pebble axes consisting of three complete examples and two fragmentary ones. Four radiocarbon dates from charcoal in hearths containing microliths range from 8980 ± 360 BP to 8475 ± 75 BP[*] and show a remarkable similarity to the Mount Sandel dates (Ryan 1980). No doubt other Mesolithic camps will become visible as the peat continues to be cut.

The Lough Boora discovery and the scatters of early flints in the south of the country suggest that Early Mesolithic people may have explored a large part of the country, perhaps entering by way of the east coast from southern Scotland and England at a time when sea level was significantly lower.

Later Mesolithic

At present there is a gap in continuity between the Early and the Later phase of the Mesolithic. The two are distinct from one another because the flint industries associated with them are very different. The flint and chert artefacts of the Later Mesolithic belong to a heavy broad-bladed industry. The technique used was

[*] Not in calibration table. Lab. nos. UB-2268, UB-2199.

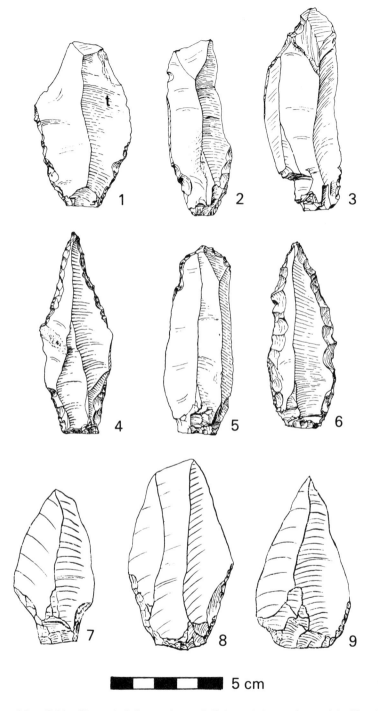

11 Later Mesolithic flints: 1–2 butt-trimmed flakes, 3 butt-trimmed knife, 4 borer, 5 scraper, 6 point, 7–9 Bann flakes (after P. Woodman)

that of direct percussion, producing large blades usually between 6 and 8cm in length. They have very well-defined bulbs of percussion and were struck from single-platformed cores (uni-plane cores), not all the way round the core, but usually across it on one surface only. Sometimes the flakes were used without any further retouch but one of the characteristics of the industry was the practice of thinning and narrowing the butt end. Flakes and blades trimmed in this manner continued throughout the Later Mesolithic until, at the end of the series, one finds the so-called Bann flakes, leaf-shaped flakes which were trimmed and retouched at the base on both edges for about 2cm after they were struck off. The fact that such blades and flakes continued to be made to a virtually unchanged pattern for such a long time shows that they were basic to the Later Mesolithic way of life. Mounted by fixing the tang into a short handle or even by just wrapping the butt in a wad of moss, as in an example in the National Museum of Ireland, they could be used very effectively as knives; mounted on shafts they became spears; mounted in pairs or in groups on a suitably forked branch, they became effective multi-pronged fish spears.

Flint axes, borers and other heavy-duty types of tool suitable for working wood are representative of the Later Mesolithic, and polished stone axes were also in use. There is surprisingly little evidence of hunting equipment but Woodman suggests that a good deal of it could have been made from organic materials and would not invariably have survived (Woodman 1977, 195–6). Microliths and transverse arrowheads are absent also; there seem to have been no projectile heads. End scrapers and burins are rare. All in all, the Bann flake and its precursors were the commonest implement type, and this seems to indicate that the Later Mesolithic in Ireland developed along insular lines, a trend which became even more marked towards the end of the period.

It is now believed that hunter-gatherer communities were dispersed throughout most of Ireland during the whole of the Mesolithic period, and clearly they were not as tied to, nor as dependent on, accessible sources of flint as was originally believed. Later Mesolithic sites are known on the east coast at Rockmarshall, Co. Louth, and at Dalkey Island and Sutton in Co. Dublin. There are also inland sites around lakes such as Derravaragh, Kinale, Iron and Allen in the northern part of the Midlands and at Lough Gara on the Sligo/Roscommon border (Mitchell 1970, 7; 1971, 276). There are other indications farther west on the Sligo coast, and there are the researches being conducted in the south where assemblages of worked flints, including Bann flakes, have been recovered through field-walking and where excavation is also beginning to bring results.

Up to the present, the best series of dates for a Later Mesolithic site has come from Newferry, Co. Antrim. The site lies in the middle of the flood plain of the Lower Bann, close to its exit point from Lough Neagh. Over the past fifty years several excavations have taken place at Newferry, which is a geographical area embracing both sides of the river. The area is an interesting one from many aspects. The broad flat flood plain of the river on both sides consists of an extensive deposit of diatomaceous earth which is commercially exploitable. It averages 1m to 1.3m in thickness but sometimes as much as 2m. In places it is covered by peat and almost everywhere rests on peat 60cm to 1m thick. Below the lower peat there is sand and below this again are deposits of glacial origin. Hearths and man-made objects are stratified at various levels in and below the deposit. Clusters of flint points have been found in association with extensive spreads of charcoal, indicating communities concerned with fishing, the catches being preserved for later use, perhaps by smoking them over smudge fires lighted on the river bank. This probably meant that the area was occupied seasonally in the summer when the water level was low and the river flowed in a confined channel. When the area flooded in winter, sedimentation took place, covering the hearths of the summer before. It is from this sequence that the series of radiocarbon dates has been obtained.

Woodman in his 1970–1 excavations at Newferry (Site 3) uncovered a series of zones, the lowest of which rested on the sandy floor of the valley as it had been *c*.8000 BP. Considerable disturbance of the various occupation horizons had occurred, caused in part by the annual fluctuations of the river level, and consequently the only way in which they could be divided into meaningful groups was on the basis of the geological changes that had taken place over the three millennia or so represented in the excavations. The lowest zone, Zone 9, merely indicated that man was present. Zone 8 had some archaeological content and in Zone 7 there was evidence of flint-working on the site itself and of extensive occupation. Each zone as far as Zone 3 produced reliable dating evidence. Neolithic pottery and flints were found in Zone 2, but Woodman does not regard the dates obtained as being reliable. He prefers to date his archaeological sequence from Zone 8 at 7630 ± 195 BP,[*] Zone 7 at approximately 7000 BP (the mean of a range of dates) up to Zone 3 a millennium and a half later (Woodman 1977). The excavator has been at pains to stress, however (*ibid.*, 184), that 'the dates from Newferry can only be taken as a general sequence rather than placing too much emphasis on individual estimations'. One of the chief reasons for this is that, owing to the situation of the site, the deposits were water-lain and consequently not invariably *in situ*. The implement assemblage was typical of that already described for the Later Mesolithic.

The final stage of the Mesolithic in Ireland is often known as Ultimate Mesolithic because it was a period of survival. There is growing evidence that the Neolithic way of life, based on domestication of animals and on crop husbandry, was being practised in Ireland during the sixth millennium BP but there is also

---

[*] Not in calibration table. Lab. no. UB-641.

evidence that the Mesolithic type of economy survived in places until at least about 5000 BP. There is thus a period of overlap which coincides broadly with the time when the sea was attaining its maximum transgression upon the land during the transition between the Atlantic and the Sub-boreal Phases.

A number of shell middens have been excavated on the east coast, broadly dating from this period. Three middens at Rockmarshall, Co. Louth, close to the modern shore, were formed by people squatting at the inner edge of the raised beach on top of deposits formed at the time of maximum transgression (Mitchell 1947; 1949). The material recovered, other than the shells, was small in amount, consisting mainly of broken beach pebbles of flint and roughly struck flakes. At various points throughout the midden there were scatters of burnt stone and charcoal, testifying to the transitory and seasonal nature of the site. Charcoal from one of the middens produced a ^{14}C date of 5470 ± 110 BP.

Another site excavated by G. F. Mitchell (1956; 1972) was farther south, at Sutton on the northern side of Dublin Bay on what was, in early Postglacial times, the island of Howth. A large midden by Irish standards was present though it was rather thinly spread. It had been formed when the sea had attained its maximum relative height and the midden was just inland from the storm beaches and had in fact been cut into in places. A Later Mesolithic assemblage including Bann flakes and polished stone axes was found, together with fish and animal bones, but no pottery. The site was reinvestigated in 1970 and some further bone fragments were recovered including one piece of a long bone which was probably that of domesticated ox (Mitchell 1972, 157). Charcoal found in the midden had a radiocarbon date of 5250 ± 110 BP.

An almost identical date was forthcoming from middens in Dalkey Island in the southern part of Dublin Bay (Liversage 1968) which lie on a wave-cut plat-form. In general the range of material found was similar to that of Sutton though the upper part of one of the middens was found to contain sherds of Western Neolithic ware. Bones of domesticated animals were also present and occupation of the site goes on into the full Neolithic.

In recent years, the traditional view of the south-west of Ireland as an area unknown to Mesolithic peoples has been overturned. The finding of a plano-convex flint knife, generally an indicator of Neolithic activity, near a shell midden at Ferriter's Cove, Ballyferriter, in the Dingle peninsula, was one of the factors which led Peter Woodman to undertake an investigation. There is an extensive series of small shell middens along this part of the peninsula. They lie on a wave-cut platform of uncertain age and have been preserved by overlying sand dunes. Coastal erosion, however, is a serious problem and since some of the middens were found to be in danger, excavations were undertaken at Ferriter's Cove, beginning in 1983 and resumed in 1984 and 1985. Three sites were chosen where small middens could be seen in the cliff face. While some flint and chert artefacts were found, the dominant raw material was greenstone. The basic industry appears to have been the production of blades about 10cm in length. There were few diagnostic implement-types though one artefact of sandstone resembled a Bann flake. There was no evidence of pottery or of domesticated animals and by and large, Woodman regards the assemblage as being fairly representative of the blade industries of the Later Mesolithic.

Wild pig and deer bones together with fish bones and fish scales have been recovered from the living or squatting areas in addition to the great quantities of shells such as one would expect in a seaside location on the edge of a rocky shore. Radiocarbon dates obtained for Sites 1 and 2, which may, in fact, prove to be part of one extensive settlement, range from 5620 ± 80 BP to 5190 ± 110 BP. Site 3 produced a somewhat similar range of dates, though these results must be regarded as preliminary since the excavations are still continuing. The excavator's tentative conclusion is that the sites seem 'to straddle the Mesolithic/Neolithic change on the western periphery of Europe' (Woodman *et al.* 1984, 8). This is borne out when the calibrated Ballyferriter dates are compared with those of the two other transitional sites, Sutton and Rockmarshall.

The way of life suggested by the discoveries at Ferriter's Cove and at other coastal sites throughout Ireland at this period is one that was practised by well-adapted hunter-gatherer communities, but concurrently other communities were already in existence, perhaps even in west Kerry (p. 36), who had adopted a life-style based on farming. In the view of many archaeologists the change from hunter-gatherer to farmer is so drastic that only immigration could account for it. The other view is that 'the Neolithic way of life was introduced by a slow and complicated process resulting from overseas contacts – there was no invasion and no arrival of a great colony of foreigners' (O'Kelly 1981, 182). It could have been introduced by Irish natives returning from travels abroad and by small family groups enticed here by what they had heard of Ireland from Irish travellers. At first, and indeed for a long time to come, the way of life must have been a mixed one. Hunting, fishing and food collection must have gone on while the practice of agriculture and pastoralism was slowly developing, so that no hard-and-fast line can be drawn between the end of the Mesolithic Period and the beginning of the Neolithic proper. This stage is not easy to demonstrate exactly in the archaeological record, largely for lack of excavated sites of the period and because of the smallness of the amount of relevant material. It has been, and no doubt will remain for some time, a matter of opinion as to whether the practices involved in the Neolithic way of life could have spread to Ireland through contacts between the natives and farming communities elsewhere or whether an influx of farmers from neighbouring Britain was responsible for the introduction of pottery, domesticated animals, forest clearance, and so on. Having regard to the paucity of evidence concerning the Mesolithic/Neolithic overlap, it is easy to indulge in too much speculation. The evidence as it stands at present tends to support Woodman's view that 'the Later Larnian, though partially contemporary with the Neolithic, is a separate tradition' (Woodman 1974, 246).

It is only fair to add a cautionary rider. One cannot help feeling that there is a constant tendency to undervalue the capacities of so-called primitive peoples to advance themselves, and to underestimate the degree of contact that could have been established through trade and travel over the years between widely separated communities. The 'new arrival' certainly had his place in the introduction of the Neolithic way of life but this was surely no sudden or single process; the Mesolithic population must have been involved also over a long period of time. It seems unlikely that the neighbouring land-masses were unknown to the coastal dwellers on each side of the dividing waters. There must have been travelling to and fro and there must have been exchange of ideas as well as of goods and peoples, and on both sides there must have been a degree of movement towards control of the environment, generally but perhaps erroneously attributed exclusively to the Neolithic economies.

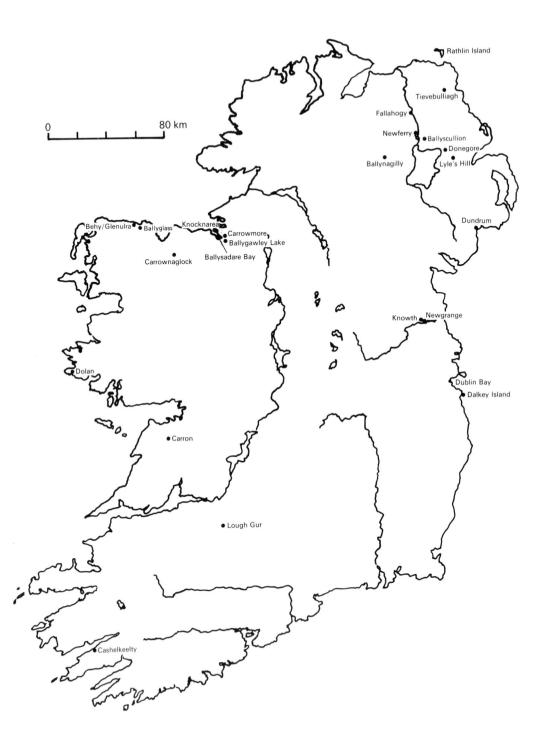

12 Neolithic sites; Late Neolithic/Beaker sites

3

The Neolithic period

The first farmers

Domesticated cattle and sheep/goat were not native to Ireland and had to be introduced from outside, and the same obtained for the cereals, wheat and barley. The wheat was of the more primitive types such as einkorn and emmer and had to be parched in order to extract the grain. For agriculture to be practised, whether tillage or grazing, an open space in the forest was a necessity and the Neolithic people either sought this out or, more probably, cleared one. Land clearance for grazing and cereals is usually called by the Scandinavian term 'landnam' (literally, 'land taking') because it was most clearly documented in Denmark (Iversen 1941). It was noted that a decline in the pollen of elm (the 'elm decline') occurred sometime after the beginning of the Sub-boreal (pollen zone VIIIa in Mitchell's zonation), dated in radiocarbon years to *c*.5200 BP. This decline which, in point of fact, involved the pollen spectra of other tree species also, coincided with an increase in weed-type pollen, particularly that of ribwort plantain (*Plantago lanceolata*), and also with herb and grass pollen. The evidence was interpreted as indicating land clearance by man to provide areas for agriculture, and this was equated with the beginning of farming.

Three stages were proposed for the landnam process: (1) opening up the forest cover; (2) farming; (3) regeneration of woodland after the particular farming episode had ceased. This 'classic' phase of the elm decline has been noted in pollen diagrams throughout north-west Europe, including Ireland and Britain, and it appears to have been relatively synchronous throughout. Though not always supported by archaeological evidence, the classic elm decline was for a long time taken by archaeologists as marking the boundary between Mesolithic and Neolithic practices.

In the forty or so years since the theory was first advanced, the elm decline phenomenon has been subjected to searching scrutiny and various reasons, including that of climatic change, have been put forward to account for it. It has been noted that the tender young shoots of elm are well known as welcome fodder for cattle, and if the young growth was being collected for use in this way, the supply of elm pollen would naturally be much reduced. It is also true that cattle will strip and eat the bark of elm trees and if this were happening to any great extent, stands of elm would quickly be killed with consequent effects on the pollen production. At the present day we have become aware of the appearance and alarming spread of 'Dutch elm disease' which has reached epidemic proportions. All over Britain and Ireland and farther afield dead elm trees are a saddening feature of the landscape. Could there have been a similar epidemic in most of temperate Europe in the fourth millennium BC? This is a matter which has been much debated and which is not fully resolved though the theory is being taken more and more seriously.

It is now clear that, whatever its cause, the classic elm decline does not represent the earliest forest clearance in these islands, and a new question has arisen, namely, could these earlier ones be attributable to Mesolithic people? Several

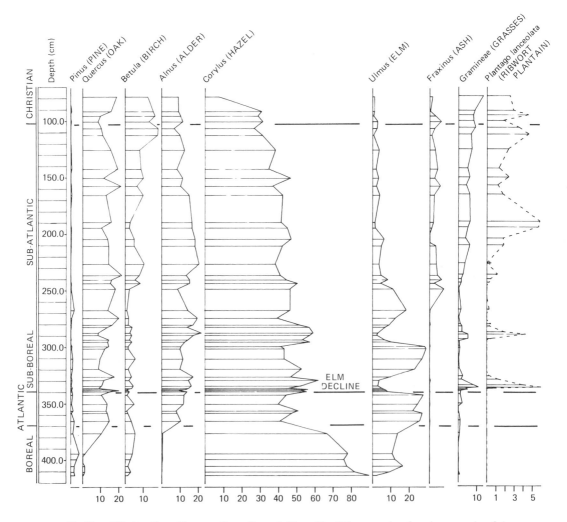

13 Simplified pollen diagram from Scragh Bog, Co. Westmeath, showing trends of the more common trees and herb species from Boreal to Recent times (after M. O'Connell)

sites in Ireland have yielded both palynological and radiocarbon evidence of earlier clearance. The majority are in the north-east; there are a few in the west and one in Co. Kerry. In the raised bog at Ballyscullion in the Lower Bann valley, Co. Antrim, pollen diagrams have shown human interference with the forest between 5815 ± 90 BP and 5530 ± 60 BP, but it is not directly associated with archaeological finds (Smith 1975). At Ballynagilly, Co. Tyrone, early dates for forest clearance were also obtained and in this case there were archaeological

14 Örup elm forest in southern Scania, Sweden, killed by disease in three years

associations. While the north-east of Ireland has long been known for its connections with early man, this is not the case with the south and therefore the results
from Co. Kerry are all the more interesting.

Dates which agree remarkably well with those above-mentioned have come
from palynological studies carried out at Cashelkeelty in the south-west of the
country in Co. Kerry by Ann Lynch. She found what she describes as tentative
evidence of two phases of human activity, the first beginning at 5845 ± 100 BP
when pollen of pine and birch was declining and that of grasses had begun to rise
steeply, signifying forest clearance. One cereal-type pollen grain (of wheat –
Triticum type) was identified in the horizon immediately following the initial
phase, and she concluded that cereal cultivation appeared to have taken place
immediately after clearance, following which grasses and allied pollen came to a
peak. The latter was interpreted as evidence of grazing. This first phase of
activity was estimated to have ceased by *c*.5500 BP, by which time woodland
regeneration had taken place (Lynch 1981, 90). A proposed second phase of
activity began *c*.5400 BP and followed the same pattern as the first. Two cereal-
type pollen grains (barley and wheat – *Hordeum* type and *Triticum* type) were
found. The phase ended at *c*.4900 BP with regeneration of woodland. The
average duration of the forest clearance phases at Cashelkeelty was about 400
years and this ties in well with studies carried out in the north of Ireland (Pilcher
et al. 1971, 560).

W. Groenman-van Waateringe (1983, 217) defines agricultural activity as
'the keeping of domesticated animals and the cultivation of cereals' and goes on
to say: 'When these are recognizable in the pollen record (as cereal, weed, and
pasture plant pollen), we may speak of the "Neolithic".' She lists thirteen sites in
Ireland for which pre-elm decline interference is indicated in the pollen diagrams
and assesses their reliability as indicators of pre-classical elm decline agriculture.
She regards two sites as producing certain evidence of agriculture: Newferry, Co.
Antrim (Smith and Collins 1971) and Cashelkeelty, Co. Kerry (Lynch 1981). Six
others are 'highly probable': Dolan, Co. Galway; Carron, Co. Clare; Ballygawley
Lough, Co. Sligo; Ballynagilly, Co. Tyrone; Ballyscullion, Co. Antrim; and
Fallahogy, Co. Derry. The six 'highly probable' sites taken with the two 'certain'
ones would appear to justify her conclusion that they 'are evidence enough that
agriculture was practised in various parts of Ireland as early as the fourth millennium BC' (Groenman-van Waateringe 1983, 227). It is clear, therefore, that the
classic elm decline can no longer be regarded as indicative of the earliest
Neolithic activity in Ireland.

Groenman-van Waateringe regards the disease theory as the most probable
of the various explanations put forward for the elm decline and believes that the
prominence which the decline has attained in the pollen diagrams is due to the
presence of a more open vegetation at that time, with consequent representation

of the pollen of the more low-growing herb species in the records. 'The increase of this pollen at the same time as the decline of elm is thus an illusion, in so far as, although the amount of pollen from arable and meadow vegetation has indeed increased in the deposit, this is not due to an increase in agricultural activity' (*ibid.*, 223).

Her 'Reconstruction of the Early Neolithic landscape' paints a vivid picture of these early clearings in the primaeval Atlantic forests and deserves to be quoted in full (*ibid.*, 227):

> One should visualise these settlements with their tiny fields and meadows tucked away in the forest, encircled, on the richer soils at least, by an out-skirt and mantle vegetation rich in edible, berry-bearing species. Given time, the mantle vegetation, consisting of prickly bushes, including hawthorn, wild roses, brambles and *Prunus* species, and creepers like *Lonicera* (honeysuckle) and *Hedera* (ivy), grows into an impenetrable vegetation strip between the arable and the woodland, thus protecting the fields against browsing by wild animals. The outskirt vegetation accompanying the mantle in the open, i.e. arable side, would consist of herb species, such as wild strawberry, characteristic of a semi-shady environment. The development of these vegetations is a natural one by which Neolithic man could profit. The only thing necessary for the propagation of these plant communities, already present on natural wood edges, such as along river valleys, etc. was the clearance activity of Neolithic man.
>
> Where the soils were not rich enough for the development of such mantle and outskirt vegetations, a poorer variety of this hedge-like vegetation will have developed, consisting mainly of bramble and furze. For the south-western and western fringes of Ireland, one can easily imagine such a vegetation, the remnants of which can still be seen to this day.

Material equipment in the Neolithic

What supplies and equipment were needed to make these forest clearances, to settle in them and to produce food? Stone, including flint or chert, would have been a prerequisite for fashioning implements for working in wood, for digging, for hunting in order to augment food supplies, and for various other pursuits. Other useful raw materials were antler and bone. It would have been necessary to know how to locate suitable clays if pottery was being made and how to temper and fire them, also how to cure and sew skins and how to preserve various foods.

It is not reasonable to expect that all these skills and implements and all this equipment were present at one time in a particular group or community. Many skills and implements must have evolved in response to the challenges of the local environment. When the resources of one site became exhausted, it was necessary to move on and perhaps to adapt to other conditions and to acquire other skills. The forest regenerated itself in the now deserted clearing and all trace of former settlement was covered over by scrub, woodland, and in many cases eventually by peat. This may partly account for the small number of Early Neolithic settlements which have been identified in Ireland. The problem would not have arisen had Neolithic communities made their houses of as durable a material as they were eventually to use for their great stone tombs.

Any account of the material equipment of a prehistoric community is bound to be biased because only the imperishable materials survive and even in these cases, the imperishability or otherwise may depend on the type of soil in which they have lain. Other factors also, such as climatic fluctuations, may need to be taken into account. Generally speaking, inorganic substances will remain when organic ones will not, though even here there is variability. Bone, antler and horn are all very resistant materials but acid soils destroy them. Wood does not preserve in Ireland except in very damp or wet conditions such as those provided by peat bogs, swamps, etc. Pottery generally preserves well, but depending on the clay and temper composition, its condition when it is brought out of the ground can vary enormously. Acid soils, again, are not favourable to it. One must always bear in mind, therefore, that the find-assemblage of any particular site rarely represents the whole content and is perhaps only a sample of the discarded material.

Flint and stone

These materials are virtually indestructible and, together with potsherds, provide the greater part of the finds indicative of Neolithic activity in Ireland. As in

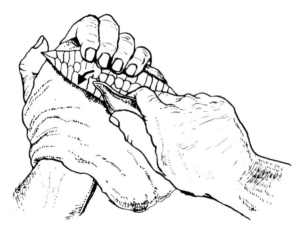

15 Technique of pressure flaking with a bone point

the Mesolithic period, both flint and chert were used but, while the ability to make good quality blades seems to have deteriorated, the range of equipment was enlarged. A new technique, that of pressure flaking, was employed. By means of skilfully applied pressure with a finely pointed bone, small flakes were successively detached from the artefact so as to bring it to the desired shape and thickness. Typical Neolithic artefacts such as leaf- and lozenge-shaped piercing arrowheads were often beautifully finished in a fine bifacial ripple-flaking

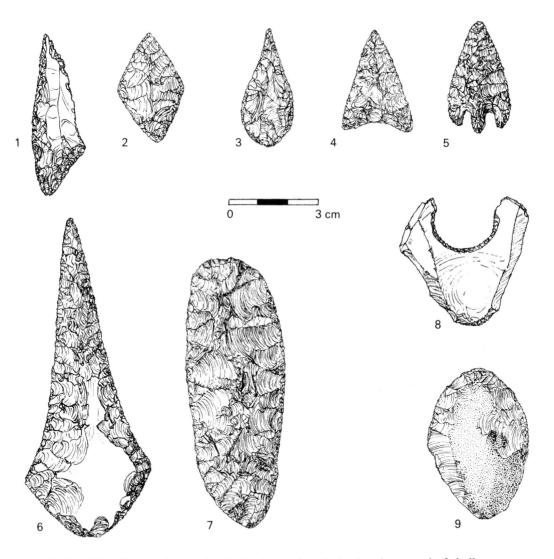

16 Neolithic flints: 1–5 arrowheads (petit tranchet derivative, lozenge, leaf, hollow-based, barbed and tanged), 6 javelin head, 7 plano-convex knife, 8 hollow scraper, 9 end-scraper (Ulster Museum; Crown copyright)

technique. Some were only 2–3mm in thickness. Pressure flaking was also used in the manufacture of large polished lozenge-shaped javelin heads and in plano-convex or 'slug' knives, flat on one surface and curved on the other.

In contrast to the Mesolithic, scrapers are among the most numerous of the flint implements and a great variety of them was used for skinning animals and in the preparation of skins and hides for clothing. They would also have been used in fine wood-, bone-, and antler-working. A type peculiar to Ireland is the very prevalent hollow scraper of which there are many beautiful examples. The working edge is a hollow or part-circular notch of varying depth worked into the edge of a flake or blade. They can be of flint or chert and have been found on most domestic Neolithic sites as well as in court and portal tombs. They could have been employed as spokeshaves when making arrow-shafts and also in cutting bone and antler for the manufacture of pins and beads and perhaps as reaping equipment. In addition, there was a great variety of blades and cutting tools for use in dismembering and butchering carcasses and for all sorts of everyday mundane purposes.

Polished stone axes were an invaluable implement in Neolithic times owing to the need for forest clearance, and they were made in many shapes and sizes. They were hafted by slotting their butts into a hole or mortice in a wooden haft.

17 Original wooden handle (pearwood) for polished stone axe, Maguire's **Bridge**, Co. Fermanagh

They may have been glued-in with resin but would also have been held in place with a criss-cross binding of rawhide, shrunk-on. Some were probably mounted in a similar type of handle but with the cutting edge set at right angles to the axis of the haft, and thus the tool became an adze. The axe was used for felling and chopping and the adze for smoothing roughly split planks, for jointing timbers in house-building, and, when mounted on a longer haft, it could become a mattock for use in tillage. Some axes were made from flint or chert, but the majority were made from other types of stone. The Neolithic people became adept at selecting rock which would not fracture as easily as flint and which could be ground and polished to a fine cutting edge. Igneous and metamorphic rocks were found to be the most suitable and rock outcrops had to be selected as sources of the raw material. While by no means the only ones, the two prime sources in Ireland are in the north-east, one near the summit of Tievebulliagh Mountain near Cushendall in Co. Antrim and the other near Brockley on Rathlin Island just off the Antrim coast (Sheridan forthcoming).

These axe factories, that is, the sites where the rough work of preparing the implements for manufacture was carried out, were brought to attention in the early part of this century by W. J. Knowles (1906). Large numbers of rough-outs, running into many thousands, were collected from exposures from which the peat cover had been eroded and from fields under plough. It was eventually recognized that the rough-outs were made on the spot from pieces broken from a special type of rock which outcropped at the surface in these two places. This raw material has been defined as 'a close-textured heavy rock of varying shades of blue-grey, often with white or black flecking . . . a porcellanite formed where the weathered inter-basaltic layer of weathered basalt has been baked at high temperature in contact with an intrusive dolerite plug' (Jope 1952, 31).

Axes made from it are superior to those of flint because, though flint is harder, it is more brittle. When a good cutting edge was produced on the stone axe, it was more lasting than that of a flint implement. Evidently man discovered the outcrops and found that their quality of rock was very suitable for making fine axes. These he roughed-out on the spot, taking his best results home for finishing by grinding and polishing with sand and water on a suitable piece of sandstone or quartz. Investigations have shown that the rough-outs at Tievebulliagh lie on clay in the base of and under a layer of peat which began to form over them at the beginning of pollen zone VIIb (in Jessen's scheme), that is, the transition from the Atlantic to the Sub-boreal climatic phase, *c.* 5200 BP.

Radiocarbon dates are not available for the Irish sites but the factories are paralleled at Mynydd Rhiw in Caernarvonshire, at Craig Lwyd in north Wales, at Prescelly in south Wales and at Great Langdale in the Lake District in England. Charcoal samples associated with axe chipping floors at Langdale Pikes in Cumbria have been radiocarbon-dated to 4474 ± 52 BP and 4680 ± 135 BP but this is regarded as the high-point of the exploitation of the site. On the palaeo-botanical evidence, Tievebulliagh would appear to have been exploited from about 5000 BP onwards. No Tievebulliagh axe has been found in a Mesolithic context, though, as already noted, stone axes made from other types of rock were in use (Woodman 1976, 300).

Porcellanite axes have also been found scattered over a wide area from Shetland to the south coast of England. Woodman, however, points out that most of the axes identified as porcellanite lie within a 40km radius of Tievebulliagh itself. Nevertheless, the distribution pattern is evidence of movement between the two islands during this period. Though the palaeobotanists have postulated a dense forest cover at the time, the axe distribution shows that overland travel as well as

18 Chipped porcellanite axes, one partly polished, Rathlin Island, Co. Antrim

water transport was important in Britain and Ireland. It has been suggested that the diffusion of axes over wide areas did not necessarily mean that an organized trading system had been developed: much of the traffic may have been carried on to satisfy the claims of kinship (Clark 1965, 26).

A number of experiments in the felling of trees by flint and by polished stone axes are detailed by John Coles (1973, 20–1). A trial clearance of oak forest by means of flint axes hafted in accordance with examples known from prehistoric times was carried out in Denmark. If the trees were more than 35cm in diameter they were girdled, i.e. a ring-cut was made around the trunk, and they were left to die. Smaller trees could be felled in about thirty minutes. Another experiment, in Czechoslovakia, showed that trees such as pine and spruce of about 14–15cm diameter could be felled with a polished stone axe in about seven minutes. As in the Danish experiments, the method adopted was to deliver a series of short downward-slanting blows around the trunk at about knee height; after felling, the cut edge had a pointed shape, like a pencil-end. Near Leningrad, a polished axe found on a Neolithic site was used to cut down a pine tree of 25cm diameter and the operation was carried out in twenty minutes.

Wood

Wood must have been the most universal raw material of all in prehistoric times. Without it the majority of the stone and flint tools and weapons – axes and arrow-

19 Hoard of 19 porcellanite axes found in the last century at Danesfort, Malone, Belfast

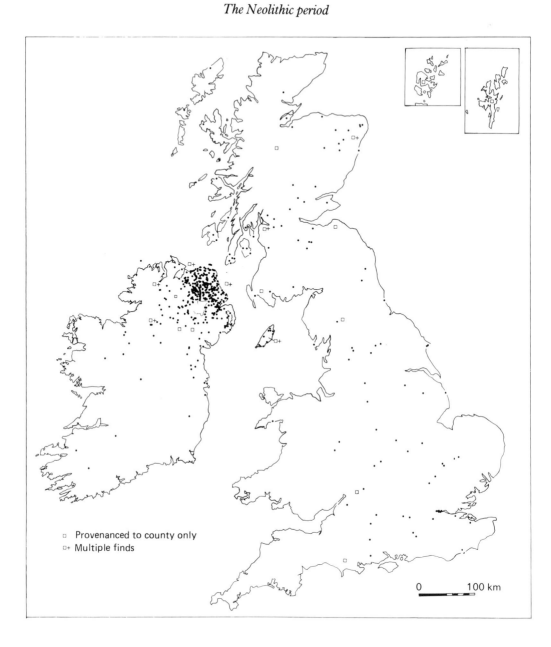

Provenanced to county only
Multiple finds

20 Distribution of porcellanite artefacts, mainly axes but including some rough-outs, chisels, flakes, etc. At least 1,300 further specimens with unknown or vague provenance are known (after A. Sheridan)

heads, for example – were useless, and, conversely, most types of woodworking could not have been carried out without the stone and flint tools. It is true that trees could be felled by burning and wood could be split by means of wooden wedges; arrowshafts could be tipped with bone or other organic material provided the edge was sharp, but nevertheless, the superiority of stone and flint for heavy duty work was undeniable. Clearly there is a correlation between the widespread use of the polished axe in the Neolithic and the felling of forest trees. Woodland clearance was necessary in order to create arable and pasturage areas, but the wood itself was necessary also, for fires, for implements, for handles, hafts and so on, and for building purposes. In time and with skilful management, Neolithic peoples must have been able to achieve a balance between the two; sufficient clearance of woodland to provide the need for food and at the same time to keep up with the ever-constant demand for timber. When, for some reason or other – climatic change, overpopulation, etc. – this balance became upset, new areas and perhaps new modes of living had to be sought elsewhere.

Pottery

Pottery is one of the distinctive features of the Neolithic period. There is no evidence from Ireland that Mesolithic people made or used it. It is normally found on every kind of Neolithic site, both domestic and funerary. It is a useful chronological indicator because while no two sites will produce identical pots there is almost always an underlying trend linking all the pottery types of a particular phase. The simplest division of Irish Neolithic pottery is into round-bottomed and flat-bottomed pots. While they overlap in time, the round-bottomed bowls are thought to be the earlier.

These bowls often have a marked shoulder at the point of junction of the neck with the body (carinated pots). In general, the earliest pottery is finely made, plain ware, well finished and smooth; ornament can occur, mainly in the upper and rim area. As time went on, ornament increased and incised or jabbed patterns appeared, and some pots were highly ornamented. Rim-forms displayed great variety. The term most generally applied to this ware is Western Neolithic because of its widespread occurrence in both Ireland and Britain at the start of the Neolithic period. It has been broken down into many different styles, often of quite localized distribution, which frequently cause confusion to all but the professional archaeologist.

The classification most frequently resorted to is that of Humphrey Case (1961) who catalogued all the Irish Neolithic pottery on the basis of rim forms. He distinguished a number of different wares and he subdivided most of the categories into styles named after various excavated sites, chiefly in the northern province. The sequence relies generally on stylistic considerations and is not

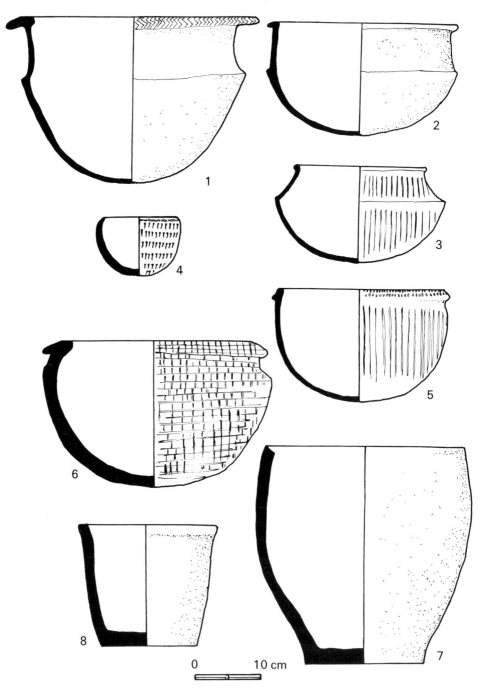

21 Neolithic pottery: 1 and 2 Western Neolithic, Lough Gur Class I(a) and Class I; 3 Ballyalton Bowl; 4 Carrowkeel Ware; 5 Sandhills Western; 6 Linkardstown-type; 7 Lough Gur Class II; 8 Kilhoyle (after H. Case)

related to radiocarbon-dated material. The earliest pottery was called the Dunmurry style, after a hearth site in Co. Antrim which contained sherds of very fine quality ware. The Ballymarlagh style, a pottery of thicker fabric, was named after the court tomb in Co. Antrim. Lyles Hill ware comes slightly later and is one of the best known pottery types of the Irish Neolithic, named after the habitation site near Belfast where a great quantity of sherds was found. The profiles are markedly angular and the necks tend to be straight. Suspension holes can be found below the rim in some pots.

Sandhills ware, in which Case distinguishes four styles, Sandhills Western, Murlough, Dundrum and Goodland, is another facies of the Western Neolithic round-bottomed pottery and is found in habitation sites and in some court tombs. Sandhills Western is no longer regarded as an early distinctive ware. The other styles occur variously in Middle and Later Neolithic contexts. Other round-bottomed pots are Ballyalton bowls, named after the court tomb in Co. Down. They have inturned rims and are decorated with incised or with impressed motifs, all-over or partially.

Carrowkeel ware is the name given to a distinctive kind of pot found in passage tombs, though it occasionally occurs in domestic contexts also. It is semi-globular in shape, of poor fabric and decorated all over with stab-and-drag incised ornament in linear designs.

What Case has termed 'Limerick style' is represented by Western Neolithic ware from various habitation sites at Lough Gur, Co. Limerick. The excavator, S. P. Ó Ríordáin, divided all the Lough Gur sherds into two groups, Class I and Class II, representing the round-bottomed and the flat-based types respectively. He subdivided Class I into I and Ia, the latter having ornament on the rim and the rims themselves becoming prominent features of the vessels. Ó Ríordáin explained the division into classes rather than into types or styles designated by site-names as an attempt to escape from 'nomenclature [which] has been successively known as Windmill Hill, Neolithic A and Western Neolithic . . . This has the further advantage that it avoids absolute identification of the Lough Gur pottery, which exhibits local developments and peculiarities, with any one of the British or Continental groups' (Ó Ríordáin 1954, 327).

The second main type of Neolithic pottery is what many prefer to call by the simple name of flat-based coarse ware and which is represented by Lough Gur Class II ware, Rockbarton ware and Kilhoyle, among others. The Lough Gur Class II ware is quite different not only in shape but in texture from Class I. As well as being flat-based, it is comparatively tall and the side walls are much less curved; also the pottery is a good deal coarser. Decoration is confined to the rim and to an internal bevel. Sometimes there is a foot, i.e. a protruding base. This was a domestic-type ware and it continued in use from the middle of the Neolithic. Rockbarton pots are named after a habitation site in Co. Limerick, not far from Lough Gur. It is comparable to Class II ware and there are sometimes cordons or bands below the rim on the outside. The decoration can be all-over or partial, consisting of incised, grooved or finger-nail impressions in herringbone and cross-hatched patterns. Kilhoyle pots are named after the wedge tomb in Co. Derry and are also found on habitation sites. They are bucket-shaped with a protruding foot and are rarely decorated.

The above represents a very simplified scheme for Irish Neolithic pottery, encompassing Early, Middle and Late periods. The different types of ware are in no way successive: some of them parallel one another in time, others overlap for part of the time. The terms given above are widely used by archaeologists to describe and define pottery other than that found at the type-site, and provided the comparison is apt and fairly exact, the Case and the Ó Ríordáin nomenclature serve a useful purpose, especially where ^{14}C dates are not available for the pottery context. The fallibility of a typological scheme based largely either on visual or associative grounds has been demonstrated very clearly in recent years. A type of decorated round-bottomed ware found with single-grave cist-like burials and known as Linkardstown-cist ware was assigned to the Later Neolithic on typological grounds. Radiocarbon dating of more recent finds of this pottery showed it to belong in the earlier rather than the later part of the Neolithic (p. 130). A fresh assessment of Neolithic pottery is badly needed, taking into account all the different scientific techniques now at the disposal of the archaeologist.

Settlement

The oldest radiocarbon dates obtained so far in Ireland for evidence of Neolithic habitation come from a site at Ballynagilly, Co. Tyrone, a few kilometres north-west of Cookstown. The site consists of a low hill of glacial gravel and sand, rising about 15m above the surrounding bog. The hill was formerly covered by peat and when this was bulldozed, flint artefacts and pottery came to light. This discovery led to the excavation of the site, commencing in 1966 and continuing until 1971 (ApSimon 1969; 1971; 1976). Four main sites were discovered. A Neolithic house had been built on top of the hill and lower down were three other sites dating approximately to Late Neolithic/Beaker times. In addition, traces of occupation prior to that represented by the Early Neolithic house were found in the form of pits and some hearth debris containing sherds of plain Western Neolithic ware. Radiocarbon dates obtained for this phase centre on 5600 BP and are among the oldest so far obtained for Neolithic domestic activity in these islands. This earliest occupation has already been mentioned (p. 35) as one of the sites producing 'highly probable' evidence of the practice of agriculture and hence of Neolithic culture. The question as to whether this phase could be due to a process of acculturation on the part of the Mesolithic population, that is, to the acquisition by it, by whatever means, of distinctive Neolithic practices, is discussed by A. M. ApSimon who maintains that (ApSimon 1976, 24): 'the un-Mesolithic facies of Ballynagilly, with pottery already the product of a confident tradition . . . is not easily explained by local acculturation'.

The main Early Neolithic occupation took place around 5200 BP and the pollen record shows evidence of 'landnam' forest clearance for that period. Two grains of cereal-type pollen suggest arable farming. This clearance is directly associated with the archaeological activity on the hilltop which was evidenced by the remains of a rectangular house, 6.5m × 6m, marked by parallel foundation trenches with a posthole at each end. The trenches, 30–40cm wide and 20–30cm deep, contained the burnt bases of radially split oak planks which had stood vertically on end. This appears to be the first find of such walls in a Neolithic context in Ireland though they are well known in central Europe. A shallow pit on the south of the house may have provided the material for clay daub which could have been plastered over the joints or used in wattle-and-daub end-walls. A ^{14}C date of 5165 ± 50 BP was obtained from charcoal from the plank wall (Smith *et al.* 1971). There were two hearths in the centre of the floor and two further postholes which would have contained posts, possibly to help support the roof. Pottery sherds and flint were found both in the floor deposit and outside the house.

22 Ballynagilly, Co. Tyrone, Early Neolithic house. South wall trench at left, north trench at right, two postholes of gable in foreground

The flint assemblage included narrow flakes and blades and six leaf-shaped arrowheads. The pottery was the classic round-bottomed shouldered bowl of the Early Neolithic, similar to the Ballymarlagh style of the Case classification.

Pollen analyses showed that open grassland conditions prevailed until the middle of the third millennium when the forest regenerated, and settlement began again towards its close when there was a settled mixed farming economy in which pastoralism and the cultivation of barley went forward side by side. This broadly coincides with the period of Late Neolithic/Beaker activity in the vicinity of the Newgrange monument, to be described later.

The circumstances of the discovery of the Ballynagilly complex may perhaps provide at least a partial explanation for the apparent scarcity of habitation sites in Ireland, not only in the Neolithic but in succeeding prehistoric periods also. Were it not that the peat cover had been stripped from the hillock on which Ballynagilly stands and that flints and pottery were discovered, the house foundation would not have been detected or even suspected. Prehistoric peoples in general were frequently more concerned to perpetuate the remains of the dead than to provide impressive earthly dwellings. Settlement sites consisting of single homesteads, built of non-durable material, leave little if any trace above ground even when they are not covered by peat, and from the time of the earliest farmers the settlement pattern in Ireland seems to have been of that order. When the surrounding land or enclosed fields had become unfit either for tillage or for pasturage the tendency was for the farmer to move on and start the pattern all over again. Most traces of settlement, therefore, have been detected accidentally, as at Ballynagilly.

A number of such traces have been found in equally unexpected circumstances, that is, beneath the mounds of chambered tombs when these were in process of excavation. They usually consist of spreads of charcoal, perhaps some flints and pottery sherds and sometimes stakeholes and postholes. Mostly the remains merely indicate the presence of an abandoned settlement, the extent or nature of which cannot or has not been ascertained, and they owe their preservation to the superincumbent tomb or mound. Frequently radiocarbon dates have been obtained for these buried horizons and unfortunately, in works of a general nature, there is a tendency for these dates to become 'attached' to the overlying structures, particularly in the case of chambered tombs, rather than to the horizons that produced them. This presents a false chronology for the chambered tombs in question, and also for Irish chambered tombs in general. In actual fact, given the substantial number of chambered tombs that has been excavated, firm ^{14}C dates are very sparse indeed.

Excavations in the Boyne Valley in Co. Meath showed clear evidence in many cases of human activity on the sites before the passage tombs were built. At Site L, one of the smaller passage tombs which adjoins the main Newgrange mound, an altered turf-line, 5–10cm thick, flecked with charcoal and containing flint, was found beneath the covering mound. Sherds of plain round-bottomed shouldered bowl were found in a hollow and the stratification was such that it was clear that domestic activity on the site had ceased before the building of the Site L passage tomb. Some evidence of pre-mound domestic activity was also found at Site Z, another of the small neighbouring tombs (O'Kelly *et al.* 1978, 293–4). Pits and flecks of charcoal were detected beneath the main Newgrange monument also and, though no ^{14}C date was obtained for what was obviously pre-mound domestic activity, it must have taken place prior to the construction of the overlying monument.

Extensive evidence of pre-tomb domestic activity was found at Knowth, also in the Boyne valley (Eogan 1984, 211–44), beneath six of the smaller satellite

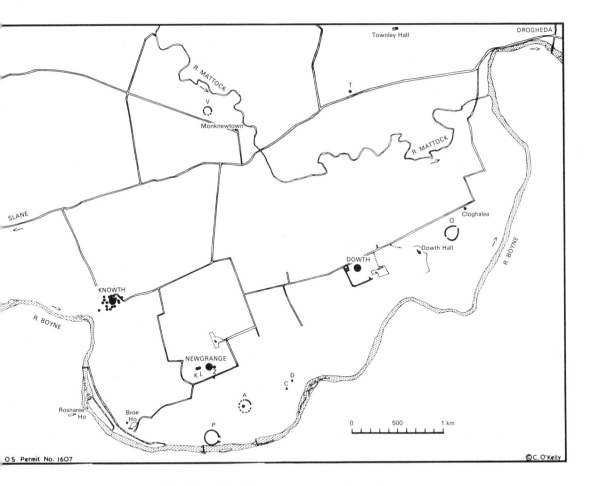

23 Map of the Boyne passage-grave cemetery

tombs. The area in question was subrectangular, 10.7m by 9m internally, delimited by an irregular trench which was interrupted at the north-east by a gap or entrance about 1m wide. There were a number of postholes in the western trench and there were pits and fire-reddened areas, but no specific hearth in the enclosed area. Sherds of Western Neolithic pottery and some flint were mixed through the fill of the trenches. Charcoal from one of the pits produced a ^{14}C date of 4852 ± 71 BP. Another of the pits predated the subrectangular structure. Eogan remarks that though the purpose of the structure remains unknown, its general shape and size suggest a house.

Another feature uncovered in the same area consisted of a pair of parallel curved trenches running north–south for a distance of about 58m. No evidence of their further extension was obtained. They were about 8m apart at the southern end and 11m at the northern. The eastern trench, which was the nearer of the two to the main mound, was the better defined. Postholes were identified in both but more specifically in the eastern trench, and Eogan envisages that they contained a series of closely set posts forming palisades. Pottery sherds and some flints were mixed through the fill of the trenches. The eastern one cuts across the subrectangular structure and is consequently later in date.

These enigmatic trenches bring to mind the on-going excavations at Donegore Hill, Co. Antrim, about 8km north of Lyles Hill. A considerable quantity of Western Neolithic pottery sherds and also flint was found by surface collection in a ploughed field on top of the hill. Subsequently, aerial photographs revealed at least two interrupted (causewayed?) ditches surrounding the summit of the hill (Mallory and Hartwell 1984). While only brief preliminary excavation results are available as yet and one, or possibly two, further seasons of excavation are envisaged, already the cultural material recovered from the enclosed area comprises over 30,000 sherds, mainly Western Neolithic though with a very small percentage of Early Bronze Age material (personal communication from J. P. Mallory). Donegore promises to be one of the most interesting occupation sites of the Early Neolithic period yet excavated in Ireland.

In the context of the Knowth trenches one must also take note of a curious feature in the field immediately east of Satellite Z at Newgrange (C. O'Kelly 1978, 48, pl. 24). It is a U-shaped structure with deep ditches running north–south, the rounded end of the U being at the south. It is upwards of 100m in length and about 20m wide and is best seen in aerial photographs. While its purpose and date are unknown, it invites comparison with cursus earthworks in Britain.

Also in the Boyne valley, evidence of primary habitation was found beneath two low mounds in the Townleyhall estate in Co. Louth, about 2km north of the Boyne passage grave cemetery. No house or hut plans were recovered but a feature of both was the large numbers of stakeholes with associated hearths, fire-reddened areas, flints and Neolithic pottery. The Townleyhall I site (Liversage 1960) was encircled by a low bank and outer ditch, and later a mound was erected over it, though not concentrically with the bank and ditch. A few cremations were found in the mound. At the Townleyhall II site (Eogan 1963), a passage grave with its covering mound was erected over the habitation layer. The interval between the two phases is not known. A ^{14}C date of 4680 ± 150 BP was obtained from 'charcoal with passage grave ware sealed below barrow of passage grave type' (*Radiocarbon* 1968, 4). The date therefore refers to the primary habitation layer where some sherds of Carrowkeel ware were found in addition to those of Sandhills type.

Similar pre-mound activity has come from court tombs such as Bally-macaldrack and Ballymarlagh in Co. Antrim and Carnanbane, Ballybriest, Co. Derry. Pits, hearths and postholes were found beneath the latter (Evans 1939) as well as Neolithic ware similar to that from Ballynagilly. A ^{14}C date of 4930 ± 80 BP was obtained from charcoal associated with the pottery. These pre-mound features have often been interpreted in the past as evidence of ritual practices, preparation of the site for burials, and so on. While this explanation may be correct in some instances it is not universally so.

Unequivocal evidence of pre-tomb habitation was found when the two court tombs, Ma. 13 and 14, were excavated at Ballyglass, Co. Mayo. In the course of the excavation, which took place between 1968 and 1970, traces of what appeared to be a house foundation became evident close to the western end of one of the two sites, Ma. 13. When these traces were followed up and the area in question was fully excavated, the foundation trenches of a rectangular house, 13m × 6m, were found. A number of postholes were set into the trenches and formed the principal structural elements of the house, while inside it was divided into a principal space and lesser compartments. Hearths were found within the house, and numerous sherds of Neolithic ware. Pits containing pottery, flint and chert were found outside the house, some of them within the confines of the tomb structure. The tomb cairn had not been constructed directly on top of the house but overlay something more than half of it and was eccentrically orientated in relation to it.

Five radiocarbon dates obtained from charcoal contained in separate wall slots ranged from 4680 ± 95 BP to 4480 ± 90 BP. It is not known how much time elapsed between the abandonment of the house and the building of the court tomb and cairn but Ó Nualláin in a preliminary report says: 'It is difficult to avoid the conclusion that the house was intentionally demolished to make way for the construction of the tomb' (Ó Nualláin 1972, 54–5).

This discovery prompted the re-examination of court tomb Ma. 14, and the foundations of two timber structures were found, one to the south of the cairn and the other in the forecourt of the tomb itself. The southern structure measured 6.5m by 3m and stakeholes instead of postholes were found in the wall slots. It seems to have extended under the cairn. The other structure was more difficult to define. Wall slots, some curved and some straight, with postholes and stake-holes were found, and associated with them were a few flint artefacts and fragments of pottery. A large quantity of struck flakes, mainly of chert, was found in the immediate vicinity of each of the structures and Ó Nualláin suggests that perhaps the latter were workshops rather than domestic dwellings (Ó Nualláin 1972a, 22). There is, however, some doubt in the matter and it must await definitive publication.

Charcoal from a wall slot in the forecourt structure was dated to 4390 ± 100 BP and a sample from another wall slot was very similar. A sample of charcoal from the top of 'a grey layer which extended from under the cairn and kerb of the tomb across the foundations of the domestic structure' was dated to 4270 ± 90 BP.

Aerial survey carried out in connection with excavations at the Carrowmore megalithic cemetery in Co. Sligo (p. 106) revealed numerous circular or quasi-circular sites on the eastern slope of Knocknarea Mountain, 2km west of the cemetery. A group of five was identified on the ground as hut sites and two of these were fully excavated in 1981–2 by members of the Swedish team operating

24 Ballyglass, Co. Mayo, court tomb with underlying habitation in foreground

at Carrowmore (Bengtsson and Bergh 1984). The group of huts was on the 275m contour some way below the summit of the mountain on which stands the great cairn known in Irish as *Meascán Méidhbh*, popularly supposed to be the grave of the legendary Queen Maeve of Connaught.

The remains of the two excavated structures were oval in shape, approximately 7m × 5m. Shallow ditches had been dug around the outsides and the material from them placed on the inside to form low banks into which structural timber posts had been set. It could be seen that the posts had been set to lean inward so that presumably they would meet at the top and be tied together wigwam fashion to form a self-supporting structure covered with thatch or with animal skins. The ditches prevented water from the higher ground from running into the floor areas. The huts had possibly been rebuilt several times. A large number of finds, mainly chert but some flint also, came from both sites. Obviously the knapping took place on site. The bulk of the finds consisted of hollow scrapers; in fact, the two huts provided the largest number – 189 and 180 respectively – hitherto found at a single site. There were also other types of scrapers together with points, knives and arrow/javelin heads. There was no pottery in Hut 2 but Hut 1 produced sixty sherds, six of which had twisted cord impressions.

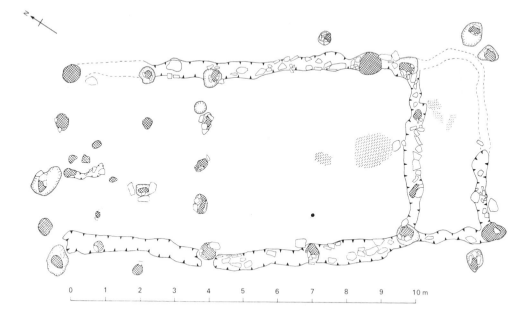

0 1 2 3 4 5 6 7 8 9 10 m

25 Ballyglass, Co. Mayo, plan of house. Single stakehole shown black, fire-reddened areas shown by broken ruling (after S. Ó Nualláin)

The presence of so many hollow scrapers could indicate that the huts served as hunting lodges which were in use over a period of time. The scrapers could have been used to prepare arrowshafts and for cutting or sawing wood or bone or preparing hides, operations consonant with hunting, but of course the function of the huts remains speculative. A charcoal sample from a layer containing finds, including two hollow scrapers, from Hut 1 was dated to 4250 ± 75 BP. There was a burnt area in the centre of Hut 2 and this produced a similar date.

At many points around the Irish coast, wind erosion of sand dunes has revealed dark layers which contain charcoal, hearths and spreads of shells and animal bones. A variety of artefacts has been found associated with them and these show that not all horizons in the sand are of the same date; indeed it is likely that some of them are as late as post-Norman times. Difficulties of dating have been created by the very nature of the dunes. As the sand is eroded by the wind, objects which properly belong to high and therefore late levels drop down into lower and earlier strata and thus confuse the picture. There are instances where the sand has been blown away completely, allowing objects from several horizons to collect together at the bottom. If the sand blows up to cover these again, as it sometimes does, they may appear to the unwary to be in a 'sealed deposit'. Careful study has revealed that in some instances along the north and east coasts of Ireland (Collins 1952; 1959; Movius 1942, 252–4), the deposits at the base of the sand overlie the surfaces of the raised beaches. Some of these contain pottery and it has been suggested (Case 1969, 16) that this type of Sandhills ware is the product of the acculturated coastal Late Larnian people. Woodman, however, regards it as 'an intrinsic part of the Irish Neolithic' (Woodman 1974, 253), and furthermore he points out that remarkably little of this 'Sandhills Ware' has been found in coastal contexts. Plain Neolithic pottery contained with charcoal in a pebble-floored hearth in the dunes at Site 12, Dundrum Nature Reserve, Co. Down, gave radiocarbon dates of 4775 ± 140 BP and 4565 ± 135 BP. Like all Irish Neolithic bowls, the Sandhills type developed in time the heavy rims and the ornament so characteristic of assemblages at Lough Gur and elsewhere. When farming activity had recommenced at Ballynagilly following the post-landnam forest regeneration, Sandhills-type ware was found in a Late Neolithic context.

Another coastal feature is the great mounds of sea shells which testify to seasonal occupation in order to exploit the marine resources during the most favourable times of the annual cycle. The excavations at Ballyferriter on the Co. Kerry coast have been mentioned above (p. 28). During the excavation campaign at Carrowmore, Co. Sligo, in the early 1980s, investigations were carried out on one section of the chain of shell middens in Ballysadare Bay. Excavations were centred on well preserved remains at Culleenamore, just south of the southern slopes of Knocknarea Mountain. The seaward edge of the midden appeared to have been eroded but in the extensive remaining parts it was found that in addition to the great quantity of oyster and other shells, there were a number of hearths stratified in the deposits together with charcoal, ash, and some remains of charred posts. Bones from domestic animals were found in the upper levels as well as those of red deer and fragments of antler. There were some pottery sherds also from the upper levels and stray finds of flint, bronze, glass and iron. The radiocarbon dates showed periodic utilization of the site from the first quarter of the third millennium until Iron Age times (Österholm 1984).

The above are only a few of the many evidences of habitation and settlement in Ireland in the third millennium. There are many others such as that beneath the hilltop cairn on Lyles Hill, near Belfast (Evans 1953), where great quantities of sherds of round-bottomed shouldered bowls, leaf- and lozenge-shaped arrowheads and hollow and round scrapers were found but no house plans were recovered. While the excavator suggested that the finds were collected from habitation sites elsewhere and ritually dumped, the more mundane explanation may be that they represent the *in situ* remains of a Neolithic settlement, preserved by reason of the superincumbent cairn. One of the best examples of Neolithic settlement is that at Lough Gur, Co. Limerick. Unfortunately most of the excavations undertaken there were carried out in 'pre-radiocarbon' times and thus absolute dates are to all intents and purposes non-existent as far as the settlement is concerned. In this present volume we have tried in the main to concentrate on sites for which absolute as opposed to relative dates are available but an exception must be made for Lough Gur owing to its great significance for Irish archaeology.

Lough Gur is a small lake in the east of Co. Limerick set among limestone hills. The lake is C-shaped and from the land at the west the peninsula of Knockadoon juts out between the two arms of the 'C'. Today there is water on three sides of the peninsula but the level of the lake was lowered by drainage in the middle of the last century so that originally the peninsula must have been virtually surrounded by water. Some of the best evidence found so far in Ireland for Neolithic settlement has come from the shores of Knockadoon. The soil is light and the land is divided up by sheltered valleys and it is warm even in winter. When cleared of scrub by the Neolithic settlers it would have been suitable for small-scale primitive tillage and in due time would have been able to support a thriving cattle-raising economy just as it does today.

Beginning in the mid-1930s and recommencing in the late 1940s, the late Seán P. Ó Ríordáin excavated the remains of at least sixteen settlement sites of Neolithic and Neolithic/Bronze Age date at Knockadoon (Ó Ríordáin and Ó Danachair 1947; Ó Ríordáin 1954). The foundations of at least ten houses were identified as well as a number of smaller, less well-defined structures. One must picture the houses as standing in ones and twos here and there in close proximity to the then lake edge. While variant house plans were recorded, the standard forms were circular and rectangular and both types were being built and lived in contemporaneously.

The first of the houses found (Site A) had a rectangular plan, preserved in the ground as a stone wall-footing, or socle, the internal dimensions being 9.7m long and 6.1m wide. The doorway was at the south-west corner and the domestic fires had been lit directly on the earthen floor in the centre of the floor-space. The latter was divided into three aisles by two lines of posts running longitudinally and this may have meant that the centre aisle which contained the hearth was used as the daytime living-space. The side-aisles may have been for storage and for sleeping quarters. Lines of posts also stood just inside and outside the wall-footings and, with the rows already mentioned in the interior, must have helped to support the roof structure and its covering of reed thatch. No remains of the actual posts were recovered but the postholes in which they had stood were clearly marked in the soil. Little evidence was forthcoming as to the material used for the superstructure of the walls but the probability is that it was either turves or mud, most likely the latter.

26 Lough Gur, Co. Limerick, looking south-west. Knockadoon peninsula is enclosed by the two arms of the lake

Quite near this house, the remains of another rectangular one, Site B, were found and just a little to the east was Site C. A large area was excavated here, and because of the depth of the habitation deposit in places, and the number of finds, particularly of pottery, this is the most important site on Knockadoon. The plans of three circular houses were identified. In two of them the mud wall had been built in the annular space between two concentric rings of wooden posts. In the third, a single ring of posts supported the roof while the wall may have been constructed in wattle work, plastered inside and out with mud. Two of the houses had internal diameters of 5.2m and the third was a little larger. Where recognizable the hearth was at or near the centre of the floor and there were pits adjacent to it. In one house the central living space around the hearth was about 2.4m in diameter, this being marked off from the rest of the floor space by a ring of wooden posts set concentrically with respect to the house wall. There were two other rings of posts, one inside and one outside the walls, and all three rings of posts supported the roof structure with its heavy thatch, probably of reed which, then as now, grew profusely at the lake edge. Around about these houses were

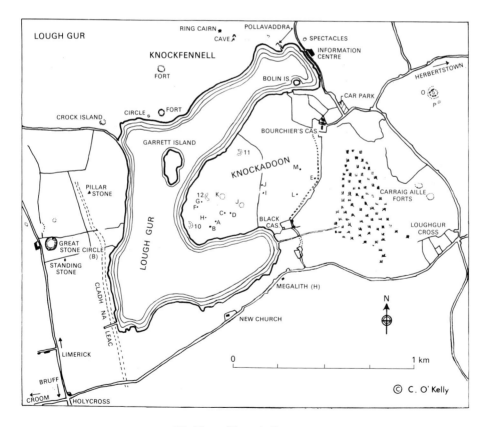

27 Map of Lough Gur area

59

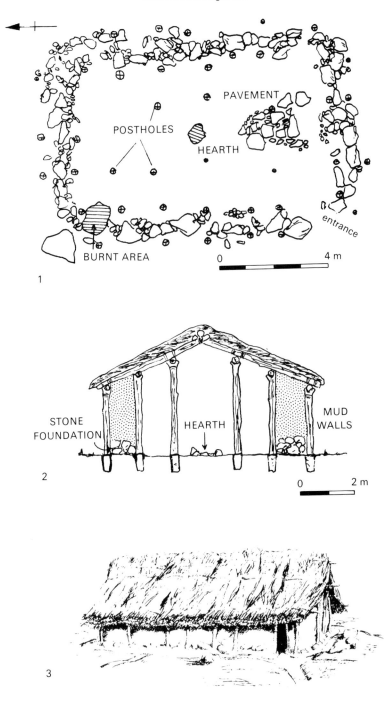

PAVEMENT

POSTHOLES

HEARTH

entrance

BURNT AREA

0   4 m

1

STONE
FOUNDATION

HEARTH

MUD
WALLS

2

0   2 m

3

28 Lough Gur, House A: 1 Plan, 2 Conjectural E–W elevation (after S. P. Ó Ríordáin),
3 Suggested reconstruction (after M. J. O'Kelly)

various irregular pits in the old ground surface which were used either as rubbish pits or for storage, and it is from them, as well as from pits inside the houses, that many of the small finds came.

There were several other similar houses and there were also some smaller structures which were more in the nature of temporary shelters. Ten sites in all were published, all but one of them prehistoric, before Ó Ríordáin's untimely death in 1957. Five further house sites, though excavated, remained unpublished. A study of these sites has recently been undertaken (Grogan and Eogan forthcoming), making use of the original field notebooks, drawings, etc. and also the finds from the sites.

These sites are an interesting group as they consist of habitation enclosures surrounding a house or houses, not for the purpose of defence against human enemies but perhaps merely to delimit the living enclosure, keep domestic animals out, and prevent some of them – goats, for instance – from climbing on to the thatched roofs. Three of the enclosures are named Circles J, K and L because in a former survey of the area (Windle 1912) they were classed as stone circles and were designated in this manner. Ó Ríordáin retained the Windle nomenclature where possible. The other three were not found by Windle, and Ó Ríordáin called them Sites 10, 11 and 12.

Circles J, K and L are the most regular in shape, the enclosing wall consisting of two concentric rings of low contiguous boulders or orthostats, the annular space between them being a metre or more wide. These acted as revetments inside and outside the base of a bank of turves or one of earth and rubble which may originally have been from 1.5 to 2m in height. Where the enclosing rings abutted on natural cliff edges or rock outcrops as in Sites 10, 11 and 12, these were incorporated in the rings. At Circle K it was found that there was a gap in both rings, and excavation not only showed that this was the entrance, but also revealed rock-cut postholes that had apparently held the jambs of some kind of wooden gates. This showed that the two enclosing rings of boulders must have retained a substantial wall. If there had been no more than the two rings of stones a gate would have been pointless as animal or man could have stepped over them into the enclosure at almost any point (M. J. and C. O'Kelly 1981, 21). In the centre of Circle K there was a rectangular building, probably a domestic house, the outline of which was marked by rock-cut postholes, and there were a number of burials within the enclosure, mostly children. Outside, but partly underlying the arc of the enclosure, was a hut site on the floor of which were further skeletal remains, again of children, and there was one adult female burial (p. 132). This hut had been a substantial structure with stone wall foundations. At J, L and Site 10 also there was evidence of domestic activity predating the sites themselves.

At Circle J so much disturbance had taken place that it was impossible to obtain house or hut plans. The area had later been used as a burial ground,

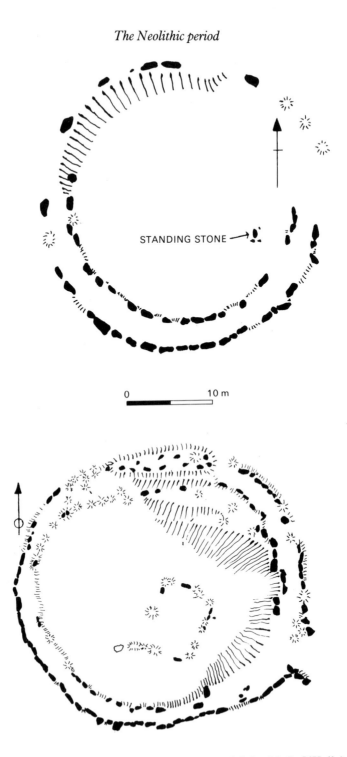

STANDING STONE →

0   10 m

29 Lough Gur, Circle J (top) and K (bottom) (after M. J. O'Kelly)

possibly in Early Christian times. These two circles, J and K, averaged 30m in overall diameters.

Circle L had an overall diameter of 22m and it contained two superimposed houses. Two ^{14}C dates were obtained from charcoal samples from the earlier occupation phase: 4410 ± 240 BP and 4690 ± 240 BP. It is unfortunate that these are the only radiocarbon dates available for the Knockadoon settlement.

Sites 10, 11 and 12 are somewhat similar to the above but are more irregular and natural features were utilized to a greater extent to augment the enclosure rings. At least one house was identified and it was evident that pre-enclosure activity had taken place at Site 10 (Grogan and Eogan forthcoming).

One of the most important outcomes of the Lough Gur excavations was the enormous amount of pottery recovered – over 11,000 sherds from Site C alone – and it was possible to reconstruct various individual groups of sherds so that several complete or almost complete vessels were available for study. No vessel was recovered intact, however. As already mentioned, two main Neolithic wares were distinguished by Ó Ríordáin, Class I and Class II.

Class I pottery consists of round-bottomed shouldered bowls with plain rims, sometimes everted, and generally known as Western Neolithic or in Britain as Windmill Hill after the type-site near Avebury in Wiltshire. The ware is hard, thin and fairly smooth, sometimes 'corky' in appearance. Class Ia is a subdivision of the round-bottomed bowls and belongs to the Sandhills-ware tradition. The rims bear incised ornament and are larger and more elaborate than in the plain ware. In section they are club- or T-shaped and can be 1.5 to 2.5cm across; in some cases lugs are present. The colour of all Class I ware varies from light brown to a very dark red. Some of the pots have a marked angular shoulder, a feature which concealed the fact that there was a joint in the wall of the pot at this point. The fabric of these pots is remarkably good and shows either that the clay was artificially refined or levigated or that naturally refined sediments were chosen for the purpose. Before beginning to make the pot, special types of temper were added to the clay so as to reduce its plasticity. A common material used at Lough Gur for this purpose was crushed calcite, a white crystalline material available locally. This strengthens clay, especially when it is limestone-based as at Lough Gur, and it acts as a glue. The use of organic material in the Lough Gur ceramics argues a high degree of technology. When the organic material burnt out during firing the 'corky' appearance mentioned above resulted. Before firing, the pots were burnished with a smooth pebble or with a piece of bone so that well-preserved pieces exhibit polished surfaces. Experiments suggest that the clay itself, derived in some cases from volcanic ash, was obtained from a deposit at most about 2.5km from Knockadoon, but possibly much more local. While the pottery can generally be referred to as round-bottomed shouldered bowl, there are many varieties, some of which have already been mentioned above.*

In the course of time at Lough Gur, the rims of the round-bottomed shouldered bowls became simpler and another type of ware appeared – flat-bottomed bucket-shaped pots which were coarsely and crudely made and which sometimes had a crudely scratched ornament below the rim. This is Ó Ríordáin's Class II ware. There are some instances of encrustation – application of decorative bands of clay to the finished pots (Ó Ríordáin 1954, 340). In these pots, made from various local clays, the tempering agent was usually crushed chert, though some were still tempered with calcite. The colour is mostly a greyish black but there are some shades of brown also. This rough domestic ware eventually became the dominant pottery and the round-bottomed wares evidently ceased to be made. The Class II ware is comparable, but in form only, to the flat-based coarse ware found in the north of Ireland where it is known as Kilhoyle ware. Both Class I and Class II wares were found together at many of the sites and were also found in association with Beaker pottery (p. 81). Apart from a couple of sites, the latter was usually present only in small amounts and occurred towards the end of a particular period of occupation. Frequently, in the latest levels, Beaker again ceased to be present, and the Neolithic Class II-type assemblage continued as before.

Apart altogether from the pottery, the range and variety of other finds were remarkable. Characteristic flint and chert leaf-shaped and lozenge-shaped arrowheads, as well as some hollow-based types, were found together with Bann-type points with thinned and narrowed butts, parallel-sided blades, scrapers and so on. There were upwards of fifty complete or almost complete polished stone axes and over 350 small fragments. They were mainly of greenstone which may have been locally obtained (Grogan and Eogan forthcoming) though a small number were of porcellanite from Tievebulliagh in Co. Antrim. A great many of the axe fragments had been adapted for other uses. Several hundred beads of bone and stone were found. Bone is well-preserved in the limestone soil of Lough Gur and as well as beads, numerous points and pins were common on most of the excavated sites.

Large amounts of animal bones – food waste – were collected (van Wijngaarden-Bakker 1974, 369ff.) and the vast bulk of them were of domestic ox. Small numbers of pig and sheep were present as well as a few dogs or wolves – it is not easy to distinguish between the skeletal remains. Bones of brown bear and red deer show that hunting was practised. Some items of bronze were found and there was also evidence of metalworking.

---

* The writer is indebted to Rose M. Cleary of University College, Cork, for technical and other information relative to the Lough Gur ware.

The dating of the Lough Gur settlement relies on the pottery typology; the radiocarbon dates obtained for Site L (mentioned above) fit the proposed chronology but cannot be regarded as definitive. A date of 4090 ± 140 BP was obtained from a trial excavation on Garrett Island (Liversage 1958) which lies in the middle of the lake to the west of Knockadoon and which also showed traces of Neolithic occupation. On the evidence of the pottery found in the excavation the occupation appeared to belong to a mature stage of the main Lough Gur settlement.

Ancient field systems and enclosures

The huts and houses of a stock-raising cereal-growing community imply the existence of field systems and farm enclosures, but of their very nature such will not survive unless protected in some way. At many places in Ireland it is known that vast areas of peat bog have grown over and hidden ancient sites and features. Instances of this at Lough Boora and at Ballynagilly have already been mentioned. In peat-bog areas in Cork, Kerry, Tipperary, Mayo and Donegal, where the peat is being cut away for use as fuel, some of the ancient pre-peat field boundaries have been revealed. Systematic investigation of pre-peat surfaces in North Mayo in the west of Ireland has been going on since 1969 when a joint survey was conducted by Michael Herity and Seamas Caulfield.

At Behy/Glenulra a series of parallel field walls divided by offset cross-walls into rectangular areas of up to 7ha in extent were found. The parallel walls were set 150–200m apart and ran from the cliff edges for distances of up to 1km until they disappeared beneath the still uncut bog. The excavator (Caulfield 1978, 138; 1983, 200) suggests that these large tracts were more suitable for husbandry than for tillage.

In 1970–1 an oval enclosure within one of the large fields was excavated. It was about 22m by 25m and was bounded by poorly built stone walls. The post-holes of a small circular hut were found. The finds included Neolithic round-bottomed shouldered pottery, a leaf-shaped arrowhead and portion of a stone axe, as well as scrapers and numerous fragments or chips of quartzite and chert. A charcoal sample from the enclosure was dated to 4460 ± 115 BP.

Behy court tomb (De Valera and Ó Nualláin 1964, 4–5) is situated about 250m to the west in another large field. It was completely embedded in peat, its foundations resting on the mineral soil. Three radiocarbon dates were obtained for the basal peat close to the tomb: 3890 ± 110 BP, 3630 ± 70 BP and 3930 ± 105 BP. The second of these dates is regarded as 'possibly largely erroneous' (*Radiocarbon* 1973, 223) due to the quality of the sample submitted. Caulfield makes the point (1978, 141) that the date of the oval enclosure is consistent with the dates for the initiation of the peat.

Excavation was begun at Belderg Beg, 7km west of the Behy field system, in 1971. The site had been largely stripped of bog which would originally have been from one to two metres in thickness over the whole area. A series of small conjoined enclosures was found. There was evidence of flint knapping, and a few sherds of pottery and a stone axe were recovered. Criss-cross dark bands, interpreted as evidence of primitive ploughing, were noted, and these were overlain in places by ridge cultivation of a type similar to that still in use in the west of Ireland. Blanket bog started to form on this surface but it was shortly invaded by secondary woodland of oak and pine. A radiocarbon date of 4220 ± 95 BP was obtained for the stump of a pine tree which had its roots resting on the mineral soil but not penetrating it. The tree, therefore, grew on a thin layer of bog.

Subsequently, after blanket bog had once more begun to form, occupation of the site recommenced. A long stone wall built on 20–30cm of peat was found, and a line of pointed stakes followed the line of the wall, in some cases situated

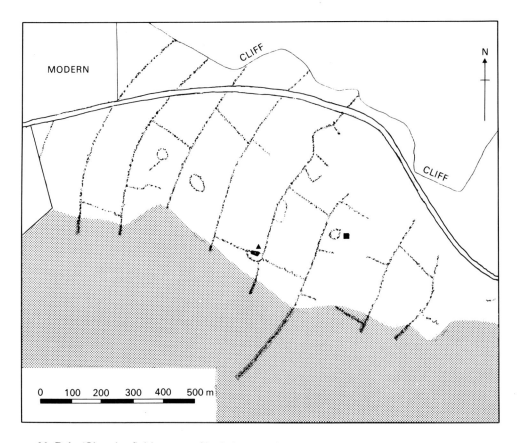

30 Behy/Glenulra field system. Shaded area at bottom shows approximate edge of uncut bog. △ = Behy court tomb; ■ = Glenulra enclosure (after S. Caulfield)

directly beneath it. One of the stakes was radiocarbon-dated to 3220 ± 85 BP and a second stake had a closely similar date. A circular stone and earth house or hut, 9m in diameter, was excavated. There was an internal wall trench and within this was a ring of postholes. Saddle querns and rubbing stones were found which would have been utilized for grinding the corn produced in the tillage plots. The amount of charcoal found suggested that the structure had burnt down. A ^{14}C date of 3170 ± 85 BP was obtained from a burnt block of wood found within the house (Caulfield 1973, 18) and this ties in well with the dates recorded for the secondary stone and stake wall.

At Carrownagloch, Glencree, also in North Mayo, Michael Herity investigated an area enclosed by a stone wall, also formerly covered by peat. There was extensive evidence of ridge cultivation and the remains of a circular hut, *c.*7m in diameter, were found. More than one period of occupation was represented at the site, because it could be seen that a 'ghost' wall ran across the enclosure and the ridge cultivation could be seen to underlie the later wall. A radiocarbon date similar to those of the second phase at Belderg Beg was obtained for a hearth underlying the final enclosing wall (Herity 1981, 37).

In Co. Kerry, on Valencia Island, a pre-bog wall has recently come to light and the radiocarbon date is similar to that of the Behy/Glenulra enclosure (Mitchell unpublished). At Lough Gur, adjacent to the Neolithic houses on Knockadoon, there are several instances of stone-faced terraces built across narrow sloping valleys, thus creating small fields. A more extensive field pattern with associated hut foundations can be seen spreading over the broad rounded ridge of Knockfennel Hill on the north side of the lake. While the Knockadoon terraced fields may well be contemporaneous with the Neolithic houses, and there is some evidence from the excavations which suggests this, the date of the Knockfennel system is unknown.

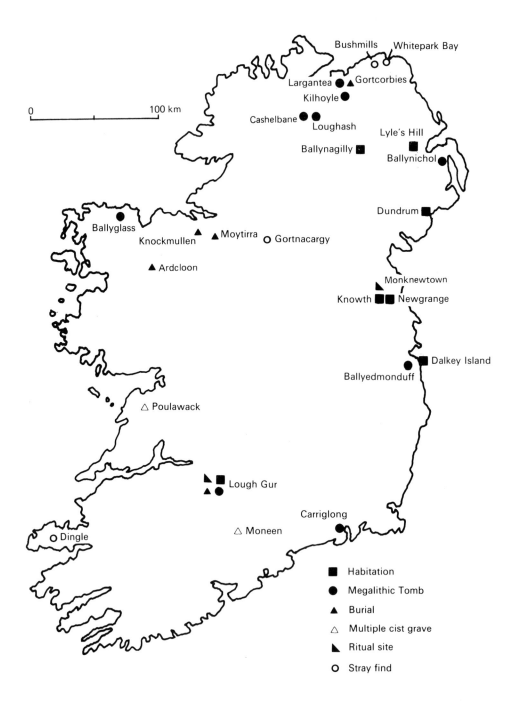

Key

- ■ Habitation
- ● Megalithic Tomb
- ▲ Burial
- △ Multiple cist grave
- ◣ Ritual site
- ○ Stray find

31 Distribution map of Beaker finds (after R. M. Cleary)

68

4

The Late Neolithic/Beaker period

Beaker pottery

Beaker pottery has already been mentioned in connection with the habitation and settlement sites at Ballynagilly, Co. Tyrone, and at Lough Gur, Co. Limerick. Nowadays, students of Irish archaeology are as familiar with Beaker ware as they are with the Irish Neolithic round-bottomed and flat-based ware. Yet it was not until the discovery of Beaker in 1939 at the Grange stone circle near Lough Gur that it began to be regarded as other than an extremely rare and exotic commodity in Ireland, confined to a few finds in the northern part of the country, its presence there being explained by the nearness of this territory to Britain, where Beaker was well known. As time went by and more and more sites in different parts of Ireland began to yield Beaker ware, an explanation for its presence was sought in terms of an invasion or migration of 'Beaker Folk' who came to exploit the country's ore deposits. This theory is very properly being questioned at the present time.

Beaker pottery is known in Europe from Iberia to Poland and from the Mediterranean Sea to the Baltic. In its original context it was the characteristic pottery of aristocratic warrior-archers who buried their dead in single graves, i.e. in pits or in cists constructed of slabs of stone covered by circular mounds of earth or cairns of stone. In the graves they placed their characteristic pottery together with tanged-and-barbed flint arrowheads, stone wrist guards or bracers (these protected the wrist from the recoil of the bow string), and in some instances there were copper knives or daggers. More rarely there were some items of gold.

Beaker ware has many different forms and it was ornamented in a variety of ways. Not surprisingly, a number of typologies are in existence, but for these islands the most widely used at the present day are those of D. L. Clarke (1970) and J. N. Lanting and J. D. van der Waals (1972). In its classic forms, Beaker is a high-quality ware, thin-walled, well-fired, well-ornamented and normally of S-profile. The classic types most frequently found in Ireland are the All-over-ornamented ware, the Bell Beaker, and two types with British affinities, namely, Wessex/Middle Rhine and North British/Middle Rhine. In the All-over-ornamented Beaker the ornament was impressed on the clay by a comb-type implement, or by a twisted cord, or by grooving. Bell Beakers were frequently ornamented in zones, and in the other two types, panels of ornament and incised

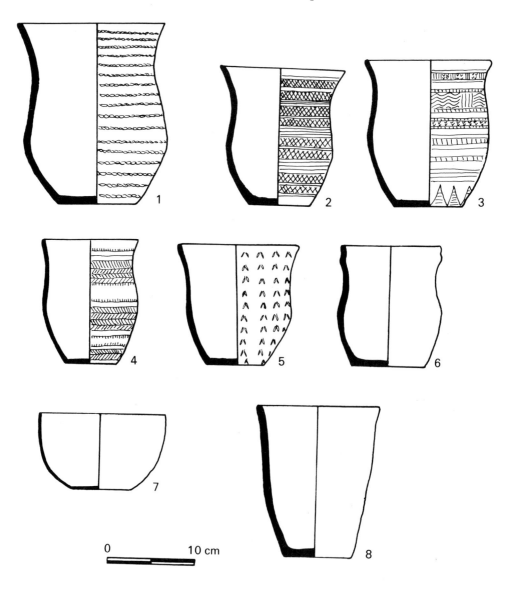

32 Beaker Ware: 1 All-over-ornamented (AOO), 2 Bell Beaker (E), 3 Wessex/Middle Rhine (W/MR), 4 North British/Middle Rhine (N/MR), 5 Rusticated Beaker, 6 Cordoned Beaker, 7 Undecorated Bowls, 8 Flat-based Coarse Ware (decorated/undecorated) (after D. L. Clarke)

lines can occur, as well as comb-stamp impressions. A number of related forms such as Cordoned Beakers, Pot Beakers, plain bowl-shaped vessels and footed or polypod bowls are also known from Ireland. While a basic continuity is evident between Neolithic and Beaker-Period pottery, some new elements appear such as the use of comb impressions and the addition of chamotte (sometimes known as grog, i.e. ground-up pottery sherds) to the clay before firing as a temper (Cleary 1983, 111). Tempering counteracted excessive shrinkage, facilitated even drying and consequently prevented cracks, etc.

In the older view, and indeed in the view still held by some archaeologists, the Beaker Folk migration theory could conveniently be used to explain a number of important changes in the archaeological record of the Late Neolithic/Metal Age transition. For instance, during the proposed Beaker Folk expansion and migration towards the end of the third millennium BC, the building of megalithic tombs (i.e. constructed of large stones) came to an end in western Continental Europe. The knowledge of metallurgy began to spread widely there and eventually in Britain and Ireland, and in the latter there was a rapid development of this new technology. Because Beaker pottery was found at the great stone circle at Grange near the western shore of Lough Gur, it was tempting at that time (AD 1939) to assume that the building of this impressive monument was inspired by newly arrived Beaker people and carried into effect by the natives under the direction of the Beaker Folk warrior aristocrats.

In Britain and Ireland since the 1970s, Beakers and 'Beaker Folk' have come to be regarded in a much more realistic light, one which is more in keeping with the facts as they are. Colin Burgess, one of the prime movers of the new approach, has pointed out that Beakers brought Britain and Ireland into touch with a widespread international tradition of which Beakers themselves were the nucleus. Various artefacts such as tanged copper daggers, V-perforated buttons, double-pointed awls, wrist guards and tanged-and-barbed arrowheads were at various times and in various places associated with them, 'together constituting the outward sign of a movement or idea, the precise nature of which may never be revealed' (Burgess 1980, 62). He refers to this as the 'Beaker package' and says that 'it was everywhere blended into local contexts alongside local artifacts, and the absence of any accompanying international social or economic system, house or settlement type, ritual or burial tradition, argues powerfully against a greater Beaker folk movement in the traditional sense' (Burgess 1980, 63).

Many excavations have taken place in Ireland since Beaker was found at the Grange stone circle at Lough Gur (p. 138), and the picture is not as clear as it then appeared to be. Beaker ware must still be regarded as something of a ceramic phenomenon, but whether introduced by way of immigrants or by way of culture contact and through the existence of trading connections with Britain and the Continent, it is as yet impossible to say with any degree of certainty. The ware was adopted by the natives but not to such an extent as to supersede indigenous forms. As a high quality, extremely decorative ware, it must have had prestige value. It could have affected the life-style of those who adopted it to the extent that it represented a higher level of technology than heretofore but there is no evidence that its introduction made any impression on their way of life. Though mainly found in domestic assemblages in Ireland, the classic Beaker types never form more than a small proportion of the whole. There are no distinctive Beaker house-types and, when the pottery occurs in non-domestic contexts, the same lack of impact is evident. It has occasionally been found in graves and in chambered tombs in Ireland, but no distinctive Beaker graves comparable to those from Britain are known, where the crouched inhumation is contained in a cist or a pit under a round mound and accompanied by a classic Beaker pot. Even in the British cases, as Burgess points out (1980, 70), the only new element in this mode and form of burial was the Beaker pot itself; the remainder was not peculiar to the 'Beaker Folk'. This idea of integration of Beaker pottery styles with indigenous ones rather than a take-over by immigrant elements has been demonstrated in habitation sites in the Boyne valley and at Lough Gur.

Apart from the Lough Gur concentration, Beaker is predominantly found north of a line running westward from Dublin Bay, taking in Dalkey Island and the Ballyedmonduff wedge tomb. Therein lies the difficulty of attributing the earliest use of metal to Beaker-using communities. Up to the present, the earliest evidence for metal working comes from the south-west of the country, the area where Beaker is virtually absent.

Settlement

At Newgrange, Co. Meath, the Late Neolithic/Beaker domestic activity took place along the front or southern part of the mound when it had fallen into decay. The sides of the cairn collapsed at some unknown date after the completion of the monument. We do not know the duration of the monument's *floruit* but it is at least possible to say that no secondary interments or any modifications of the structure, such as occurred at many chambered tombs, were discovered here. Whether the collapse of the sides of the cairn and consequent concealment of the entrance of the passage tomb were the factors which led to its abandonment or whether it was first abandoned and then left to the mercy of wind, weather and animals is not known. When it collapsed, the stones and layers of turves of which the cairn was composed spread out all around and over the kerb of the monument for an initial distance of 4–7m. Later slides extended even farther. Excavation showed extensive evidence of settlement on and beyond this collapsed material. There was no evidence of domestic activity beneath the earliest layers of the collapse.

About two-fifths of the perimeter of the cairn in the entrance area were excavated between the years 1962 and 1975, and the domestic activity was found throughout the whole extent of the area. It was in no way connected with the monument itself and even if the 'squatters' were aware of the nature and former status of Newgrange as a great 'public' monument, no attempt was made to interfere with it by digging into it or in any way altering it. The squatting was a continuous process extending both circumferentially around the edge of the collapse in the area excavated and outward from it to the limit of the excavation, a distance of over 20m from the kerb of the monument. It was also clear that the activity continued into the unexcavated areas to the east and west and beyond the southern limit.

The settlement consisted of a series of living floors strung around the edge of the collapse, each with a hearth at the centre. The hearths were usually rectangular in plan, one metre long by half a metre wide, and were outlined with carefully set stones. Each floor had numerous pits and holes, some of them postholes. Potsherds and flints (both artefacts and the very numerous waste pieces resulting from flint-knapping on the spot), as well as large quantities of animal bones, were concentrated on the floors and around the hearths. It was not possible to reconstruct with certainty any specific house plans; the most convincing were two parallel arrangements of postholes at the western limit of the excavation and an L-shaped foundation trench in the Central Area. In the main, it appeared that the people were squatting in rather flimsy structures set up in the shelter of the high

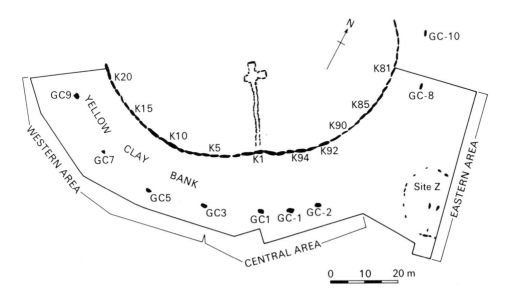

33 Newgrange, Co. Meath, areas excavated 1962–75

73

cairn. As one house or hut became unusable, perhaps due to prolonged occupation or to a further slide of stones from the mound, others were set up, and the way of life continued as before (O'Kelly *in* O'Kelly *et al.* 1983).

Two features in particular remained unresolved after the final season of excavation in 1975, a multiple arc of large pits in the Eastern Area and a bank of boulder clay in the Western Area (*ibid.*, 16–21 and 26–9 respectively). The pits, averaging 1.5m in diameter and 1–1.5m in depth, were dug to a rough but fairly organized pattern consisting of three concentric arcs which extended across the eastern part of the excavation. The multiple arc certainly continued beyond the limits of the excavation on the eastern side of this area. It was not concentric with the kerb of the Newgrange cairn but, on the contrary, swept away from it towards the southern limit of the Central Area of the excavation. It may have continued on in this direction, but since this part was excavated in the first season, the pattern of pits, if such existed here, was not then obvious. About seventy pits in all were identified in the multiple arc. It was clear that they had not held posts. After a pit was dug, it was backfilled quickly, some charcoal, animal bone food waste and sherds of pottery being sometimes thrown in with the soil. Charcoal samples from three of the pits yielded ^{14}C dates (*ibid.*, 21). Another group of sixteen pits very similar in every respect was found between the multiple arc and the

34 Newgrange, Co. Meath, one of the Beaker squatting areas

kerb of Site Z. In 1982 a cutting was opened close to the road boundary of the site under the auspices of the National Parks and Monuments Branch of the Office of Public Works in advance of a proposed tourist facility (Sweetman 1985) and an extremely complex series of features was uncovered, probably of Beaker date. On a visit to the excavation it was apparent to the writer that none of the pits which were then exposed resembled in any way those of the multiple arc or those of the smaller group.

The bank of boulder clay commenced in the Western Area, almost opposite the tomb entrance, as a low narrow ridge of stoneless light yellow clay, more or less parallel with the kerb of the monument and 5–6m distant from it on average. It ran westward to the limit of the excavation at the west side and presumably beyond. The Beaker settlement was already in existence when the bank was heaped up and it continued to exist afterwards as the Beaker occupation layer ran not only beneath the bank, but also up along its northern shoulder. This feature and the multiple arc will be elucidated only when further full, not partial, excavations are undertaken.

Six radiocarbon dates, including the three obtained from the multiple arc of pits, and ranging from 4050 ± 40 BP to 3875 ± 90 BP, were obtained from Beaker-associated charcoal in the Eastern Area. The dates are later by approximately 400 radiocarbon years than dates obtained for the structure of the tomb. The duration of the Beaker occupation is not known.

The animal bones, the food waste of the squatters, are of special interest. A study (Van Wijngaarden-Bakker 1974; 1986) has shown that domesticated cattle predominated, though pig and sheep/goat were also present in significant amounts. Other domesticated species were the dog and the horse. There is proof that the latter were eaten though they were not a primary food source and they were also probably used as pack and/or riding animals. Their number was not large. Among the wild species represented were red deer, mountain hare, fox, brown bear, wild cat and wild boar, none of which were found in significant amounts. Neither fish nor bird bones were present, possibly because conditions were not favourable for preservation.

An in-depth study of the pottery was undertaken by Rose M. Cleary (*in* O'Kelly *et al*. 1983). The total number of sherds was over 3,600 and almost 200 vessels were represented. Technical processes, such as polished briquette section, spectrographic analysis and petrological examination, among others, were employed. In the excavated area five main pottery concentrations were identified but in spite of the number and diversity of vessels the whole assemblage constituted a homogeneous entity. It consisted of classical Beaker, Beaker-associated ware, Coarse ware, Grooved ware and Late Neolithic-influenced domestic ware. Studies of the raw material suggested local manufacture of the assemblage. Cleary feels that 'it is better to consider the Newgrange

Table 2 *Newgrange: Late Neolithic/Beaker Pottery Types*

	Classification	Type	Minimum no. of vessels represented
I	Classic Beaker	All-over-ornamented	14
		Bell Beaker	10
		Wessex/Middle Rhine	8
		North British/Middle Rhine	8
II	Typically associated with classic Beaker forms in Irish habitation sites	Cordoned Beakers	15
		Pot Beakers (rusticated)	10
		Undecorated bowls	7
		Flat-based bucket-shaped	15
III	Beaker-influenced	Containing elements of classic beaker techniques and ornament	53
IV	Coarse domestic	Flat-based coarse domestic ware, decorated (grooved/bird-bone, impressed/lugged) or undecorated	31
V	Domestic ware with Neolithic affinities	Thick coarse undecorated flat-based ware	11
		Bowl forms	6
VI	Possible Neolithic connections	Whipped cord impressed	1
VII	Possible Grooved ware connections	Rilled and lug-ornamented	9
VIII	Grooved ware (Rinyo-Clacton)	Internal grooving	2

assemblage as one complex, spanning at least 200 years, rather than one resulting from three or four migrations into the Boyne valley' (*ibid.*, 63). The pottery with Late Neolithic affiliations and similarities 'can be considered to be the rough domestic ware used in conjunction with the Beaker ceramic range and can be seen as a continuation of the Neolithic pottery tradition in Ireland' (*ibid.*).

The classic Beaker forms represented at Newgrange consist of All-over-ornamented pots, the ornament achieved either by comb or twisted cord impressions or by grooves; Bell Beaker, a title which is self-explanatory, also ornamented; and two further types with British/Rhine affiliations in which the ornament is zonal, the zones alternately filled with incised herring-bone motifs or with comb impressions with incised fringing; the polypod vessels are classed as Wessex/Middle Rhine. The above descriptions are extremely simplified ones. Other wares are present which are typically associated in habitation sites with the classic Beakers. These are Cordoned Beakers, the cordons (bands) being pinched up around the circumference of the pot – very occasionally they are applied; Rusticated ware, the so-called Pot Beakers, in which the decoration consists of fingernail impressions; and also flat-based bucket-shaped pots and undecorated bowls.

The flint work was studied by Daragh Lehane (*in* O'Kelly *et al.* 1983). The assemblage contained over 11,000 pieces of flint that had been humanly modified, and nodular flint was the raw material used, probably picked up from the drift in the neighbourhood. The proportion of implements to waste flint was 8.6 per cent, indicating that the flint was worked in the area. There were just over 800 finished implements. Of these, scrapers constituted 54 per cent, 438 in all. There were thirty-six blades and flakes with edge retouch for use as knives; thirty butt-thinned forms; and twenty-two artefacts which are known as arrowheads of petit tranchet derivative type but which are much more convincing in the role of knives held in the hand. There were six true arrowheads consisting of leaf-shaped, triangular and hollow-based forms (one of each), and there were three barbed-and-tanged examples; the latter are usually associated with Beakers, while the others demonstrate Neolithic continuity.

As with the pottery, the most noticeable feature of the flint assemblage was again its homogeneity and its continuity. It showed no new traits throughout and was typical of Late Neolithic and Beaker assemblages in Britain. Comparison could not be made with other Irish material, as qualitative analyses of the type undertaken at Newgrange were not available.

Amongst other finds were a flat metal axe and a number of stone objects which were taken to be the equipment of a metal worker (O'Kelly and Shell 1979). They were covered by a considerable depth of collapse from the cairn in a part of the Eastern Area where there was a typical Beaker living floor with central rectangular hearth. The axe was a high-tin bronze, cast in an open mould and finished by forging, grinding and polishing. It lay about 6m from two of the pits of the multiple arc from which radiocarbon dates were obtained, and it was argued that by association the axe could be of similar date. This is clearly earlier than the date generally envisaged for similar axes – Type Killaha in Harbison's typology (1969a) – particularly when the dates are calibrated.

The Knowth monument, which lies about 1km to the north-west of New-grange, also produced evidence of Beaker activity, consisting of four areas where finds of flint and pottery were present, as well as cremation deposits loosely associated with Beaker ware, and there were also many isolated finds of pottery. The total number of pottery sherds recovered and the number of vessels rep-resented by them are approximately the same as those from Newgrange (Eogan 1984). From the pottery and flint assemblages it would appear that the Knowth occupation was of a domestic nature and was similar to that at Newgrange. No house plans were recovered, but pits and hearths were present and in general the material from the various concentrations appears to represent domestic debris (Eogan 1984, 245).

The Eastern concentration covered an area 19m by 14m, its western limit being terminated by one of the satellite passage tombs, Site 15. A number of pits and depressions were found, two of them containing sherds of Beaker. In addition, sherds of Beaker were found in a large oval pit in the same area. There were two reddened areas which could have been hearths but neither was defined by any form of setting; only one contained charcoal. The pottery sherds came from both fine and coarse Beakers and some pieces of Western Neolithic ware were also present. About thirty-four vessels were represented. Flint was being knapped on the site, mainly in the production of scrapers, as at Newgrange. No food waste in the form of animal bones was found.

The Western concentration lay in a layer of dark material flecked with char-

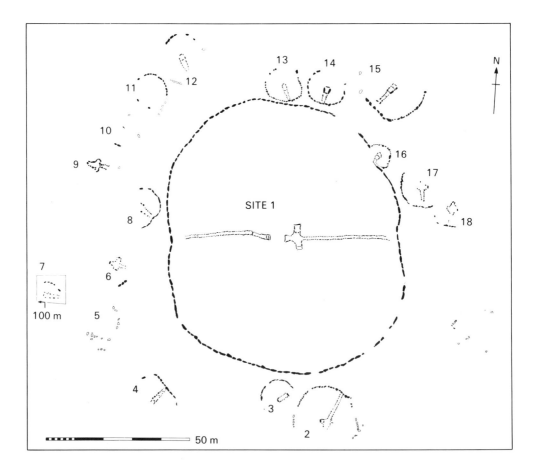

35 Knowth, Co. Meath, Site 1 and satellite passage tombs (after G. Eogan)

coal, possibly a layer of turves. The sherds represent about thirty vessels which come variously within the Beaker classification. The pottery was well fired and finished. Cord and comb-stamp ornament was rare and the great majority of sherds were decorated with incised lines. There were some Cordoned Beakers. As at Newgrange, flint was being worked on the site.

A deposit of cremated bone covering an area 44 by 30cm was found in the passage of the satellite tomb, Site 15, which adjoined the Eastern concentration. It was contained in a layer of silt-like material with small stones mixed through it, 40cm in maximum thickness. Eogan says that this may have filtered in through the roof of the passage. The layer was covered by soft earth and stones which, according to the excavator, may have accumulated when the roofstones of the tomb passage were removed (in antiquity). The layer containing cremated bone was 30–40cm above the old ground surface. There was no evidence of a pit but an attempt had apparently been made to provide a compartment by placing small stones against two of the unprotected sides, the other sides being formed of the structural stones of the passage. Sherds of a Beaker were found in and close to the cremation, not all at the same level in the fill. Some were on the cremation itself, others were in the fill above the deposit, and the main concentration was outside the 'compartment'. The sherds fitted together and almost an entire undecorated Beaker was reconstructed. Eogan places the vessel within the Bell-Beaker group (*ibid.*, 311). He says that 'the presence of sherds with the cremation indicates that they were associated. It is likely that the vessel was placed beside the burial but got broken, probably when the tomb was wrecked. This destruc-tion also appears to have disturbed the upper part of the silt layer' (*ibid.*, 312).

In another of the satellite tombs, a cruciform example, Site 6 (1984 numer-ation; formerly Site 9), near the western concentration of pottery, a cremation was found in one of the three side-chambers. Around the edge of the deposit and partly sunk into it were sherds of a Beaker vessel of coarse ware with incised orna-ment. Eogan comments that the pottery in the nearby concentration was much finer, and he suggests that the coarser vessel may represent an isolated find. He says that 'it cannot be established if a complete vessel was deposited although sherds could have disintegrated at the time of the destruction of the site' (*ibid.*, 312). A mixed deposit of pottery sherds, flints, charcoal, animal bones and part of a human skull was found overlying the flag in the left-hand recess of another satellite, Site 18.

Radiocarbon determinations obtained from charcoal in two of the Beaker concentrations were unfortunately anomalous, probably due to contamination of the samples (*ibid.*, 321), but at the Monknewtown embanked enclosure, a few kilometres to the north (discussed below, p. 134), a Late Neolithic/Beaker Period squatting area of the same type as those at Knowth and Newgrange produced radiocarbon dates similar to those from Newgrange. The flimsy nature of the

Beaker habitations on the one hand, and the durability and wealth of the Boyne megaliths on the other, form a striking contrast. At Newgrange at least, the radiocarbon dates show a gap of about five hundred years between the two. Elsewhere we have speculated about the aftermath of the Newgrange monument (O'Kelly 1982, 145) and have wondered how far the enormous quantities of turves used in the building of this and of the neighbouring satellite mounds had become the undoing of the rich Neolithic farmers. The same turf stripping had taken place at Knowth. Grass would eventually have become re-established and possibly there would have been some regeneration of woodland in the form of hazel and birch scrub, but the Boyne valley was far too fertile an area ever to remain unpopulated for long. By the end of Late Neolithic times, the communities may have been poorer but they herded cattle and raised pigs and were engaged in cereal cultivation. W. A. Caspari (*in* O'Kelly *et al.* 1983) identified eight grains of naked barley and one grain of emmer wheat in a sample of charcoal associated with Beaker ware at Newgrange. A ^{14}C date of 3885 ± 35 BP was obtained from the charcoal. Cereal grains were also identified at Knowth though no ^{14}C date was available.

Louise van Wijngaarden-Bakker, in her final report on the animal remains from the Beaker settlement at Newgrange (1986), draws some interesting conclusions relating to the palaeoeconomy of Newgrange, and by inference, that of the Boyne valley in general. She remarks that the turf stripping activities of the passage tomb builders would have resulted in a deterioration of the cultivation areas and a greater emphasis on animal husbandry. Consequently, in the succeeding period the emphasis of the economy would perforce have been mainly directed towards the breeding of the primary food animals. She notes the absence of querns and grain rubbers in spite of the evidence for cereal cultivation mentioned above. The latter implies, however, that in some part at least of the catchment area the humus layer was sufficiently developed to support cereal crops, or alternatively, cereals could have been acquired through exchange. In order to support the large herds of food-producing animals, transhumance may have been practised, orientated perhaps towards the rich coastal regions. Van Wijngaarden-Bakker remarks in particular on the widening of the subsistence base in the course of the Beaker occupation with the introduction of the horse and the increased importance of sheep/goat. She concludes that:

> The Beaker settlement at Newgrange formed part of an exchange network involving the movement of subsistence products such as live cattle, horses and possibly smoked pork as well as raw material such as flint and antler. The extensive grazing of large herds would have increased the contacts with neighbouring communities, while the favourable position of the settlement on the border of the River Boyne stresses the importance of transport by water. (Van Wijngaarden-Bakker 1986, 102)

It has already been mentioned that at a time broadly coinciding with the Late Neolithic/Beaker settlement at Newgrange, occupation of Ballynagilly, Co. Tyrone, recommenced. The change in the pollen diagram suggested clearance of birch scrub and the establishment of a mixed farming economy in which pastoralism and the cultivation of cereals went forward side by side. This is similar to the findings from the Boyne valley. Some distance downhill from the Early Neolithic occupation area, three habitation sites were found. Just as in the case of Newgrange, although there were extensive traces of domestic activity in the form of hearths, pits, postholes and stakeholes, there was no definite house or hut foundation.

The Beaker ware included All-over-comb and All-over-cord, Bell Beaker, Wessex/Middle Rhine and North British/Middle Rhine. Seven radiocarbon dates from charcoal associated with the pottery range from 4050 ± 50 BP to 3780 ± 70 BP and agree with those obtained for similar associations at Newgrange. One pit contained pottery of Late Neolithic/Sandhills type. The flints were of broad flake type and contained a variety of scrapers though small convex ones were in the majority. Lozenge-shaped pressure-flaked arrowheads were present, and a few tanged-and-barbed examples. Since only preliminary reports have appeared as yet the site as a whole cannot be fully evaluated.

One of the Beaker dates, 3860 ± 50 BP, refers to a pot with a combination of comb and false relief decoration. The excavator suggests that this appears to represent 'an early stage in the evolution of the Beaker-derived "Irish Bowl" Food vessel series' (ApSimon 1976, 22). (The latter pottery type will be described below.)

Lough Gur, Co. Limerick, has already been mentioned in connection with the extensive Neolithic occupation on the Knockadoon peninsula. No dates are available for the beginning of the settlement but one could perhaps think in terms of a few centuries earlier than the building of Newgrange. One of the remarkable features of Lough Gur was its continuity of occupation from its beginnings until some time in the Bronze Age. Unlike Ballynagilly, there was no discernible break in the settlement pattern. Houses continued to be built and to fall into decay and be reconstituted, so that most of the houses and the house-enclosures contained Beaker pottery in addition to the Neolithic wares. It was frequently difficult to establish the stratigraphical succession of the different phases, particularly where there was little depth of occupation debris or where so much continuous activity had taken place over a prolonged period. Pits had been dug into earlier levels, and pottery and other finds were often not in their original context as a result.

The largest assemblage of Beaker sherds was at Site D and the variety of ornament, thickness, and texture suggested that a large number of vessels was represented. Apart from this site, the amount of Beaker in the settlement was not considerable but was fairly consistently present and, as at Newgrange and elsewhere, was associated with Neolithic wares. The round-based shouldered bowls of Class I and the coarse flat-based ware of Class II were everywhere associated with Beaker in the later phases. Associated metal objects included a small gold disc – probably a button cap – from Site D. Bronze pins, a few awls and some other items of bronze were found at some of the sites. At Circle K (Grogan and Eogan forthcoming) the bronze objects came from the sod or immediately beneath it and glass beads and fragments came from a similar horizon. Outside the enclosure some unidentifiable fragments of clay moulds were found. A Neolithic/Early Bronze Age date was proposed by Ó Ríordáin (1954, 354–8) for glass beads found at Site C, but Grogan and Eogan believe that they are unlikely to be earlier than the Late Bronze Age and bear comparison with those found at the Rathgall hillfort (discussed below, p. 313). One must thus question not only the contemporaneity of the glass beads with the main occupation phases on Knockadoon but that of the bronze objects and clay moulds also, at least as far as the above-mentioned sites are concerned. Continuity of occupation on the Knockadoon peninsula may have persisted for a much longer period than was envisaged by Ó Ríordáin thirty years ago.

The continuity of occupation on Knockadoon was made possible by the soil and climatic conditions on the peninsula. The light warm limestone soil of Lough Gur was very favourable to cattle raising and once the initial clearance was completed, forest regeneration would scarcely have presented a problem. In the settlement, cattle bones accounted for almost the total assemblage; only about five per cent were pig and sheep/goat. Horse bones were found at Sites A, C, D and Circle K, each time in Late Neolithic/Beaker contexts (Van Wijngaarden-Bakker 1974, 368ff.).

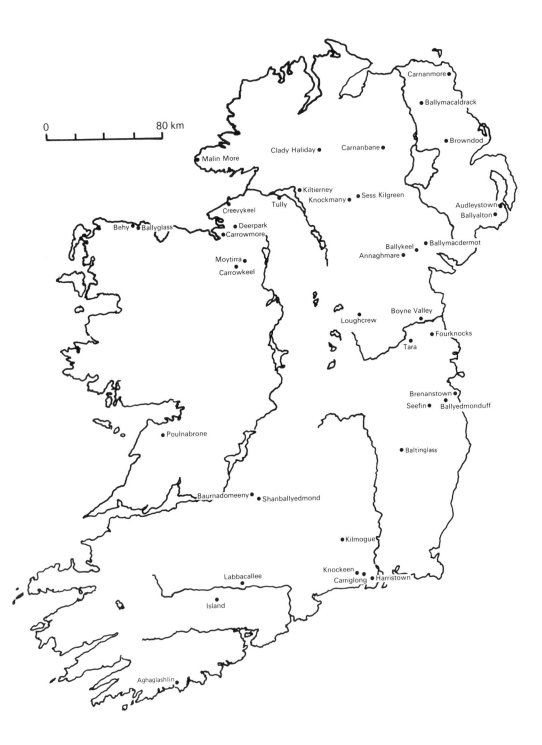

36 Megalithic sites

5

Megaliths

Megalithic tombs

In most parts of Ireland tombs built of great stone slabs, megalithic tombs, are well known. While many have been destroyed in the past and many more in recent times, reliable estimates place the surviving number at about 1,200. There are many variant forms but it is possible to classify them into four main types: court cairns (formerly known as horned cairns), portal dolmens, passage graves and wedge-shaped gallery graves, or, to use the newer nomenclature, court, portal, passage and wedge tombs.*

Court tombs

A count has placed the number of tombs of this class at 329 (Ó Nualláin 1979), all of them, except for about a half dozen, lying in the northern third of Ireland. Of the outliers, two are in Co. Clare and there is one in each of the Counties Tipperary, Kilkenny and Waterford. The northern distribution is therefore very marked. Within that area there are strong local concentrations, particularly heavy ones in the coastal regions of Mayo, Sligo and Donegal in the west and north-west and a lesser concentration in Down and Louth around Carlingford Lough in the north-east. These two areas are connected by a strong spread of tombs across the midlands of Ulster. Related tombs are to be found in Scotland, the Isle of Man and on both sides of the Severn estuary in Britain (De Valera 1960).

The name court tomb arises from its most prominent feature, the court-like area from which access is gained to the tomb chamber. The cairn averages about 30m in length, 15m wide at the front and about 7m at the rear. The long straight sides are usually marked by a revetment of stones standing on end (orthostats), though dry-built stonework is also known, as at Audleystown, Co. Down (Collins 1954; 1959a). The tomb or gallery, also built of orthostats, is placed

---

* In the 1950s a survey of the megalithic tombs was initiated by the archaeological section of the Ordnance Survey, at first under the direction of Dr R. De Valera and subsequently under that of Dr S. Ó Nualláin. To date, four volumes of this valuable work have appeared: Vol. I, 1961, Co. Clare; Vol. II, 1964, Co. Mayo; Vol. III, 1972, Counties Galway, Roscommon, Leitrim, Longford, Westmeath, Laois, Offaly, Kildare and Cavan; Vol. IV, 1982, Counties Cork, Kerry, Limerick and Tipperary.

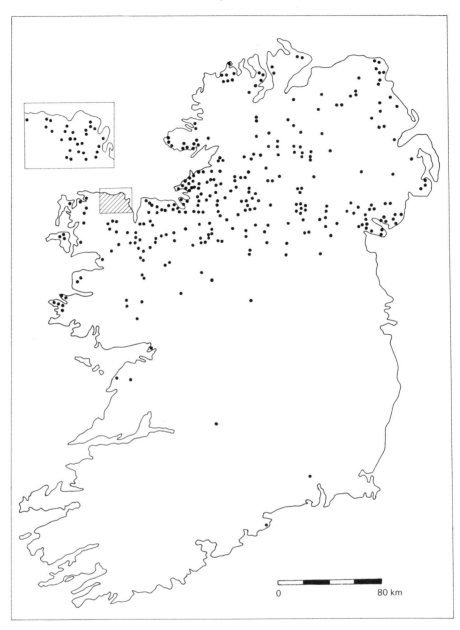

37 Distribution map of court tombs (after S. Ó Nualláin)

axially within the cairn and, in about 70 per cent of the known cases, has two compartments divided from each other by jamb-stones or by jamb and sill stones. Some three- and four-chambered galleries are known: e.g. Clady Halliday, Co. Tyrone, Browndod, Co. Antrim, and Annaghmare, Co. Armagh. The corbel technique was used in the roof. Slabs were laid flat, one on the other, each oversailing the one beneath until the space could be closed by one or two further stones. Entry to the tomb chamber or gallery was from the unroofed court, a feature usually defined by standing stones, though it can also have dry-built stone walls as at Behy, Co. Mayo. The court can be oval or circular and fully enclosed with a narrow entry, as in the Deerpark and Creevykeel, both in Co. Sligo; these are full court tombs. In others the court is U-shaped, as at Shanballyedmond, Co. Tipperary; or semicircular as at Cohaw, Co. Cavan. The U-shaped and semi-circular forms are the commonest. Circular or full courts, as they are called, are found in the western part of the distribution.

The tombs normally have an eastern orientation. In the majority of the known examples there is a single court and a compartmented gallery and these are placed at the broad end of the cairn. In dual-court tombs a court and a gallery

38 Creevykeel, Co. Sligo, court tomb, after excavation and conservation

are placed at each end of the cairn, as at Cohaw and Audleystown, and there is a variant in which the court occupies the centre of the cairn and the tomb galleries open longitudinally from it towards each end. This type is well exemplified at the Deerpark and at Ballyglass (Ma. 13). Sometimes subsidiary chambers are found opening separately on to the cairn edge, as at Annaghmare, Co. Armagh, or into the court, as at Malin More, Co. Donegal (De Valera 1960). A few galleries have transept chambers, as at Behy.

It is in the nature of things that complex sites such as dual court tombs or those with subsidiary chambers opening on to the sides of the cairn, or elsewhere, could have been built over a period of time and that not all parts may be of the same date. It is more obvious in some than in others that additions were made. The added subsidiary chambers in the Annaghmare court tomb and the various additions and improvements to Creevykeel (Hencken 1939) are instances. Likewise, the plan of the Deerpark, Co. Sligo (Ó Nualláin 1976, 99, 102–3), suggests that this is at least a two-period site.

Evidence on the nature of the burial rite is unsatisfactory as yet because less than forty tombs have been excavated and some of them were only partially dug. In the majority of the excavated sites, one cremation was found in the tomb and in a number of cases, this was a young male. In one tomb, however, Clady

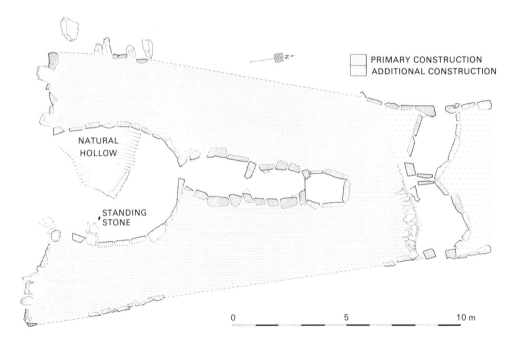

PRIMARY CONSTRUCTION
ADDITIONAL CONSTRUCTION

NATURAL
HOLLOW

STANDING
STONE

0   5   10 m

39 Annaghmare, Co. Armagh, court tomb (after D. M. Waterman; Crown copyright)

Halliday (Davies and Radford 1935–6), there were two; Audleystown contained thirty-four burials, thirty of which were unburnt, and another tomb at Bally-alton, Co. Down (Evans and Davies 1933–4), had eight unburnt burials.

Excavators have tended to interpret the mixture of stones and earth in the courts outside the tomb entrances as remnants of an original blocking of the openings, but it can also be interpreted as material which fell from the highest part of the cairn into the court. In a somewhat similar fashion, what used to be called 'extra-revetment material', namely, the stones lying outside the edges of the cairns, is now seen to be merely the collapse of the upper parts of the cairn revetment walls, or else slip of the cairn material itself. If the tomb doorway was closed at all, it is likely that this was done by means of a stone slab as at Newgrange, Co. Meath (O'Kelly 1982, 98), or at Cairnholy I and II in Scotland (Piggott and Powell 1948–9, 113, 125), or with timber, particularly if it was intended to open it again for the insertion of further bodies.

The evidence from Behy, Co. Mayo, is of particular interest in this regard (p. 65). The whole monument had become completely enveloped in a growth of peat which was 2m thick at the time of excavation (1963–4). While a hole had been dug through the peat in modern times to gain access to the chamber, the court area had remained hidden by the peat and thus had suffered no recent disturbance. Of this area the excavator says: 'The large quantity of stones found within the court and outside the revetments was clearly collapse from the dry-walling of the court and kerbs, and no deliberate blocking of the court or built extra-revetment material were present' (De Valera 1965, 6). Of course, this monument does not necessarily represent the totality of court tombs.

The pots found in the excavated tombs are round-bottomed bowls with or without shoulders, some decorated, some plain. Coarsely made flat-bottomed bucket-shaped vessels also occur. The characteristic flints are leaf- and lozenge-shaped arrowheads and hollow scrapers. All of these items have already been noted from Neolithic habitation sites. Javelin heads are also found; over a dozen are listed from excavated court tombs (Collins 1981, 116–17). Polished axes of stone have been found and stone beads have come from eight excavated sites (Ó Nualláin 1979, 8). It has occasionally been found that, where sufficient investigation was carried out, evidence of pre-tomb activity came to light, as at the two Ballyglass sites (p. 53). The excavator in question, Ó Nualláin, rightly suggests that in view of the discoveries at these two sites and of the fact that habitation refuse has been found under many other court tombs, more extensive investigation of the precincts might be called for.

Total excavation of the court tomb at Shanballyedmond, Co. Tipperary (O'Kelly 1958), did not uncover underlying habitation but it did reveal structural details of great interest and showed how much may have been missed in the partial excavations at other sites. The gallery had two chambers built of orthostats and it was surrounded by a U-shaped setting of sixteen non-contiguous orthostats set at an average distance of 3m outside the sides of the tomb. The area between would have contained cairn material but much of it had been robbed. The spaces between these orthostats were filled by dry-walling creating a post-and-panel effect. About 2.3m outside this again, thirty-four postholes were found, set to a U-shaped plan concentric with the U-shaped post-and-panel setting. Clearly this edge of the monument had been marked by wooden posts, a feature completely new in this or in any other type of Irish megalithic tomb. The ends of the arms of the timber 'U' curved inward to connect with the ends of the horns of the forecourt to give approximately flat fronts (on plan) to the cairn material which would have come forward on either side of the court. A ^{14}C date of 4930 ± 60 BP was obtained from charcoal from postholes on the south front of the entrance.

Outside the orthostatic post-and-panel-type kerb there existed on the north side an extensive spread of smaller cairn stones which had become covered by hill-wash from the steep slope above the monument. This outer low cairn material terminated along such a definite line that it appeared likely that its edge had originally been marked in some way. As excavation proceeded this surmise proved correct because it was only then that we first came upon the U-shaped setting of postholes already described. The ^{14}C date of 3475 ± 40 BP obtained for charcoal from the base of the cairn-spread in this area is however completely at variance with that obtained from the entrance area. Neither of the two samples

40 Shanballyedmond, Co. Tipperary, court tomb, conjectural reconstruction

submitted to the Groningen laboratory was collected with radiocarbon-sampling in mind and it is therefore possible that the latter sample was contaminated in some way. If not, it raises interesting questions as to the possible structural phases of the monument.

The only burial found in a primary and undisturbed position was that of a youth aged between ten and fifteen years. The cremated remains had been deposited in a rectangular, partly stone-lined, pit or cist dug in the floor of the end chamber. Before the deposit was made, a fire had been lit in the cist and allowed to burn for two to three hours (the duration of the fire was estimated from experiments made on the site). The cist was then swept clean, the cremated bone put in place and the whole covered by a flagged pavement. A similar fire had been lit in the front chamber but there was no evidence of burial.

The finds included some small poorly preserved scraps of pottery of round-bottomed-bowl type, some undoubtedly from primary positions, and some fine leaf-shaped arrowheads in flint and chert. These latter objects had been burnt and were found as several scattered fragments under the edge of an area of cobbled pavement in the front of the forecourt.

Few firm radiocarbon dates are available as yet for Irish court tombs and in respect of some of those that are available it is difficult to know what aspect of the tomb's history is being dated, some dates applying to pre-tomb activity and others to later interference. The radiocarbon dates from Carnanbane, Bally-briest, Co. Derry (Evans 1939), are from a black layer beneath the cairn and are connected with pre-tomb activity; and one from Ballyutoag, Co. Antrim (Herring 1938), has a standard deviation of 300 years. The dates for Annaghmare, Co. Armagh (Waterman 1965), were disappointing as, whereas one of 4395 ± 55 BP was obtained for 'charcoal sealed behind the primary block-ing of the forecourt', those from the chambers were anomalous.

Despite two excavations (Evans 1938; Collins 1976) it has been admitted that the monument at Ballymacaldrack (Dooey's Cairn), Co. Antrim, is not yet fully understood. Behind the outer stone chamber was a feature unique in Irish court tombs, but found at Lochill in south-west Scotland, that is, a stone-lined trench containing three deep pits. Evidence of intense burning was forthcoming from the trench and the stones themselves. A large quantity of charcoal and lesser amounts of cremated human bone were found on and under the paving of the trench, to which the name of a 'cremation passage' has been given. A. E. P. Collins's excavation provided two charcoal samples from the trench: 4940 ± 50 BP and 5150 ± 90 BP. Charcoal from the lower part of the forecourt blocking gave a date of 4630 ± 130 BP. Collins remarks: 'From these it would appear that the "cremation passage" saw extensive burning . . . and that part at least of the forecourt blocking deposit was put in position about 500 years later.' A series of eight samples from the cairn, forecourt blocking and chambers of the court tomb at Ballymacdermot, Co. Armagh (Collins and Wilson 1964), provided dates which were totally inconsistent.

Six samples of charcoal were submitted from the court tomb at Tully, Co. Fermanagh (Waterman 1978, 12), and the excavator regarded two samples from Chamber I and one of the forecourt samples as providing dates for the construction and use of the monument. These are: 4890 ± 65 BP; 4785 ± 85 BP; and 4960 ± 85 BP.

Ó Nualláin (1972) adduces the dates of the Ballyglass court tombs, Ma. 13 and Ma. 14, from the dates of the structures which underlay them, and he is of the opinion that no great amount of time elapsed between the abandonment or decay or demolition of the structures and the erection of the court tombs. Nevertheless, given the radiocarbon dates quoted for the habitation structures, the associated court tombs are rather later in date than one might expect.

It is unfortunate that none of the ^{14}C dates obtained so far for court tombs show a consistent pattern which relates strictly to the construction of the monuments. The earliest acceptable dates at present seem to be those from Tully and the single Shanballyedmond date. There are no exact Continental prototypes for the court tombs or for their near relatives in Scotland, and they are best regarded as an insular development evolved through the fusing of diverse traditions which constituted the way of life in the northern part of Ireland and neighbouring Scotland in the Neolithic Period.

Portal tombs

The latest figure for the number of portal tombs (Ó Nualláin 1983) is 163 and, as in the case of the court cairns, the majority are in the northern half of the country. There are, however, important concentrations in Clare and Galway in the west and along the east side of Ireland as far as Waterford in the south. One is known at Aghaglashlin, near Rosscarbery, Co. Cork, and another at Ardarawinny near Schull in the same county.

The portal tomb has a straight-sided chamber, often narrowing towards the rear. The entrance is marked by a pair of tall portal stones set inside the line of the side slabs. The chamber is usually covered by a single capstone of enormous size, poised high over the entrance, resting on the portal stones at the front and sloping downward towards the rear where it rests on the back-stone of the chamber, or, in a number of cases, on a lesser capstone which is supported on the chamber orthostats. Usually, though not always, a slab closes or partly closes the entrance, standing recessed between the portals. The tomb entrance tends to be orientated roughly eastward, but tombs facing in various other directions are also known.

The portal tomb at Kilmogue in Co. Kilkenny, known by the picturesque

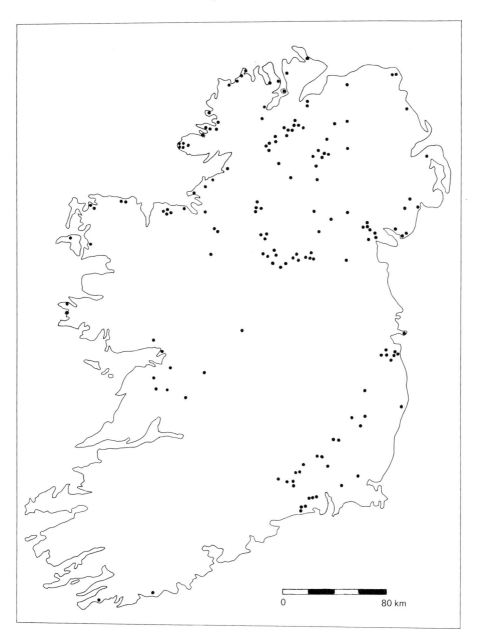

41 Distribution map of portal tombs (after S. Ó Nualláin)

name of *Leac an Scáil*, 'the stone of the champion or hero' – though some would translate it as 'stone of the shelter or shade' because there is ample shelter under it – is, as the name suggests, a very remarkable, indeed a spectacular example of the type. Like most portal dolmens it favours a low-lying situation, in this case, as in many similar examples, beside a stream. It is orientated approximately north–south with its front facing north. The two 3.6m-high portal slabs have a 2.7m-high septal or dividing slab recessed between them. The single chamber measures about 3m by 2m and its side- and end-stones are about 1.3m high. These support a small horizontally laid capstone subsidiary to the main one which is an enormous slab, 5m long by 3.6m wide by 60cm thick (the *leac* of the champion), laid at a steep angle, its tail resting on the subsidiary capstone and its front resting on the tops of the portals and sailing up over them so that its front edge is nearly 5m above the ground. Some remains of the base of a cairn still exist and excavation of this might well yield useful information. The chamber floor is covered in stones and debris of recent date.

Another very impressive example is that at Knockeen, Co. Waterford. In this case the portals and the recessed septal slab face west. Other well known examples are Poulnabrone in the Burren country in Co. Clare, Proleek in Co. Louth, Brenanstown in Co. Dublin, and the remarkable group at Malin More in Co. Donegal. In fact, every county in Ireland, as is shown by the inventory compiled by Seán Ó Nualláin (1983, 89–103), except Kerry, Kildaire, Laois, Limerick, Offaly and Westmeath, contains examples of this most picturesque monument.

No portal dolmen is known where an appreciable amount of cairn survives;* in many cases no trace of cairn is perceptible. It is probable that portal tombs did not have high mounds to begin with, just enough stones around the bases of the orthostats to hold them firm. A high mound, even if it did not cover the capstone, would have taken from the magnificent appearance of the great soaring roof-slab. In about twenty-five examples there is evidence for the presence of a long cairn, but the siting of some chambers, e.g. in one of the long sides or even within the body of the cairn, raises the question as to whether the two features, i.e. the tomb and the long cairn, are of the same building phase. The excavation of a portal tomb at Dyffryn Ardudwy, Merionethshire, Wales (Powell 1963), showed that it originally had a round mound and that a long mound was added later.

An Irish portal tomb which has been partially excavated is that at Ballykeel, Co. Armagh (Collins 1965). It was set at the southern end of a long cairn which, before excavation, was about 30cm in height, 30m in length and about 9m in width. At the time of excavation, the chamber structure had been reduced to five

---

* The recent (1986) excavation of Poulnabrone (not yet published) has revealed definite traces of a low cairn (Ann Lynch, pers. comm.).

42 Kilmogue, Co. Kilkenny, portal tomb (*Leac an Scáil*)

43 Poulnabrone in the Burren, Co. Clare, portal tomb

stones, the two portals with the recessed closing-slab, the back-stone of the chamber and the capstone. There were no side slabs but it is convincingly argued that they had been present originally. In many respects, such as siting and content, Ballykeel is a fairly typical example. A radiocarbon date of 3350 ± 45 BP was obtained from charcoal collected in layer 4 of the cairn structure, a stratum lying on top of the lowest cairn stones and containing abundant sherds of coarse flat-bottomed pottery. According to the excavator a date '600 years earlier would have seemed more likely' (*Radiocarbon* 1970, 292). If this charcoal is not due to a secondary disturbance, it may mean that the long cairn is an addition to a pre-existing site as at Dyffryn Ardudwy, a possibility made more likely by the presence of a cist at the tail of the cairn. This feature may perhaps be compared with the secondary chamber in the added cairn at Dyffryn. The Ballykeel cairn was sectioned only, not fully excavated, the only way in which it might have been possible to determine its date-relationship with the primary dolmen. Many hundred sherds of pottery were recovered from the chamber area. These included plain round-bottomed shouldered bowls and three decorated carinated bowls of Ballyalton type, but the greatest number of sherds were of flat-based coarse ware analogous to Ó Ríordáin's Class II wares from Lough Gur (Collins 1965, 69).

The evidence from the twenty or so portal tombs which have been excavated suggests that the burial rite was cremation. The finds (from thirteen tombs only) consist in the main of similar type pottery to that from Ballykeel together with leaf-shaped arrowheads and hollow scrapers. In view of the similarity in several

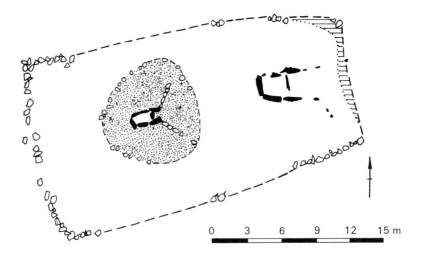

44 Dyffryn Ardudwy, Merionethshire, Wales, chambered cairn. Simplified plan (after T. G. E. Powell)

respects between the court cairns and the portal tombs in the northern third of Ireland (the presence of long cairns and also the similarity between the tomb assemblages), the question has frequently been debated as to whether one is not derived from the other. The problem is compounded by the absence of a range of firm and convincing radiocarbon dates for either.

Very similar tombs are known in Wales and Cornwall, and perhaps also in the Cotswold–Severn region. The 'Whispering Knights' in Oxfordshire is considered to be a portal tomb (Corcoran 1969, 96). The Irish Sea part of the distribution is well shown on a map by F. M. Lynch (1969, 146). According to Lynch:

> The presence of strikingly similar portal dolmens in both countries, Ireland and Wales, reveals that contact must have been close, whether it was a case of derivation one from the other, or of two parallel streams emanating from some common source as yet unidentified. The existence of portal dolmens in Cornwall should not be forgotten. (*ibid.*, 169)

Passage tombs

Estimates (Ó Nualláin 1979, 11) place the probable number of passage graves in Ireland at about 300 tombs, and until much more excavation has been done, a more exact figure will not be available – there are many unexcavated hilltop cairns which may or may not contain passage tombs. Although the exact number is not known, the main distributional spread is clear. While this is in the northern half of the country, the most impressive examples lie in a cross-country band from the Dublin/Drogheda coast on the east to Sligo in the north-west. Passage tombs differ from all the other classes of megalith in that they are built on hilltops or on whatever was the highest point of land available; also, there is a marked grouping of the tombs into cemeteries. The four great cemeteries, those of the Boyne and Loughcrew in Co. Meath and Carrowkeel and Carrowmore in Co. Sligo, all lie on the cross-country band above-mentioned. There are small, more scattered groups in the Dublin/Wicklow mountains, in Donegal, in north Antrim and in Co. Waterford, and there is a single site in Co. Limerick. A slab bearing typical passage grave art, now in the Cork Public Museum (O'Kelly 1949), is regarded as being the only surviving evidence of a presumed site on Clear Island off the coast of south-west Cork. Interestingly, in quite recent times a site has come to light on that island which, though as yet unexcavated, bears every indication of being a passage tomb.

Probably the best-known cemetery is that which lies within a great bend of the River Boyne near Slane, in Co. Meath (Eogan 1968, 1974a, 1984; O'Kelly 1982). Here, in an area of something over 4km by 3km there are the three great mounds of Newgrange, Dowth and Knowth, all of much the same dimensions and strikingly situated on hilltops so that they can be seen in silhouette against the

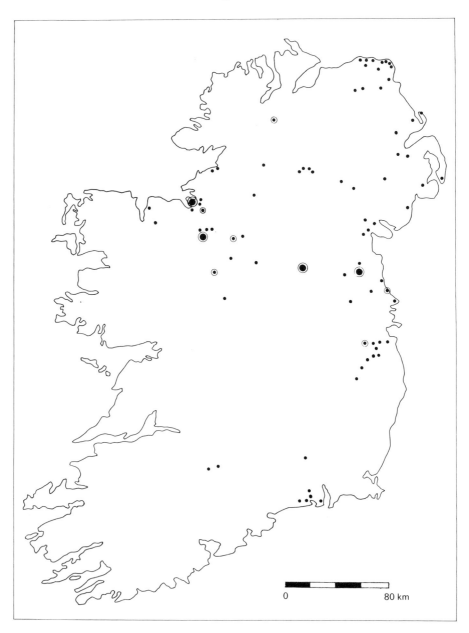

45 Distribution map of passage tombs (after S. Ó Nualláin)

46 Clear Island, Co. Cork, slab bearing passage-grave ornament

sky from many vantage points in the neighbourhood. While only one tomb is known in the Newgrange cairn, Knowth contains two, one opening from the east side of the cairn and the other from the west. Dowth also contains two tombs, both opening from the west side of the cairn.

Immediately west of Newgrange on the same ridge are two smaller passage graves, Sites K and L, and immediately east of it is another one, almost completely destroyed, Site Z. All three have been excavated (O'Kelly *et al.* 1978). Twelve massive orthostats, irregularly spaced, stand outside the perimeter of the main mound. The four opposite the entrance are of striking height and appearance. As well as the two passage tombs within the main mound of Knowth, seventeen smaller tombs, some almost destroyed, were uncovered by excavation around or close to the main monument. All contained tombs of passage tomb type, some simple in plan, others more complex. Smaller passage tombs such as these, which surround or are adjacent to a larger one, have come to be known colloquially as 'satellites'.

About 40km west of the Boyne valley, in the Loughcrew Hills above Old-castle, Co. Meath, there is another important cemetery where twenty-five tombs

47 Newgrange, Co. Meath, standing stones in front of the entrance

survive in various stages of preservation. They are magnificently situated and some of them can be seen from a long way off. At Sligo on the west coast there are two cemeteries, Carrowkeel in the Bricklieve Mountains, consisting of fourteen tombs, and the other at Carrowmore. The latter is something of an anomaly and will be discussed later. The Carrowkeel cemetery lies in an area of great scenic beauty and some of the tombs are dramatically situated on peaks with cliff sides. Excavations of a very cursory nature were carried out there by R. A. S. Macalister *et al.* (1912). There is a passage tomb (unexcavated) and a number of satellites in another dramatic situation on the summit of Knocknarea Mountain not far from Sligo town.

Without exception, Irish passage tombs are found in circular cairns which vary in diameter from about 85m in the largest, as in Newgrange, Dowth and Knowth, to as little as 8m (site W at Loughcrew) in the smallest examples. Many cairns are now much denuded, having been used as stone quarries in the past, but several are remarkably well preserved and a few remain to a height of 10m or more. Most of them seem to have had massive orthostatic kerbs but among the exceptions are Fourknocks I, Co. Meath, and the Mound of the Hostages at Tara, also in Co. Meath, where kerbs of this type did not occur.

Excavation (1962–75) has revealed that when Newgrange was completed, an almost vertical retaining wall, about 3m high, stood on top of the kerb. On the north side this was built of ordinary cairn stones but on the south or entrance side it was built of white quartz and grey granite boulders. This revetment is the first of its kind to be investigated and restored in Ireland though examples are well known in Brittany. One of the most recent excavations in the latter region

48 Carrowkeel, Co. Sligo, hilltop cairn

revealed a series of dry-stone facings at each side of the entrance to the passage tomb at Gavrinis, Larmor Baden, in the Morbihan. This tomb is the one most frequently compared to Newgrange on the basis of the ornament carved on the structural stones (Le Roux 1981; 1983). From various accounts of past excavations, however, it is clear that revetments were sometimes present in Ireland also but had not been recognized for what they were: Baltinglass, Co. Wicklow, Cairn T at Loughcrew, Cairn B at Carrowkeel, for example.

The name 'passage tomb' comes from the nature of the tomb structure which consists of a passage of varying length leading into a chamber which may be circular, as at Dowth South (O'Kelly and O'Kelly 1983); oval, as at Fourknocks

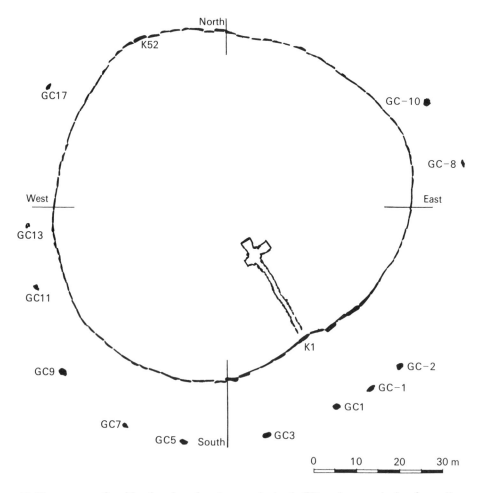

49 Newgrange, Co. Meath, plan showing tomb, kerb (K) and great circle of standing stones (GC)

50 Newgrange, Co. Meath, after conservation

51 Gavrinis, Larmor Baden, Brittany, passage tomb showing revetments discovered at each side of the entrance during recent excavations

I (Hartnett 1957); or polygonal, as at Cairn G at Carrowkeel. Often two side cells and an end cell open off the chamber to give a cruciform plan, as at Newgrange and in the eastern tomb at Knowth, Site 1. More complex plans also occur, as at Cairn L, Loughcrew, and Cairn K, Carrowkeel, where pairs of opposed side cells give a transepted plan. Sometimes too there is little if any distinction between passage and chamber, only a slight widening of the latter distinguishing the two. These are often called undifferentiated passage tombs or V-shaped passage tombs or, in the case of a group of five near Tramore, Co. Waterford, entrance graves (to be discussed below).

Passage tombs are built of orthostats. The passage is usually roofed by means of lintels laid across the tops of the orthostats, though corbels or supporting stones are sometimes employed to give height to some of the lintels. The chambers are usually corbelled, though small chambers may have capstones laid directly on the orthostats. One excavated site, Fourknocks I, which had an unusually large oval central chamber, was partly roofed in corbels and probably finished in timber, the latter supported on a centrally placed wooden post (Hartnett 1957, 251). Sill-stones frequently divide the passages into segments and are also found across the entrances to the chambers and side chambers.

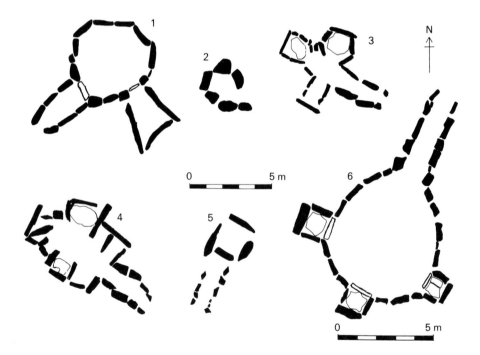

52 Irish passage tombs: 1 Dowth South, 2 grave 7, Carrowmore, 3 and 4 Loughcrew H and L, 5 Knowth, Site 14, 6 Fourknocks (all Co. Meath except no. 2, Co. Sligo)

The older excavations, of which there are about thirty, were unscientific and badly recorded, but the information from them and from more recent investigations gives some notion of the burial practice. Cremation seems to have been the normal rite in Ireland though unburnt primary burials are also known. The skeletal material was placed in the side and end cells of the cruciform tombs, and on the floor of the passage and chamber in the less elaborate types. At twelve sites there are one or more shallow stone basins and the bones were presumably laid into these. In some of the tombs at Loughcrew and Carrowkeel, stone slabs on the floors of the cells perhaps served the same purpose. At Fourknocks I, the side and end cells contained masses of mixed burnt and unburnt bone, packed in and sealed down with little stone slabs deliberately and carefully placed on top. Unburnt bones were defleshed beforehand; the persons had been dead for some time and perhaps had been temporarily buried or otherwise stored before they were placed in the tomb. It was possible to count twenty-four people (men, women and children of varying ages) from the bones in the three recesses. The evidence indicated that all these bones had been put into the tomb at one time, a single collective burial, after which it was closed. Similar evidence has come from the passage tomb known as the Mound of the Hostages at Tara, Co. Meath. There, not only did the passage and chamber contain a great quantity of cremated bones, but also a mass of them had been placed against the outside of the tomb structure before the cairn was heaped up over it (De Valera *in* Ó Ríordáin 1985, 27–8). The most recent evidence is that from Newgrange. The bone fragments of a small number of people, at least four, two of whom were cremated and two unburnt, were found in 1967 in the course of the excavations, embedded in the floor of the tomb chamber near the basins, but this may be only a fraction of the original deposit. The tomb has been open to visitors since 1699 and we do not know what may have been removed as souvenirs or in various cleanings-out of the interior.

A distinctive group of objects is generally found in passage tombs and is usually mixed through the masses of bone. The pottery, known as Carrowkeel ware after the Sligo cemetery, is a coarsely made round-bottomed fabric of poor quality with much incised and jabbed ornament. Many bone and antler pins occur, some of them very long and made from deer antler, the best known of which are the 'mushroom' and 'poppy-head' types. Others have a herring-bone pattern carved on their shanks as at Fourknocks I (Hartnett 1957, 241–3), and a very striking specimen from Site 3 (1984 numeration; formerly Site 12) at Knowth has a helical U-shaped groove running from top to bottom, interrupted only by a vertical channel also running from top to bottom. Both this and the herring-bone example from Fourknocks I are warped and damaged from heat and it may be surmised that they were with the bodies during cremation. A stone object very similar to the bone or antler example from Site 3 at Knowth was found near Site 1 though not associated with any particular burial deposit (Eogan 1984, 29 and 163 respectively). The decoration on these objects is paralleled at other Irish passage tombs such as Carrowkeel and the Mound of the Hostages at Tara, where little groove-decorated stone pendants have been found. Other types of pendant are hammer- and pestle-shaped, as in examples found at Newgrange. Also noteworthy are the 'marbles', small spheroids cut from chalk which is sufficiently hard to take on a very smooth surface amounting to a polish in some cases. As well as several of these chalk examples, Newgrange has produced two 'marbles' made from serpentine. No objects of everyday use are found in passage tombs, such as flint or stone implements or domestic pottery. On the other hand, these objects are well known from the court tombs and from some portal and wedge tombs.

A distinctive feature of many passage tombs is the engraved ornament found on the structural stones (p. 110). Some of the finest examples are in the Boyne valley where over twenty tombs contain ornament, and Loughcrew where there are thirteen. Ornament is also found at Fourknocks I and at the Mound of the Hostages at Tara, both in Co. Meath, and at sites in Co. Tyrone, Co. Antrim, and Co. Wicklow. There are two isolated decorated slabs from the Newgrange area which have had to be relocated for reasons of safety, one in the National Museum of Ireland and the other inside the Newgrange enclosure (O'Kelly 1967) and there is the single slab from Clear Island. Ornament is absent from the Sligo cemeteries.

Of all the megalithic tomb types in Ireland, passage tombs appear to have the least fixity of orientation of the entrance, though there appears to be some preference for the south-eastern quadrant. At Loughcrew, of the eleven tombs for which plans are ascertainable, six face south-east, including the two principal ones, Cairns L and T. In Brittany, where there are many variants of the passage tomb, all those with a long passage face south-east, including Gavrinis, Ile Longue and the tombs of Barnenez South. Of the remaining Breton tombs, the great majority also face towards the south-east quadrant (Giot 1960, 48; L'Helgouach 1965, 282–4).

The entrance to the Newgrange tomb faces south-east and it has been found that, at the time of the winter solstice, 21 December, and for about a week before and after that date, the rays of the rising sun strike into the tomb as far as the end-chamber. Situated above the tomb entrance is a structure known as the roof-box and the direct rays of the sun pass through a slit in its floor and in the form of a very narrow pencil of light, strike across the chamber floor to the front edge of the basin stone in the end recess, dramatically and brightly illuminating the tomb (O'Kelly 1982, 123–4). Investigation of the phenomenon has led to the conclusion that the orientation of the tomb was deliberate (Patrick 1974).

The Carrowmore cemetery is situated on a low-lying gravel ridge in contrast to the hilltop situation of the other cemeteries. Each individual monument stands on its own little eminence. Not all of the sites are megalithic tombs. Of the forty-five known sites which can be traced today – and this is only about half the number present over a century ago – thirty-two can be recognized as megalithic monuments (Kitchin 1983). Many are best described as boulder circles since they consist of a circle of boulders of the local stone, gneiss, placed either directly on the ground or in very shallow sockets and packed around with small stones so as to form a continuous filling along the line of the circle. Within the area enclosed, there can be a dolmen, consisting of uprights covered by a capstone; or a small cist or chamber also covered by a capstone; or, in most cases (eighteen examples), no trace of a central structure is visible. All, or almost all, the monuments have suffered severely at the hands of 'diggers' in the last century and they were also devastated by local people in search of stones and gravel. It cannot be said with any certainty what, if any, type of central structure was present originally in these eighteen examples.

Four sites were excavated between 1977 and 1979 (Burenhult 1980; 1984). All were boulder circles and contained respectively: a polygonal dolmen (no. 7), a small chamber or cist (no. 4), a cruciform chamber (no. 27), and a central

53 Newgrange, Co. Meath, sun shining through slit in the roof-box at the winter solstice

cremation without any central structure (no. 26). None of them had the passage-feature normal in the classic Irish passage tomb. A very interesting series of radiocarbon dates was obtained for three of the excavated sites. At present, these are the oldest radiocarbon dates quoted for megalithic constructions in Ireland. No date was forthcoming for the primary construction of the fourth site, no. 26. Charcoal from a pit or posthole in the centre of the chamber of no. 7 (which also marked the centre point of the boulder circle itself) provided a ^{14}C date of 5240 ± 80 BP. The cruciform chamber of no. 27 was very much disturbed and, in addition, secondary interments of both Bronze and Iron Age had been inserted inside the boulder circle. The central chamber was surrounded, and probably supported, by a stone packing, and charcoal samples from between and under the lowest layers provided ^{14}C dates of 5040 ± 60 BP; 5000 ± 65 BP; and 4940 ± 85 BP (Burenhult 1984, 62). Grave no. 4 is the smallest megalith in the cemetery and, because of the complexity of its construction and the extremely early radiocarbon date of 5750 ± 85 BP quoted for the small central chamber or cist, is also the most controversial (Caulfield 1983, 206–13; Burenhult, 1984, 62–4). There was clear evidence of intense activity at Grave no. 4, reflected not only

54 Carrowmore, Co. Sligo, Grave no. 7, with Knocknarea Mountain in the background

in the considerable quantity of megalithic-type grave goods recovered – over sixty-five fragments of antler pins, including seven pieces with mushroom-shaped heads – but also in the amount of cremated human bone, which weighed over thirty kilos.

There is only one monument in the Carrowmore cemetery which comes within the classic passage tomb definition. This is no. 51, known as 'Listoghil'. It is centrally placed with regard to the other tombs and is at a somewhat higher elevation. It consists of a large stone cairn, between 35m and 41m in diameter at present, with remains of a kerb. At the centre is a rectangular chamber roofed with a single limestone capstone, 3m by 2.75m, and the cairn must originally have covered it.

The early Carrowmore dates run counter to those obtained for other Irish passage tombs. The latter are admittedly meagre in number and many of them date the pre-monument horizon, not the monument itself. This is the case at the Mound of the Hostages at Tara, Co. Meath (unpublished), where three radio-carbon dates centring on *c.* 4000 BP were obtained from charcoal beneath the mound. The same phenomenon has already been mentioned in connection with Townleyhall II and some of the Knowth satellite tombs. Another interesting example is the monument on the summit of Baltinglass Hill, Co. Wicklow, a much-damaged site consisting of the remains of a cairn which originally covered several small passage tombs and where there were at least two building phases. It was excavated in the 1930s (Walshe 1941). Some of the stones bear ornament similar to that of Boyne valley art. Underlying the cairn was a black layer containing a good deal of charcoal, carbonized wood and charred hazel-nut shells and nearby was a polished stone axe (*ibid.*, 227). It may be suspected that this is a pre-passage tomb horizon.

No radiocarbon date has so far been forthcoming for either of the two passage tombs within the main mound of Knowth (Site 1). The radiocarbon date of *c.*4745 BP quoted for 'basal redeposited sod-like layer of mound' was obtained from charcoal samples combined from two separate cuttings in the mound, collected at intervals two years apart (*Radiocarbon* 1971, 453). A more informative date as far as Site 1 is concerned came from a satellite tomb, Site 16 (Eogan 1984, 109–32). This tomb was in existence before the main mound and kerb were built and in fact it lay on the line of the kerb at the eastern side and the satellite had subsequently to be modified to allow of its construction. Charcoal within the mound of Site 16 provided a ^{14}C date of 4399 ± 67 BP. This date is almost identical with two dates obtained for the structure of the Newgrange tomb, and on present evidence, therefore, it would appear that the main Knowth mound and kerb (Site 1) are later than Newgrange. This agrees well with stylistic criteria because the motifs engraved on the Knowth kerbstones are so much more sophisticated than the Newgrange ones that one must automatically assume a later date for them. If, however, as there is reason to believe, Site 1 is a multi-period monument, earlier dates may emerge for one or both of the two tombs which it contains.

Two radiocarbon dates were obtained for the Newgrange tomb from a putty-like mixture of burnt soil and sea sand used to caulk the interstices between the slabs forming the roof of the passage (O'Kelly 1969, 140; 1972, 226). The samples came from two separate locations in the roof and provided dates of: 4425 ± 45 BP and 4415 ± 40 BP. At the back (north side) of the mound an already con-solidated turf mound underlay the cairn of the main monument and vegetation (mainly moss) taken from the transported turves gave a ^{14}C date of 4480 ± 60 BP.

Of all the different types of megalithic monument, passage graves are those which have the best claim to be international. Examples are known in Scan-dinavia and Denmark and all along the 'Atlantic façade' from the tip of Scotland to the Iberian peninsula. The earliest radiocarbon dates come from Brittany; a few early ones are known from Iberia but the latter do not provide a representa-tive picture because radiocarbon dates for megalithic tombs are sparse in the peninsula.

Entrance graves

This is the name usually given to a group of five tombs situated inland from Tramore Bay in Co. Waterford which are distinct in their distribution, separated as they are from the main body of passage tombs in the northern half of the country. Many morphologically similar examples are found among the passage tombs and they are usually known as undifferentiated or V-shaped tombs because the side walls generally diverge outwards from one another from the entrance inwards. A sill stone may demarcate the inner or chamber end and others may occur in the 'passage'. Many of the Knowth satellites are of this type, and also Site K at Newgrange.

Because of its location on the south-east coast the Waterford group is often compared to similar tombs in Cornwall and in the Scilly Isles. Two of the group have been excavated, Carriglong (Powell 1941) and Harristown (J. Hawkes 1941), but no evidence of the primary date was forthcoming. At Harristown cremated bones representing possibly two persons were found in a primary position but a number of secondary burials were discovered also, dating to the Bronze Age. One of these, an Urn burial, was accompanied by a bead of faience (p. 187).

Passage grave art

Among the best known features of the Irish passage tombs is the 'art' which is engraved on many of the structural stones and is so well exemplified in the Boyne

and Loughcrew cemeteries, and at Fourknocks I, all in Co. Meath. It does not
occur at Carrowkeel or Carrowmore, the two Sligo cemeteries. One site, Clover
Hill in the Carrowmore area, is often mentioned as providing an example of the
art, but the structure is not a passage tomb and the devices on its stones do not
resemble anything in the repertoire of the passage tomb artist. Other examples
of the art are found at King's Mountain and Tara (Mound of the Hostages),
Co.Meath; at Seefin, Baltinglass and Tournant,* Co. Wicklow; at Sess Kilgreen
and Knockmany, Co. Tyrone; at Carnanmore and Lyles Hill,[†] Co. Antrim; at
Kiltierney, Co. Fermanagh; at Drumreagh, Co. Down and at Clear Island,[‡]
Co. Cork (Shee Twohig 1981, 202–27). Seen on a map, this distribution is
markedly eastern and northern in extent if one regards the Kiltierney and Clear
Island sites as outliers.

The devices on the stones are geometrical in concept and non-
representational and while it is probable that they are symbolic, religious or
magical in content, it is unlikely that we will ever discover what any of them
meant since we cannot know the minds or the emotions of a people who did not
know how to write and who are separated in time from us by more than four
thousand years. Not everyone accepts the non-representational nature of the
motifs, and interpretations of their meanings are many, but it is our belief that
these are not only purely personal, but are also conditioned by the strength of the
interpreter's imagination and by the climate of thought and psychology in which
he or she has grown up. Certainly none is overtly representational, whatever may
have been the original intention.

There is no means of knowing whether the carvings were meant to be art in
our modern sense of the term or even whether they were thought of at all as ornament or decoration (C. O'Kelly 1973, 262–3). In some instances it is obvious that
the carver was aware of the shape of the slab and that he laid out an overall pattern
to fit the available space. The outstanding example of this is the entrance stone
(KI) at Newgrange, where an integrated pattern of lozenges, spirals and concentric arcs was exactly fitted not only into the outline of the stone but also to its
surface curvature. This carving is regarded as one of the great achievements of
prehistoric art in western Europe. Kerbstone 52, which is diametrically opposite
the entrance stone, has much of the same quality and may well have been carved
by the same master hand. Other examples at Newgrange which bear patterns
designed to fit the respective stones are the relief saltires on the leading edge of
the lintel of the roof-box and the 'false relief' pattern of lozenges, triangles and
zigzags on a corbel in the western cell of the tomb. The entrance stone of the western tomb at Knowth has an organized pattern of boxed rectangles fitted to the

---

* Now in the National Museum of Ireland.
† In the Ulster Museum, Belfast.   ‡ In the Cork Public Museum.

shape of the stone (Eogan 1967) and this 'hurdle' pattern is repeated on two other stones within the western tomb itself. There are two other kerbstones equally compelling in their sense of organized design, both situated to the left of the entrance to the other tomb, the eastern one (Eogan 1977). One of them, which could be called the 'sun-dial' stone, is a *tour de force* of technique and design and, as in all the best examples, the motifs are fitted effortlessly to the unwieldy shape of the stone. A few similar instances of this skill are to be found at Fourknocks I, notably the stones lettered a, b, c, e and f (Hartnett 1957, 224–7).

The actual carving was done by picking the surface of the stone so as to make a series of little picks or pit-marks. The implements used were most probably flint points and a wooden mallet. The motifs most commonly found in Irish passage grave art can be conveniently divided into ten groups, though each of the groups can have numerous subdivisions (C. O'Kelly 1973, 364ff.; Shee Twohig 1981, 170ff.). These are circles, dots-in-circles, arcs, spirals and serpentiforms, all curvilinear. Rectilinear devices consist of lozenge/triangle, chevron-zigzag, radials, parallel lines and offsets or comb devices. Cupmarks, that is, round-bottomed depressions, when artificial or partly so, may also be included. The numerical incidence of the above motifs varies from site to site. For example,

55 Newgrange, Co. Meath, the Entrance Stone. Roof-box is above mouth of passage

lozenges and chevrons are common at Newgrange and offsets and independent groups of arcs are rarer. At Loughcrew, on the other hand, these latter motifs occur frequently while lozenges and chevrons are scarce.

It is strange that none of the other Irish types of megalithic tomb have any comparable art work. One court cairn at Malin More, Co. Donegal (Shee Twohig 1981, 235, fig. 281), has some picked designs on two structural stones, but like

56 Newgrange, Co. Meath, Kerbstone 52, detail

113

57 Knowth, Co. Meath, 'hurdle' stone at entrance to western tomb, Site 1

58 Knowth, Co. Meath, 'sun dial' stone near entrance to eastern tomb, Site 1

those on the Clover Hill structure at Carrowmore, Co. Sligo (*ibid.*, 235, fig. 282), taken as a whole, they could be of Iron Age or Early Christian Period date. A number of the wedge tombs have artificial cupmarks on some of their capstones, but there are no picked devices which would compare with those of the passage graves. In two instances, Baurnadomeeny, Co. Tipperary, and Scrahanard, Co. Cork, there are crudely incised criss-cross patterns on structural stones (O'Kelly 1960, 91). The Baurnadomeeny example is certainly ancient but there is some doubt about the other.

Irish passage grave art is often said to be derived from Iberian and Breton examples but the overtly representational nature of much of the Breton art in particular indicates a fundamental difference. Only a very small number of motifs is held in common and one is led to the conclusion that, as in megalithic architecture itself, Ireland followed its own distinctive insular path.

Wedge tombs

These are the most widespread of the megalithic tomb types found in Ireland. About 400 are known and the distribution shows a marked western and southern bias. The counties of Clare, Cork, Kerry, Limerick and Tipperary contain between them over two hundred tombs and more than one hundred are in one county, Co. Clare (De Valera and Ó Nualláin 1961; 1982; Ó Nualláin 1979, 15). This pattern of spread is all the more notable when it is realized that in the same five counties only four court tombs, seven portal tombs and two passage tombs are known. The remaining wedge tombs are dispersed through the areas in which the main concentrations of the other three types occur.

The name 'wedge tomb' arises from the fact that the tomb chamber is usually wedge-shaped in plan and in longitudinal section profile, that is, it is wider and higher at one end. This wider, higher end contains the entrance and faces south-west in the great majority of cases, an orientation directly opposite to that of the court tombs and of some portal tombs, and one which is remarkably fixed when compared to the seeming lack of a rule of orientation in the passage tombs. The gallery is built of orthostats and roofed with slabs laid directly on them. While pad-stones may be used on occasion to bring up the height of a low side-orthostat, corbelling proper does not occur. The galleries vary greatly in length, from as little as 2m to almost 14m in the splendid example at Labbacallee in Co. Cork.

It has been customary to divide the wedge tombs into two sub-groups, northern and southern wedges, so-called at a time when it was thought that the two sub-types had a mutually exclusive distribution, the one group in the northern part of Ireland, the other in the south. It is now clear that this pattern is not correct, and in abandoning it, some archaeologists have also abandoned the sub-division of the class as a whole. This, however, is to take up a position in the

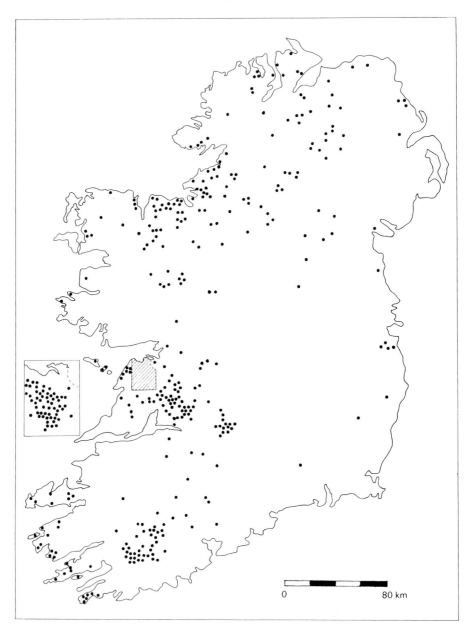

59 Distribution map of wedge tombs (after S. Ó Nualláin)

opposite extreme because such a sub-division remains a valid concept even if the old names and patterns of spread are to be changed.

In the 'northern' wedges the gallery is entered through a 'portico' or 'ante-chamber' marked by two tall well-matched portal stones. This element is divided off from the rest of the structure by a sill-stone or by a septal slab. The east end of the gallery may be roughly rounded in plan and is sometimes converted into a small closed chamber by a septal slab set across the gallery. Outside the gallery and 50cm to 2m distant therefrom is a U-shaped setting of orthostats, completely hidden when the covering cairn was in place. The portico-entrance is flanked on either side by a flat or very slightly concave façade of orthostats which extends outward to form the front of the cairn. The latter is horseshoe- or heel-shaped and may have either an orthostatic or a dry-built kerb at its edge. Cairn length at 10 to 15m is much shorter than that of the court cairns.

In the 'southern' wedges the gallery sometimes has a portico or ante-chamber, but this is usually cut off from the rest by a high septal slab so that it may not be possible to pass from this front element into the main part of the chamber behind, as it is often possible to do in the 'northern' wedges. Sometimes there is a small closed cell at the east end of the gallery which is square-ended, not rounded. The sides of the tomb are normally built of double rows of orthostats set close together. The available evidence suggests that this type was set in the centre of a circular or short oval cairn which had an orthostatic kerb at its edge. Thus when the cairn was complete, the tomb was totally hidden from view. Circular cairns up to 15m in diameter are known. It will be seen therefore that while there are obvious points of similarity in the two sub-groups, there are also differences in detail.

Despite the fact that the wedge tombs are the most numerous of the four main classes, the number of sites excavated is very small in proportion (about twenty), and since a number of these produced no finds, our knowledge of the burial practice is very unsatisfactory. Cremation seems to predominate but unburnt burials have been found in the same tombs side by side with the cremations.

A good example of the 'northern' type wedge tomb in the morphological sense is that at Island, near Mallow, Co. Cork (O'Kelly 1958a). Excavation revealed that the tomb chamber consisted of a U-shaped orthostatic gallery lying SW–NE, entered at the south-west between two tall portal stones, the internal width being greater at the entrance than it was towards the north-east end. A second U-shaped setting of orthostats was placed outside the tomb gallery at a distance of about 1m therefrom. This was finished at the north-east end in a rounded heel and at the south-west the ends of its arms were linked with those of the tomb gallery by orthostats set so as to give a more or less flat façade to this part of the monument. The western portion of the plan was given a more marked wedge-shape by further external settings of orthostats. To close the spaces between the ends of the outer 'U', two further slabs were set into the façade.

Outside all of this were found the sockets of a setting of non-contiguous orthostats which, presumably with dry-walling in between them, had formed a revetment at the edge of the cairn. This was round-heeled in plan and flat in front so as to articulate with the flat façade already described. In front of the façade, a trench with two sockets adjacent to each end of it, similar in character to the kerb sockets, evidently had held stones which marked off a semicircular area in front of the tomb entrance. The overall length of the monument was 11.5m and the width was 9.5m.

The upper fill of the chamber was mainly of field stones but below them was a tightly packed layer of yellow soil and stones, an original feature put in to seal the burial deposit. There were three lots of cremated human bone, two of them

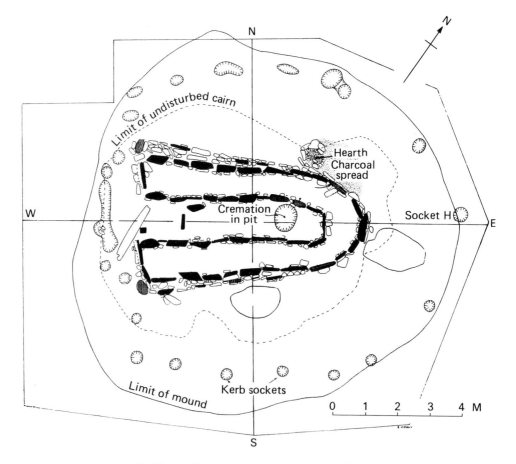

60 Island, Co. Cork, wedge tomb, general plan

too small to enable any useful conclusion to be drawn but the third lot was probably that of a female sixty to seventy years old. The finds were meagre – a few flint scrapers – and the total absence of pottery was disappointing.

A 'southern' wedge-tomb is well seen at Baurnadomeeny, Co. Tipperary, where total excavation of the site revealed many interesting details (O'Kelly 1960). The tomb gallery, orientated WSW–ENE, was in two parts: a main chamber at the east end and a portico at the west end, completely cut off from the chamber by a high septal slab. There was an extensive area of incised markings running roughly vertically and horizontally on the inner face of one of the portico orthostats. These had been made after the orthostat was set up but before the burial deposit was put in place. The chamber was well constructed of massive slabs in the close-set double-wall technique usual to these tombs, but the eastern closing stone was missing. The overall axial length of the tomb was 7m and the maximum width was 3.65m. The chamber had been dug out in recent times and nothing survived of the original contents except a few small fragments of burnt human bone and one sherd of featureless pottery. There were five cremation burials in the portico. Sherds of pottery accompanied one of the burials which was in a slab-like cist, but again, the ware was featureless.

The whole tomb had been encased in built stonework bedded in yellow soil before the loose cairn cover had been thrown up, the encasement being held at its base by two arcs of boulders. The cairn edge had been marked by large slabs set in a circle 15m in diameter. The tomb was centrally placed within it and it was clear that when complete the cairn covered and hid the whole tomb structure. A further fifteen cremated burials were found, twelve in diminutive cists under the cairn and three just outside the kerb. Otherwise finds were few. The cairn base produced some sherds from flat-based pots of the domestic-type functional ware similar to that labelled Class II at Lough Gur. There was no Beaker.

Of the twenty excavated wedge tombs, no primary pottery was reported from eight. Eight further tombs produced Beaker ware, all except one site (Lough

61 Island, Co. Cork, wedge tomb, conjectural reconstruction of front (E. M. Fahy)

119

Gur) being north of a line from south Co. Dublin to Galway. Sherds of 'thin well-baked pottery decorated with incised lines' were found in Labbacallee wedge tomb, Co. Cork, which was excavated in 1934 (Leask and Price 1936, fig. 6) and these are also claimed as Beaker ware (De Valera and Ó Nualláin 1982, 3) though not listed as such by D. L. Clarke (1970) in his *corpus* of Beaker. The Lough Gur wedge tomb (Ó Ríordáin and Ó hIceadha 1955) was excavated in 1938 and produced about 250 sherds with recognizable Beaker ornament. Other pottery represented was Class II ware, a small amount of Class I and some Food Vessel sherds. Fragments of a crucible and a stone mould for casting bronze spearheads were found as well as other stone objects. The human remains were very fragmentary and there were large amounts of animal bone. It would appear that a good deal of disturbance and possible secondary use had taken place.

The Bell-Beaker ware found under the pavement in the wedge tomb at

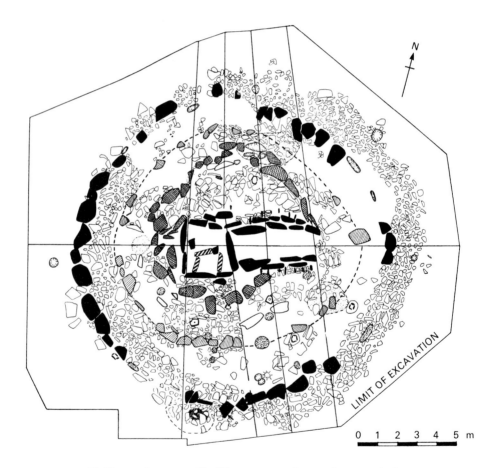

62 Baurnadomeeny, Co. Tipperary, wedge tomb, general plan

Ballyedmonduff, Co. Dublin (Ó Ríordáin and De Valera 1952), and in the tomb at Moytirra, Co. Sligo (Cremin-Madden 1969), belongs to the All-over-ornamented Pan-European type, and the closest parallels are British (Waddell 1978). Waddell goes on to say that (*ibid.*, 124): 'the occurrence of demonstrably earlier Beaker in some wedge tombs in the northern half of the country . . . suggests . . . that the earliest wedge tombs lie in this part of Ireland. Thus, certain court-tomb elements in northern wedges take on a new significance.' He mentions sill- and jamb-segmentation and a frontal façade as being among these features. Another Beaker association, tanged-and-barbed arrowheads, is found in three tombs only, all in the northern province.

In view of the virtual absence of Beaker ware from excavated wedge tombs in the south, one is forced to speculate that they are perhaps later in date, and the evidence from the Island, Co. Cork, wedge tomb would seem to bear this out. Three radiocarbon dates have been obtained. The first sample was submitted to the Dublin laboratory in the late 1950s and consisted of charcoal from a spread outside orthostats 32, 33 and 34 in the outer ring of the gallery on the north side. A ^{14}C date of 3110 ± 140 BP was obtained and at the time it was viewed with an understandable amount of reservation. In 1979 two further samples were submitted, this time to the Groningen laboratory. One of these was from the same extensive charcoal spread as the Dublin sample and the date obtained, 3050 ± 35 BP, was very similar. The other sample came from the bottom of socket H at

63 Baurnadomeeny, Co. Tipperary, wedge tomb after excavation and conservation

the heel of the cairn where some large pieces of charcoal had been placed while still hot enough to redden the soil at one side of the pit (O'Kelly 1958a, 5). A ^{14}C date of 3090 ± 30 BP was obtained.

It is possible that the people of Clare, Cork and Kerry in particular may have continued the megalithic burial tradition at a time when it had been superseded elsewhere. Unfortunately, the few wedge tombs which have been excavated in the south have been singularly unproductive as regards datable finds. Four sites excavated in the Iveragh peninsula in Co. Kerry (Herity 1970) produced no grave goods nor any evidence of date. A cremated burial was found in one of the tombs. On the basis of present evidence, therefore, the wedge tombs of the south and south-west cannot be shown to be monuments which 'belonged to a widespread and numerous beaker-using community' (De Valera and Ó Nualláin 1961, 116) nor can one regard them as of general Late Neolithic-Early Bronze Age date (De Valera and Ó Nualláin 1982, 120) since one of them at least has been shown to date to the Early/Late Bronze Age transition.

So far, no certain example of a wedge tomb has been found in Britain and only one or two sites have been claimed as such (Daniel 1950, 154). Ó Nualláin (1979, 15) holds that the *allées couvertes* or gallery graves of Brittany provide prototypes for the Irish wedges, seeing in the small ante-chambers and in the outer walling of the Breton tombs parallels for the porticos and double walling of the Irish ones. He adds: 'The finds from the Breton tombs include Beaker and flat-bottomed ware akin to that found in some Irish tombs as well as barbed and tanged arrowheads, and support the view that the *allées couvertes* are ancestral to the Irish series.' John Waddell (1978, 124–5), however, is of the opinion that there is no good reason to derive the wedges from the Breton galleries. In fact, he claims that the fundamental morphological differences between the two, such as the rectangular and consistently parallel sides of the Breton galleries, together with their eastern orientation, rule out a 'parental connection'. One is therefore drawn to the conclusion, on present evidence at least, which is admittedly scanty, that Daniel's tentative suggestion (1972, 244) that the Irish wedges are an indigenous development is correct.

The megalith builders

It must be realized that the fourfold classification of Irish megalithic tombs is a convenience designed to make easier the study of this great body of material, and it should not be thought that the different kinds of tomb were being built by groups of people who were unknown to each other. Indeed this cannot have been so and when one lists the various points of similarity in the tomb types rather than the differences, it emerges that there must have been many contacts between the various and varying groups. The court tomb and the portal tomb builders were living and working at about the same time in the northern half of Ireland, for, in so far as excavation has revealed them, the objects placed with the bones of the dead in both types of tomb were the same. Similarly, a transepted court tomb gallery has, in effect, a cruciform plan similar to that of many Irish passage graves, though there are differences of detail. The shallow façades of court tombs can be compared with the slightly dished fronts of some wedges, and some of the latter have circular cairns with orthostatic kerbs like those of the passage tombs. It may be argued that these comparable features are not valid evidence of influence by one group on another, but there must have been communication since there is distributional overlap both in space and time, and the basic effort for all the builders seems to have been the construction of a House for the Dead. But while there is distributional overlap of tomb types, there is also evidence of mutual exclusiveness, particularly amongst the court tombs and the wedges. The virtual confinement of the court tombs to the northern third of the country and the preponderance of wedge tombs in the south must mean that these areas were differentiated from one another in some way in their social structure.

It seems to the writer that there is little or no necessity to invoke influxes of colonists from Britain and the Continent to explain the phenomenon of the megaliths or to explain why some of the Irish types resemble types found outside Ireland. At one time it was believed that the practice of building megalithic tombs emanated from the eastern Mediterranean by a process of diffusion, but radiocarbon dating of tombs in Brittany and elsewhere in the West has shown that the practice began earlier there than in the East. From the Early Neolithic onward Ireland cannot have been isolated from the rest of the world, awaiting the influx of colonists to point the way to the next step. The practice of erecting Houses for the Dead would have become known through two-way contacts with Britain and the Continent. These houses are of two basic kinds wherever they are found in the West, gallery graves and passage graves, and by a process not understood, one social group adopted one type and a different group adopted another, each community developing its own variant or variants of the basic types. The idea of a House for the Dead could have been a familiar one long before the first megaliths were erected in Ireland and it could have lain dormant until the conditions were right, that is, until there was a well-fed settled population with time and reserves of wealth in food and labour sufficient to undertake enterprises on such a scale.

If one looks at the Boyne valley, for example, from the fourth millennium BC the land was being progressively cleared. It is believed that though the climate had become less moist and less warm than previously, it was still warmer than that of the present day. The character of the woods was changing also due to a combination of climatic and anthropogenic influences. Woodland clearances were increasing in number and extent from now on, and by the time the great

Boyne passage graves were built in the middle of the third millennium BC, clearances were being sustained in some areas at least and were no longer being swallowed up by forest or woodland regeneration. Pollen and seed analytical work undertaken at Newgrange and Knowth showed that an open landscape prevailed in the neighbourhood (Groenman-van Waateringe and Pals *in* O'Kelly 1982; Groenman-van Waateringe *in* Eogan 1984). Samples from the turves used in the building of the mounds show that the proportion of tree to non-tree pollen was about 1:3, and evidence of both animal and crop husbandry was demonstrated by the presence of faunal remains and of cereal grains. Both wheat and barley were identified. The woods in the neighbourhood consisted of oak, and on high ground of oak, birch, alder, pine, willow and hazel. At Newgrange there was evidence of ash.

Clearly the Boyne valley was capable of supporting a sizeable community and there can be little doubt that in this community some were more wealthy and more powerful than others and were able either to secure or to exact the labour necessary to build the monuments. Only a society with great material and intellectual reserves could have envisaged the monuments in the first place, and perhaps spiritual reserves were needed as well. These large edifices are surely the concrete embodiment of a belief in the hereafter, in the necessity of providing a House for the Dead so that some spirits at least would live on to perpetuate the memory of the builders and of the community as an entity. Though few of the other monuments are as grandiose as those of the Boyne, a somewhat similar motivation must have inspired even the humblest of them, and the perpetuation of the practice well into the Bronze Age argues for a very powerful residual tradition in parts of Ireland.

The figure of 1,200 megaliths known at present for the whole of Ireland may seem excessively large but it must be remembered that as far as our present knowledge goes they were being built over a span of at least a millennium and a half – almost as long a period as the present duration of the Christian era. Even if one were to bring up the number of monuments to about 1,500 to allow for all those destroyed and if these are spread over the period of time postulated, the average building rate per year is still very low. We have seen that, apart from a few exceptions, the number of individuals interred in each tomb was small; in several of the court tombs, for instance, only a single youth was found. This leads one to speculate either that the monuments were built to house 'special' people or that the structures themselves fulfilled the main requirement and that the burials were of a token nature. In either event, they cannot have served all the burial needs of the community. They must have represented some element unrelated to the utilitarian requirements of the vast majority; whether this was to house a particular person or family or to symbolize temporal and/or spiritual powers one does not know.

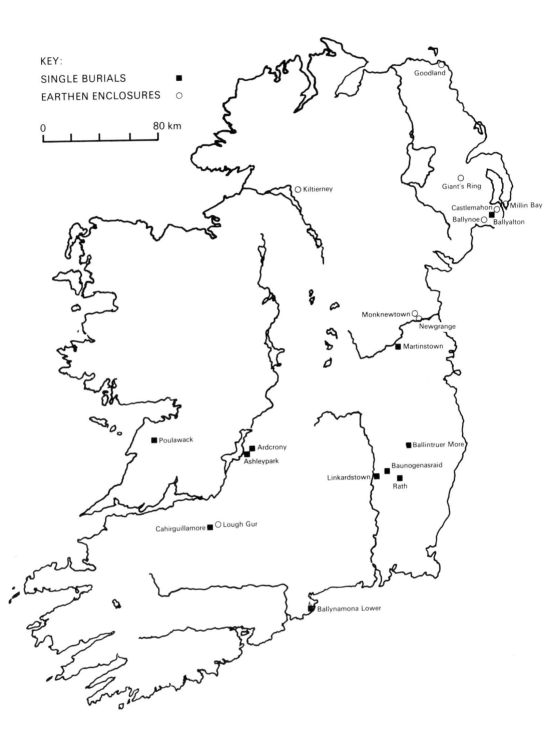

KEY:

SINGLE BURIALS ■

EARTHEN ENCLOSURES ○

0   80 km

Goodland ○

Kiltierney ○

Giant's Ring ○

Castlemahon ■   Millin Bay ○

Ballynoe ○   Ballyalton ■

Monknewtown ○

Newgrange

Martinstown ■

Poulawack ■

Ardcrony ■

Ashleypark ■

Ballintruer More ■

Baunogenasraid ■

Linkardstown ■   Rath ■

Cahirguillamore ■ ○ Lough Gur

Ballynamona Lower ■

64   Neolithic single burial; earthen and stone enclosures

126

6

Single burials and earthen and stone enclosures

Neolithic single burials

It may seem that an undue amount of space has been devoted to megaliths but they constitute the most visible reminder of prehistoric times in Ireland. Also, the finest of them, such as the great Boyne monuments, the court tomb at Creevykeel, Co. Sligo, the portal dolmen at Poulnabrone, Co. Clare, the wedge tomb at Labbacallee, Co. Cork, and so on, are of great intrinsic interest. They tend, however, to distract attention from a number of very interesting burials of the Neolithic and the Late Neolithic/Beaker period in which both burnt and unburnt bodies were being deposited in very much simpler tombs and graves. Perhaps these were the last resting places of the 'not quite so special' people who were nevertheless considered to be of sufficient means and importance to have a grave of their own or a family grave. On the other hand, they may have been a separate people from those who practised the megalithic tradition, but at the same time, had their own distinctive ways of honouring the dead.

The Linkardstown cist

A very interesting example is the Linkardstown cist-type burial, so-called after an excavated example at Linkardstown, Co. Carlow (J. Raftery 1944). The body or bodies, unburnt, were placed in a cist or small chamber of large slabs or boulders which were arranged on the ground surface, generally in a polygonal plan. The Co. Carlow cist was 2m by 2.3m at ground level but examples smaller than this are known, some of them less than a metre in length and width. The side slabs were slanted inwards so that the dimensions at the top were less than at ground level. All spaces between the side slabs were usually infilled with smaller pieces of stone and other slabs were placed against the outside. A capstone or capstones closed the top. A small cairn surrounded the structure and then the whole was covered with a circular mound of sods or earth bounded by a kerb. The mounds vary in diameter from about 35m to 20m. The normal burial consisted of one or two male bodies, sometimes flexed or crouched, and in some cases it was clear that the limbs had been disarticulated beforehand. In one case, a cist contained a cremation and an inhumation. The type as a whole is well exemplified in the primary phase of a fairly recently excavated example at Baunogenasraid, Co. Carlow.

It had been thought that the distribution of these cists was restricted to an area in the east of the county, running from Co. Dublin southward to Co. Wexford, but two examples are now known from north Tipperary, Ardcrony (Wallace 1977) and Ashleypark (Manning 1985). The Ardcrony tomb contained two disarticulated, defleshed male skeletons with a round-bottomed highly decorated pot placed on the paved floor of the tomb chamber or 'cist' midway between

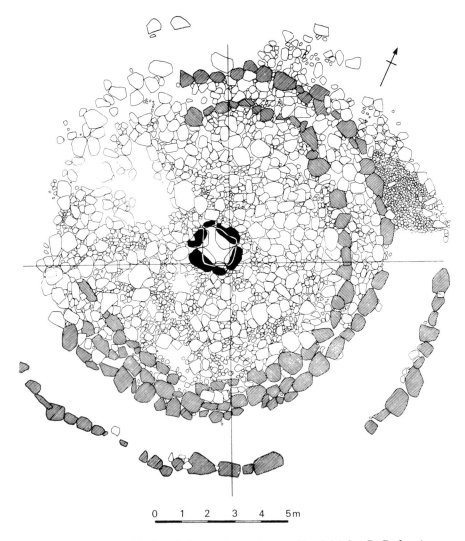

0   1   2   3   4   5m

65 Baunogenasraid, Co. Carlow, cairn and central burial (after B. Raftery)

128

them. At Ashleypark, the bones of an adult male and a child were accompanied by some typical decorated sherds of Linkardstown-type as well as plain Neolithic ware and cord-ornamented ware.

Michael Ryan (1981) has listed a number of sites which contain burial chambers similar to the type described above. In the list he includes Poulawack, Co. Clare, a site dug by Hugh O'Neill Hencken in the 1930s when the Harvard Archaeological Expedition was in Ireland (Hencken 1935). Interestingly, though Poulawack was a multiple cist cairn, or, in the terminology now preferred, a cemetery cairn, the central burial feature was identical with some of the Linkardstown-type cists. It lacked, however, the distinctive pottery. The feature which singles out certain cists from others, therefore, is the presence of a round-

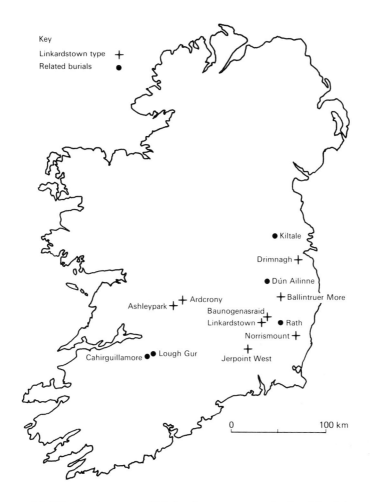

66 Distribution map of Linkardstown-type and related burials

bottomed highly decorated Neolithic pot, or sherds thereof, similar to that found at Ardcrony and elsewhere. Only some of the sites listed by Ryan contained this distinctive ware (Brindley *et al.* 1983), and Poulawack is not among them. In the Brindley paper it is contended that only when this specific ware is present can the cist or tomb be referred to as of Linkardstown-type.

Radiocarbon dates for bone samples from Ballintruer More, Co. Wicklow (J. Raftery 1973) (a similar type of cist which also contained this ware), Ardcrony and Ashleypark are as follows: Ballintruer More 4800 ± 70 BP; Ardcrony 4675 ± 35 BP; Ashleypark 4765 ± 40 BP. At present, therefore, early dates such as these can be taken as referring only to the cists in which the distinctive decorated pot is part of the grave furniture. The pots are round-bottomed and shouldered and the ornament consists of channelled grooves, executed with a blunt point in geometric panels, a series of oblique strokes being frequently employed. The decoration covers the whole vessel, often extending to the base also. A plain round-bottomed shouldered bowl is found with the decorated pot in some cists. The decorated ware is also found in contexts other than these particular cists; for example, it is similar to pottery found in the court cairn at Ballynamona Lower, Co. Waterford (Powell 1938) and that in a burial pit at Martinstown, Kiltale, Co. Meath (Hartnett 1951). It bears a strong resemblance to the decorated Western Neolithic ware classified as Ballyalton by Humphrey Case (1961) and mentioned already in connection with the Ballykeel portal tomb.

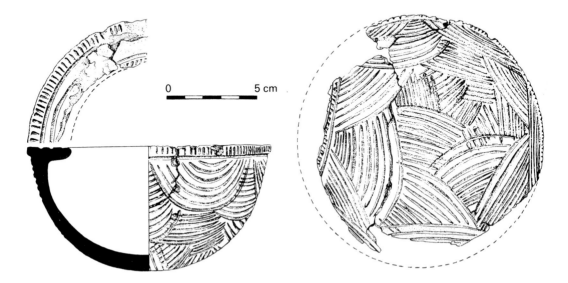

67 Baunogenasraid, Co. Carlow, decorated pot found with central burial (after B. Raftery)

As for the cists themselves, it is now clear that the Late Neolithic date hitherto ascribed to them, and to the decorated pottery contained in them, can no longer be sustained in all cases. The construction techniques of the graves, however, i.e. the corbelled effect displayed in some cases in the chambers, the round mounds and revetments and the efforts to seal off the cist, all argue links with passage tomb traditions.

The pit burial at Kiltale which has been mentioned above provides an interesting insight into modern man's reaction to the burial customs of his remote ancestors. In 1949, during sand-quarrying operations, workmen reported the discovery of a human skeleton buried in a cavity in the sand in 'something like thick canvas'. The Health Authority ordered the skeletal remains to be interred in the local graveyard and two pieces of the supposed canvas were handed to members of the staff of the National Museum of Ireland. The 'canvas', in fact, represented sherds of a decorated Neolithic bowl which had accompanied the burial. There was some suggestion that a large stone may have closed the top of the burial pit (Hartnett 1951, 1). When the human remains were subsequently examined it was found that they represented the almost complete skeleton of a male between fifty and sixty years, but whether it was interred in a crouched or in an extended position could not be ascertained. A few further sherds of pottery recovered by the Museum staff established the pot beyond question as a decorated round-bottomed Neolithic bowl with a flat rim overhanging inward, of the kind that has come from the cists of Linkardstown type described above.

The burial at Rath, Co. Wicklow, can also be placed in the Neolithic period. It was contained in a stone cist in the centre of a circular mound of sand which was about 60m in diameter. The cist was a double one, being unequally divided into two compartments. In the larger compartment there was a decorated pottery vessel and in the other a pile of cremated bone but no other finds (Prendergast 1959). Nearby, there was a broken pot similar to the one in the cist but larger. The cremated bone represented the remains of a young male. The ornament on both pots consisted of whipped-cord or cog-wheel impressions in horizontal rows around the vessels, and the smaller one was decorated on the base also. The profile of the larger vessel has been compared to that of the reconstructed pot from Linkardstown but the resemblance may be more apparent than real.

Another example of Neolithic burial comes from Cahirguillamore, Co. Limerick (Hunt 1967). During blasting operations in a quarry, a small burial chamber was discovered, formed in the angle between the rock face and a large boulder leaning against it. The cavity was full almost to the top with disarticulated human bones, representing fourteen persons. Sherds of pottery and bone pins and beads were mixed through the deposit. No stratification could be discerned. The pottery was a mixture of Western Neolithic and Beaker ware. Some of the bone pins resembled those found in passage tombs. Outside the entrance to the little chamber or cavity there was a crouched inhumation accompanied by a round-bottomed decorated Neolithic bowl. According to the excavator (*ibid.*, 30): 'the evidence of the grave goods seems to anchor it somewhere between the Neolithic and the Bronze Age'.

A number of burials contemporary with the habitations was found at Lough Gur. All were inhumations and the majority were those of children. Four were in the crouched position, that is, the body was tightly flexed, the legs drawn up and the hands close to the head. In the northern part of Site C, on Knockadoon, a youth of about fourteen years was buried in this position in a large and deep pit (Ó Ríordáin 1954, 371, 374). The bottom of the pit had been scooped out subsequent to the period of the primary utilization of the site and the burial inserted, accompanied by a decorated pot of typical Limerick Western Neolithic style (*ibid.*, 454, fn. 156). There was no protective covering over the burial. A total of nine or ten burials was found at Circle K; all but one were of children. The exception was the crouched burial of a woman accompanied by the bones of a foetus. It is thought that she died during delivery. Stone and bone beads were found with two of the child burials. Two other burials, again of children, were found near one of the houses in Site D, and an adult burial in extended position was found outside Circle L (Grogan and Eogan forthcoming). All these burials were associated with Neolithic or Neolithic/Beaker levels.

Earthen and stone enclosures

This omnibus term covers a wide variety of structures and, in so far as their date is known or can be inferred, covers diverse periods from the Neolithic on into the Bronze Age. Some are assumed to have served ritual and ceremonial purposes, others are sepulchral and some of the stone monuments in particular are nowadays being hailed as solar and/or lunar observatories.

Embanked enclosures

These have attracted particular attention in recent years mainly because some see in them possible parallels for the henges which are ritual or ceremonial sites well known in Britain and well exemplified at Stonehenge. The orthodox henge consists of a bank and ditch, the latter usually internal, surrounding a roughly circular area within which may be features such as stone settings, postholes, burials and so forth. G. J. Wainwright (1969, 131–2) listed thirteen examples for Ireland, five of them reputedly in the Boyne valley. One of the latter, however, 'a small ring with an internal ditch east of Dowth', is modern and two others near Knowth seem to be ringforts or ring barrows of platform type. Only the remaining two, Sites P and Q (C. O'Kelly 1978, 51–2, 56) approximate to the classic definition. Site P, on the bank of the Boyne due south of Newgrange, consists of a circular saucer-shaped area surrounded by a bank. Its estimated diameter varies between 125m and 140m. The average height of the bank at present is only about 1.5m but judging by the great spread of bank material it must originally have been of impressive size. There is no trace of a ditch and if present at all it must have been inside the bank as, unless the river has drastically

68 Newgrange, Co. Meath, aerial view. Newgrange mound in foreground with U-shaped feature at left and satellites K and L at right; River Boyne at top of picture; Site P to right of figure-of-eight-shaped depression; Site A nearer to centre of picture at left

changed course, there would not have been sufficient space on the southern side between it and the enclosure. Aerial photographs clearly show a light-coloured band inside the bank and this may denote either a ditch or a collapsed wall-facing. Photographs also show that in the ESE the bank appears to be interrupted, the two ends being prolonged outwards at right angles, giving something of a keyhole shape to what may have been the entrance.

Site Q is east of the passage grave mound of Dowth, which is *c*.2km NE of Newgrange. Like Site P it is oval rather than circular and it is larger – 180m by about 150m in diameter. The surrounding bank, in places 3–4m in height, is now pierced by two opposed openings but in the first edition of the Ordnance Survey map of 1837 and in the Fair Plan, which represents the actual field survey of the time, only one opening is shown, that in the south-west, the present north-east opening being marked on the map only by a dotted circle and symbols denoting bushes and scrub. Even today this opening is narrower than the other and one is led to the belief that it was breached in modern times to facilitate the movement of farm machinery, as the enclosure has been constantly under tillage. There is no trace of an interior ditch. The enclosure is on a slope and the interior was obviously scooped up to form the bank; at the same time it was brought to a more horizontal level than the ground outside, so that the bank is much higher at one end than at the other. The level of the interior is also much lower than that of the surrounding field.

The other two comparable sites in the Boyne valley (not included in Wainwright 1969) are Site A which lies between Newgrange and Site P, and a site at Monknewtown a few kilometres due north of Newgrange. Only a small segment of the bank of Site A remains but it must originally have been at least 140m in diameter. A considerable number of worked flints have been picked up from the vicinity of the bank (O'Kelly 1968). Eccentrically placed within the enclosure is a tumulus about 25m in diameter and 6m in height. The complete ring of the enclosure can be seen in aerial photographs, and there seems to be a close similarity between it and Site P nearby, the same keyhole feature, if that is what it is, being present on the east side. None of these sites has been excavated.

The Monknewtown site is, or was originally, also an embanked enclosure, but it is only about half the size of the three discussed above. The bank, only a quarter of which remains, was formed by scooping up the surface of the interior. There was no inside ditch. A section excavated through the bank showed evidence of pre-enclosure activity (Sweetman 1971, 135). The interior, about 85m in diameter, was badly disturbed, pottery of eighteenth- and nineteenth-century date being found in the top soil. Since the latter lay directly on the fluvio-glacial gravels and all cultural activity took place on the gravels, any interpretation of this difficult site on the basis of stratigraphy had to be ruled out.

For purposes of excavation, which was initiated as a rescue operation in 1970–1, the interior was divided into four sectors and various portions of each were investigated (Sweetman 1976). In the two northern sectors, adjacent to the remaining segment of the bank and in one case cut into what was the original edge of the bank, eleven pits were found, all within less than 10m of the original edge of the bank. They were not arranged in any pattern and varied in size, shape and construction. Although all are referred to as 'burials' (*ibid.*, 28), only three contained any evidence of such. Pit no. V was lined with upright stones giving it a bucket-like shape and a small amount of cremated bone rested on the bottom flagstone. There were no artefacts. Pit no. VI was covered by a capstone and the pit was partly lined with upright stones. The remains of a cremation were found on the basal flagstone. There were no artefacts. Pit no. VIII was unlined and contained the remains of a large crude bucket-shaped vessel with estimated height of about 30cm and base diameter of 16–17cm. It was flat-rimmed, undecorated and heavily gritted with pebbles, some of them nearly 1cm thick. A few large pieces of cremated bone were found in the remains of the pot. Apart from a few fragments of cremated bone from one of the remaining pits and a piece of flint from another, all the rest were empty. The most interesting find from this half of the interior was a Carrowkeel bowl containing some cremated bone representing the remains of a child. It lay, not in a pit, but in a shallow hollow or depression scooped out of the gravel. It had no covering other than a reddish brown clay which extended outward from the bank over the whole of this northern area for a distance of 6–10m. This red layer, which was not a natural accumulation, had been deposited after the construction of the bank and after the digging of the above-mentioned eleven pits.

At least six hearths were found in the northern area, as well as sherds of Neolithic and Beaker ware. Some of the latter were in a grey layer on top of the red deposit, others lay directly on the gravel, as did some of the hearths. Of five ^{14}C samples from the primary cultural layer directly on the gravel, one was dated to 3465 ± 80 BP, which fits in well with the pit burial containing coarse pottery. Of the remainder, two are anomalous and the others are up to a millennium later. The excavator estimated that they 'may represent termination of activity on the site' (*Radiocarbon* 1974, 270).

A habitation area was found in the south-western sector close to the original line of the bank, and it seems to have been a squatting area somewhat similar to that found at Newgrange, where the Late Neolithic/Beaker occupation was clustered close up against the ruins of the cairn. Evidence of habitation came from a curious pit-type structure, *c*.5m by 7m, scooped out of the gravel within which were a number of irregularly spaced postholes with a hearth almost centrally placed. The floor of the pit was up to 50cm below the level of the top edge. More than 4,000 sherds of pottery were found in or near the pit and they compare closely with the assemblage from similar occupations at Newgrange and Knowth. A ^{14}C date of 3810 ± 45 BP was obtained for charcoal from the hearth.

A few metres from the habitation area there was a small shallow ring-ditch enclosing an area *c*.4.5m in diameter. There was a small shallow pit almost in the centre containing some cremated bone and a few small sherds of pottery similar to the coarse ware found in pit burial no. VIII. A sherd of finer ware was also present. A secondary hearth was found in the ditch and a single sherd of Beaker. No ^{14}C date was forthcoming.

A good deal of space has been devoted to Monknewtown, firstly, because any excavation in the Boyne valley is of particular significance, and secondly, because it is the only one of these curious Boyne enclosures that has been excavated so far. It is clear that they are far from being understood and the restrictive 'henge' label is not helpful until further work has been done. At least nine other similar enclosures have been noted in surrounding areas. A limited excavation carried out at a similar type of enclosure, the Giant's Ring, Ballynahatty, Co. Down (Collins 1957a), produced no evidence of date. A single burial containing cremated bone was found in a small dolmen eccentrically placed within the circle of the enclosure.

Ritual enclosures

The site on Goodland townland, Co. Antrim, just south of Fair Head in the north-east corner of Ireland, is about 240m above sea level and lies on one of the few patches of chalk that survive, hence the name of the townland. A group of one hundred or more Late Medieval transhumance or booley huts was being investigated here in the 1950s and 1960s (Case *et al.* 1969). These are upland sites that were seasonally occupied from spring to autumn, and the practice is one that continued well into living memory. In the course of the work, traces of Neolithic occupation were discovered at the edge of the encroaching blanket bog and clearly running beneath it. Excavation showed that several extensive settlements were present in prehistoric times. Flint was abundantly available, porcellanite and quartz were also to hand, and before the blanket bog started to form, an environment very suitable for Mesolithic and Neolithic people prevailed. We are concerned here with the enclosure ditch of which the excavator (Case 1973, 178) says: 'It is hardly possible rationally to look beyond a ritual explanation for the enclosure and many of the associated pits.'

Excavation revealed traces of a segmented enclosure ditch, about 14m by 12m, as well as pits, post- and stakeholes and enormous quantities of flint and pottery. Some eight irregular segments of ditch were found and over 170 pits, all of which had been filled in again shortly. The filling of the ditch incorporated forty-four deposits, the more elaborate ones consisting of glacial boulders which had sherds of pottery and struck flint flakes packed around them in a matrix of dark soil, itself rich in sherds and flints. The pits contained similar deposits. Over 6,000 sherds of pottery, representing perhaps 266 vessels, were recovered, mainly of Western Neolithic or Sandhills-type ware resembling sherds from Townleyhall II (pp. 52–3). Over 13,000 struck flints were recorded, as well as artefacts of quartz, porcellanite and other kinds of stone. A study of the sherds indicated that complete pots had not been deposited, either whole or deliberately broken, but rather that the pits and deposits contained material gathered up from scatters of domestic soil where sherds and flints would occur naturally; in other words, settlement rubbish. Case suggests that the reason for depositions of this sort was that settlement rubbish or debris was associated in the minds of the Neolithic inhabitants with fertile soil, and its deposition would ensure recurring fertility.

A ^{14}C date of 4575 $\pm$ 135 BP was obtained for charcoal in a pit with mature Sandhills ware, and the base of the overlying peat was dated to 4150 $\pm$ 200 BP. Reference has already been made to the suggestion that the pits and associated artefacts found beneath many mounds and cairns may represent ritual deposits, but the question has not been satisfactorily resolved in all cases up to the present.

Stone circles

The Grange stone circle at Lough Gur, known as Circle B in the Windle (1912) survey of the area, is situated near the western shore of the lake and is one of the most impressive examples of its kind in the country. It is one of a group of monuments which were formerly present in the vicinity consisting of several stone circles, some standing stones and a few 'dolmens', as all megalithic tombs were previously known. Most of these monuments have now totally or partially disappeared except for Circle B, which remains in a remarkably well preserved state. The monument consists of an unbroken level space, 45.7m in diameter, surrounded by a ring of 113 contiguous orthostats. Built against the stones on the outside is a broad bank of earth, 9m wide and up to 1.5m high measured from the interior. The tops of most of the stones are level with the bank but some are higher and very large. There is one which must weigh at least fifty tonnes. In the north-east there is a narrow entrance passage lined on each side by contiguous standing slabs. Since there is no external ditch, the material for the bank must have been scraped up from the surrounding area. The same is true of a thick layer of soil, averaging 45cm in depth, spread over the interior to conceal the packing stones in the sockets of the orthostats.

The monument was excavated in 1939 (Ó Ríordáin 1951). Two opposing quadrants in the interior were completely excavated and portions of the other

137

two, and a number of cuttings were made through the bank at different points. Apart from a posthole in the centre of the interior, perhaps used as a marker in setting-out the circle, the only structures found were portions of five enclosures delimited by shallow trenches, 6–8m across. Some were circular and others were irregular in shape, and it could be seen that not all were contemporaneous. Two separate fragments of clay pipes were found in one of the trenches covered by a large stone so that any slip from the surface was ruled out. The pipes dated to the seventeenth century AD and Ó Ríordáin believes (1951, 45) that the enclosures belong to some activity which took place in the circle around this time.

Two hearths were found on the old ground surface of the interior and sherds of pottery were connected with them. Some thousands of sherds were found in all, some in the cuttings through the bank but most of them in the interior, mainly in the fill and in the packing around the uprights. Sherds were also found in the sockets in which the uprights had been set. The sherds represent the round-bottomed bowls of Class I, the coarse flat-based pots of Class II, and in addition there was both Beaker and Bowl Food Vessel.

One Beaker pot which could be reconstructed from the surviving sherds is closely similar to one from Wick Barrow, Stogursey, Somerset, which D. L. Clarke places in the Late Southern Beaker group, S3(W) 821 (Clarke 1970, 399, fig. 957). The Grange Beaker can also be equated with Step 6 of Lanting and van der Waals' scheme (1972). C. B. Burgess (1980, 68) remarks that in Britain 'for steps 5 and 6 there are dates between *c*.1850–1473 BC from vessels found as far apart as Suffolk and the Outer Hebrides'. This does not take us very far towards

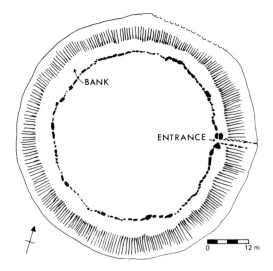

69 Lough Gur, Stone circle B at Grange (after S. P. Ó Ríordáin)

138

ascertaining even the approximate date of the Grange example. Sherds of this pot were found in one of the sockets of the orthostats and others lay nearby, covered by the filling in the interior.

Several hundred pieces of flint and chert were found. Among the artefacts were arrowheads (hollow-based and tanged-and-barbed), scrapers, and some asymmetrical knives similar to those found in the secondary occupation at Newgrange. A stone axe and some fragments were recovered and there were a few items of bronze, one of them an awl and another a mounting of some kind, perhaps for a sheath. There were some human bones but none constituted a formal burial. Animal bones scattered through the fill of the interior and in the bank cuttings represented cattle, pig, sheep/goat, horse, dog and hare.

S. P. Ó Ríordáin considered the site to have been a sacred and ritual one, citing in support the absence of habitations and burials and also the number of broken pottery sherds found near the uprights of the circle, presumably to be regarded as a ritual breaking. We are no nearer now to deciding whether his interpretation was the correct one or not.

In the field adjoining Circle B are the remains of two other circles. One was originally 16–17m in diameter and the other, largely destroyed, may have been about 55m in diameter (M. J. and C. O'Kelly 1981, 36). There are two other monuments east of the lake which are known as Circles O and P in the Windle nomenclature (*ibid.*, 28–9). These were the first sites to be excavated by Ó Ríordáin at Lough Gur when he came there in 1936 but unfortunately they remain unpublished.

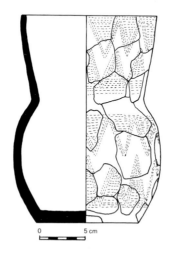

0   5 cm

70 Conjectural reconstruction of Beaker from Grange stone circle, Lough Gur (after S. P. Ó Ríordáin)

Circle O is the more impressive of the two. It is 56m in overall diameter and consists of an outer earthen bank faced inside and out with large stone slabs. The position of the original entrance is not known. Within is a ditch which provided the earth fill for the bank. Concentrically placed within the area enclosed by the ditch is an inner circle of contiguous orthostats, 15.3m in diameter. There were no diagnostic finds nor were there any burials. Ó Ríordáin concluded that it was a ritual site.

Circle P is 10.7m in overall diameter and consists of twenty-nine contiguous stones which form a kerb around a platform of stones and earth. There was no entrance feature. Two cremation burials accompanied by large flat-based coarsely made unornamented pots were found below the base of the platform. It may be, therefore, that this monument is not a stone circle proper but rather a burial tumulus of which only the kerb and basal portion of the mound now survive. The pottery vessels may be related to the flat-based domestic coarse ware

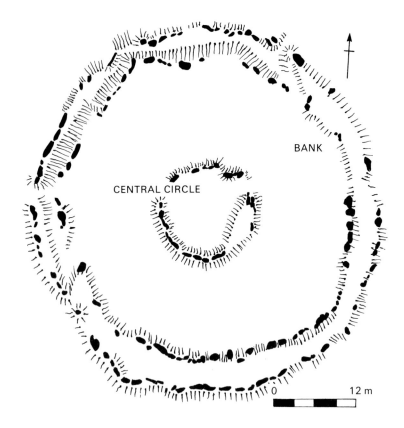

71 Circle O, Lough Gur

140

so prevalent in the Lough Gur district and which occurs widely in Bronze Age contexts also.

The series of widely separated standing stones encircling the Newgrange monument has been mentioned above (p. 100). Undue claims have been made for this feature; firstly, in accepting without question that it was originally complete and consisted of thirty-five to thirty-eight orthostats, and secondly, that it was erected subsequent to the monument itself in Beaker/Early Bronze Age times. Only twelve widely and irregularly spaced stones are present, situated at varying distances from the kerb of the cairn and extending from the north-eastern perimeter around to the north-west. There are no stones in the northern arc. When the monument was first brought to notice in AD 1699, only the same twelve stones were present.

With regard to the supposition that the circle was originally complete and consisted of from thirty-five to thirty-eight members the position is best summed up as follows: 'It must be stressed . . . that very little evidence was forthcoming in the excavated areas for the presence of the "missing" stones . . . one must be prepared to accept the thesis that the circle may never have been complete' (O'Kelly 1982, 79; O'Kelly *in* O'Kelly *et al.* 1983, 9–10). As for the second assumption, that the stones are of Beaker Period date, 'everywhere in the excavations along the southern perimeter it was found that the existing orthostats were in position before the [Late Neolithic/Beaker] habitation began . . . ' (O'Kelly 1982, 82).

Eight standing stones were excavated and another one on the north-east which was lying prone was also examined. The base foundations were investigated in all cases. Some, such as GC−2 opposite the tomb entrance (O'Kelly 1982, fig. 11), were resting on the old ground surface and in the case of this stone the old turf line could be traced beneath it, dipping slightly beneath its enormous weight. The edge nearest the monument was propped by large boulders with an accumulation of smaller stones which had been thrown in in more recent times. On the opposite side of the stone a short sloping trench ran partly under the base, and this was interpreted as a ramp for allowing the orthostat to be slid into place. While this is suppositional, at least the trench was shown conclusively to be connected with the erection of the standing stone and was not a later feature, of which there were many in this part of the site, i.e. south of the line of circle orthostats. These included a particularly disturbed habitation area, medieval trenches, and cultivation trenches running N–S and cutting through earlier strata. Another stone, GC3, stood in a deep socket-hole wedged by large stones, but further excavation showed that it had been erected on top of a great filled-in, pre-existing, man-made hollow. As a consequence, this stone, exceptionally, had tilted from the upright.

Two explanations which can be put forward for the presence of the standing stones are either that they were already present before the cairn was built and were perhaps connected with an earlier monument (there is a pre-existing turf mound beneath the great cairn) or else that they had been brought on site by the passage grave builders and found 'surplus to requirements' and were therefore set up along the southern half of the perimeter. Perhaps future excavation will reveal a more intimate association between the two monuments than exists at present.

One other point may be raised. The Newgrange circle in recent years has attracted attention from the growing body of people interested in the laying-out of such structures and in the possibility that mathematical and geometrical formulae were involved. Far too few stones are present in the Newgrange circle and their distribution is too irregular for any meaningful exercise of this nature. Even when the possible positions of 'missing' stones are plotted, no axis of symmetry can be found. The circle echoes the shape of the mound to some extent, that is, it is broader at the southern or front part, but at the east and west sides the stones are not equidistant from it. While it may well be that stones were removed from the southern part of the circle it is possible that none was ever present in the northern part, that is, at the back of the mound (O'Kelly 1982, 83–4), thus rendering its status as a stone circle in the true sense of the term ambiguous.

Anomalous sites

While some monuments, such as that at Grange in Lough Gur, fit into the category of stone circle and others into that of embanked enclosure, and so on, there are a few which do not seem to come within any morphological grouping. Two examples of this type are in Co. Down, the Millin Bay cairn (Collins and Waterman 1955) and the Ballynoe Stone Circle. The latter was excavated in 1937–8 by A. E. van Giffen but remained unpublished until, many years after his death, his notes were put in order by Groenman-van Waateringe and Butler (1976). Both are complex sites and it is doubtful if the full answer to the many problems posed by them is yet known.

The Millin Bay site consisted of an oval elongated cairn, 23m by 14.9m, and about a metre in height. A number of irregularly spaced orthostats were disposed around the mound, eleven of which have survived. Centrally placed beneath the mound was a long stone cist-like structure in a pit in the ground, and it contained the disarticulated remains of fifteen individuals and a single cremation. The cist was carefully built, covered by lintel stones, and the whole was covered and surrounded by a mini-cairn, oval in shape. This was retained at its perimeter by a setting of small standing slabs. Sixty-four stones in all, both earth-fast and loose ones, bear some degree of engraved 'ornament' though its nature is such that it does not compare closely either with Irish passage grave art or with Irish rock art. There were several other burials in the mound and some short cists. Some sherds of Carrowkeel-type ware were recovered from the pre-cairn surface. The site is clearly a multi-period one as appears to be the case also at Ballynoe.

The Ballynoe site consisted of a long cairn, 21m by 9m, surrounded by a ring of closely set standing stones. A small stone cist was present at the east end of the cairn and another at the west end. The latter was subsequently augmented by two more chambers and this necessitated an extension of the cairn at this end. Cremated bone was found in the cists, and a sherd of Carrowkeel ware. Settings of what van Giffen in his notes called 'baetyl stones' were found in several places beneath the mound. Owing to the fact that the excavator himself did not publish his findings it was extremely difficult to interpret many of the features and for this reason a number of alternative interpretations are included in the report (*ibid.*, 87–9).

Another Co. Down site, situated at Castle Mahon Mountain (Collins 1956), owed its excavation largely to the fact that traces of a small stone circle appeared to be present, a type of monument rare in that county. There were five widely

72 Millin Bay, Co. Down, after excavation and conservation

spaced stones, and a small cist containing the cremated bones of a child, together with a plano-convex flint knife, were found near the centre of the enclosed space. There was a pit nearby, the bottom of which had been intensely burnt. Another pit on the line of the arc of standing stones contained sherds of Neolithic pottery of Lyles Hill type. Again it must be asked if a multi-period site was not in question.

An area very rich in prehistoric remains was the Archdall deerpark in the townland of Kiltierney in Co. Fermanagh, but past 'excavations' and modern farm 'improvements' have sadly depleted them. A site marked 'carn' on the Ordnance Survey map of 1907 may have been a passage tomb. The two decorated stones which remain bear ornament characteristic of that type of monument though some of the motifs are closer to those of Millin Bay than to the usual run of such devices. In the course of farm improvements in 1974, an earthen fort, a linear earthwork and a stone circle were destroyed, and excavation was subsequently undertaken to salvage whatever remained (Daniells and Williams 1977).

The stone circle, which had contained seven large irregularly spaced boulders before destruction, lay about 250m from the presumed passage grave or 'carn'. It differed from the usual Ulster type of stone circle (p. 232) and was closer to some of the embanked ones. A number of burials in pits were found within the circle and some of the finds, such as sherds of Carrowkeel ware and hammer pendants, were more appropriate to passage tomb burials than to the kind of Early Bronze Age cemetery suggested by the interments themselves. The excavators concluded that the evidence suggested that Carrowkeel ware and hammer pendants continued in use beyond the Neolithic period and that the stone circle did in fact represent an Early Bronze Age cemetery. Its resemblance to the site at Castle Mahon was also noted because of the similar widely spaced orthostats found there, together with pits and artefacts of Neolithic and Early Bronze Age date.

Scale bar: 0 — 80 km

Labels on map:
Drumbest
Castlederg
Topped Mountain
Tedavnet
Moylough
Lough Gara
Latoon
Roscommon
Tara
Athlone
Clonmacnoise
Dalkey Island
Athenry
Somerset
Frankford
Derrinboy
Dowris
Bishopsland
Gleninsheen
Gorteenreagh
Coolmanagh
Rathgall
Mooghaun
Killaloe
River Shannon
Rear Cross/Holyford
Enniscorthy
Lough Gur
Carrickshedoge
Clogher
Bunmahon
Ross Island
Killaha East
Bantry
Mount Gabriel

73 Bronze Age tools, weapons and ornaments

146

7

The Bronze Age

Chronology

Many attempts have been made to establish a chronological framework for the Irish Bronze Age and while each has its merits, none is wholly satisfactory. The number of radiocarbon dates for Bronze Age burials is increasing, based mainly on charcoal associated with the burial or on samples of bone therefrom, and in this way some order is coming into the burial chronology. The number of settlement sites that has been identified is low by comparison and dates are scarce as a result. The greatest difficulty arises, however, when attempts are made to provide absolute dates for the metalwork. The vast majority of the artefacts are chance finds made in the course of land development works such as gravel digging, drainage, peat cutting, and so on, and furthermore there has been very little accurate recording of the circumstances of the finds. Very few of them come from datable graves or other such associations. A number of burials containing Bowl Food Vessels are associated with typologically early metal objects; for instance, a Bowl from Corkey, Co. Antrim, found with a dagger and one from Carrickinab, Co. Down, found with an awl and a dagger (Harbison 1968, 44, 46; 1969, 8, 17). Over twenty burials, the majority in Urns, contained bronze razors (Binchy 1967, 47) but these examples are comparatively few in number in relation to the whole. To all intents and purposes the metal artefacts of the Bronze Age have no context capable of providing absolute dates at present.

It has been necessary, therefore, to look to evolutionary typologies, to association with or derivation from British and Continental models and to the few reliably recorded hoard associations in the attempts to provide a relative chronology for the metalwork, that is, one in which it is argued that a particular type of object is earlier or later than another of the same type by virtue of the relationship between them. The dates assigned to the various developmental phases are conventional ones measured in calendrical or solar years BC. While radiocarbon dating has greatly altered traditional thinking on other aspects of the Bronze Age, particularly the ceramics, the traditional framework for metal artefacts is virtually unchanged from that put forward by George Coffey, one-time Keeper of Irish Antiquities at the National Museum of Ireland, in his work on the Bronze Age published in 1913. He proposed five stages as follows:

1 2000–1800 BC Flat copper axes, copper knife-daggers and the earliest halberds.

2 1800–1500 BC Flat bronze axes, flanged and with expanded ends, small daggers, lunulae.

3 1500–1250 BC Flanged axes with stop-ridges, tanged spearheads, larger daggers.

4 1250–900 BC Palstaves, socketed axes, rapiers, early leafshaped swords, looped and leafshaped spearheads, gold torcs, disc-headed pins, bronze razors.

5 900–350 BC Socketed axes, swords with notches below the blade, sword chapes, socketed sickles, spearheads with lunate openings in the blade, gold fibulae and gorgets, horns. Towards the close of this stage iron had come into use.

By and large very little has changed today, either in the sub-divisions or in the objects assigned to them. One cannot but contrast this with the enormous changes that have overtaken traditional thinking in other aspects of archaeology and Coffey provides an interesting example of this. In his fourth division (1250–900 BC) he says (Coffey 1913, 5): 'In this period must also be placed the building of the great tumuli of the New Grange group', a statement which reflected the traditional thinking of his day. By the time excavations began at Newgrange in 1962, a certain amount of updating had already taken place in traditional thinking and the Boyne 'culture', so-called, was being linked with the Wessex culture of southern Britain and with Mycenaean Greece. A date centring on 1500 BC was the one generally proposed for the Boyne tombs. As we have seen, Newgrange was again updated in the course of the excavations when radiocarbon samples provided dates which, when subjected to tree-ring calibration, are equivalent to *c.*3000 BC in calendrical years. One wonders what revelations might be forthcoming were it possible to apply absolute dating to the almost monolithic chronology of Irish Bronze Age metalwork.

During the past two decades in particular a substantial amount of research has been undertaken on the techno-typology of the period. Spanning as it does almost two millennia, it encompasses an enormous body of metalwork such as axes, daggers, halberds, spearheads, swords, and so on, as well as a great variety of gold and other objects. The period has been divided up either into Early, Middle and Late, or into Earlier and Later, and to each of these divisions phases have been assigned named after the find-places of hoards of metalwork in which significant associations or type-changes have been detected. For example, for the earlier part of the Bronze Age Peter Harbison (1973, 95–125) distinguishes four phases, three of which are named after hoard-sites, and he associates various metal artefacts with each, arranged in typological sequence. For the later part of the Bronze Age, George Eogan (1964) distinguishes three phases, each named after a well known bronze hoard: Bishopsland, Roscommon and Dowris. These sub-divisions are very useful in the ordering of such a large body of material provided too great an emphasis is not placed on the terminology. The latter tends to straitjacket the artefacts themselves and to cause one to lose sight of the fact that they were the product of human beings and that the latter in turn were to a large extent the product of the type of society in which they lived. A. M. ApSimon identified the problem some years ago when he wrote (1969a, 57–8):

> Metal-working has been seen in terms of traditions and industries, which though often poorly defined, can be arranged in a succession of stages. Settlements and burials have been used to define cultures whose inter-relations delimit periods and phases. But, because metal finds are so rare among grave goods and in settlements, it is practically impossible to combine bronzes and cultures in a single detailed chronological scheme and unhelpful to use a system of 'ages' which ignores one line of evidence.

Nor is the problem confined to the archaeologists. I. C. Goddard (1974, 46) has described the difficulties encountered when he endeavoured to relate a radiocarbon chronology for Late Bronze Age forest clearances to the chronology proposed for the metalwork of the period. He found that the Irish chronology was based on the English and that it in turn was based on that of Europe. He goes on to say: 'The European chronology appears to be an arbitrary division into equal periods whose initial and terminal dates are ultimately derived, I would presume, from more distant historical chronology. Clearly the Irish "chronology" is meaningless in the strict sense of the term. The "dates" are simply arbitrary pointers to steps in a sequence.' Goddard stresses that this not a cricitism of the compilers of the chronology but is due to the lack of data which makes it impossible to provide an absolute chronology.

The conventional framework of the Irish Bronze Age

The most generally accepted division of the period as a whole nowadays is into Early Bronze Age (EBA) and Late Bronze Age (LBA) though, as far as the metalwork is concerned, there is a somewhat 'grey' area towards the end of the EBA which is regarded by some as a Middle Bronze Age (MBA). Colin Burgess (1980, 126), for instance, sees 'a significant metallurgical response in Britain and Ireland, which, in traditional terms passed from "Early to Middle Bronze Age" *c*. 1400 BC'. He includes the Bishopsland Phase dated by Eogan to 1200–900 BC in the second half of the MBA and would begin the LBA after this point. Eogan, while recognizing the existence of a middle phase beginning *c*.1400 BC and demonstrated by the introduction of palstaves, rapiers and socket-looped spearheads with ribbed, kite-shaped blades (Eogan 1962, 45), states (*ibid.*, 57) that: 'The first section [of the middle phase] emerges as a continuation of the Early Bronze Age, while the second section stands out as an incipient Late Bronze Age that saw the introduction of new types that were to continue and become standard forms.' In his 1964 paper Eogan uses the term 'Later Bronze Age' to define the period which begins this second section, *c.*1200 BC, and ends in the course of the first millennium BC when the knowledge of iron working had been introduced. The terms Early and Late Bronze Age are used below and the sub-divisions of the EBA are those proposed by Harbison (1973, 95–125) and of the LBA by Eogan (1964, 323–5). All the various sub-divisions are named after hoards except EBA 4. The dates are not radiocarbon-based.

Early Bronze Age
  1 Knocknagur* *c.*2500–2000 BC
  2 Frankford-Killaha-Ballyvally *c.*2000–1550 BC
  3 Derryniggin *c.*1550–1400 BC
  4 *c.*1400–1200 BC
Late Bronze Age
  1 The Bishopsland Phase *c.* 1200–900 BC
  2 The Roscommon Phase *c.* 900–700 BC
  3 The Dowris Phase *c.* 700 BC (duration uncertain).

The techno-typology and the dates of the various artefacts given below reflect as far as possible a consensus of the views of the most prominent workers in this particular field at present – ApSimon 1969a and 1976; Burgess 1974 and 1980; Eogan 1962 and 1964; Harbison 1969 and 1973 – as well as those of specialists in the Antiquities Division of the National Museum of Ireland.†

A matter that has been discussed extensively by the authors above-mentioned and by others is the question of foreign or outside contacts and influences. Beyond doubt these must have been present throughout the Bronze Age. The very nature of the requisite raw materials implied the exploitation of metal sources from many different areas. Ireland possessed copper and gold, and possibly some tin was also available, perhaps sufficient for the earliest stages of the bronze industry (J. S. Jackson 1979, 122), but even if the copper- and gold-bearing ores were much more readily accessible than we know them to have been, they still could not have supplied the whole of the Irish market. Ireland

---

  * A placename misspelt as 'Knocknague' by previous writers (information from John Waddell).
  † Particular reference is made below to two catalogues published in connection with an exhibition of the 'Treasures of Ireland', the first in 1977 by the Metropolitan Museum of Art, New York, and the second in 1983 by the Royal Irish Academy. The Bronze Age section in the Metropolitan catalogue is by Peter Harbison and that in the Academy catalogue by members of the staff of the Antiquities Division of the National Museum of Ireland. Another compendium referred to below, published in 1973, was written by A. T. Lucas, the then Director of the National Museum.

would inevitably and eventually have been drawn into the trade and exchange networks linking her with the outside world. In the earliest part of the period it is believed that the Atlantic influences predominated, that is, Brittany and Iberia, in addition to her nearest neighbour, Britain. In the later part of the Bronze Age an extraordinary expansion in production took place and Irish gold was being obtained from central European and more easterly sources, the Atlantic trade routes having declined by then. Other strong influences came from Denmark and the Baltic, perhaps partly via Britain.

Conspicuous wealth was very evident from the early part of the first millennium BC onward. The range of weaponry and of items of personal adornment in gold is remarkable and one cannot but reflect that more of the material ingredients of Ireland's so-called 'Heroic Age' were present in the Dowris Phase of the LBA than in the period around the close of the millennium where some scholars place it (K. H. Jackson 1964).

Technology

The earliest known metal was copper, and it is perhaps a measure of our lack of precise knowledge of when and how it first came to be used in Ireland that the conventional influx of immigrants is often invoked to account for it, though less so than formerly. The knowledge of metal working is generally thought to have accompanied the introduction of Beaker pottery but there is no evidence of direct involvement of one with the other in Ireland. In a few instances stone objects recognized as metal workers' tools have been found in contexts containing Beaker pottery (Butler and van der Waals 1966, 63; O'Kelly and Shell 1979). The bronze axe from the Beaker settlement at Newgrange has been mentioned above (p. 77), and also the fact that a radiocarbon date of *c.* 2000 BC has been argued for it though, it must be made clear, not on the grounds of direct radiocarbon-dated evidence.

The transition from stone to metal must have been a long-drawn-out process, comparable in ways to that which accompanied the Mesolithic/Neolithic transition. A considerable period may have elapsed between the first awareness on the part of the natives of the existence of these new and exotic copper artefacts, acquired through exchange, trade or travel, and the time when they began to manufacture them themselves from their own native ores. Brian Scott makes the interesting point that 'while in no way retreating from the view . . . that indigenous Irish invention of smelting and melting of copper is an attractive but untenable hypothesis, we may yet see that acquaintance here with copper and its ore minerals is one way in which the development of indigenous copper production could have been accelerated' (Scott and Francis 1981, 36–7). Stone Age people were dependent for many of their tools on knowledge of the properties of the various rocks and their trained eyes may have already been aware of the bright green/blue staining associated with the presence of copper ores long before its metallurgical possibilities were demonstrated. Alison Sheridan (1983) has reviewed the various theories relating to metallurgical origins.

The location of the ore was but the first step in the complex manufacturing process. However and from wherever they received their initiation into the mysteries of metallurgy, a flourishing industry eventually developed in copper and bronze working as well as in the manufacture of objects in gold. It has been said that 'the earliest metallurgists in Ireland were very highly skilled. Not only could they select the right deposit, hand-pick, wash and concentrate the ore; they could control the roasting, smelting and possibly refining processes in a very competent way, and eventually alloy' (Coghlan and Case 1957, 97).

The Metal Age began with a copper period, that is, a time during which unalloyed copper was used as the raw material for the objects manufactured. Analyses have shown that this early Irish copper contained appreciable traces of arsenic, antimony and silver as well as other trace elements, and there are ore deposits in Munster which could have given such a metal. There is even the possibility that this typical Irish metal was a *regulus alloy*, that is, an intermediate product resulting from the alloying of a Munster ore of the *fahlerz* or grey copper type, rich in arsenic, antimony and silver, with a purer copper smelted from Munster or other ores. The arsenic improved the quality of the resulting metal. Evidence of this early metallurgy in Ireland is of a number of kinds: primitive mining of copper ores; evidence of smelting; stone moulds in which objects were cast; and finally, the objects themselves.

Mining of copper ores

Important copper deposits are found in the counties of Cork, Kerry, Tipperary, Waterford and Wicklow, and occur in lesser quantities in Clare and Galway and in some of the more northerly counties. A strong local tradition of what appears to have been primitive mining remains in a number of areas but in most cases the physical evidence has been obliterated, often by post-medieval mining. Stone mauls used as mining hammers and of a type common to primitive mining every-where have been found in the past in the Rear Cross–Holyford area of Tipperary, at Bunmahon, Co. Waterford, on Ross Island in Killarney, Co. Kerry, and at Mount Gabriel, Derrycarhoon and Ballyrisode, Co. Cork. It is these latter areas, situated on the coastal peninsulas of the south-west, that provide the clearest evidence.

The commonest of these hammers were made from beach cobbles of sizes convenient to the hand and used without hafts as pounders. They were apparently selected for their oval shape and when found at the mines display at each end areas that have become abraded in use. Others have a chiselled equatorial groove in which was placed a withy or pliable tree-root, the two ends of which were bound tightly together to form a haft or handle. In other examples the ends of the equatorial groove stop at each side of a carefully made flat area. Experiments suggest that this type was hafted by driving a wooden wedge between the end of the handle and the flat so as to take up any remaining slackness. It has been suggested also (Jovanovič 1979, 107–8) that the ungrooved mauls were used in removing ore from small cracks or channels, whereas the largest grooved ones were used to crush the broken blocks of ore. Owing to the confined working space and also because of the weight of the pebbles, a stable wooden handle could not be employed and the binding of the mauls by a rope or roots enabled the worker to deliver vertical and circular strokes by lengthening or shortening the flexible handle.

The best evidence of mining activity has come from Mount Gabriel and

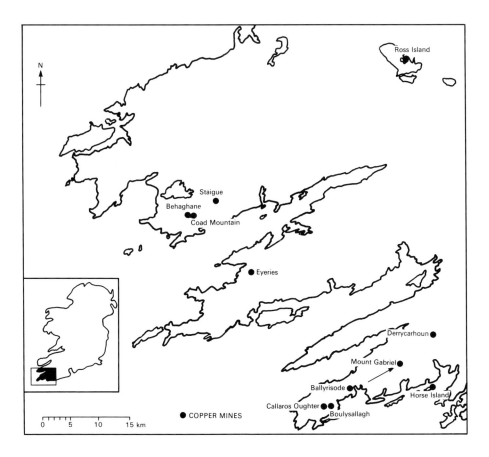

74 Distribution map of west Cork/Kerry copper mines (after J. Jackson and W. O'Brien)

Derrycarhoon near Schull in south-west Cork. At Derrycarhoon in the last century, when a four-metre thickness of peat had been cut away for fuel, six old mine shafts were discovered and in them were found various objects used in the mining process, such as a wooden ladder, wooden shovels and stone mauls. Only the mauls survive. Pioneering work by John Jackson in the 1960s resulted in the identification of twenty-five mines (Jackson 1968), and present-day ongoing research by W. O'Brien has augmented the number to at least thirty-four. These shallow workings are almost totally inaccessible owing to flooding and to blanket peat infill, the latter suggesting the antiquity of the workings as well as helping to ensure their survival. The mines appear as small tunnels driven into rock scarps for varying distances of up to 10m. Some of the mine-shaft walls show the characteristic spalling produced by the technique of fire-setting. The rock was heated by building a fire against it and was then rapidly cooled by spilling water on it. This shattered the rock which was then removed by pounding with the stone mauls, many of which, both broken and complete examples, have been found in the shafts and in the tip-heaps outside their entrances.

The copper-bearing rock was brought from the mines and crushed by hammering to enable concentration to be done by hand-picking and washing the richer material out of the gangue. It is this latter waste material which makes up the tip-heaps outside each mine. As yet no evidence of smelting has been found adjacent to the mines and it must therefore be assumed that the ore concentrate was taken elsewhere, though not necessarily very far away, for further processing. In 1966 a trench was cut through the tip-heap of mine no. 5 and the char-

75 Mount Gabriel, Co. Cork, entrance to mine no. 27

coal from two separate carbonaceous layers was amalgamated for radiocarbon analysis (Jackson 1968; 1984) giving a date of 3450 ± 120 BP.

It was recognized that further research was needed and in 1970 a limited examination was undertaken in the area (Deady and Doran 1972). Between 1982 and 1985, detailed field survey by W. O'Brien was carried out at the Mount Gabriel mines and at eight additional areas in the south-west. In 1984, excavation of the interior infill deposits of mine no. 24 on the eastern slope of Mount Gabriel produced waterlogged, partly charred wooden material which bore the marks of tooling. This represented the remnant of firesetting operations. A sample of this material has produced a ^{14}C date of 3130 ± 80 BP. The tip heaps or dumps outside some of the mines were excavated by O'Brien and in the following year a living area on the hillside outside one of the adits or drivings was similarly investigated. Postholes and a trough into which water had been diverted, possibly for use in firesetting, were identified. The excavation is expected to continue (O'Brien, unpublished).

Smelting

Since the ores are sulphides they must first have been roasted to remove the sulphur. This would have been done by interlayering the ore concentrate with wood charcoal and by keeping the pile burning at a low temperature, perhaps for several days. Skill and experience were necessary to do this for not only had the temperature to be controlled but the pile had to be so constructed, maintained and vented that there was free and even access of air to all its parts throughout the roast. No direct evidence of the carrying-out of this process has so far been found in Ireland. The roasted ore was then smelted in a furnace which also used charcoal as a fuel. Though no actual smeltery has been found, some of the cakes of raw copper produced are known and these give some indications of the nature of the furnace used. Cakes from Carrickshedoge, Co. Wexford, for instance (Bremer 1926, 89), are from 10cm to 20cm in diameter and about 1cm thick.

It is thought that the furnaces were of the simple type in which the ore and charcoal were interlayered in, and mounded over, a shallow circular bowl-shaped hollow dug in the ground and lined with clay. When a tuyère or clay funnel-shaped nozzle had been fixed on the side of the bowl and the charge had been fired, a dome-shaped clay cover was put on over the charge. This had a small vent at the top for the release of the furnace gases. A continuous controlled air blast was supplied through the tuyère from a pair of bellows. As the ore was reduced, the metal particles became molten, ran together and passed down through the charcoal to the bottom of the furnace, there to be moulded to the form described above by the shape of the bottom of the furnace itself. Subsequently, this cake, or ingot as it may be called, provided the metal from which axes and other objects were made. Pieces cut or broken from it were re-melted in a clay crucible and poured into the requisite mould. If the alloying with tin had not been done during the smelting process, it could now be done in the crucible. Fragments of shallow dish-like crucibles believed to be of Bronze Age date have been found on Dalkey Island in Dublin Bay (Liversage 1968, 89–91) and elsewhere.

While the Irish craftsmen were using the arsenical coppers, whether obtained by careful ore selection or by deliberate alloying, no problems other than those of a technical nature arose, for the raw materials were obtainable in Ireland. But when it came to the making of tin-bronze (approx. 90 per cent copper, 10 per cent tin) a new problem was immediately encountered, namely, where to obtain the necessary tin ore or metallic tin. The presence of tin associated with alluvial gold in Co. Wicklow has long been known. It occurs as mineral tinstone or cassiterite (SnO_2) in the alluvial gravels along the Goldmines River and other streams in the area, having been transported thither, possibly by glacial action, in the form of cassiterite crystals. No satisfactory parent source has yet been found. Spectroscopic tests have shown the presence of trace amounts of tin in the Allihies copper lodes in Co. Cork and minute traces have been detected in soils and peats, but no locality has been recognized that might have been exploited even by the painstaking methods of the ancients.*

Even if some tin had been obtained from native sources it is doubtful if it could have been enough to meet the developing demand, and so a trading or other arrangement must have been set up to obtain sufficient of the metal, probably from the Cornish mines, if not from somewhere farther afield. This means that travel to and fro across the sea was continuing at this time and that some materials were exported from Ireland in exchange for the tin, unless one envisages each Irish smith going himself to Cornwall to mine the ore, smelt it and bring away enough metallic tin to supply his needs for a given length of time. Another possibility is that there was a constant movement of itinerant smiths between Ireland and Britain, each one bringing his stock-in-trade with him.

Stone and clay moulds

Moulds have been found in various parts of the country and were used for the casting of a variety of artefacts such as axes, knives and daggers, spearheads, and so on. There are both single and bivalve moulds. The bivalve mould was in two parts so that after casting, the completely shaped object could be taken out by separating the two parts. The single valve or open mould shaped only one face of

* Information supplied by courtesy of M. A. Cunningham of the Irish Geological Survey.

the object being cast and the other face had to be shaped by hammering and grinding.

The open moulds for casting axes are probably amongst the earliest to be made and used in Ireland and are of great technological interest. The Doonour mould from near Bantry, Co. Cork (O'Kelly 1969a), was discovered when a small field near the seacoast was being reclaimed. There was no evidence of a furnace or other associated structures. It is a roughly rectangular block of grit, 31cm by 22.5cm by 14cm in maximum length, width and thickness respectively. Its form is partly natural and partly artificial. Parts of faces 1, 2 and 4 and all of face 6 show clear evidence of shaping, the work having been done by percussion, probably by means of a pointed chisel and a mallet. The stone was selected because it is a fine-grained freestone and therefore reasonably easy to carve, and the source could be immediately local. There are matrices for five different sizes of axe and for two chisel-like implements. There is no evidence that any kind of lid was fitted to any of the matrices to convert them into closed moulds when they were being used. Hot metal was certainly poured into some of the matrices, and the colour change in, and the friable nature of, some of the internal surfaces

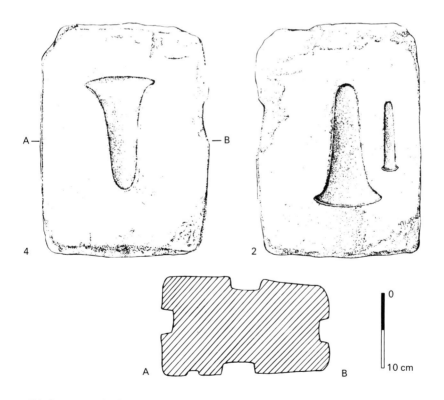

76 Stone mould for axeheads from Doonour, Co. Cork, showing faces 4 and 2

indicate that the depth of the metal may have been about 8mm. As none of the opposing faces of the block is parallel, each matrix had to be set level before pouring so as to ensure that the metal would distribute properly in the matrix. In all cases the floor surfaces of the matrices are curved in two directions and the deepest parts are usually centred on the long axis but much nearer to the cutting-edge ends than to the butt ends. If therefore the matrix were set level and metal poured in to fill it to the requisite amount, the downward surface of the metal would have been moulded to the double curvature but the upper surface would have remained fairly flat. Both the cutting edge and the butt end would have been thick and blunt. In fact, the objects cast in such moulds can have been no more than rough-outs for axes to be finished by hammering and grinding.

Peter Harbison (1969a, 22–4) lists 60 objects which he calls 'ingots'. They have an ovoid or trapezoidal shape with flat or slightly rounded unhammered rough faces and sides. In some cases, one face is almost flat and the other a rounded bump. The distribution is widespread but there is a concentration in Antrim. As illustrated in his catalogue, they appear to be just such rough-outs as those postulated here. The hammering would also have hardened the metal and this would have enabled a better cutting edge to be developed. The shapes of the matrices in the Doonour mould seem to have been designed to produce rough-outs for axes of the kind called 'Type Ballyvally' by Harbison (1969a, 32), that is, thin-butted with sides curving outwards to the cutting edge. About half of the known examples bear incised linear ornament.

In due time, bivalve moulds in both stone and clay came into use, the stone often being the easily carved steatite instead of the sandstones used for the open moulds. Evidence exists that wooden models of the objects to be cast or even examples of the objects themselves were used on which to build up bivalve clay moulds for artefacts such as spearheads and swords. In the case of a bronze sword in the Ulster Museum the grain of the wooden pattern which had impressed itself on the mould is clearly visible on the bronze. For socketed tools and weapons and for such items as the elegant curving trumpets or horns of the Late Bronze Age, bivalve clay moulds were used with a core to make hollow castings. When the clay mould had been made and hardened or burnt in the fire a clay core had to be supported within the mould in such a way that the molten metal could be poured freely around it. Clear evidence of traces of the clay core remain inside the tube of some of the horns (Coles 1963, 335) and in the chaplets or small metal supports positioned on each side of the horn to hold the core in place.

Perhaps too, the *cire perdue* or 'lost wax' process of casting was employed but evidence of this is not easy to find since the clay mould had to be broken to remove the newly made metal object. In this process a wax model of the object to be cast was encased in clay and baked. The liquid wax escaped through specially contrived holes or vents and the molten metal was poured in through these. When the clay mould was broken away an image in metal of the wax model remained.

As well as the fragments of crucibles recorded from Dalkey Island, fragments of clay moulds for socketed spearheads, knives and perhaps an axe and a sword were found in the same area of the island, Site V. At the Rathgall hillfort, Co. Wicklow, an LBA workshop area or smithy was uncovered by excavation in which were hundreds of clay mould fragments, indicating extensive manufacture of bronze implements (B. Raftery 1976, 345). In addition to crucible fragments, portions of stone and clay moulds were found in the Knockadoon habitation settlement at Lough Gur. At Site F, for instance, the total number of fragments of clay moulds was about one hundred. Among the recognizable pieces were moulds for spearheads and rapiers (Ó Ríordáin 1954, 420–2). Many of the different types of mould are illustrated in Coghlan and Raftery (1961). A number of bronze moulds are also known.

One other bronze-working technique remains to be mentioned, the manufacture of sheet bronze. It was employed in some of the most striking objects of the LBA such as the bronze cauldrons. The cake or ingot of bronze was laid on an anvil and beaten with a heavy stone hammer to render it as flat as possible. After a certain amount of hammering the metal became brittle and had to be reheated or annealed so as to make it more malleable. Annealing was a 'trick of the trade' which had to be acquired by the Irish smiths either empirically or by imitation. When the sheets were thin enough – this could be as little as 5mm – they were further hammered to bring about the required curvature, as for example in bowls and cauldrons. In the latter case the requisite number of sheets was riveted together and, as so often in the best metalwork, what was a utilitarian necessity was often turned into an aesthetic feature in its own right (Brannon 1984, 56). The heads of the rivets were beautifully shaped and arranged in pleasing patterns. In some cases sham rivets in the shape of conical spikes were attached to the sides of the vessels to enhance further the decorative appearance. It is also thought that the prominent rivets helped to transfer heat from the fire to the sides of the vessel during use.

Bronze objects

Early Bronze Age

Large numbers of the metal objects made in the various types of mould have survived in Ireland. A count of the axes of the early part of the Bronze Age (Harbison 1969a) shows that some 2,000 have come down to us (this does not include numerous palstaves and related items nor the socketed axes of the LBA). The axe was a basic tool in continuous use and because of this a techno-typological sequence can be observed from the earliest broad thick-butted copper examples (Type Lough Ravel) through the improved half-flanged bronze axes to the socketed ones. The developments were principally attuned to the more efficient attachment of the haft or handle to the axe, to the provision of a more efficient cutting edge, and also to a more economical use of metal, as for instance in Sub-type Ballybeg where the butts are thinner and more rounded. In the next development the sides became more curved and the cutting edges began to be widely splayed. Instead of slotting the axe into a wooden handle and maintaining it in place by a shrunk-on rawhide binding, a new method of hafting was evolved. Flanges, very low at first, were hammered-up along the sides of the axe (Types Killaha and Ballyvally) and a haft bent to an approximate right-angle, a knee-haft, began to be used. The butt was thrust into a slot in the end of the knee, the side-flanges holding it in place with the addition of a binding. Decoration begins to appear on the faces and sides.

Towards the second half of the EBA, haft-flanged axes, that is, axes cast with more pronounced flanges, came into use (Type Derryniggin). A further development was a ridge or stop on the flat surface of the axe to prevent further move-

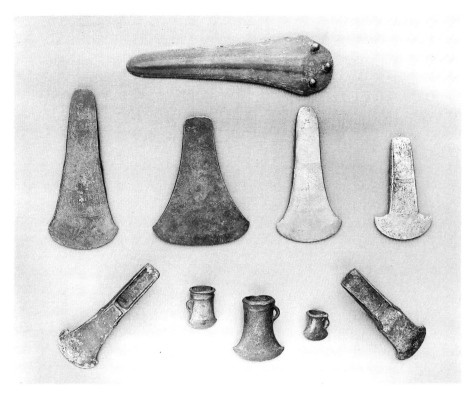

77 Bronze halberd and axeheads

ment of the haft. In time, the flanges were drawn out and curved somewhat inward from each side so as to grip the ends of the knee more firmly and, in the later examples, the metal of the septum or enclosed portion was thinned so that the stop-ridge became a pronounced ledge-like feature. Sometimes, too, the ends of the flanges were continued downward on to the face of the blade to form a pointed ornamental feature. While it is possible that this type evolved into something like the West European palstave or the corresponding British MBA version in which the flanges and stop-ridge coalesced to form haft-pockets on each side of the septum, it is probable that the palstave was a fresh introduction into Ireland to be copied, though not extensively, by the Irish smiths. The palstave form continued in use throughout the remainder of the EBA. A loop was added through which a cord was passed behind the angle of the haft so as to secure it further. Some Irish palstaves have two opposing loops.

Many of the flat and low-flanged axes are decorated with various incised linear designs and some of them are so beautiful that one can hardly imagine these axes ever having been used for any kind of rough work. Many of the motifs, chevrons, triangles, etc., are similar to those found on the Food Vessel pottery of the EBA but it is not possible to say which copied which, if indeed there was any copying at all.

A point that has to be borne in mind in regard to the axe typology and that of various other artefacts is that while, broadly speaking, the various stages are typologically and chronologically progressive, the concept itself is schematic and artificial. In real life, some products would have been much more long-lived than others and would have been in use contemporaneously with very much more

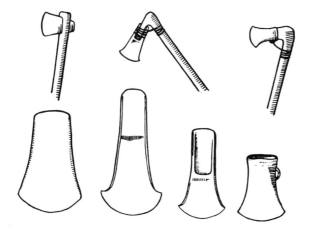

78 Types of copper and bronze axeheads and various hafting methods (after J. Raftery; copyright NMI)

161

progressive types of the same object. It must also be appreciated that there would be regional differences and preferences. For this reason, a very broad tolerance in the matter of date must be allowed in respect of individual unassociated finds.

Irish daggers are diverse in style, dimensions and shape and their classification is therefore difficult (Harbison 1969). Harbison is of the opinion that all the daggers found in Ireland (about 142 in all) are of Irish manufacture, though the idea of making daggers and many of the dagger shapes did come from outside. The earliest Irish dagger is tanged and has its nearest parallel in England, and from this introduced idea came the daggers with from two to six rivets in the butt which helped to attach it more firmly to the bone or wooden handle. Other developments included grooves running parallel to the edges. A small triangular-shaped grooved dagger, *c.* 14cm in present length, from Topped Mountain, Co. Fermanagh, was found in a cist grave with an inhumed skeleton and a Vase Food Vessel. Near the dagger was a piece of gold pommel-binding. In some

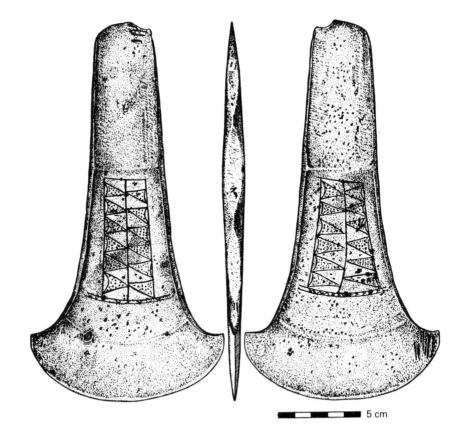

5 cm

79 Decorated bronze axeheads (copyright NMI)

162

examples the blades were ornamented by means of designs picked out in dots (pointillé ornament) and the handles themselves were cast in bronze. The second half of the EBA saw the introduction of the rapier, indicating the more advanced typology displayed about this time. The rapier evolved through a lengthening of the dagger blade, spurred on by Continental and British influence and crystallizing in a remarkable series of local developments, as, for instance, the rapier from Lissane, Co. Derry which is 79cm in length.

80 Bronze daggers

In most cases, the daggers are unassociated; some have been found in graves, usually inhumation burials in cists, sometimes with an accompanying pottery vessel, but these are only a very small proportion of the known EBA burials.

The spearhead with its socket extending into the blade probably came into use also about this time, and the native smith applied the hollow-casting technique embodied in it to the earlier type of tanged and part-socketed dagger-shaped spear to produce eventually the fully socketed spearhead with ribbed kite-shaped blade of EBA 4. This type usually had loops on the socket for tying it to the shaft, and in later examples the loops became incorporated into the bases of the blade-wings.

One of the most remarkable and perhaps enigmatic artefacts of the first half of the EBA in Ireland is the halberd (Ó Ríordáin 1937; Harbison 1969), a sturdy dagger-like blade, sometimes scythe-shaped, usually of copper, with a strong midrib. Examples vary in length from *c.*20 to 40cm. It was mounted at right angles to a long haft by means of rivets. In Ireland the haft seems always to have been of wood, while in central Europe some examples have tubular metal handles. Well preserved halberd blades show little evidence of wear or re-sharpening and the points, which would have been very susceptible to damage, are remarkably perfect in many examples. It is not known whether the halberd was used as an implement, as a weapon, or merely as a symbol of office or ceremonial object. The lightness of the riveted mounting, and the frequent absence of characteristic wear or damage from use, suggest that it was not intended to be used in any strenuous activity.

Its distribution in Europe is widespread. It is found from southern Italy to Scandinavia and from Hungary to Poland and it is depicted on rock carvings, as

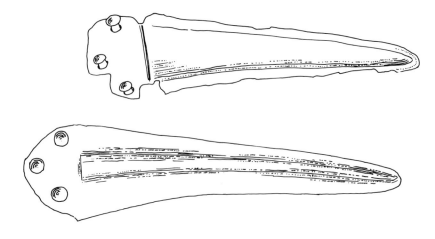

81 Bronze halberds, Ireland. No locality; scale ⅓ (after S. P. Ó Ríordáin)

164

for instance, those at Val Camonica in northern Italy (Anati 1962). Its exact place of origin is not known and the matter has been widely discussed, Italy being one of the sources considered (Barfield 1969, 79–80), but since about 40 per cent of all the known halberds are concentrated in Ireland (about 150 in all), it could be argued that it was invented and developed independently here. About a dozen are known from hoards and one only from a grave, a cist burial at Moylough, Co. Sligo, which contained cremated bones but no pottery (Waddell 1970, 129). The cist cover is decorated (see p. 242). Of those found in hoards, two, from Frankford, Co. Offaly, and Killaha East, Co. Kerry, respectively, are associated with flat axes and daggers of types prevalent in EBA 2.

Other artefacts developed in the EBA are double- and single-pointed awls, razors and razor knives of Class I (Binchy 1967). Apart from gold ornaments, which will be discussed later, there were bronze and jet beads and spacer-bead necklaces of jet and amber as well as many types of pin fashioned from bronze, bone, etc. Even though new forms such as the palstaves, rapiers and socket-looped spearheads with ribbed kite-shaped blades appeared towards the close of the EBA, they were mainly developments of existing types and did not represent totally new directions or stimuli. While stone moulds of both single and bi-valve form continued in use, two-piece clay moulds were involved in the technique of hollow-blade casting.

Late Bronze Age

This is distinguished from the preceding period by the presence of a considerable number of new tools such as socketed axes and hammers, punches, gravers, knobbed sickles and so forth, and also by technological advances and the almost universal use of clay moulds. It is believed that the character of the metal industry changed and had perhaps become more of a specialist craft. The Bishopsland Phase, which is taken as initiating the LBA, is so named after the hoard of a specialist craftsman. A few of the tools and weapons of the EBA persisted but assumed fresh development. The socketed axe, core-cast in a clay mould, was probably a development from the earlier fully flanged one, and the loop for binding purposes continued to be used. Similarly with the spearheads; small lunate openings with raised edges occur towards the base of the blade. A very fine example, 29cm in length, with ornamental openings in the blade, was found in the River Shannon, near Athlone, Co. Westmeath, dated *c*.700 BC (Lucas 1973, 40–1). By this time (the Dowris Phase), the leaf-shaped or lanceolate spearhead had become the dominant form. It was attached to the shaft by means of peghole rivets. There are some very elegant examples which are so long and slender that one must question their efficacy as weapons (RIA 1983, 95). Traces of ornament in the form of bands of sheet gold hammered into grooves in the sockets of two

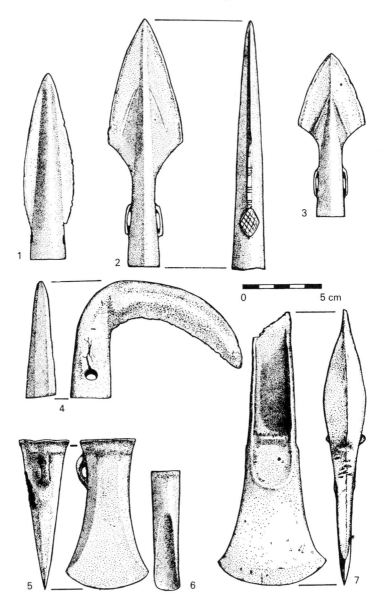

82 Bronze objects: 1–3 spearheads, 4 socketed sickle, 5 socketed axehead,
6 gouge, 7 flanged axehead with stop-ridge. From Charleville demesne,
near Tullamore, Co. Offaly (copyright NMI)

166

spearheads, one of them from Lough Gur, have been noted (Coles 1971, 94–5) and again one must question their role as weapons. Numerous examples are known of the moulds in which these various types of artefact were cast (Coghlan and Raftery 1961).

About 1000 BC another weapon made its appearance, namely, the flange-hilted or grip-tongue sword of which more than six hundred examples have been catalogued by George Eogan (1965). After casting, the edges of the sword blade were hardened and sharpened by hammering and the whole surface was ground on a whetstone. If decoration was required it was applied at this stage before the final burnishing of the surface was carried out. The hilts consisted of separate plates of wood, bone or horn riveted to the tang but due to their perishable nature only a few have survived. In 1970 a bronze sword found in a bog at Reask, Co. Galway, had a small piece of wood still in position at the junction of blade and hafting plate (NMI 1973, 184). Only four swords in all retain traces of the hilt plates.

Eogan has divided the Irish bronze swords into six classes. The earliest date from the beginning of the first millennium BC and he derives them from proto-types in England with an ultimate origin in the Erbenheim and Hemigkofen sword-types of Germany. Eogan's Class 3, of which there are about twenty examples, is an insular version of the Hemigkofen broad blade V-butted sword, widespread in southern and eastern England and in hoards of the 'Wilburton complex' of these areas. These swords are ancestral to Class 4, the commonest Irish type, which accounts for about three-quarters of the known total. Class 4 swords, the Ewart Park type in Britain, have a graceful leaf-shaped blade, often with a raised rib or ridge parallel to each edge. Well-preserved examples are from 45cm to over 60cm in length. The flanged tang widens gradually towards the butt and there is usually a ricasso or notched indentation where the flange meets the blade. The terminal, or top of the tang, is straight-ended, and rivets were inserted through the tang to hold the hilt-pieces in place. A very well-preserved example from Shinrone, Co. Offaly, *c.*800 BC, 48cm in length, demonstrates the above features (Lucas 1973, 40–1) but there are numerous variations.

Class 5, though represented by only about forty examples, is of particular interest because swords of this kind are the first to reflect far-reaching changes that had been taking place on the Continent where iron-using communities of the Hallstatt culture came into prominence. Though Ireland was still, culturally speaking, in the Bronze Age, the Class 5 Hallstatt C-type bronze swords show the penetration of new influences, or perhaps 'fashions' is a better word. Whether the industry that produced them was a separate one from the more traditional elements or whether both old and new types were made in the same workshops according to demand is not known. None of the new sword types has been found in hoards. If they represented separate traditions one might expect localization, but this is not so. About a half dozen have been found in the River Bann in the north-east, three in the Shannon and eight or nine in the central region of Roscommon/Westmeath. It must of course be said that distribution patterns do not tell the whole story because they so often merely reflect the areas where, due to the presence of peat, lack of modern development, and so on, preservation is at its best.

The prototype of the Irish Hallstatt C-type sword is the short Gündlingen variety found on the Continent, but the Irish swords are believed to be local copies of examples found in southern Britain (Eogan 1965, 14). By comparison with other types, they are fine long weapons, the complete examples being from 60cm to over 70cm in length, with blades that are parallel or nearly so for most

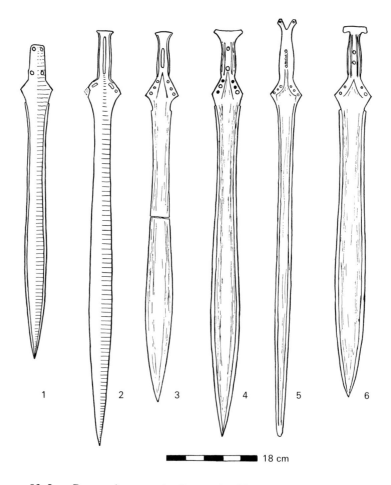

18 cm

83 Late Bronze Age swords, Eogan classification (after G. Eogan)

of their length and there can be a central swelling which gives an almost oval cross-section. The tang is the most distinctive feature because the terminal is forked or 'eared'. One of the finest examples, dated to *c*.600 BC, found in the River Shannon at Killaloe, Co. Clare (RIA 1983, 94–5), exemplifies the classic type. It is 77cm in length. Sword scabbards or sheaths were of wood or leather and the ferrule or chape at the tip of the sheath was usually of bronze and attached by rivets. There is considerable variety in their design, some long and tubular and others bag-, boat-, or wing-shaped.

Shields must have been largely of organic materials, as few bronze examples are known from Ireland. One found at Athenry, Co. Galway, is now in the British Museum, and another, now in NMI, came from a bog near Lough Gur. The latter is just over 70cm in diameter and it is decorated by means of repoussé work, the ornament being hammered-up or punched or incised, as the case may be, from the back, the front surface meanwhile resting on a yielding surface such as wood or lead. The repoussé work consists of a raised central boss surrounded by concentric rounded ridges separated from one another by continuous rows of small semicircular bosses. The metal is so thin that it can scarcely have been designed as other than a display or ceremonial weapon. Attention has been drawn to two hitherto unknown bronze shields (B. Raftery 1982a). One was found by a scuba diver on the bed of the River Shannon at Athlone, Co. Westmeath, in 1981 and the other was brought to Raftery's notice shortly after. This had been found about twenty-five years previously on the west shore of Lough

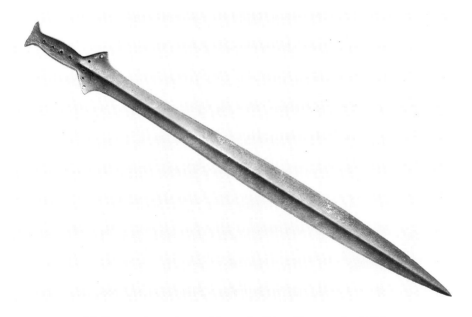

84 Bronze flanged sword from the River Brosna, Co. Offaly

169

Gara in Co. Sligo and was in private hands. These two examples bring to eight the number of known shields from Ireland. The Lough Gara shield compares closely with the one from Athenry mentioned earlier.

Two wooden shields, of alder, are known from bogs in Cloonlara, Co. Mayo, and Annandale, Co. Leitrim, respectively. The central boss surrounded by raised concentric ribs characteristic of all extant Bronze Age shields is present, but the ribs are interrupted at one point by U-shaped notches. The only Bronze Age leather shield known in Europe today was found in a bog at Cloonbrin, Co. Longford. The leather is 5–6mm thick and the shield was originally *c*.50cm in diameter. The central boss is covered by a stitched-on leather cap and in this case the notches in the surrounding ribs are V-shaped (Lucas 1973, 40–1). Two wooden moulds for the production of leather shields similar to the Cloonbrin example are known; both display the V-shaped notches (Coles 1962, 180–1). The U-notch is characteristic of northern and central European shields and the V-notch of the Mediterranean world (*ibid.*, 157–8). Grips of varying kinds are provided behind the central boss, and in the leather shield mentioned above this consisted of a piece of leather stitched on.

Cauldrons made of sheet bronze combined utility with beauty of design and technical expertise. A complete example was found in the Dowris hoard, and portions of two others. One of the best known cauldrons is that found in a bog at Castlederg, Co. Tyrone, dated *c*.700 BC. It is 56cm in maximum diameter and

85 Bronze shield found in a bog near Lough Gur, Co. Limerick

curves sharply inward towards the rim; the latter is strengthened by a reinforcing ring. Two free-moving suspension rings are fitted into two loops which are brazed and riveted to the cauldron and were prevented by curved reinforcing strips from any possibility of tearing loose. Cauldrons are derived from proto-types in Greece and the Orient; about thirty-two are known in Ireland in various stages of preservation.

The Irish bronze trumpet-horns are the single largest group of such instru-ments known and belong to the same horn family as the North European *lurer*. About 120 specimens, of which ninety are extant, some very fragmentary, have been recorded from Ireland. There are both end- and side-blow examples and John Coles distinguishes two classes: end- and side-blow types occur in each class (Coles 1963; 1967). The side-blow horns are unique to Ireland. Class I horns are confined to the northern third of Ireland and Class II are concentrated in the south-west; both classes are found in the Dowris hoard (p. 185 below). In the Class I end-blow horns there is an inserting flange on the bell portion which slips inside the short tubular end-piece which is then used as a mouth-piece. In two

86 Bronze cauldron, Castlederg, Co. Tyrone

examples, from Drumbest, Co. Antrim, there is a cast-on mouth-piece and the instruments measure almost a metre in length. The side-blow examples, two of which were also found at Drumbest, are flat or slightly domed at the closed end where there is often a ring and loop, with another on the tube itself. The ornament on Class I horns can consist of ribs, grooves, zigzags, domes or spikes on the bell, and the bodies are usually plain. Class II horns have plain bodies and conical spikes at bell and mouth as a rule. The end-blow examples have an enclosing flange or socket at the end of the bell yard which fits over a long straight tube with an inserting flange, with four holes in each, at each end. None of the mouth-pieces survive. The tube is ornamented with spikes and ribs and has a loop and ring. In the side-blow examples there are usually two loops and the closed end has a stepped pyramidal form with a loop and ring attached and another on the tube. This class is best exemplified in a hoard of six found in a bog

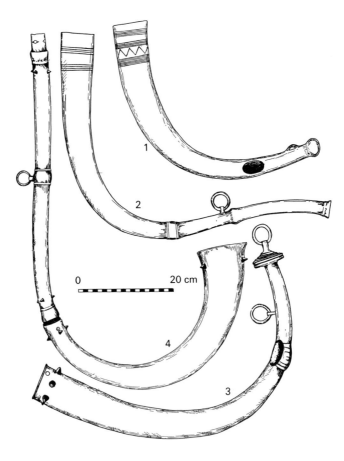

87 Horns: 1 and 2 Class I (side-blow and end-blow), 3 and 4 Class II (side-blow and end-blow) (after G. Eogan)

near Chute Hall, Clogher, Co. Kerry (Coles 1963, pl. 30), consisting of both side- and end-blow types. The Dowris hoard contained no less than twenty-four horns in varying degrees of preservation, the majority of them of Class I, some of them now in NMI and others in the British Museum. The Dowris hoard and another from Co. Clare provide the only two instances where Irish horns were found in association with other metal objects and for this reason it is difficult to assign a range of dates for the instrument.

Both John Coles and Peter Holmes have demonstrated the high level of technology involved in the casting processes, and the latter has also shown that the instruments were by no means restricted to the production of, at best, a few notes but that, when the correct playing technique was applied, a fairly extensive range of sounds could be produced (Holmes 1979, 180).

Bronze was also used to fashion ornaments such as rings, bracelets, pins, etc. There is great variety in the latter from the simple straight-shanked pin with a swelling on the head, often ornamented, to the plain disc-headed pin with side-loop on the stem. In the Dowris Phase the disc on the head of the pin has a central knop surrounded by fine concentric grooves, and in some examples the disc is attached so as to be parallel to the line of the pin. These are known as sunflower pins. Eogan distinguishes another type of pin in the Dowris Phase, the cup-headed pin, of which at least nine are known in Ireland. Instead of a disc, the top of the pin, at right-angles to the shank, has a slight depression or cup-like hollow, undecorated.

Gold

When discussing the source of Bronze Age tin, mention was made of the alluvial gold of Co. Wicklow. It has often been assumed that this was the source of the metal for all the gold objects of the Irish Bronze Age but when one comes to consider the matter, this is manifestly impossible. As Axel Hartmann has pointed out (1979, 215), the amount of gold used in Ireland at that time must have been anything up to a hundred times more than the amount which has been recovered. A great many objects must have been lost or melted down or are still hidden in the ground in the form of hoards and so on. The alluvial gold of Wicklow even if combined with the ores of the north of Ireland could not have provided the raw material for such a vast quantity of objects. Analysis has shown (Hartmann 1970; J. Raftery 1971) that the gold had diverse origins.

In the 1960s a programme of analysis of almost 1,500 gold objects from Europe, of which 507 were of Irish provenance, was undertaken, and it was thus possible to compare the gold of one region with that of another and the gold of one type of object with similar ones elsewhere. On the basis of the various analyses it was concluded that the proportion of native Irish gold used (only nuggets of

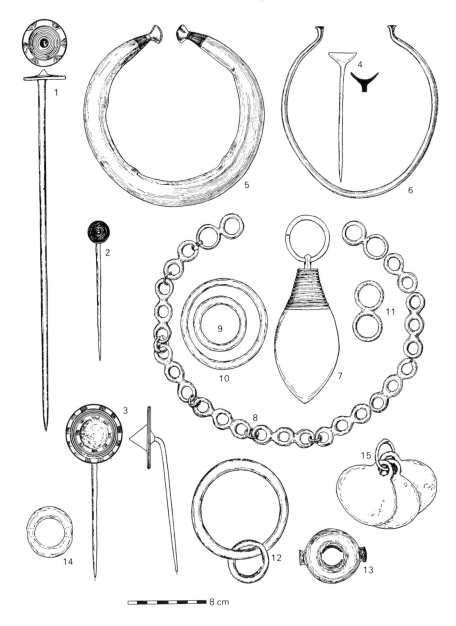

88 Late Bronze Age artefacts: 1–4 pins, 5 and 6 collar and neck ring, 7 crotal, 8 chain, 9–14 various ring forms, 15 rattle pendants (after G. Eogan)

Wicklow gold were analysed for purposes of comparison) was confined to the earliest gold objects, lunulae, sun discs and a few others, and that there was a strong possibility that the proportion was small. The composition of much of the gold showed such resemblances to that of the earliest gold from Iberia that Hartmann was of the opinion that contacts with that peninsula were very strong during the period in question and that there was a trade in gold between the two, that is, from Iberia to Ireland. It is only fair to add that Hartmann's conclusions have not received unreserved support (Harbison 1971; Scott 1976; Hartmann 1979).

In the LBA, however, the period of the great gold hoards and the one most prolific in gold ornaments, Hartmann gives central Europe or points east of it as the source of the gold used in Ireland, the Atlantic trade route having declined in importance by then. Hartmann sums up by saying (1979, 227): 'The intensive exchanges of material which occurred during the lunula period between Ireland and Iberia were superseded during the Late Bronze Age . . . by connections between those areas and Central and Northern Europe.'

While the analytical results must now be taken into account in any discussion of the Irish gold ornaments, many questions remain unanswered, but wherever the metal came from there is no doubt of Ireland's great wealth in gold ornaments during the Bronze Age. There are now reckoned to be about 600 ounces of pre-historic gold in NMI – a figure of 570 ounces was given by George Coffey in 1898 (Armstrong 1933, 3) – and this does not take into account various pieces in private hands and in collections outside Ireland. Armstrong (*ibid.*) remarked that only Athens surpassed NMI in the richness of its gold collection. If we add to this all those objects that are known to have been melted down or otherwise lost or destroyed, it is not surprising that the period has been called Ireland's 'first golden age' in a literal as well as in a metaphorical sense.

Techniques

Similar techniques to those of the worker in copper and bronze were employed by the goldsmith. Nuggets of gold or ingots of the metal were beaten into thin sheets. A bronze anvil showing traces of gold is in the Ulster Museum. Gold wire was made by cutting a narrow strip from the sheet and twisting it, or else by rolling it with a flat piece of stone or bronze on an anvil (Maryon 1938, 186). This wire could be wound over a leather thong to form a necklet, as in an example from the Derrinboy hoard, Co. Offaly, or used to attach the terminal discs to the collar, as in the famous Gleninsheen gorget from Co. Clare. Wider, thicker strips of various shapes were twisted to make neck torcs, bracelets and earrings. Pen-annular rings were made from cylindrical bars of solid gold bent around almost to a circle; in later stages, the cores of these rings were often of lead or copper, as in the gold-plated lead ring from Killyleagh, Co. Down. Gold was also used to cover other metal objects, e.g. the lead pendant or bulla from the bog of Allen, the decorated bronze discs of the sunflower pins, and so on.

As in the bronze objects, repoussé work was commonly employed, the thin sheet-gold readily lending itself to this medium. Compasses were used on sun discs, gorget terminals, pin-heads, and so on. Two pieces of metal could be joined by stitching with gold wire, or, in the LBA, by soldering. In the latter case the two pieces of metal were joined by melting on to them another metal or alloy of a lower melting point. Thus, copper was often added to gold to make the solder (Maryon 1938, 191). In the Dowris Phase copper was often alloyed with gold to

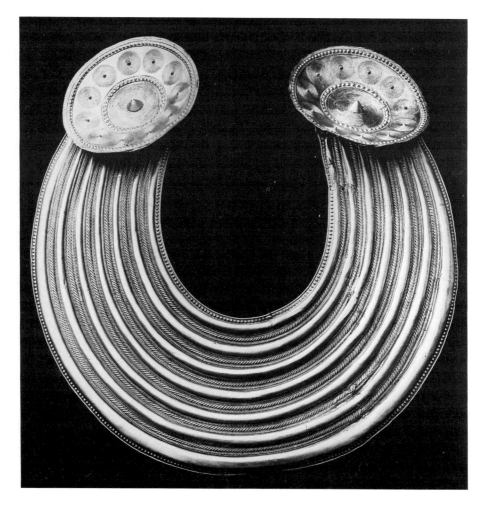

89 Gold gorget found in the 1930s in a rock crevice at Gleninsheen, Co. Clare

176

a maximum proportion of 8 per cent so as to 'stretch' it, and this also gave it more elasticity and a richer hue.

Casting techniques were also employed, the molten gold being poured from crucibles similar to those used for copper and bronze. Dress-fasteners (fibulae) were sometimes cast in one piece, that is, the two conical terminals and the connecting curved bow, and after casting the terminals were finished by

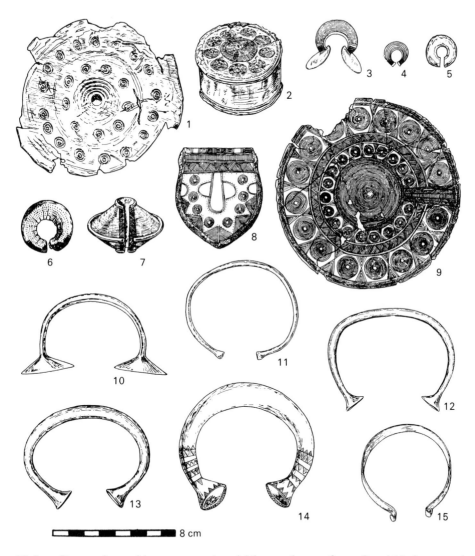

90 Late Bronze Age gold ornaments: 1 and 2 box and part of one, 3 and 10 sleeve- and dress-fasteners, 4 penannular ring, 5 and 7 tress/lock rings, 6 gold-plated ring, 8 bulla, 9 Lattoon disc, 11–15 bracelets (after G. Eogan)

177

hammering to the required shape. Maryon (1938, 201) demonstrates how a four-part mould could be used to cast an example with hollow terminals. The ingenuity and expertise displayed in these attractive ornaments is one of their remarkable features.

Gold objects

Probably the earliest of the Irish gold ornaments are the thin discs of various sizes from about 1cm to 12cm in diameter. A small plain disc, 11mm in diameter, with two perforations near the centre was found in the excavation of Site D, Lough Gur (Ó Ríordáin 1954, 410–11), in a horizon containing Late Neolithic and Beaker sherds as well as a number of objects in copper and bronze. Gold discs (now lost) were found with wristguards at Corran, Co. Armagh. The majority of discs are ornamented with very low repoussé geometrical motifs arranged in cross-in-circle patterns or in concentric patterns of plain or zigzag lines. A few of the smaller discs of this type have Beaker and EBA associations in Britain. Apart from the Lough Gur example, all the known Irish discs are chance finds and little or nothing has been recorded of the circumstances in which they were found. It is known, however, that twelve were found in pairs in different parts of the country. About twenty discs are known in all. It was originally assumed that the discs were the same sort of object as the gold-plated bronze disc mounted on a little six-wheeled bronze waggon found at Trundholm Moss, Zealand, in Denmark in 1902 (Eogan 1981, 157). A bronze figure of a horse stands on the front part of the waggon and the whole is thought to be a cult object representing a 'sun chariot'; hence, the Irish discs have been called 'sun discs'. The comparison between it and the early Irish discs, however, is not an apt one. The perforations at the centre of the Irish discs suggest that when glued to a wooden or bone backing, they could be sewn on to the clothing in pairs as ornaments or as ornamental buttons.

Two discs from Roscommon are similar to a pair from Oviedo in Spain and may indicate Irish–Iberian contact (Taylor 1968, 261). A beautiful pair, *c*.11cm in diameter, were found in the roots of an oak tree at Tedavnet, Co. Monaghan, and have been dated to *c*.2000–1800 BC. They are made like the others from sheet gold, ornamented in the typical manner, and have two perforations (RIA 1983, 16–17, 80). A disc which is different from the rest was found in a peat bog at Lattoon, Co. Cavan, with two gold bracelets and two dress fasteners, an association which indicates that it belongs to the Dowris Phase. It is large, 12.1cm in diameter, and has an all-over decoration made up of an elaborate pattern of concentric circles, triangles and herring-bone devices (Eogan 1981, 148–9). There is another such find which can be also attributed to the Dowris Phase, a disc from near Enniscorthy, Co. Wexford (*ibid.*, 148–50).

Of EBA date are the earrings made from sheet gold in various designs, some like little elongated baskets, which unfortunately are unlocalized. A similar pair was found in a Bell Beaker grave at Radley in Oxfordshire, England (Piggott 1965, 101). Another type has parallels in Portugal and may be further evidence of Irish–Iberian contact (Taylor 1968, 261).

The most characteristically Irish of the EBA gold ornaments is the lunula, a crescentic collar made from thin sheet gold. While a few are completely unornamented, normally there is a finely incised pattern of triangles, lozenges and chevrons near the points of the crescent and along the edges of the broad part of the plate. This ornamentation is so fine that it is visible only on close examination. When being worn the lunula evidently relied for effect on its sheer expanse of glittering metal. A study of the type by Joan Taylor (1970) lists eighty-one lunulae as having been found in Ireland. Of these, forty-five are in NMI, nine in

91 Gold lunula, Taylor's classical type, Ireland, no locality

the British Museum, four in the Ulster Museum, seven in private hands and seven are now known to be lost; the remainder are located in museums and collections outside Ireland. In addition, twenty-two lunulae are known which are not of Irish provenance, eleven in Britain, nine in north-west France and one each in Luxembourg and Germany. Since an Irish origin for the type as a whole is hardly disputable, these latter may be exports, or some may have been made by travelling Irish craftsmen. Taylor (1970, 58) compares the ornament on some of the Irish lunulae to motifs on Beaker pottery and considers Beaker influence on the collars to have occurred between 1700 and 1600 BC. A lunula found at Newtown, Co. Cavan, was contained in an oak box, and examples of wooden containers for other precious ornaments are also known.

The most prolific period for gold ornaments is from 1200 BC onwards, and many gold hoards are known. The remarkable hoard of gold objects from

92 Schematic representation of panels of lunula decoration, classical type
(after E. C. R. Armstrong and J. Taylor)

Derrinboy, Co. Offaly, dates to the Bishopsland Phase, *c*.1200–1000 BC. Among the objects were two very fine gold armlets with raised ribs alternately plain and decorated with punched ornament (MMA 1977, pl. 5, 50). Prototypes are known in southern Britain and in Scandinavia. In the same hoard was the very curious and apparently unique necklet mentioned earlier (p. 175). This consists of a leather core of cylindrical cross-section, 4mm in diameter, made from a continuous thin strip folded along its length and sewn with gut. This was covered all over with a closely wound gold wire of D-section, 1mm wide and half that in thickness. The full length of unbroken gold wire measures, when uncoiled, 15.24m. The two ends of the gold-covered leather were thrust into a gold cylinder or ferrule where they were held in place by a rivet, now lost (J. Raftery 1961, 56–7).

The technique of twisting ribbons and bars of gold to form torc-shaped ornaments has already been mentioned (p. 175). The concept was introduced to Britain and Ireland from the Continent and earrings, bracelets and necklets were fashioned by this method from the close of the EBA onwards. A pair of gold earrings from Castlerea, Co. Roscommon, *c*.1200 BC (MMA 1977, pl. 3, 49), are flange-twisted, that is, the angles of a gold bar of rectangular section were hammered into four thin flanges on an anvil and the whole was then twisted. The two so-called Tara torcs, *c*.1200–1000 BC (Lucas 1973, 26; MMA 1977, pl. 4, 49–50), were made in a similar manner. The terminals, which consist of thin rods of gold, are bent back so as to hook one around the other, but in these two torcs the terminals are more elaborate than usual because one of the bars in each example has a thinner expansion rod attached to it. The larger torc is 36cm in diameter and the other is *c*.21cm. Torcs of various forms continued to be made

93 Gold torc (privately owned)

181

throughout the Bronze Age, and in later times also, bar-twisted, flange-twisted and ribbon-twisted being the commonest types (MMA 1977, pl. 6, 50). In 1978 two torcs, one flange- and the other ribbon-twisted, were found during the disc-harrowing of a marshy field at Coolmanagh, Co. Carlow. One was three-flanged and remained untwisted, possibly because damage had occurred during manu-facture. The flanges had been hammered-up and were 1cm in height and 1mm in thickness on average. The ribbon torc was 21.75cm in diameter and had been twisted twenty times (Manning and Eogan 1979). Thirty-one examples of torcs of the bar form, with or without flanges, are known in Ireland, the greatest number for any one country, and about sixty ribbon torcs (Eogan 1967a; 1983).

By association, the Coolmanagh ribbon torc should belong to the Bishops-land Phase, but two others are known of Iron Age date, i.e. one found at Clonmacnoise in Co. Offaly with a gold buffer torc and another in the Somerset, Co. Galway, hoard. (Both are discussed on pp. 278–9.) Another factor which complicates the dating of ribbon torcs is that Axel Hartmann's gold analyses show that these artefacts belong to the same category as a group of forty-four objects, mainly torcs, of which the datable examples can, with one exception, be ascribed to the La Tène Iron Age (J. Raftery 1971, 103). Barry Raftery, in sum-ming up the evidence (1984,180), states: 'While it is possible to disagree with Hartmann's views on the source of Irish prehistoric gold . . . it is difficult to ignore the fact that the ribbon torcs belong to a metal group which differs con-sistently from that of all the gold objects alleged to be contemporary with them and which, both in Ireland (where datable) and on the Continent, is essentially a La Tène phenomenon.'

After the lunulae of the EBA, the gorgets of the LBA are probably the most spectacular items of Irish gold ornament. Like the lunulae, these also are collars of crescentic shape and only eight are extant (Powell 1973–4, 11). The crescent is decorated all over in rounded relief-bands, sometimes separated by rope mouldings, lines of dots and other devices, achieved by the repoussé technique of hammering-up from the back. The ends of the crescent are affixed to discs ornamented in patterns of concentric circles and repoussé dots. The most splendid specimen is perhaps the Gleninsheen Collar, found in 1932 in a rock crevice in the Burren in Co. Clare. It is *c.*31cm in maximum diameter and is dated to *c.*700 BC. The discs were sewn to the crescent by means of gold wire. Another fine specimen, 26cm in maximum diameter, came from Ardcrony, Co. Tipperary (MMA 1977, pl. 10, 51–2). Gorgets are an insular development, unique to Ireland.

Another type of gold ornament of the LBA is the so-called lock or tress ring, found principally in Ireland and Britain, with a few examples in France. They are biconical in shape, formed of two opposing cone-like face-plates bound together in which there is a gap or slit which runs from the outer circumference towards the centre. The latter is formed of a hollow tube in which there is also a slit to match the slit in the cones. About twenty examples are known in Ireland, mainly from the area round the lower part of the River Shannon and they are usually found in pairs. It has been suggested (J. Raftery 1967, 63) that they were used to hold a long lock or tress of hair, and the repoussé bosses found on the inner surface of the tubes in some examples give weight to this argument as they would assist in gripping the hair. They display a very high level of workmanship. George Eogan has examined sixteen Irish examples (1969, 103) and in all but one instance the face-plates were made of individual gold wires soldered together without a backing. In others, the surface is of sheet gold covered with minute parallel grooves drawn with a compass while the metal was still flat (Lucas 1973, 26, 39–40). Two lock-rings were included in the hoard of gold objects found in 1948 at Gorteenreagh, Co. Clare, which is dated to *c*.800–600 BC (J. Raftery 1967). In both examples the face-plates were of gold wires soldered together. They average 9.75cm in diameter and the central tubes or cylinders are *c*.5cm in length with internal diameter of 1.35cm (MMA 1977, pl. 11, 52). A gorget was included in this hoard as well as two bracelets and a fibula or dress fastener.

The gold dress-fastener (fibula) is an Irish adaptation of the fibulae of Northern Europe. The latter, however, unlike the Irish ones, had a pin attachment. In essence, the Irish examples consist of two hollow conical terminals connected by a curving bow. It is believed they were worn on the chest to fasten two sides of a garment together by means of loops slipped over the discs and on to the ends of the bow or bar. In this way the discs would be fully in view. The two most splendid examples are from Castlekelly, Co. Galway and Clones, Co. Monaghan, 28cm and 21cm respectively in maximum width, dating to *c*.700 BC (Lucas 1973, 34, 47; MMA 1977, pl. 7, 50). The terminals of the Clones dress-fastener are decorated with a series of small concentric circles surrounding central depressions or dots. Many different techniques were employed. Sometimes the bow and terminals were cast in one piece, as already mentioned, and sometimes the terminals were either soldered or cast on to the bow. The latter may be hollow or solid (RIA 1983, 84). A dress-fastener from Killymoon, Co. Tyrone, was found in a wooden box made from a single block of alderwood.

A very much smaller but similar type of object has been given the name 'sleeve-fastener' by Eogan (1972). The bow is semicircular and usually less than 2.5cm in maximum diameter and contains longitudinal parallel scores or striations which end just short of the terminal discs, the intervening space being decorated with criss-cross hatching. There are no prototypes known outside Ireland.

Penannular rings, equally small and also striated, but without the terminal flat discs, are also present. Eogan has catalogued eighty-seven examples of the sleeve fasteners and fifteen of the rings (Eogan 1972). In addition, there are a number of very small plain penannular rings to which the name 'ring money' has often been applied.

Hoards

Hoards have frequently been mentioned in connection with artefacts of the Bronze Age. Sometimes they consist of objects of the same type, e.g. the hoard found at Cappeen, Co. Cork, which contained six copper axes, all of Harbison's Lough Ravel type. Others contain objects of varying kinds, such as that of Frankford, Co. Offaly, where two axes of different types, a dagger and a halberd, were found together. Hoards can contain artefacts of copper, bronze and gold, both finished and unfinished, both whole and broken; they can also contain strips and pieces of metal, stone moulds and objects of stone, wood, amber and so on. Some can be categorized as founder's hoards consisting of scrap collected for melting down. One of these is the hoard of at least two hundred pieces found in Co. Roscommon which gives its name to Eogan's LBA 2. Others, such as the Bishopsland hoard from Co. Kildare (LBA 1), represent the stock-in-trade of craftsmen, and yet others were probably those of merchants. As well as the

94 Gold dress-fastener and wooden box, Killymoon demesne, Co. Tyrone

above, some undoubtedly were items of treasure buried for safe-keeping and eventual retrieval. It is tempting to place the gold hoards in this category but in actual fact one cannot know for certain what the motive was. It has also been suggested that some were ritual deposits, especially those found in rivers or in wet places, as for example, the hoard of gold ornaments found in a river in Co. Waterford near New Ross which consisted of a fibula and four penannular bracelets with hollow terminals (RIA 1983, 21, 90).

The Dowris hoard (Eogan 1983a, 117–42) is the most remarkable of the bronze hoards. It was found in AD 1825 or, according to other accounts, AD 1833, by two men trenching potatoes (Armstrong 1922, 134) in the townland of Whigsborough, Co. Offaly, at a place variously called Derrens or Dowris. It included more than two hundred items of which about 190 are extant, 111 in NMI and seventy-nine in the British Museum. E. C. R. Armstrong (*ibid.*) gives a full account of the find, its content and the manner of its dispersal. H. S. Crawford (*in* Armstrong 1924, 14) itemizes the various objects, naming forty-four spearheads, forty-three axes, twenty-four trumpets and forty-four crotals, the latter a type of musical instrument not known outside Ireland. These are gourd-shaped objects, grooved at the narrow top and fitted with a suspension ring, and their function was that of bells or rattles or perhaps harness-jingles. They contain a loose clapper or a piece of metal or stone and emit little sound. An exotic item in the hoard is the Kurd-type bucket made of sheets of bronze riveted together, which is believed to have been a Continental import (Eogan 1964, 317). Two other buckets are present which are native copies. The remainder of the hoard is composed of objects in common use in Ireland in LBA 3.

John Coles (1971a, 164–5) makes the interesting suggestion that perhaps the Dowris finds were objects which had been deposited in a central offering place and not a hoard in the true sense. One of his arguments is based on the presence of artefacts such as the bronze horns or trumpets, of which both types, Class I and Class II, were found together but which are normally mutually exclusive. In Coles' interpretation, there would be no positive association of one object with another such as is assumed in a hoard because, if the objects were offerings, they would have been brought to the site at different times and from a variety of places.

There are some remarkable gold hoards, a few of which have been mentioned already, and if only one is to be singled out, perhaps it should be what became known as The Great Clare Find of 1854. Armstrong (1917) gives a graphic account of the discovery, its content, and the sad details of its dispersal in so far as these could be ascertained. The discovery was made in the townland of Mooghaun North by men working on the construction of the West Clare railway. According to one account, the objects were found in a mound of stones – some said these were the burnt stones of what is known in Ireland as a *fulacht fiadh* or cooking place and in Britain as a burnt mound – but according to others the hoard was contained within a stone-setting of some kind, one stone of which had protruded from the side of the cutting. When the stone was pulled out, a cascade of gold ornaments followed. There was an immediate scramble and groups of them were sold at once in various places and many, no doubt, subsequently melted down. From contemporary accounts it is known, however, that the hoard contained at least 138 penannular bracelets, six collars, two neck-rings, two lock-rings and possibly two torcs, all of gold. Of these, thirteen items are in NMI, one of them a splendid gold collar, and thirteen or fourteen pieces are in the British Museum; a few may have survived in private collections but the rest have disappeared from the record (Armstrong 1917; 1933, 14ff; Eogan 1964, 335, and 1983a).

Other materials

Some wooden vessels have survived from the Bronze Age, recovered from watery places and from bogs. Wooden shields, scabbards, handles or hilts, moulds and boxes have already been mentioned, but these in no way represent the extensive use to which wood was put during the period. One has only to recollect that practically every tool and weapon required a handle or shaft of some kind and that this was most commonly of wood. In addition, wood must have been used to fashion vessels and implements for preparing and conserving food. Bone and horn would have been widely used also, as they are both decorative and durable, but neither survives except in exceptional circumstances.

Two other more exotic substances were also used, amber and jet, mainly for decorative purposes such as beads, buttons, etc. Amber is a fossilized resin formed from the fluid secreted by pine trees in Tertiary times. It forms in irregular nodules and when these become washed out from the strata in which they occur, they collect on the seashore. The southern shores of the Baltic provide the largest supply, and it is believed that this was the main source of amber in ancient times though the substance is also known from the east coast of Britain.

In 1943 two amber beads and a gold mount for a glass bead were discovered in peat at Milmorane, Co. Cork. The casts of the amber beads and of the glass one (a few fragments of which were recovered) could clearly be seen in the sods of turf at the site (Mitchell 1951, 180). A radiocarbon date of 4040 ± 150 BP was obtained for blanket bog around the necklace. A comment on the date (*Radiocarbon* 1961, 36) is to the effect that the pollen diagrams of the bog agree with the radiocarbon date and that 'evidently the necklace was buried in the bog'. The date, therefore, is a *terminus post quem* for the necklace.

Jet is a soft black stone related to lignite (brown coal) and was used for decorative purposes throughout the Bronze Age. Some very fine multi-strand necklaces were fashioned from jet beads with spacer-plates separating the strands in such a way as to give the whole a crescentic shape. It has been suggested (Childe 1949, 124) that the lunula was a translation into gold of the crescentic jet necklaces found in graves in Scotland and northern Ireland, but it can equally well be argued that the jet necklace is a copy in a cheaper material of the gold lunula, or that both are twin manifestations of one idea (Hawkes 1940, 324).

In a Bronze Age cemetery at Keenoge, Co. Meath, one of the graves contained forty-one jet beads. Amber beads and one of jet were found with secondary interments in the mound of the passage tomb at Tara known as the Mound of the Hostages. In one inhumed burial, four segmented faience beads, eight tubular bronze beads and one of jet were found near the neck of the skeleton, obviously the components of a necklace. The inhumation was that of a youth and it had been inserted in the clay covering which topped the mound of cairn stones (Ó Ríordáin 1955).

Faience is a distinctive glassy substance, blue-green in colour, well-known in ancient Egypt and the Mediterranean world, and widely exported and imitated. The Tara beads were not true faience but composed of powdered blue glass or glaze which was mixed with quartz grains and moulded before firing (*ibid.*, 170–1). Faience beads are the subject of a certain amount of debate since an indigenous origin was proposed a few decades ago for the many examples known from Bronze Age contexts in Britain, as opposed to the traditional view that they had been imported from the Near East.

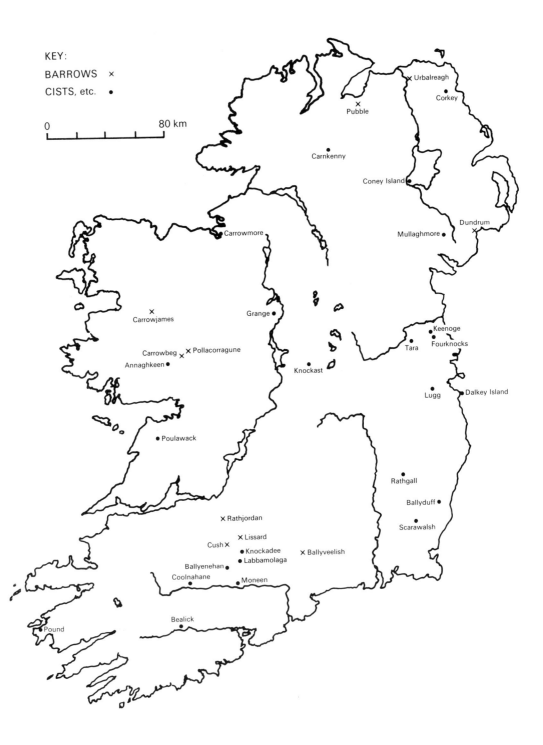

KEY:

BARROWS   ×

CISTS, etc.   ●

0   80 km

× Urbalreagh

● Corkey

× Pubble

● Carnkenny

Coney Island ●

Dundrum ×

Mullaghmore ●

Carrowmore ●

× Carrowjames

Grange ●

● Keenoge

● Fourknocks

Tara ●

Carrowbeg × × Pollacorragune

Annaghkeen ●

Knockast ●

Lugg ●

● Dalkey Island

● Poulawack

Rathgall ●

Ballyduff ●

Scarawalsh ●

× Rathjordan

× Lissard

Cush ×

× Ballyveelish

● Knockadee

● Labbamolaga

Ballyenehan ●

Coolnahane ●

● Moneen

Bealick ●

● Pound

95 Bronze Age cist and pit burials; barrows

188

8

Bronze Age burial

Apart from the metal objects, burials provide the most prolific evidence for the archaeology of the Irish Bronze Age. The burial rite of the EBA was largely a single grave one, either in a stone cist (or 'stone coffin', as it was sometimes called in the past) or in a pit, perhaps without any surface marking or sometimes beneath a mound of earth or a cairn of stones. Sometimes the burials were grouped in cemeteries. There could scarcely be any greater contrast to the practice of the preceding Neolithic Period when great stone tombs were erected to house the dead. Even though, as we have seen, there is evidence for single grave burial during the period of the megalithic tombs, it does not appear sufficient to account for the change represented by the EBA funerary practice. Some see it as reflecting influence from the Beaker burials in Britain and on the Continent.

Cist burial

Cists are box-like structures set into the ground, the sides lined with stone slabs placed on edge. They were normally covered by another slab or slabs and sometimes the floor was paved. The commonest cists of the EBA are those of the short rectangular type, about 80cm long, 50cm wide and 50cm deep on average. Some polygonal cists and a few long cists are also known from the Bronze Age. In the case of the short cist, when the body was interred unburnt it had to be placed on its side with the knees drawn up to the chin – perhaps it was even tied or trussed in that position – and literally rammed into the grave. A single pot (exceptionally two or more) was placed near the head, and as it was presumed by early archaeologists that it had contained an offering of food or drink for the spirit of the deceased, the name Food Vessel was coined for the type as a whole, though no conclusive evidence has survived to show that the pot was so used. Other types of pot such as the tiny Pygmy Cups or the large pots, the Urns, are also found, though cist burial can be said to be chiefly a Food Vessel phenomenon.

Cremations are about twice as common as inhumations. In these cases the fragments of burnt bone, twisted and distorted out of shape during the cremation, are found in a little heap on the floor of the cist, the pot, when present, standing close by, usually empty unless it had subsequently become filled with soil which had been washed into the grave. In the later burials of this kind the Food Vessel may actually contain the cremated remains. When the burial

189

ceremony had concluded, the capstone was laid over the grave and the soil originally dug from the pit was filled back on top. Since not all the earth dug out would now go back because of the space occupied by the cist, the position of the grave must have been marked for a time by a slight mound which would have become less noticeable as the loose earth consolidated and would hardly have been visible at all once the vegetation had become re-established; or, indeed, it may be that the surplus earth was scattered rather than mounded up over the grave. The above is a description of what might be called the classic type of short cist burial, but in actual fact, there are many variants such as compartmented cists, double cists, cists beneath mounds or cairns or inserted in pre-existing mounds. The majority of burials now known have been found by chance in the course of gravel quarrying, ploughing, or other work on the land. They often occur in groups or cemeteries, i.e. flat cemeteries unmarked at the surface, and also in cemetery mounds (or multiple cist cairns, as they were formerly known).

John Waddell in a survey of the published literature and of records in NMI compiled an inventory listing 637 cists considered to be of EBA date (Waddell 1970). This figure has, of course, been augmented since then, but Waddell was able to draw interesting and valuable conclusions from the data that were available up to 1970. He remarks that his figure is a minimum one and that the recorded cists must represent only a fraction of those actually found in the past. In those cases where the shape of the cist was mentioned in the record, the vast

96 Cist grave, Clonickillvant, Co. Westmeath

190

majority were of the short rectangular type. There were a few dozen of polygonal shape which are, in effect, little more than circular pits in the ground lined with slabs or boulders. Only about half a dozen long stone cists were recorded, approximately 2m in length and 1m or less in width. In general, long stone cists are of Early Iron Age date or later. Some examples of long cists containing Bronze Age pottery are listed by A. B. Ó Ríordáin (1969, 130–1), and also instances of extended burial in unprotected graves. Sometimes a circular mound or cairn was heaped over them. A number of extended burials, many in long cists, are known in Scotland and were accompanied by artefacts of Bronze Age type but the Irish examples rarely produce such evidence.

While single burial was the norm in the short cists, inhumations consisting of an adult and a child are occasionally found, whereas two or more adults is a fairly infrequent occurrence. In cremation burials, which, as already mentioned, are

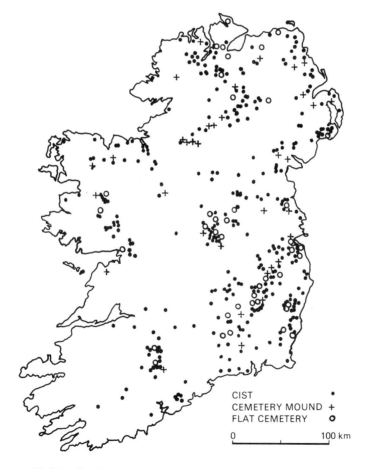

CIST •
CEMETERY MOUND +
FLAT CEMETERY O

0   100 km

97 Distribution map of Bronze Age cists (after J. Waddell)

191

about twice as common (in so far as the records give such information), two or more individuals are sometimes present. Occasionally, also, it has been found that a cist was re-opened to admit another burial. It can be seen, therefore, that no single rigid rule prevailed but that many different customs were accommodated within the overall rite of cist burial.

The record was found to be far from complete in the matter of cist orientation, though where recorded, it appeared that the long axes of the cists generally favoured an E–W or approximate E–W orientation, though N–S was also found to a lesser degree (Waddell 1970, 93).

Something over half of the 637 recorded cists listed by Waddell contained one or more pots. There were about 217 Food Vessels, forty-seven Cinerary Urns and fifty-nine unidentified 'Urns'; and five cists contained only Pygmy Cups. Grave goods other than pottery are rare and, of course, only durable objects will have survived. Materials represented are bronze, jet, stone, bone, flint, faience and gold. The latter was found in one grave only, a short cist within the Topped Mountain cairn in Co. Fermanagh. It contained an inhumation accompanied by a Vase Food Vessel and a bronze grooved dagger with a gold pommel-binding of a type familiar in Wessex in southern England. At one end of the cist there was a cremation. Another cremation in the cairn was accompanied by a polished stone axe. A flat cemetery at Keenoge in Co. Meath contained fourteen graves, six of them in cists. One of the latter contained a crouched inhumation, two Bowl Food Vessels and a razor-knife (Binchy 1967, 58). A bronze dagger was found in a Bowl Food Vessel in a cist at Corkey in Co. Antrim (Harbison 1968, 46). A bronze dagger and a bronze awl were found in the Annaghkeen, Co. Galway, cist grave and another dagger, similar to that from Topped Mountain, together with part of its bone pommel, at Grange, Co. Roscommon. Other occasional grave finds are plano-convex flint knives, flint flakes and scrapers. Bone objects such as pins and pendants sometimes show traces of fire as if they had been on the clothing before cremation (O'Kelly 1950, 17). Another example of this is a two-segment faience bead, badly burnt, found with cremated bone and a Food Vessel in a cist at Ballyduff in Co. Wexford (Hartnett and Prendergast 1953).

A distribution map of cist graves is included in Waddell's study (1970, 103). The map shows a fairly general representation of the type throughout the country though with a definite bias in favour of the eastern half. It shows cist burials as less plentiful in the west and north-west, scarce in west Cork and absent from the coastal areas of Kerry. The true picture may be, however, not that cist burial was not practised in the extreme south-west but that owing to the mainly pastoral nature of the farming economy and the presence of blanket bog over large portions of the area, the burials have not come to light. As mentioned earlier, most of them have been discovered in the course of ploughing, drainage and gravel digging.

A cist grave at Pound, Co. Kerry, on the north coast of the Iveragh peninsula, was reported in 1984 after it had been uprooted by a mechanical excavator during the clearance of a field fence (Cleary 1985). It was a short cist paved with stone slabs, but no capstone was present, at least at the time of excavation. Twenty fragments of cremated bone were recovered, representing at least two individuals, together with the base of what appears to have been a Pygmy Cup resembling a miniature Food Vessel. Cleary cites over a dozen other possible cist graves in the county, many of them on the Dingle peninsula where they have been located by the Dingle Archaeological Survey team either in the field, from local information, or from records.

Pit and Urn burial

Another type of Bronze Age burial is the pit burial which can contain burnt or unburnt remains and sometimes had a slab laid over the top. These burials can be unmarked at the surface and can occur in groups, i.e. in flat cemeteries, but they can also be found beneath or in mounds and cairns. Frequently, the pit contains an Urn, a specific kind of large pot, which was inverted over the cremated remains; and sometimes the pit was floored by a paving slab. Short cists were also used. Again, Urn burials can occur in groups unmarked on the ground surface; in pre-existing mounds such as those built to cover chamber tombs; and in barrows.

Food Vessels

About five hundred pots of this kind are known in Ireland. The ware is also well known in Britain but not on the Continent. In general it is coarser, thicker and heavier than the classic Beaker type and rougher to the touch. The pots average about 10 to 16cm in height depending on type and are strong, hard and well-fired. Though there is a lot of variety in the shapes, two distinct forms predominate, the Bowl and the Vase, both flat-bottomed.

The Bowl is mainly characterized by its form and decoration. The classic type is semi-globular and squat in proportion to its height, which averages 8–12cm. The ornament was usually impressed with a comb on the clay before firing so as to produce a characteristic series of raised zonal designs in false relief. Running chevrons in false relief are common and decoration can also occur on the bevelled inner lip and on the base. Food Vessels of this tradition can also have a tripartite profile or they can be ribbed, that is, with horizontal ribs or mouldings, and some also have lugs. Bowls are found with both unburnt and burnt remains; more than three-quarters of all known examples were found in short cists and the remainder in pit burials. The Bowl is essentially an Irish development, and while there is

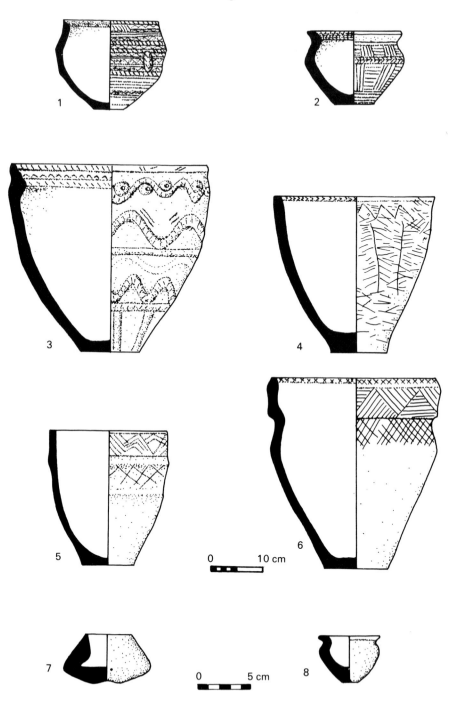

98 Bronze Age funerary ware: 1 Bowl Food Vessel, 2 Vase Food Vessel, 3 Encrusted Urn, 4 Vase Urn, 5 Cordoned Urn, 6 Collared Urn, 7 and 8 Pygmy Cups

undoubted Beaker influence it is probable that it was also influenced by Late Neolithic wares (ApSimon 1969a; Waddell 1976).

The Vase type of Food Vessel tends towards a biconical rather than a globular form and can be up to 16cm in height. The ornament was usually incised or scored in a series of short lines in herringbone patterns or in a series of filled triangles. However, the same motifs executed in the same way can be found both on Bowls and on Vases. The majority have been found with cremations in short cists, though a small number have come from pit graves. They stood mouth upward and sometimes contained the cremated remains. It must be said, however, that several examples are known where both the Bowl and the Vase were in an inverted position.

Though primarily a funerary ware, Food Vessel pottery has been found in domestic contexts, e.g. at Dalkey Island (Liversage 1968, 157); on what appears to be a habitation site on Coney Island, Lough Neagh (Addyman 1965, 84); and there were a small number of sherds in the Late Neolithic/Beaker assemblage at Newgrange (Cleary *in* O'Kelly *et al.*, 1983, 108). It was also present in the presumed ritual site at Lough Gur, the Grange stone circle (p. 137).

Cinerary Urns

These were formerly classified into four types: Enlarged Food Vessels, Encrusted Urns, Collared Urns and Cordoned Urns. It has been demonstrated by ApSimon and Waddell, among others, that the first two types are merely different and larger versions of the Vase, and the enlarged type is now more aptly called a Vase Urn, since the majority retain the vase profile and the type of ornament is also similar. In height, however, the Vase Urn is 20cm or more and was inverted over the cremated remains. Upwards of ninety examples are known, the vast majority from funerary rather than domestic contexts. They have been found in cists and in pits in about equal numbers; the cists are usually of polygonal shape.

There are about one hundred examples known of Encrusted Urns, and the burial rite with which they are associated is similar to that of the Vase Urns, though pit burials are marginally more common (Waddell 1976, 291). In the Encrusted Urn, ribs or bands of clay were applied in geometrical patterns to the finished vessel and luted down before firing. Often these encrustations covered the whole vessel from rim to base and some pots have encrusted rosettes set within the angles of an encrusted zigzag band below the rim. The rosettes and bands were often further emphasized by slashed incisions. Often too, the internal slope of the rim had a number of parallel ridges and grooves marked with the same incisions. The rim diameter and the height of the pot are often the same, seldom less than 30cm, and by contrast, the flat base is of small diameter, leading one to conjecture that the pots were never intended to stand upright, as in the example from Coolnahane (O'Kelly and Shee 1974). A study of this type of urn and also of the Collared and Cordoned types has been made by Rhoda Kavanagh (1973; 1976 respectively).

It has been suggested that some of the ornament on these pots may be skeuomorphic, that is, copying the form of another object. In this case the arrangement of applied ribs may represent the poles bulging through the hide covering of a wigwam-like tent or hut; and some basketry patterns, like those on a Vase and an Urn from Labbamolaga, Co. Cork (O'Kelly 1950), may likewise represent the wicker mats used in some forms of house construction. This in turn suggests that perhaps the mouth-downward urn was thought of as a hut or house for the dead rather than as a mere bone-container. Some urns have holes drilled near the rim (Kavanagh 1973, 513) and these might have been used in tying a skin or cloth cover over the mouth of the urn if the cremated bones had been put into the pot before inverting it in the grave pit, but they may also be 'soul holes' through which the spirit of the dead could come and go.

Often found with Vase and Urn burials are Pygmy Cups, very small pottery vessels of various forms which may have had some ritual use (ApSimon 1969a, 47; Kavanagh 1977). Kavanagh has listed seventy examples from Ireland. Many have perforations in the side walls (Kavanagh 1977, 73). The vessels are rarely more than 5cm in height and the biconical form is the commonest. Some of them, however, resemble miniature Bowl or Vase Food Vessels. They accompany

99 Urn burial, Coolnahane, Co. Cork

cremation burials, frequently in cists; in fact, their function was to accompany the cremation burial and the cremation pottery, whether Vase or Vase Urn or Encrusted Urn, and only rarely was the Pygmy Cup the sole pottery accompaniment to the burial (Kavanagh 1977, 73). In decorated examples the ornament is distinctive, consisting of incised chevrons and lozenges, and the bases are also decorated with criss-cross and similar motifs.

While Collared and Cordoned Urns have certain traits in common, both appear distinct from urns of the Vase tradition. More than fifty of each type are known. They are all big vessels averaging about 35cm high and 30cm in diameter at rim or shoulder, but in common with the Vase type, they have disproportionately small bases. They are somewhat coarsely made. The walls are thick, and crushed stone grits of large size were often added to the clay. Many of them were built up from coils of clay and the vessels tend to break along the lines of junction of the rings.

The Collared Urn is so called because its 'overhanging' rim not only looks like a collar but was often achieved by applying a collar of clay to the top of the pot. Ornament when present is geometric in type, executed by incisions or by twisted

100 Encrusted Urn, Coolnahane, Co. Cork, detail from area below rim

cord impressions, and is normally confined to the upper portion of the urn, that is, to rim and collar areas. The inverted urn was usually placed in a simple pit and contained only one cremation.

The Cordoned Urn has two parallel ribs or cordons of applied clay that encircle the vessel in its broad upper middle part. Occasionally three or more cordons are present. Again, decoration is restricted to the upper part of the vessel and is cord-impressed. While it is mainly a funerary ware, many sherds of what undoubtedly appears to be Cordoned Urn have been found on habitation sites, e.g. Meadowlands, Downpatrick, Co. Down (Pollock and Waterman 1964; ApSimon 1969a, 48–50). A radiocarbon date of 3575 ± 70 BP was obtained from the bottom habitation layer that contained the Urn sherds. On the basis of associated artefacts A. B. Ó Ríordáin (1967, 44) dates the Cordoned Urn in general to *c.*1400 BC, but in view of the Meadowland evidence perhaps this should be up-dated.

The distribution of Urns is interesting. Taking the most numerous group first, the Encrusted Urns, about seventy are in the provinces of Ulster and Leinster. Seventeen of the remainder are in Munster and are mainly concentrated in a band running N–S along the eastern borders of counties Limerick and Cork (Kavanagh 1973, 521, 617). None is known from Clare and Kerry and indeed the midlands and west of Ireland generally have very few. The distribution of the Vase Urns corresponds with that of the Encrusted Urns and in origin both probably owe much to the EBA Food Vessel tradition as well as to the Late Neolithic flat-based coarse wares, some of which were already showing applied or encrusted ornament. The Collared Urns are found mainly in the north-east as are also the cordoned types, though both are found in Leinster and farther south in Co. Cork and in Limerick. A very good cordoned example is that from Knockadea, Ballylanders, Co. Limerick (now in the Cork Public Museum). These types of Urn may also have been influenced by the Late Neolithic coarse wares as well as by the coarsely made bucket-shaped domestic pottery of the Beaker Period.

This distributional pattern accords well with that of Bronze Age objects in general. Urn burial in Ireland parallels that in Britain, and, like the Food Vessels proper, probably stems in both countries from the single-grave practice which was already established in the Neolithic Period. The exact relationship of urn-burial practice to that of the Food Vessel makers is not altogether clear. In Britain there is some evidence of a Beaker Period overlap (Smith and Simpson 1966, 132–4) and of contemporaneity with Food Vessels both there and in Ireland (Longworth 1961, 282). The Encrusted Urn at Labbamolaga, placed in a simple pit grave, was stratigraphically later than a cist with Vase-type Food Vessel which also had the basketry motif but incised rather than 'encrusted'. At the time these burials were excavated (1948), urns were believed to be LBA in date while Food

Vessels were EBA. Nonetheless, owing to the juxtaposition of the two burials and the fact that each of the pots carried the basketry motif, it was felt even then that the interval between the two burials was not a long one (O'Kelly 1950, 20). At Bealick, Co. Cork, an Encrusted Urn and a Vase Food Vessel were found together in a cist grave (O'Kelly 1944).

These various forms of burial practice may have continued throughout the whole of the EBA and conceivably into the LBA, but associations which would clearly establish this are not known. Some hold that there was a change in funerary custom at the end of the EBA (just as there was a change in metal technology) after which time the practice of placing objects in the grave with the dead ceased

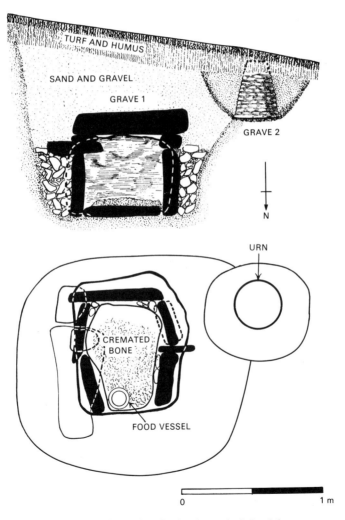

101 Labbamolaga, Co. Cork, cist and pit burials

199

(Burgess 1969, 22–3). The unaccompanied pit burials found in flat cemeteries, in cemetery mounds, in barrows and enclosures and in a variety of anomalous contexts may therefore be the successors of the Urn and Food Vessel pit burials rather than their contemporaries. In the absence of datable grave goods or suitable materials for radiocarbon measurement it is very difficult to place a particular burial in its proper context. As Raftery has pointed out, the up-dating of the urns to the EBA leaves us with a problem, namely, 'what form did the burials of the Late Bronze Age in Ireland take?' (J. Raftery 1963, 108).

Flat cemeteries

The so-called flat cemeteries can as a rule contain from three to a dozen graves, both cists and pit burials. Forty-one such cemeteries have been listed (Waddell 1970). There is usually no surface indication of their presence and they come to light by accident, very frequently during sand or gravel quarrying. Such a cemetery in a gravel quarry at Scarawalsh, Co. Wexford (Rynne 1966), was found during bulldozing operations. There were five pit burials and one cist. The latter contained an Encrusted Urn which was inverted over a cremation. One of the pits also contained a similar urn together with sherds of what was possibly a Vase Food Vessel. One pit contained no pottery and others contained two Collared Urns and a Vase Urn. Other than the pottery, which was very fragmentary, there were no grave goods. No inhumations were found.

Occasionally these cemeteries are more extensive, as at Ballyenahan North, Co. Cork (Fahy 1954). A number of graves became exposed in the vertical side of a gravel pit during quarrying operations and two years later, a bulldozer which was being used to recover topsoil from the gravel deposit exposed and destroyed several more. As far as could be ascertained after the event, there were about seventeen graves originally. Of this number it was possible to excavate only six. Four were cists and two were pit burials. One pit contained a cremation and an inverted Bowl Food Vessel of tripartite form, and another one which was much disturbed contained an inhumation together with a flat round-heeled riveted bronze dagger. One of the cists, though there was no pot, contained cremated bones, and mixed through them were sixteen small bronze rivets; obviously the object or objects to which the rivets belonged had perished. A Vase Food Vessel was recovered from the general area of the cemetery but could not be connected with any specific burial.

Cemetery mounds

Cemetery mounds and cairns are usually circular in shape and defined by a kerb or kerbs; they usually contain a maximum of about a dozen burials. A most exceptional example was the cemetery cairn at Knockast, Co. Westmeath (Hencken and Movius 1934), which had approximately forty-four burials of which five were in cists.

Two of the cemetery cairns (or multiple cist cairns, in the older terminology) are of particular interest in relation to present-day studies: Poulawack, Co. Clare (Hencken 1935) and Moneen, Co. Cork (O'Kelly 1952). Poulawack contained seven cists; the central one – and in the opinion of the excavator, the principal one – was a double cist erected on the ground surface in the exact centre of the cairn, which was revetted by two kerbs. A series of inclined slabs standing on edge supported the sides of the cist and others were laid on the capstone. Four unburnt burials were present, very much disturbed, and the space that contained them was so small that Hencken was of the opinion that the bodies had been exhumed from elsewhere and laid in the double cist. Two other cists, and possibly a third, were also primary. The remaining cists were clearly later insertions, two in the top of the cairn and the third at its perimeter. The pottery recovered from the cairn was almost entirely fragmentary, but one sherd of indeterminate Beaker (Clarke 1970, 525) was found in a crack between the floor and side stone of one of the cists.

In an earlier chapter (p. 129) Poulawack was mentioned in connection with burials of Linkardstown type, and undoubtedly it shares various morphological features with them. The 'odd man out' is the pottery – or lack of it. Some would argue that only burials containing the highly decorated round-based Linkardstown-type bowl should be included in this category (B. Raftery 1974; Brindley *et al*. 1983) but in view of the scarcity of reliable information about this particular burial mode it might seem to be too early to indulge in such fine distinctions. Perhaps when the position is clearer through more excavations and further ^{14}C dates, the process of dividing one group from another can be tackled more meaningfully.

Moneen (O'Kelly 1952) is another example in which the central cist and the primary burials contained therein resemble those mentioned above, though it too lacks the diagnostic Linkardstown-type pot. It was excavated in 1948 and was revealed as a multi-period site. In the primary phase a ditch surrounded a circular area, the material from the ditch being spread over the enclosure. There was no central feature associated with it. A number of pits and stake-holes were found though they formed no recognizable lay-out. There were also scattered fragments of pottery and in one part of the enclosed area a large pot was found that had been crushed flat and completely fragmented. It lay partly on what was then the surface of the enclosure and partly beneath it and was embedded in a charcoal spread. Very close by there were portions of a human skull, some showing traces of burning. These were the only human bones found in this primary phase. A number of flint flakes, mostly waste pieces, and a few fragments of quartz, one worked, were also found. In addition, sherds representing at least thirteen other vessels have since been identified by R. M. Cleary who has noted the remarkably unweathered nature of the assemblage. She regards it as coming within the range of Late Neolithic/Beaker wares.

The second phase of the site commenced when the ditch or fosse had partly silted up. A cairn bounded by a kerb was constructed eccentrically within the enclosed area. It was designed to cover a central cist of megalithic proportions and there were three other simpler cists clustered together in one part of the area, also believed to be primary in relation to the cairn. The central cist contained two inhumations but at some stage after the cairn had been heaped up these were disturbed and the bones partly scattered so as to enable a cremation to be inserted in the cist. No grave goods were found in any of the cists.

In the process of the excavation the cairn material was removed and frag-

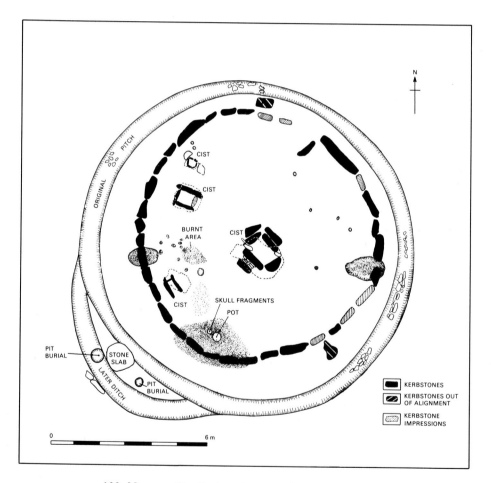

102 Moneen, Co. Cork, primary and secondary phase

ments of two vessels were found in two different areas of the basal layer of the cairn above the old turf line. It was felt that they may have been deliberately broken and thrown in when the base of the cairn was being constructed. They were not associated with cremated bone or other burial deposit. One of the pots has been identified as belonging to Clarke's North British (N3) Beaker group (Clarke 1970, 542, 525) and R. M. Cleary has confirmed that two of the fragments from the vessel found in another part of the cairn are very similar to Food Vessel.

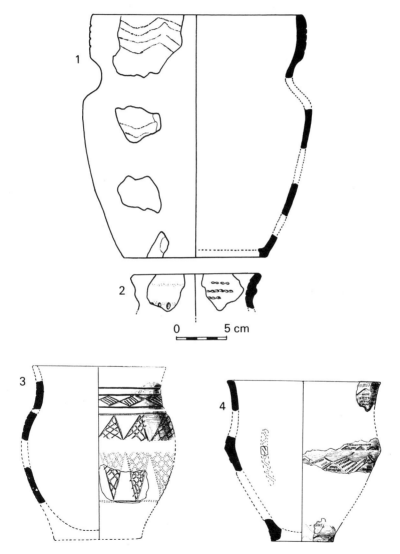

103 Moneen pottery: 1 and 2 primary phase, 3 Beaker from cairn of second phase, 4 Food Vessel from Burial 5 (1: conjectural restoration after R. M. Cleary)

Other finds made during the removal of the cairn material consisted of broken saddle querns and grain rubbers, probably discards; a bone point and a bone pendant; and a stone axe-hammer with a well defined central groove similar to that on the mauls used in primitive copper mining. This example showed no signs of use.

With the removal of the superincumbent cairn material, a full investigation of the ring-ditch feature was possible. It was found that when the ditch was already partly silted-up a short arc or loop of fosse had been added so as to enclose a small area. It appeared that during the digging of this arc, the workers had encountered a large slab which they overturned. A deep pit containing a cremation and two Food Vessels lay beneath. Instead of changing direction, the workers broke the pots, pulled out the cremated bones and threw all into the partly silted primary ditch. Having completed their extension, they placed an Urn burial within the little enclosed space just outside the primary ring-ditch. The burial pit was just large enough to take the Urn which was inverted over the cremation. Black ashes were packed in around the sides of the pot – an Encrusted Urn – and the pit back-filled. On the edge of the pit they placed a second pot and the whole was then covered by a heap of boulders. The scant respect shown for the remains of those already buried in what must even then have been regarded as a cemetery or area devoted to burial is nothing new, and we have seen in our own day, in old graveyards, bones of even quite recently-dead people being pulled out and thrown aside to make room for newer interments – and no disrespect intended!

In 1979, two samples were submitted for ^{14}C analysis in the Groningen Laboratory by courtesy of Dr J. N. Lanting and A. Brindley. One was from a charcoal spread under the edge of the cairn, the spread in which the large pot of the primary phase was embedded. A radiocarbon date of 3960 ± 60 BP was obtained. The second sample was of human bone from the primary interment in the central cist and the radiocarbon date of the sample was 3755 ± 30 BP.

Pre-existing mounds

A type of mound sometimes used for secondary Bronze Age interments was one covering a chambered tomb, frequently a passage tomb, and in some cases even the tomb itself was reused. At the Mound of the Hostages at Tara, Co. Meath, approximately fifty secondary burials were inserted in the clay mantling of the cairn (B. Raftery 1969, 13). All but one were cremations and only one was in a cist. Since the excavation is unpublished, details are scant but apparently both Food Vessel and Urn burials were present (Kavanagh 1973, 555–8; 1976, 350–1; 1977, 86). The inhumation burial has previously been mentioned (p. 187) as it was accompanied by a necklace of faience and amber beads. The cist cremation was accompanied by a stone battle axe that had been burnt, a Collared Urn, a Vase Food Vessel and a triangular bronze dagger (Harbison 1968, 59). Another cremation burial in a Collared Urn was also accompanied by a bronze dagger. Part of the tomb chamber had been emptied of the original deposits and several crouched burials with Food Vessels, a bronze awl and V-perforated buttons of jet and stone were substituted (De Valera *in* Ó Ríordáin 1985, 27–8).

Similar secondary Food Vessel and Urn burials were found in the mound of the passage tomb at Fourknocks, Co. Meath. Re-use of other types of chambered tomb is also known, e.g. a court tomb at Doohatty Glebe, Co. Fermanagh, a portal tomb at Aghnaskeagh A, Co. Louth (Evans 1935) and a wedge tomb at Kilmashogue, Co. Dublin (Kilbride-Jones 1954).

The secondary burials in the Entrance Grave at Harristown, Co. Waterford (J. Hawkes 1941), have been mentioned previously (p. 110). One of these consisted of a cremation accompanied by a Cordoned Urn, a bronze razor-knife, a perforated bone pin and a quoit-shaped faience bead. A similar urn stood upright and contained a cremation and an undecorated Pygmy Cup.

Barrows

Another type of burial mound is one which comes under the loose classification of barrow, of which there are many variants. The mounds are generally slight. This is due in part, at least, to progressive deterioration and cultivation, and on account of this the burials have frequently been destroyed. Generally speaking, barrows are round mounds, totally or largely of earth, usually encircled by a ditch and sometimes by an external bank. They range in date from perhaps Late Neolithic to the Early Iron Age. The average size varies from *c.*10 to 15m in diameter and sometimes more than one building phase is present and also more than one interment. Barrows are very numerous but they often go unnoticed unless the existence of the ditch is betrayed by a circular hollow or by crop marks seen from the air. The name ring-barrow is applied to examples with a very slight mound and external ditch and the name ring-ditch when no mound remains, if such had been present, but there is no hard-and-fast rule about the terminology as applied to the Irish sites. The terms bowl-barrow and tumulus are also employed.

Another characteristic is that many occur in groups: for example, ten at Carrowjames, Co. Mayo, at least six at Rathnarrow, Co. Westmeath; and one of the greatest concentrations was found on the Limerick/Tipperary border. Seán P. Ó Ríordáin (1936) excavated twenty-one barrows in the neighbourhood of Lissard in Co. Limerick in 1934–5 and a group of four at Rathjordan in the same part of the county in the 1940s. Numerous other barrows grouped together were noted in this border area in 1983 during a survey of a proposed gas pipeline from Cork to Limerick.

The Ó Ríordáin excavations were singularly unrewarding and in fact the very first one to be excavated, that at Lissard, was the only one to produce a Bronze Age interment. It had a very low earthen mound less than 7m in diameter and the badly preserved remains of a Vase Urn were found on the old ground surface in the centre, inverted over a minute portion of cremated human bone. Preservation conditions were clearly extremely poor. No evidence of function was forthcoming for the remaining Lissard barrows. Of a group of four excavated at Rathjordan in Co. Limerick (Ó Ríordáin 1947; 1948), three produced pottery of Western Neolithic type and the fourth had sherds of Beaker and Food Vessel, a ceramic assemblage common at Lough Gur a few kilometres away. No human remains were discovered though in one of the barrows there was a central conical pit and in another a series of pits, holes, short trenches and dark areas, none of which formed a recognizable lay-out. Ó Ríordáin remarked that, if burials had been deposited on the old ground surface unprotected in any way, they would be unlikely to survive, given the slight amount of cover provided by the low mound and also taking into account the acidity of the soil in the area.

Not far from Lissard, in Cush townland, there were three circular tumuli close together amid a complex of ringforts, field boundaries and other features. Tumulus I was smaller and more insignificant than the others and it had previously been interfered with. An Encrusted Urn burial was found about 30cm below the surface. Traces of a fosse were found during the excavation (Ó Ríordáin 1940, 133–7) and also part of a kerb at the perimeter of the mound. A layer or 'paving' of small stones covered part of the mound about 45cm below the surface. A long cist grave was found below the old ground level at the centre and Ó Ríordáin interpreted this as the primary burial. Although no skeletal material was recovered from the cist, with the exception of some fragments of teeth, he regarded the sherds of pottery present as being those of a Vase Urn. Waddell (1970, 123), however, classes them as anomalous. Ó Ríordáin associated the kerb with this phase and suggested that the incomplete fosse had been dug when the other Urn burial was inserted in the mound. The other two tumuli will be described in a later section (pp. 329–30).

At Carrowjames, Co. Mayo (J. Raftery 1938–9; 1940–1), there were two groups of tumuli. Each of the three making up the first group was surrounded by a fosse and was about 15m in overall diameter. There was a central pit burial in each; two of them contained Cordoned Urns and all three were accompanied by bronze razors (one razor and two razor-knives, all of the tanged Class I type). In the second group of seven, six were excavated and pit burials found in some. There was no central burial in the largest and most distinct mound of the group, Tumulus 4, which was 21.35m in overall diameter. Scattered cremation deposits were found and there was a Cinerary Urn burial at the outer edge of the external bank surrounding the fosse. It is the only burial of this type at Carrowjames II, i.e. in the second group of mounds, and the excavator suggested that it might be pre-mound in date (J. Raftery 1940–1, 20). Another one of this group, Tumulus 8, will be described in a later chapter (p. 330).

Two mounds, situated on an esker or gravel ridge in the townland of Pollacorragune, Co. Galway, were excavated in the 1930s (Riley 1936). The first, known as 'Carnfanny', contained a Cordoned Urn burial accompanied by an ornamented tanged bronze razor. In the uppermost levels of the mound animal bones and fragments of burnt bone were found and near the centre, at a depth of about 30cm, seven tiny blue glass beads were recovered but there was no trace of an accompanying burial. Similar beads have been found in association with burials elsewhere and an Early Iron Age date is assumed for them though, as Barry Raftery remarks (1984, 204), they 'require specialist study before their significance can be assessed'. In addition, they are not exclusive to Iron Age burials but have been found in Late Bronze Age contexts also. The second mound at Pollacorragune is of Early Iron Age or later date (p. 330).

Two mounds excavated at Carrowbeg North in Co. Galway (Willmot 1938–9) resembled some of those at Carrowjames. Each had a fosse and was *c.*17m in overall diameter. The primary cremation at Mound I was contained in a pit and was accompanied by a bronze razor or razor-knife. The pit had been dug through an overlying layer of charcoal and cremated bone, similar to that found in Tumulus I at Cush and other sites, and it is regarded as the remains of a funeral pyre. In the second mound a small hollow at the centre contained a few fragments of human bone and some animal ones and nearby was a short cist containing the cremated remains of an adult. The cremation was accompanied by a plano-convex flint knife. Both mounds were either added to or re-used subsequently (p. 332).

A site at Urbalreagh in Co. Antrim (Waterman 1968) consisted of a ring-ditch, penannular in shape, enclosing an area 5.6m in diameter. There were three burials at the centre, two of them close together in Urns – one a fine Cordoned example – which had been inverted over the cremated bones; the third burial was somewhat apart. A small earthen mound may originally have covered the burials but no trace was present at the time of the excavation. Burial 1 was at the centre and mixed through the cremated bone in the Cordoned Urn were fragments of bronze which could be pieces of a razor. The burial pit was sunk in the ground and the floor showed evidence of burning. The second burial pit was partly dug through the first one and the base of an Urn was found which contained the cremated remains of a child. Burial 3 was that of a youth, accompanied by a burnt flint flake. It was in a shallow pit and would have protruded above ground level unless protected in some way. A similar ring-ditch in the Dundrum sandhills in Co. Down contained a cist in which was some cremated bone (Collins 1952).

Radiocarbon dates were forthcoming for a ring-ditch at Ballyveelish, near Clonmel, Co. Tipperary. Three sites were excavated here as part of the archaeological investigation in 1981–2 of the area designated by Bord Gais Eireann (the Irish Gas Board) for the construction of a natural gas pipeline from Cork to Dublin. The earliest phase at Ballyveelish consisted of a shallow ring-ditch enclosing an area 11m in diameter. A pit, 1.14m in diameter at the top, narrowing to 90cm at base and 1m deep, had been dug into the old ground surface in the centre of the enclosure. A polygonal cist had been constructed in the pit and fitted comfortably within it. The top of the cist was 52cm below the top of the pit and its base was the natural floor of the pit. There were two capstones, one of them a well-made saddle quern which had crushed an Encrusted Urn lying directly beneath it. The Urn was inverted over cremated human bones. The cist was filled with a mixture of soil, charcoal and further fragments of cremated bone. There were some 4,500 fragments in all, representing a minimum of five individuals (two adults and three children) as well as a few fragments of animal bone, also burnt. There were two Pygmy Cups at different levels in the cist, one biconical and plain and the other decorated and resembling a miniature Bowl Food Vessel. When the side stones were removed it could be seen that the sides of the pit were oxidized to a bright red colour and it is possible that a fire had been lit before the cist was constructed. A ^{14}C date of 3580 ± 50 BP was obtained from a sample of charcoal inside the urn.

A ring of eight, or possibly nine, postholes surrounded the burial, which was slightly off-centre with respect to it. The area enclosed by the ring was 7 by 5.1m.

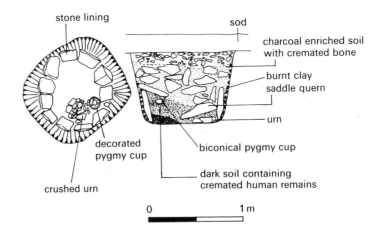

104 Ballyveelish 3, Co. Tipperary, central burial pit (after M. Doody)

The postholes varied considerably in size and depth, the largest ones being approximately 40 by 60cm in diameter. Two slot trenches, 15cm in width, formed a D-shaped porch-like feature at the south-east side which was broken at the centre by an entrance with two substantial postholes at each side. The excavator (Doody, unpublished) tentatively suggested that the central posthole-feature with attached porch could have been a mortuary house. The slot trenches contained a good deal of charcoal, possibly derived from a wattle wall or fence. The adjacent portion of the ring-ditch contained large pieces of charred wood, probably part of the burnt wattle wall. A ^{14}C date of 3485 ± 40 BP was obtained from a sample of the charred wood. The date relates to the porch-like feature and probably to the central posthole structure also, rather than to the ring-ditch. The date is not necessarily discrepant with that from the cist if the standard deviations are taken into account.

There were several pits in the enclosure outside the area of postholes. One large oblong pit which contained dumped refuse was radiocarbon-dated to 2810 ± 90 BP. Another secondary feature was a deep sub-rectangular ditch which cut through the posthole feature and coincided with the ring-ditch at north and south sides. No finds were recovered other than a saddle quern.

In 1968, the excavation of a barrow at Pubble, Co. Derry, which had been covered by peat showed it to consist of a circular mound surrounded by a shallow ditch and low outer bank. There had been several phases of construction and alteration and samples for pollen analysis and ^{14}C determinations were taken throughout the investigation. A small stone cist which had originally occupied a central position in the mound was found to have been removed and there were several other ancient disturbances. Pre-dating the construction of the cist, a central pit had been dug in the old ground surface and re-filled, but no trace of a burial deposit was recovered. Perhaps this was part of the preliminary ritual or

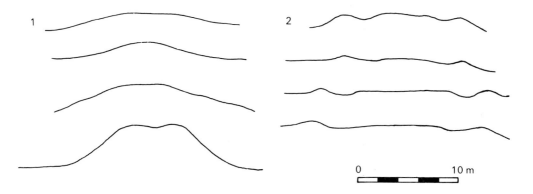

105 Carrowmore peninsula, Co. Sligo, barrow profiles (after M. Timoney)

perhaps an inhumation was formerly present. The series of ^{14}C dates together with all other details relating to the extensive excavation and investigation of the site are published in Smith *et al.* 1981. The authors concluded (*ibid.*, 53) that 'The barrow was certainly built . . . after *c.*1900 BC, indeed, probably after *c.*1600 BC, and before *c.*1400 to 1300 BC.' These are radiocarbon dates expressed notionally on the Christian calendar (*ibid.*, 31).

Between 1967 and 1974 Martin Timoney undertook a field survey of earthen monuments in the Carrowmore peninsula in the west of Ireland (Timoney 1984). He identified at least seventeen earthworks which could be classed as barrows and found that the majority were either bowl type, that is, with a perceptible central mound, or ring type, which have a bank and fosse and in which the bank is approximately the same height as the barrow. He excavated one of the bowl barrows in 1977 but the results were somewhat negative as, apart from the finding of two skeletons, there was no evidence of date.

Late Bronze Age burial

In the seeming absence of any specific identifiable burial tradition it can only be assumed that in the later part of the Bronze Age the practice of formal burial gradually waned and the custom of placing the bodies of the dead, or the cremated remains, in pits or graves unaccompanied by grave goods replaced the ancient rituals. Such burials can, in certain circumstances, be virtually undatable and may perhaps account in part for the meagre nature of the record.

A few examples are known where the formal element has not entirely disappeared and these provide the bulk of our knowledge of LBA burial customs. An enclosure within the Rathgall hillfort, Co. Wicklow, is among the most interesting of these (B. Raftery 1973; 1981). The enclosure was *c.*18–19m in diameter and was delimited by a shallow ditch of V-section. Centrally placed within it was a pit which had been dug through an area subjected to intense heat, interpreted by the excavator as the site of a cremation pyre. A stone slab surrounded by fist-sized stones lay on the bottom of the pit and burnt human bones representing the remains of a young adult were placed on the slab and covered with the fire-reddened material that had been extracted in the initial digging of the pit. Enclosing the pit was a U-shaped setting consisting of a dense mass of small, very closely spaced stakeholes, some 1,500 in all, forming an irregular band about 2m in width. A portion of a blue glass bead was found within the stakehole complex. A small pit burial at the tip of one of the arms of the U-setting contained the cremated remains of a child. Another burial (no. 2) was between the U-setting and the ditch and was contained in a well-made funnel-shaped pit. A coarse bucket-shaped pot in which were the cremated remains of an adult and a child stood upright in the bottom of the pit and a flat slab had been laid over the mouth of the vessel and covered by a larger stone which completed the sealing of the deposit. Dense black organic material which appeared to the excavator to have come from a cremation fire was packed around the pot (B. Raftery 1974a, 29).

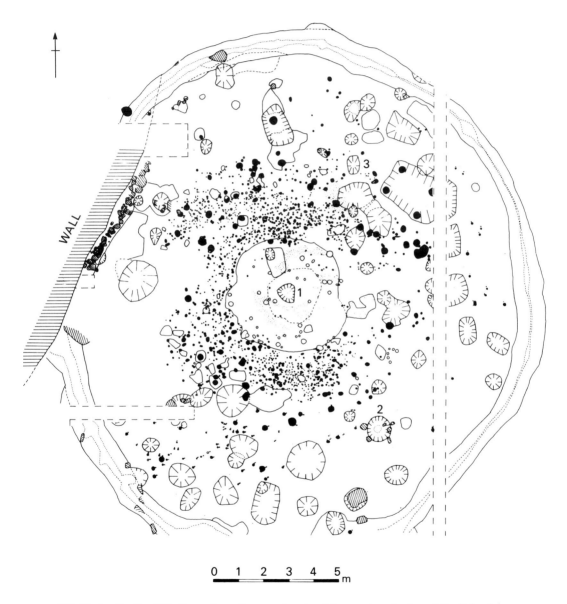

106 Rathgall, Co. Wicklow, Late Bronze Age burial complex: 1, 2 and 3 pit burials
(after B. Raftery)

There were numerous other pits in the area between the U-setting and the ditch and in one of them metal artefacts were found, all of bronze, consisting of a small chisel, part of a socketed spearhead and a portion of the blade of a leaf-shaped sword. The excavator noted that not all pits had been dug at the same time. The central pit is regarded as the focal point of the enclosure and it is attributed to the LBA, but fuller details will emerge only when the final report is published.

One of two ring-barrows excavated at Mullaghmore, Co. Down (Mogey and Thompson 1956), bears a certain similarity to the Rathgall site and also to the Pubble barrow (p. 209). Mullaghmore A was about 21m in overall diameter with fosse and outer bank and raised central portion. A cremation burial representing four people was found at the centre and it was accompanied by numerous sherds of coarse pottery, mostly in minute fragments. Some sherds bore 'pin-pricks' or tiny perforations below the rim, made before firing, a feature also found in pottery from a settlement horizon at the Rathgall hillfort (p. 313). The exterior and interior of the pots were 'slurried over', giving the effect of a coating or slip (*ibid.*, 24). A single tiny blue glass bead was found with the central burial. Close to the barrow a setting of four standing stones surrounded another cremation contained in an upright pot, the top of which was missing, probably ploughed away. The pot contained the remains of an adult, and the cremated remains of a child were scattered nearby. No date could be established for either of the

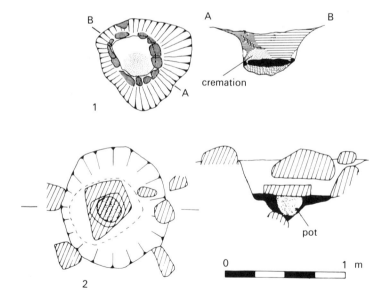

107 Rathgall, Co. Wicklow, Burials 1 and 2 (after B. Raftery)

212

burials. The excavators proposed an Early Iron Age date on the basis of the glass bead, but on account of the similarity to the Rathgall burials Barry Raftery (1981, 176–7) suggests that the Mullaghmore interments may be earlier than this. Mullaghmore B was similar in form but smaller, and the only feature discovered was a central posthole. There was no pottery.

Another burial site attributed to the Early Iron Age but which Raftery also believes is earlier is that at Lugg, Co. Dublin (Kilbride-Jones 1950), excavated in 1939. It appears to have been a composite monument – three phases were proposed – with hearths and a great number of postholes. The postholes and most of the pottery were said to have belonged to the two earlier phases, and the final one referred to two cremation burials near which a few sherds of 'early Iron Age ware' were found (*ibid.*, 325). This site will need re-evaluation before any final conclusions can be reached.

A site unusual in Ireland was excavated in 1970 in the townland of Carnkenny, Co. Tyrone (Lynn 1973–4). There was a very low circular outer bank of stones, 15m in diameter internally. The bank overlay a large patch of burnt soil and charcoal mixed with a good deal of burnt bone which the excavator tentatively suggested might represent a cremation fire. At the centre of the enclosure there was a scatter of seventeen small pits which had been dug through an area of disturbed soil. The pits contained dark earth, charcoal and flecks of burnt bone. Sixteen small stakeholes were found around one of them. In addition, there were two larger pits, one of which contained two stone discs and some fragments of coarse pottery. One of the large pits and all but one of the small ones were covered by a roughly laid spread of stones which was not substantial enough to be called a cairn.

The excavator suggested that the cremated remains had been distributed in the soil of the disturbed area in the centre and in the fill of the small pits, and that only a few individuals may have been represented. A sample of charcoal from the burnt area under the bank gave a ^{14}C date of 2815 ± 50 BP. While the site has been called a 'ring-cairn' it does not fall within the definition as applied to monuments of ring-cairn type in Wales and other parts of Britain. A denuded cairn can have the appearance of a ring-cairn, and Frances Lynch (1979, 2) makes the point that it is only when the ring has a regular inner edge that one can speak of a ring-cairn.

The record of LBA burials is singularly slender and unsatisfactory. No single type or burial mode can be isolated as characteristic. The formal approach to interment shown in Neolithic and EBA times seems to have been superseded by less easily detectable funerary traditions, e.g. graves in pits unmarked at the surface, or where marked, within an enclosing ring or in ring-barrows, frequently in secondary positions. It is unfortunate that so many of the important sites were excavated at a time when the radiocarbon-dating technique was still in the future.

In these cases, unless diagnostic grave goods were present, something which was the exception rather than the rule, there is no way at present of isolating a definitive LBA burial tradition, assuming that one existed. Perhaps the true solution is, as has been suggested (B. Raftery 1981, 177), 'that the dead were cremated and interred without gravegoods in pits, thus rendering them, under normal circumstances, archaeologically undatable'.

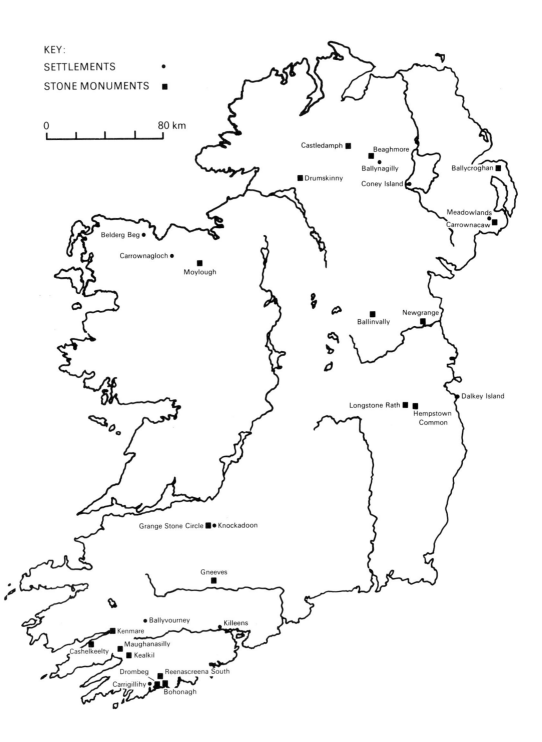

KEY:

SETTLEMENTS ●

STONE MONUMENTS ■

0   80 km

Castledamph ■

Beaghmore ■

Ballynagilly ●

Ballycroghan ■

Drumskinny ■

Coney Island ■

Meadowlands ■

Carrownacaw ■

Belderg Beg ●

Carrownagloch ●

Moylough ■

Ballinvally ■

Newgrange ■

Longstone Rath ■

Dalkey Island ●

Hempstown Common ■

Grange Stone Circle ■ ● Knockadoon

Gneeves ■

● Ballyvourney

Killeens

Kenmare ■

Maughanasilly ■

Cashelkeelty ■ Kealkil ■

Drombeg ■ Reenascreena South ■

Carrigillihy ●

Bohonagh ■

108 Bronze Age settlements; stone monuments

9

Bronze Age settlement and stone monuments

Occupation sites

There is evidence that a number of sites such as Ballynagilly, Co. Tyrone, the Knockadoon peninsula at Lough Gur, Coney Island in Lough Neagh, and Dalkey Island, Co. Dublin, were occupied either continuously or sporadically from Neolithic and even earlier times down to the Bronze Age and later. Some centuries after Beaker Period habitation at Ballynagilly had ceased, renewed forest clearance took place and occupation horizons consisting of hearths and pits were found in another part of the site. Sherds of Bowl Food Vessel were present. Another occupation area somewhat later in date produced well-made plain bucket-shaped ware about 1cm in thickness which appeared to have belonged to pans or jars of very large diameter, up to 50 cm. Thereafter blanket peat covered the entire site, but pollen evidence in the neighbouring bog showed that renewed clearance took place about 1200 BC.

The obliteration of prehistoric sites in North Mayo by blanket bog has been noted in a previous chapter (p. 65). At Belderg Beg and at Carrownagloch, Glenree, evidence of occupation dating to the mid-second millennium BC (calibrated) was found. The spread of peat bog over large areas of the country undoubtedly accounts in part at least for the notable scarcity of Bronze Age settlement sites. It has been suggested that there was a deterioration in climate *c.*2000–1700 BC and that this assisted the development of peat on hitherto cultivated land. There is also the possibility that human activity played an even greater role. The clearance of forest and the over-cultivation of soil led to deterioration and podsolization, a leaching of the soil such as can be seen in heath and moorland, and the eventual triumph of peat cover. Increased woodland clearance due to superior tools and possibly to greater pressure on the land to produce food, leading in turn to over-grazing and over-cultivation, could have triggered it off even without climatic change. No doubt different factors affected the diverse areas in a variety of ways.

The continuity of occupation at Lough Gur from Neolithic times into the EBA and later, has been mentioned (p. 81), particularly at Sites C and D and at some of the enclosure circles. Site F was probably connected with the final phase of the EBA. Excavation revealed a house of roughly rectangular plan, 8.2m by 6.4m, built against a vertical rock face 1.8m high which formed one wall of the structure; it was erected on top of an earlier occupation horizon. Outside the later house but associated with it was a hollow containing a hearth in which several fragments of clay moulds and bronze-casting waste were found. With these materials and within the house itself were numerous sherds of the well-known flat-based coarse pottery (Class II), showing that this continued in use at least to the end of the EBA, because where the mould fragments were big enough, it could be seen that they were used for casting rapiers and socketed looped spear-heads. Fragments of moulds were scattered down the hillside as well, up to one hundred fragments in all. Presumably this was the house of a worker in bronze (Ó Ríordáin 1954, 415ff.). A small amount of Beaker ware was also found, but one of the problems at many of the Lough Gur sites was the difficulty of sifting one horizon from another owing to the continuity of occupation and the relative absence of deep stratifications. In the case of Site F the excavator remarked (*ibid.*, 420) that the depth of deposit was not great and that in this stony material stratification was not reliable.

At Site D there was intensive evidence of occupation showing continuity from Neolithic through Beaker times to a mature phase of the EBA, if not later. Two wooden houses were associated with the Neolithic Period and they were replaced by a stone-built house with a central posthole. This site has previously been mentioned (p. 81) in connection with the proportionately large quantity of Beaker ware recovered, though Class I and Class II ware was present also in other levels (Ó Ríordáin 1954, 390). A few items of bronze were found together with the small gold disc previously mentioned (p. 82). Fragments of clay moulds for spearheads and a portion of a stone mould for a palstave were also recovered (Ó Ríordáin 1954, 384ff.).

Another site which gave evidence of human activity at various periods from the Mesolithic down to the Bronze Age is Coney Island, between the estuaries of the Rivers Bann and Blackwater in the south-west corner of Lough Neagh in the north-east of Ireland (Addyman 1965). Some traces of an EBA site were found on the southern edge of the island. Here basal sand layers containing Mesolithic flints had been partly cut away to accommodate what appeared to be the remains of rectangular structures. These were marked by trenches cut into the sand and were filled with dark charcoal-bearing soil, though one cutting contained a silt-like white soil representing the base of a leached sod wall. Nearby were substantial blocks of burnt timber. The trenches seem to represent two structures 2.7m in length, and 6m and 3.3m in width respectively. The fill of the trenches contained sherds of Food Vessel but because of the difficulties of the site only a small part of the occupation area connected with the Food Vessel ware could be excavated. There were a number of pits and hollows also which contained Food

Vessel sherds, mainly from Bowls decorated with comb-impressions and occasionally with false relief. A plano-convex flint knife and some small scrapers were also present. A sample of carbonized wood from a deposit containing Bowl Food Vessel has given a ^{14}C date of 3350 ± 80 BP, a date that 'seems rather young for this pottery and in isolation is not of great significance' (Smith *et al.* 1971, 99). Later deposits contained occasional stray sherds of cord-ornamented Cordoned Urns but there were no associated structures or features.

Evidence of LBA occupation overlay the Food Vessel deposits in places, consisting of thin charcoal-rich sandy material. The pottery recovered was very thick and coarse, often with large grits protruding from the surface, and it represented large flat-based bucket-shaped domestic pots. The excavator compared this so-called 'flat-rimmed ware' with material found in Navan Fort (Emain Macha), Co. Armagh, less than 20km away.

In the winter of 1961–2 preliminary work on a new housing estate, now called Meadowlands, in the town of Downpatrick, Co. Down, revealed a habitation area of considerable extent. Because the building scheme could not be held up it was possible only to excavate a single cutting across the centre of the prehistoric area (Pollock and Waterman 1964). The cutting for the most part was a minimum of about 2m in width and it was 43m long. In certain areas, however, it was possible to make lateral extensions. Within the cutting the ground plans of two round houses were partly uncovered as well as slots, postholes and pits. These features were not all in use contemporaneously. More than half of House A was uncovered. The floor was nearly 4m in diameter, with a central hearth, and its perimeter was marked by postholes. House B was of similar though more irregular circular ground plan and nearly 7m in diameter. The perimeter was determined by a gully on the north-east and by postholes elsewhere.

All the pottery found, including the sherds from the undisturbed occupation levels, is 'representative of the Cordoned Urn type of Bronze Age cinerary vessel' (*ibid.*, 41) and can be readily matched on Cordoned Urns from sepulchral contexts. The radiocarbon dates obtained from charcoal are in agreement with the findings of the excavators. The four dates range from 3795 ± 75 BP to 3265 ± 80 BP, representing a lower and an upper level respectively. There was some Beaker in the lower level.

Traces of intermittent occupation from Late Mesolithic times through the Neolithic Period and into the Bronze Age have been uncovered by excavations at Dalkey Island in Dublin Bay. Middens which post-dated the maximum transgression of the sea have already been noted (p. 28). Unfortunately artefacts were more plentiful on the site than were traces of man in the shape of houses, shelters and so on. Pottery however has confirmed occupation in the Bronze Age, as has the finding of fragments of clay moulds and crucibles (Liversage 1968).

An interesting two-period site was excavated at Carrigillihy, a sea-coast site near the village of Union Hall in south-west Cork (O'Kelly 1951). Here a well-built stone wall 2.7m thick was constructed to an oval plan, the axes measuring 24.4m and 21.3m to the internal facings. Where best preserved it stood to a height of 1.2m but must originally have been higher. The entrance lay on the east and faced the sea, and the opening originally had carefully built jambs with a wooden post set against each of them to act as hanging- and meeting-stiles for a wooden gate. The holes in which the posts had stood were found.

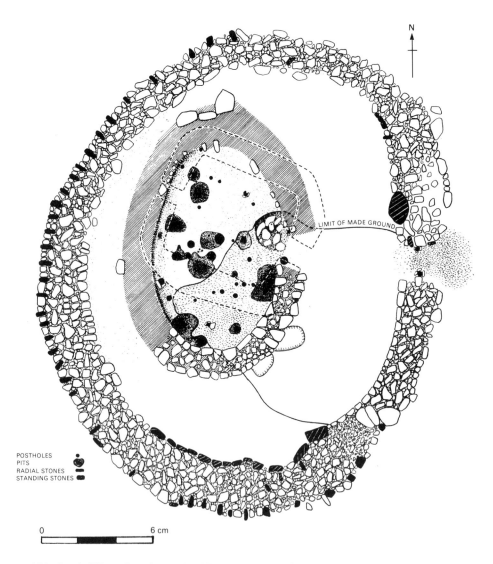

POSTHOLES
PITS
RADIAL STONES
STANDING STONES

0   6 cm

109 Carrigillihy, Co. Cork, dwelling site: plan of primary stratum; secondary house shown by dotted lines

Within the enclosure the remains of two strata were distinguished, the lower containing the foundations of an oval stone house coeval with the enclosure wall, while the upper contained the remains of a square stone house superimposed on the ruins of the earlier one. The secondary house was poor in finds; only a few portions of saddle querns and part of a shale bracelet were present, and there was no pottery.

Where best preserved the wall-base of the primary house remained to a height of nearly 60cm and delineated a floor measuring 10m by 6.7m. Strangely, no hearth site was found, but there were several postholes which gave some indication of the way in which the thatched roof may have been supported. The doorway was on the east side directly opposite the entrance to the enclosure and against the jambs here also were the postholes of the door frame.

All over the floor of the house and spreading out through the door as far as the enclosure wall and the entrance through it was a layer of domestic refuse, black from the amount of finely fragmented charcoal mixed through it. This layer contained numerous fragments of pottery and in the same horizon was found a bronze awl of the single-pointed type with a chisel-like tang. It came from a spot about 60cm inside the enclosure, sealed below a grey-white leached layer and some collapse from the wall (*ibid.*, 81), and was adjacent to a group of potsherds.

110 Carrigillihy, Co. Cork, scale model of primary house and enclosure (E. M. Fahy)

There were several pits in the floor together with scoops of various sizes and depths, all filled with dark soil. Most of the pottery came from the pits.

Within the past few years some samples of charred twigs which had been collected during the excavations were sent to the Groningen laboratory by courtesy of Dr J. N. Lanting and A. Brindley for purposes of radiocarbon dating. Sample 1 came from a pit inside the oval (earlier) house and the charred twigs gave a ^{14}C date of 3100 ± 50 BP. Two small samples from the habitation layer in the primary house were combined for the second analysis and the ^{14}C date was 2810 ± 50 BP. The first date is possibly the more accurate of the two and when calibrated places this primary phase of the site at the EBA/LBA transition.

In view of the great advance which has taken place in the in-depth study of pottery over the thirty-five years since the site was excavated, Rose M. Cleary was asked to undertake a fresh examination of the 166 sherds which comprised the main assemblage. It was possible to make a partial reconstruction of nine vessels, representing globular bowls, straight-sided vessels and one S-profile bowl. A small proportion of sherds was decorated with cord and comb impressions and incised lines and strokes. The sooty accretions on a majority of the sherds may indicate that the pottery was mainly cooking ware.

For the Late Bronze Age some settlement sites are known, though the evidence is fairly scant. A few, as at Coney Island and Dalkey, represent the continuation or reoccupation of areas settled intermittently from earliest times while others are the early occupation phases of sites that were to have a long history in Iron Age or in Early Christian times. In the latter category must be placed lakeside settlements and crannogs and also hilltop settlements, some of which were later encircled by banks and ditches, the so-called hillforts. One of the difficulties of identifying sites of the period lies in the scarcity of diagnostic artefacts. In spite of the wealth in gold and bronze which we know to have been current at this time, particularly in the Dowris Phase, very little has been recovered from field monuments, whether domestic, burial, ritual, etc. The pottery such as it is is unhelpful also and consists, as far as a definitive type can be isolated, of coarse domestic flat-bottomed bucket-shaped ware with no outstanding characteristics. The archaeologist is more than usually dependent therefore on reliable samples for radiocarbon and other dating mechanisms.

Pollen analytical studies (Mitchell 1976, 135) show a renewal of forest clearance and a rise in farming activities *c.* 1200 BC, the start of the Bishopsland Phase. This was evident, for example, in studies carried out at Ballynagilly, as mentioned already. The Bishopsland hoard itself showed a wide range of bronze implements such as socketed axes, hammers, gouges, chisels, and so on, which would ensure greater efficiency in woodworking techniques; and the socketed bronze sickle would likewise ensure higher yields from cereal cultivation. Evidence of another upsurge of agricultural activity has been noted for the period *c.* 700 BC, the start of the Dowris Phase, in spite of the fact that widespread climatic deterioration involving increased humifaction and declining temperatures has been observed all over Europe for the period in question. A number of lakeside settlements of this period have been identified and in each case the occupation was terminated by flood waters. How far this was due to climatic deterioration or how far it was caused by the blocking up of natural drainage outlets owing to the expansion of the raised bogs is not clear (*ibid.*, 159). It is also possible that some sites had outlived their usefulness.

Some archaeologists see a decline *c.*500 BC leading to a Dark Age which lasted almost to the end of the millennium but not all envisage such a speedy termination of Dowris prosperity and would extend it to the third century BC. While this may hold good for the artefactual evidence based on typologies, the examination of the sites themselves has done little to resolve the question one way or the other. It is not a practical proposition to attempt to isolate settlement sites on the basis of industrial phases such as Bishopsland, Dowris, etc. As T. C. Champion has pointed out (1971, 17), 'there is no necessary connection between the start of a settlement type and a change in metal typology'. Some sites, such as lakeside settlements, and other monument types, including hillforts, appear to bridge the transition from Bronze to Iron Age which took place in the course of the first millennium BC and these are discussed in a later chapter (p. 297) under 'Later prehistoric settlement'.

Cooking places

A type of archaeological site found in large numbers in Ireland is the *fulacht fian* or *fulacht fiadh*. While *fulacht* refers to the cooking place, *fian* or *fiadh* can mean variously 'deer' or 'out of doors' or 'of the wild'. In Britain and the Isle of Man these sites are known as boiling mounds or burnt mounds. They are generally so unobtrusive as to go almost unnoticed or to be mistaken for a mound of field stones or the foundation of a ruined hut. They usually have the appearance of a somewhat crescent-shaped grass-covered mound and are always close to a water source. It is not unusual to find several clustered together. Some of the British examples are similar and served the same purpose, that is, as outdoor cooking places. Over 2,000 examples have been identified in Ireland (Ó Drisceóil 1980), and the number is increasing as more county field surveys are undertaken. The majority are located in the south of the country, over 1,000 in Co. Cork alone.

The first of these sites to be scientifically excavated in Ireland were two at Ballyvourney in 1952 and three at Killeens in 1953, all in Co. Cork (O'Kelly 1954). Before the excavation of the first site, Ballyvourney I, its true nature was not apparent as it had the appearance of a small circular ruined house with a sunken area in the centre, similar to a hut site nearby which had just been excavated by the writer. When uncovered, the site was found to consist of a rectangular wood-lined trough filled with water that seeped in from the surrounding peaty area. As well as this, there were two hearths, a stone-lined pit or oven and the foundation postholes of a small wooden hut. The whole complex was almost

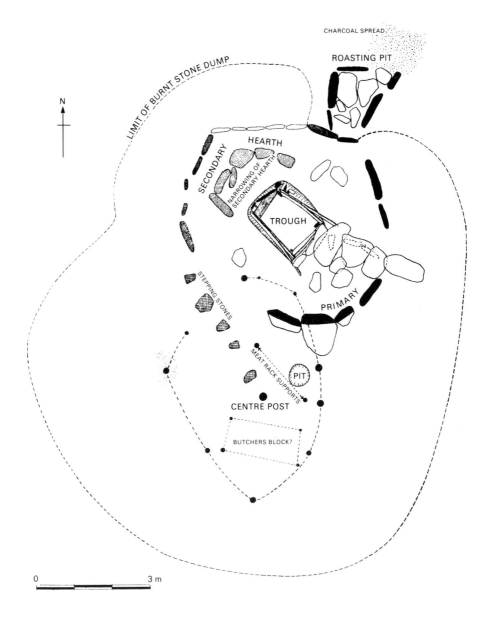

111 Ballyvourney I, Co. Cork, general plan of cooking place after excavation

completely surrounded by a dump of broken burnt stones intermixed with charcoal and ash.

The cooking method employed was to heat stones in a fire beside the trough until they became red hot and to drop sufficient of them in the water until it came to the boil. Thereafter, an occasional stone was added to keep the water at boiling point. The joint of meat was placed in the boiling water, probably wrapped in straw in accordance with the ancient practice as related in references in Irish literature (O'Kelly 1954, 122) and kept at boiling point for the requisite length of time. Before another 'cooking' could take place, the trough had to be cleared of broken fragments of stones and a succession of these makes up the large dumps surrounding the trough and hearths.

We tested the method on the spot at Ballyvourney and found that the fill of the trough, about 450 litres, could be brought to the boil in 30 to 35 minutes. A 4.5kg leg of mutton was boiled in the trough in under four hours, by which time it was cooked through and highly edible. We also tested the stone-lined pit which we suspected had been used as an oven. It was pre-heated with red hot stones, cleaned out, and a joint of meat inserted. The results were equally satisfactory. Judging by the amount of broken burnt stone that resulted from the cooking experiment, it was estimated that about fifty 'cookings' had been carried out at the site.

No datable finds came from any of the five sites but a sample of oakwood from the Killeens I trough was sent to the then newly set-up Libby laboratory at Chicago. A ^{14}C date of 3506 ± 230 BP was obtained. Understandably, doubts were cast on the validity of the date and in 1979 a further sample of wood from the same site was forwarded to the Groningen laboratory. The date of 3115 ± 35 BP that was obtained is now regarded as definitive. Several other Irish *fulachta* excavated in more recent times have given almost identical dates to Killeens I, and the same is true of some of the British sites. It must be said, however, that since the known sites can be numbered in thousands, the thirty or so excavated examples in Britain and Ireland cannot be regarded as a satisfactory sample. It has been found that the troughs are chiefly of wood – planks, branches and twigs, and hollowed-out tree trunks being used – but stone troughs are also known.

While cooking is the activity that best fits the available evidence, archaeological and otherwise, it has also been suggested that some of the sites may have been used as sweat houses (Lucas 1965; Barfield and Hodder 1981). The sites could have been devised to produce large quantities of hot water and steam for curative purposes and the almost complete absence of animal remains from most of the excavated examples could support the suggestion. On the other hand, one would not expect to find much food residue in the neighbourhood of a cooking place, given the scavenging propensities of the hunting pack, and therefore its absence does not in itself prove the sites were devoted to other uses.

112 Ballyvourney I, conjectural reconstruction

113 Cooking experiment: the joint of mutto

116 Removing the meat

117 The carving

114 The meat wrapped in straw

115 Boiling the water

118 The eating

Stone monuments

Ireland is fortunate compared to some other countries in the number of stone monuments which have survived from prehistoric times. Many have been preserved due to being in peaty or mountainous areas and some are sufficiently commanding in appearance to inhibit destruction. Two in the latter category, the standing stones around the great Newgrange cairn and the stone circle at Grange in Lough Gur have been described above (p. 137). Broadly speaking, stone monuments can consist of single standing stones, lines or rows of stones (alignments) and stone circles. One or other of these elements is frequently found in proximity to, or connected with, another.

Standing stones

These are the simplest kind of stone monument, consisting of a stone set upright in the ground, and can vary in height from less than a metre to 6m or so. They are a familiar sight in the Irish countryside, particularly in the south-west, where there are about 600 examples, but in fact they have been recorded from almost every Irish county. The Irish name for them is *gallán* or *dallán* though there are many local variations and some have been given specific names. Two adjacent to the Grange stone circle, for instance, are known respectively as 'The Pillar Stone' and 'Cloghavilla' (M. J. and C. O'Kelly 1981, 36). Some may have served as boundary markers and some marked the sites of graves. It is also true to say that some serve as very convenient scratching posts for cattle and a few may have been erected for that very purpose.

Of the excavated examples it has been found that some had cist graves at their base. The Longstone Rath, at Furness, Co. Kildare, an embanked enclosure with external fosse resembling a ringfort, contained at its exact centre a granite monolith, 5.3m in height above ground level and 6.4m in total length. At its base was a long cist, much disturbed, which contained the cremated remains of two adults. There were three sherds of pottery (possibly those of a Cinerary Urn) as well as a stone bead, a flint scraper and fragments of what was identified as a stone wristguard or bracer, which would seem to argue a Beaker/EBA date for the cist at least. The excavation (Macalister *et al.* 1913) did not establish the status of the enclosure. The Long Stone at Punchestown in the same county is 7m in total length and there was a short cist at its base which was empty and without grave goods (Leask 1937, 252). At Carrownacaw near Downpatrick in Co. Down, excavation was carried out at a 'Long Stone' about 3m in height (Collins 1957). It stood outside the fosse of what may have been a destroyed ring-ditch. A sherd of pottery and some flints of possible Neolithic/EBA date, together with some specks of cremated bone, were recovered from the fosse. Another 'Long Stone' at Drumnahare in the same county was little more than a metre high above ground level. The cremated bones of an adult were found but no grave goods (Collins 1957). A third stone at Ballycroghan had a short cist at its base.

To the ESE of Newgrange and visible from the mound are two standing stones. The area around the base of the larger one, Site C, has been excavated (Shee and Evans 1965) and while some eighty pieces of flint were found, there were no diagnostic artefacts. Because the field has been tilled repeatedly in the past it is not certain that any of the finds were directly associated with the standing stone. Similar flints can be picked up in any ploughed field in the area. The date and purpose of erection, therefore, remain indeterminate.

119 The Long Stone, Punchestown, Co. Kildare

Stone alignments

There are two major concentrations of stone alignments, one in the north in
Derry, Tyrone and Fermanagh, and the other in west Cork and Kerry. In the
latter area the distribution of alignments and of stone circles coincides closely
with that of wedge tombs. There are some alignments in Clare, Limerick, Mayo,
Tipperary and Waterford also. A study (Lynch 1976) of the west Cork/Kerry
examples defined an alignment as three or more standing stones intervisible and
lying in a straight line. Out of a total of four hundred sites examined, about thirty-
seven fitted this tight definition. Many had to be classed as ruined alignments
because one or more of the stones had fallen.

There are a number of differences between the two major concentrations.
Those in Cork/Kerry have impressively tall stones, 2–3m high on average, and
there are some alignments where the stones are up to 5m high. The number of
stones ranges from three to six. In the main, they stand isolated from other monuments. The Derry/Tyrone group is found in close proximity to stone circles and
cairns, the stones are markedly smaller, being from 50cm to 1m in height, and
there can be as many as twenty-four stones in the row. The two groups are there-

120 Seisreach, near Donoughmore, Co. Cork, stone alignment

fore separate. Alignments are known in Britain also, and the Scottish group provides the closest parallels for the southern Irish examples. The Irish alignments, on the whole, do not compare well with those of Brittany.

The Cork/Kerry alignments are consistently orientated NE–SW, as are most of the wedge tombs. The stone circles have a similar orientation. Ann Lynch's researches have shown that of thirty-seven sites which came within her definition of an alignment, twenty-three had significant solar or lunar orientations and a few others may have been orientated on the planet Venus or possibly on the limits of the zodiacal belt (Lynch 1982). She suggests that the alignment builders were aware of the more obvious events in the solar and lunar cycles, as, for instance, mid-winter sunset and midsummer sunrise, and their observations of these points would not have required any detailed scientific knowledge but would have become quite obvious to a farming people who must have spent much of their time in the open during both day and night. There is nothing, therefore, to suggest that the alignment builders had made an organized systematic study of the movements of the celestial bodies. Lynch notes that only one instance of an equinoctial orientation has been recorded, that at Gneeves, Co. Cork (Lynch 1981a, 25).

Three-stone alignments are by far the most common and their average total length is 4.7 ± 1.5m. No quantum of measurement could be established for the monuments such as, to take but one example, the megalithic yard proposed by Alexander Thom (1967). It is possible that they were set out by pacing. It has often been stated that the stones of the alignments were graded in height, the tallest being at the north-east end, but this is not so: the stones are not consistently graded in any particular way. The alignments of the south-west are found on hillsides, not on the crests, and there are marked concentrations of them at the head-waters of such rivers as the Lee, the Bandon and the Ilen in Co. Cork. The fact that many are orientated on significant solar and lunar positions does not explain why they were built and if an answer to this question is ever to be obtained, much excavation must be done.

The dating of alignments is in an uncertain state. Few have been excavated – three in Ireland: Maughanasilly in Co. Cork, Cashelkeelty in Co. Kerry and Beaghmore in Co. Tyrone; one in England at Cholwichtown, Lee Moor in Devon (Eogan 1964a) and one in Scotland at Duntreath in Stirlingshire (MacKie 1973). There was little direct evidence in the way of finds to date any of these sites. The Beaghmore complex of circles and alignments became peat-covered and began to become visible only as the peat was cut away for fuel (Pilcher 1969). Radiocarbon dates were within the very broad date bracket of 3485 ± 55 BP and 2725 ± 55 BP.

The Cashelkeelty site is about 20km west of Kenmare in Co. Kerry, at an altitude of 110m Ordnance Datum. The monuments are situated on a peat-covered ledge on the slope of a mountain and before excavation commenced they could be seen to consist of a stone circle with a recumbent stone and two standing stones; to the south was an alignment of three tall standing stones; to the west were the remains of another circle. Excavation revealed that the alignment originally consisted of four stones and that the circle had five stones. In the centre of the circle there was a cremation burial. The circle to the west, though almost completely destroyed, had originally contained eleven to thirteen stones (Lynch 1981, 65).

Pollen analysis showed that the earliest activity on the site was a period of cereal cultivation, radiocarbon-dated to the beginning of the third millennium BP. The first stone circle was erected shortly after, according to dates obtained from charcoal embedded in the old ground surface and in the stony soil above it. From stratigraphic evidence it was estimated that the alignment had been erected before the circle. No traces of settlement were recovered.

The Maughanasilly alignment of five standing stones is situated on a peat-covered hillock 213m OD. Lynch (1981, 71) concluded from her investigation that the circles and alignments were connected with funerary activities and that the construction period lay within a very similar date-bracket to that obtained for Beaghmore.

The Beaghmore site is situated in the foothills of the Sperrin mountains in Co. Tyrone near its border with Co. Derry. It was first excavated by A. McL. May between 1945 and 1947 when turf cutting had begun to expose the various monuments. He said of it:

> Extensive areas of hillside are covered still by blanket peat. In one such bog we found our complex slowly appearing as the local farmers stripped the peat. For miles around, on land denuded of turf, standing stones, now leaning or prone, push their tops through the heather; here and there imposing heaps suggest larger structures wrecked thoughtlessly or wantonly long ago. (May 1953, 174)

Elsewhere (*ibid.*, 175) he remarks: 'The visible standing stones number 1269, and cover some acres. The full extent of the complex must remain a matter for conjecture until all the turf has been cut.'

The site was re-examined in the 1960s and a far-reaching investigation carried out involving excavation, extensive pollen analysis, radiocarbon sampling, and so on, in order not only to date the site but to endeavour to give as full an environmental history as possible. Although the chief concern here is the archaeological content, it must be mentioned that the palaeoecological record (Pilcher 1969) makes impressive reading. It gives a history of the vegetational changes which occurred in this particular area west of Lough Neagh from about 7000 BP until the present day. Of particular interest is the period between AD 1700 and 1850 when it was shown that intensive potato cultivation had spread over areas never previously tilled. The dependence on this food source was to be the undoing of the population when the Great Famine broke out between AD 1846 and 1848.

At present the exposed part of the complex covers something over half a hectare, and in all seven stone circles, eight alignments and twelve cairns are visible. Three others can no longer be seen. Neolithic pottery was recovered by McL. May from hearths beneath the stratum to which the complex belongs, and he recovered a Tievebulliagh axe from a cist in one of the cairns. Other than the above, finds were meagre (Pilcher 1975). Several circles have tangential alignments and some of the cairns contained cists with bone fragments. In the main, all the stones used were small and the cairns and circles were of small diameter,

121 Part of the Beaghmore, Co. Tyrone, complex of stone circles, cairns and alignments after conservation

233

being about 3–8m. One circle was completely filled with hundreds of small boulders carefully set upright. McL. May examined ten alignments and noted that each ran in an E–W direction and that all led up to within a metre or so of one of the cairns. Six of them were in pairs. It is not easy to understand or explain the various features of this site but Pilcher (1969, 89) says that it may be assumed that: 'In the absence of evidence to the contrary, the circles, alignments and cairns were built at one time . . . in the later part of the Bronze Age.'

In the 1960s also, conservation was carried out at a stone circle at Drumskinny, Co. Fermanagh (Waterman 1964). In the course of the work it was discovered that a small cairn or setting of stones was also present near the circle. Aligned on the centre of the cairn and extending southwards for about 15m was a row of small stones which were twenty-four in number originally. No evidence of date was forthcoming nor was there evidence of burial.

Drumskinny is only one of many such complexes in mid-Ulster, notably in Co. Tyrone, but they also occur in Derry and Fermanagh. A stone circle excavated at Castledamph in Co. Tyrone (Davies 1938) produced a cist containing cremated human bone beneath a cairn within the circle. Again, this circle and others nearby were associated with cairns and alignments. A feature of the mid-Ulster sites appears to be that they are found above the 152m contour.

Stone circles

As well as the stone circles mentioned above which are part of a complex of features, this type of monument is found sporadically in other parts of the north of Ireland and also in Dublin, Wicklow and Limerick, and there is a major concentration in west Cork/Kerry. The latter were surveyed during 1970–3 by Seán Ó Nualláin on behalf of the Archaeological Branch of the Ordnance Survey (Ó Nualláin 1975; 1984) and he located ninety-three examples. Some of the circles are damaged but most are well preserved. Forty-five are of the five-stone type and forty-eight have, or have had, more than seven stones (Ó Nualláin 1984, tables 1 and 2). Ó Nualláin refers to this group as multiple-stone circles. The number of stones in the latter ranges from seven to nineteen, though circles with nine, eleven and thirteen stones predominate. The diameters range from 2.5m in the five-stone circles to 17m in the largest at Kenmare, Co. Kerry, which has fifteen stones. All the stones are free-standing and are in uneven numbers.

The circles possess a feature so far not recorded elsewhere in Ireland. Two adjacent orthostats are taller than the rest and mark the entrance. Diametrically opposite, in the south-west quadrant of the circumference, is a recumbent stone (Ó Nualláin terms this the 'axial stone'), that is, one in which the long axis is usually horizontal instead of vertical. The name 'recumbent stone circle' was applied to these monuments by Vice-Admiral Boyle T. Somerville who became interested in the west Cork stone circles and as early as 1909 he noted the orientational significance of the Drombeg stone circle (Somerville 1930). He also noted the similarity of the circles to the recumbent stone circles of north-east Scotland. It might be felt, therefore, that Somerville's terminology should be retained as a tribute to his pioneering work.

The circle orthostats normally decrease in height from the portals to the recumbent stone and a diameter drawn centrally between the portals and across the centre of the recumbent forms an axis of symmetry for the circle. John Barber has shown a number of ways in which the axis may be emphasized. He has also shown (Barber 1973) that the axis was orientated on significant solar and lunar events and perhaps also on a few of the brighter stars, the planet Venus, and the limits of the zodiacal belt, the same orientations as Lynch found in the stone alignments described above (but see Heggie 1981, 183). In three excavated sites in Co. Cork, the axis of one, Drombeg (Fahy 1959), when projected to the local horizon marks the point of sunset at the winter solstice and in another, Bohonagh (Fahy 1961), sunset at the equinoxes. In the third, Reenascreena South (Fahy 1962), the axis lay 24° to the south of the point of equinoctial sunset and a convincing orientation was not determined.

Much discussion of this aspect of the stone circle problem has taken place in recent times and Alexander Thom and others have made some remarkable claims

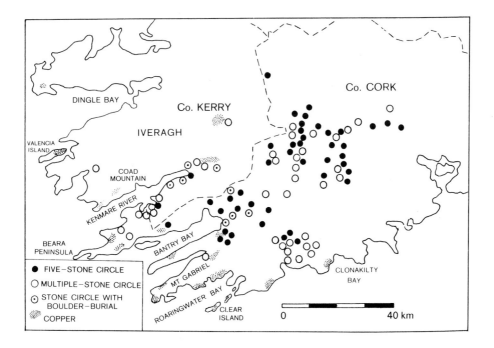

122 Distribution map of west Cork/Kerry stone circles (after S. Ó Nualláin)

for certain sites. There seems to be no doubt that orientation was important to Neolithic and Bronze Age peoples, not alone in stone circles, but also, as we have seen earlier, in megalithic tombs. But whether the more extravagant claims that have been made will ever be substantiated or not, it is difficult to say in the present state of our knowledge. The work of Barber and Ó Nualláin has shown that, apart from the five-stone group, the west Cork/Kerry circles are for the most part fairly true circles, though Barber found that there was no evidence that a metrical quantum such as Thom's 'megalithic yard' (83cm) was used in their construction. Internal monoliths are present in ten of the multiple-stone circles. Such monoliths are not centrally placed. External monoliths are present at three multiple-stone circles and at four five-stone ones. These and other associated features are detailed in Ó Nualláin 1984, table 3.

Each of the three West Cork sites excavated by Edward Fahy was found to contain a single cremation burial, centrally placed at Drombeg and Bohonagh but quite eccentrically at Reenascreena South. The latter site, though resembling Drombeg in many respects, was dissimilar in that it was encircled by a ditch and outer bank. The circle consisted of thirteen stones, and the axis of symmetry

123 Drombeg, Co. Cork, recumbent-stone circle

passes from the centre of the recumbent stone through the portal gap. At Drombeg the bones were contained in a pottery vessel but there were no grave goods in the other two sites. The pot seemed originally to have been about 26cm in height with a flat base and the ware was not unduly coarse. A slurry, some of which survived, had been applied to the outer wall of the pot (Fahy 1959, 12). Charcoal found with the bones unfortunately gave anomalous radiocarbon dates in the first millennium AD. A five-stone circle excavated by John Barber in the 1970s at Cashelkeelty had a cremation burial in a slab-covered pit at its centre but there were no grave goods. It must come within the date bracket established for the Cashelkeelty complex as a whole. If these stone circles were centres of ritual or of some cult practice or other there is as yet no evidence as to the nature of the rites performed, and the same is true of circles elsewhere in Ireland.

Boulder dolmens

Before going on to discuss stone circles elsewhere in Ireland, boulder dolmens (or 'boulder burials' in Ó Nualláin's terminology) must be mentioned as they are intimately connected with the stone circle complex of west Cork/Kerry. They consist of a large boulder capstone of megalithic proportions resting on three or

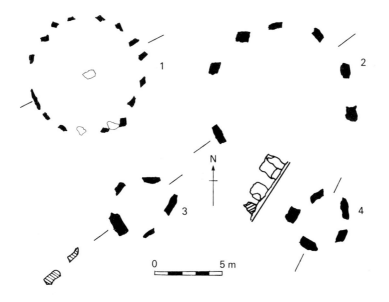

124 West Cork/Kerry stone circles, methods of emphasizing the axes:
1 radial portals, 2 normal method, 3 outlying stones on line of axis,
4 decrease in height from portals to recumbent stone (after J. Barber)

more low boulders. Only one has been excavated, at Bohonagh, Co. Cork (Fahy 1961). This is one of a group of three which are almost within sight of one another. The excavated example was 18m east of the Bohonagh stone circle mentioned earlier. It had a large boulder capstone resting on three low boulders and there was a clearance of only 35cm between the capstone and the ground. A cremation burial in a shallow pit was found beneath the capstone, but there was no evidence of date.

In the course of the 1970–3 survey of the stone circle complex, fifty-two boulder dolmens were identified and a summary of the findings together with a very useful catalogue of all the sites has been published (Ó Nualláin 1978). Eight examples occur within stone circles, there seems to have been no special rule of orientation and there is no evidence of the existence of a mound or cairn. Ó Nualláin remarks (1978, 79–80; 1984, 8) that boulder dolmens occur in areas in west Cork and Kerry where copper deposits are known and he links the stone circles and the wedge tombs in the same area with these copper lodes. He states that these three types of monument 'together occupy most of the copper-bearing districts of south-west Cork and Kerry and . . . there is a dominance of particular classes of monuments in certain of these districts' (Ó Nualláin 1978, 80). He notes that the boulder dolmens are associated with a greater number of copper-bearing areas than either stone circles or wedge tombs and goes on to say (*ibid.*):

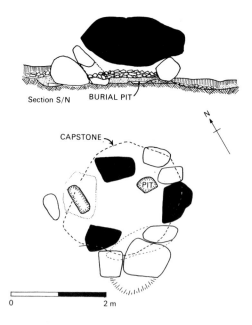

125 Bohonagh, Co. Cork, boulder dolmen (after E. M. Fahy)

'Indeed the close correspondence between their distribution and the copper lodes suggests that they may well represent specialist groups of prospectors.'

While there may be a connection of some kind between these different types of monument and the exploitation of copper, it must be borne in mind that the number of excavated sites is small in the extreme and that datable finds were virtually absent. Only four circles have been excavated in Co. Cork, that is, the three mentioned earlier and one at Kealkil (Ó Ríordáin 1939), and in Co. Kerry, there are the two excavated examples at Cashelkeelty. There has been only one excavation of a boulder dolmen and two of alignments. Of the wedge tombs, four were excavated in the Iveragh peninsula in Co. Kerry (Herity 1970), in the heart of a copper-bearing area, but produced no grave goods nor any evidence of date. A cremation burial was found in one of them. It seems to the writer that it is premature to formulate wide-ranging conclusions from the few snippets of firm evidence available at present.

Other stone circles

While the Cork/Kerry and the mid-Ulster sites are the best known, the Lough Gur area has also been mentioned (p. 139) in connection with stone circles of various types. There are a number of examples in the east of the country in Co. Louth, Co. Wicklow and on the Kildare–Wicklow border. In the west there are some in Co. Mayo and Co. Galway (Ó Nualláin 1984, 77). In the main, very little is known about them. The majority of circles are deemed to lie within the Bronze Age, but the kind of painstaking investigation applied to Beaghmore and to some of the west Cork/Kerry sites has not yet been undertaken.

Rock art

A form of art comparable in some ways to that found on passage tombs is known as rock art, so called because it is found on natural rock exposures and outcrops but also on loose stones and on some standing stones. The best and most prolific examples are in the south-west of Ireland in Cork and Kerry (O'Kelly 1958b; Anati 1963; Shee 1968; Shee and O'Kelly 1971), where, incidentally, no passage tombs are known. Rock art is found intermittently in Ulster and Leinster and there are a few examples in Connaught. It is well represented in the north of England and in south-west Scotland. The devices were executed in the same way as those of passage grave art, that is, picked on the stone with flint or quartz points. There is some incised rock art but its status is not established and it is possible that some or all of the known examples are recent.

While the commonest motif is the cupmark, stones that contain only this are not considered here as representative of rock art unless the motif is further

126 Distribution map of stone circles (after S. Ó Nualláin)

augmented by the addition of concentric or penannular circles or curves and so on. Dots are common, sometimes in clusters, and also radial patterns, ovals, and even spirals similar to those of passage graves can be found, particularly in Scotland.

There is an undeniable similarity between some passage grave art and rock art since there is a degree of overlap between their respective repertoire of motifs, but in general there are more differences than similarities. Which came first, or were both contemporaneous but expressing separate artistic traditions? Elizabeth Shee (1972) describes three decorated stones from the townland of Ballinvally, Co. Meath, all three now on display in NMI. One was found in a fence in the late 1800s, another during land reclamation in 1969 and the third formed the cover of a cist grave which contained a cremation and a Vase Food Vessel. Notwithstanding the fact that all three came from within a few kilometres of the Loughcrew passage grave cemetery where there is a substantial body of passage grave art, as Shee points out, the two 'loose' stones belong stylistically to

127 Rock outcrop at Derrynablaha, Co. Kerry, showing characteristic rock art motifs

the rock art group. She remarks that: 'one might have expected the presence of so many decorated tombs in the Loughcrew cemetery to have influenced the rock art, provided, of course, that the tombs are earlier in date than the rock art, and this is by no means proven' (*ibid.*, 231).

In attempting to forge a connection between rock art and passage grave art, one of the difficulties concerns the almost total exclusiveness of the distribution of the two types, apart from the example quoted above and a few others. It has been argued that Irish rock art had its immediate origin in the rock art of Galicia in north-west Spain and that of northern Portugal, this in turn deriving from the Mediterranean. The reverse may equally well be true, because certain of the devices of Gallego-Atlantic rock art seem more closely related to the Irish art than to anything that preceded them in Iberia (Shee and O'Kelly 1971, 75). The passage grave connection still remains unclear as it is undeniable that, for instance, certain stones at Loughcrew bear rock art motifs (Shee 1972, 229) and a good deal of what has been termed the 'hidden' ornament at Newgrange resembles rock art in some respects (C. O'Kelly 1973, 363–4).

Researches in Scandinavia suggest a passage grave origin for the earliest examples of the rock art of Sweden. In the Scandinavian countries as well as in the north of Italy the practice of decorating exposed rock surfaces goes on through the Bronze Age, when elaborate pictorial scenes replaced the earlier geometrical patterns. In some instances the later pictures can be seen to overlie the earlier spirals and circular motifs. Also, the techniques used by the Bronze Age artists differ from those employed in the earlier, more abstract type of rock art.

All the Irish rock art motifs are geometrical, as are the passage grave ones. A full corpus of the Irish material is needed before any degree of finality can be reached in the matter of the interaction of influences and also in the matter of date. There are over eighty recorded examples of rock art in Ireland, confirming the marked concentration in Cork and Kerry (Shee 1968, 144).

Three short stone cists have decoration on the underside of the covering slabs: Ballinvally, Co. Meath; Moylough, Co. Sligo; and Hempstown Common, Co. Kildare. The repertoire of picked motifs is limited to circles, arcs and lozenges, and Shee (1972, 231) regards it as closer to the passage grave repertoire than to that of the Irish rock art. She compares it to similar motifs found on the cover and side slabs of decorated cists in the north of England and in south-west Scotland where eleven decorated cist-covers are known, all but two in Scotland (Simpson and Thawley 1972, 100–2).

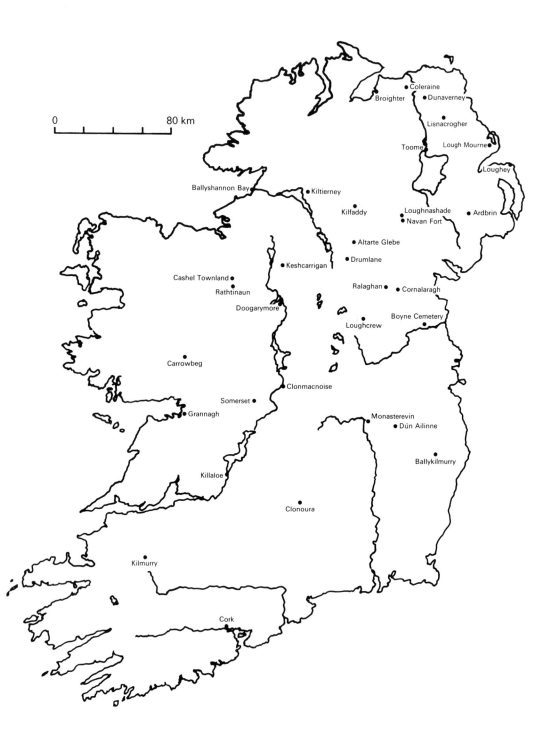

128 Early Iron Age weapons, tools and ornaments

10

The Iron Age

This is probably the period in Irish archaeology about which there is least certainty and most speculation. Its beginnings merge with the so-called Dowris Phase of the LBA and, in the absence of a Roman period such as is present in Britain, it shades almost imperceptibly into historic times with the coming of Christianity in the fifth century AD. The period is such a nebulous one that fixed points of reference are well-nigh absent, and instead attempts have been made to ally developments in Ireland with those in central Europe where two major well-defined phases of Iron Age culture can be recognized. It is becoming increasingly evident that Ireland, while susceptible to influences emanating from Europe and from Britain at this time, did not witness either wholesale invasions or folk-movements or large-scale importations of manufactured objects. Nothing beyond the normal amount of intercourse and contact – and perhaps movement – between Ireland and these regions can be detected in the archaeological record at present. Admittedly the record is very inadequate; settlement and burial sites are limited in number and the artefactual evidence is almost entirely of an unassociated nature, without context, and as often as not, without provenance. Apart from what can be gleaned from relative typologies and comparisons with documented material elsewhere, the industrial aspect of the metal industry stands alone.

The European Iron Age

Hallstatt

By about the middle of the second millennium BC knowledge of iron had come to central Europe following a slow spread westward from ultimate origins in the Near East. At first its use was sporadic; it was employed mainly as a decorative material, as for instance on the hilts of bronze swords, but by the beginning of the seventh century BC it began to occupy an important place in the economic life of the communities in the areas now known as Bohemia, Bavaria, Upper Austria, Switzerland and eastern France. The material culture of these iron-using peoples is given the name Hallstatt after an important cemetery near a village of that name in Austria. The cemetery contained upwards of 2,500 graves, a majority of which can be dated to the oldest phase of the European Iron Age. Hallstatt was an

245

important station for the export of salt, and it is not surprising that some of the graves indicate by the richness and variety of the objects deposited with the dead, particularly in the great number of metal objects, that a rich and evolved society was in question, handling and frequently imitating objects imported not only from the great classical civilizations but from the extreme corners of Europe. Nor was the cultural traffic all one-way because Hallstatt influences reached as far as Iberia, Britain and Ireland.

The Hallstatt culture is associated with an aristocracy. The dead, presumably the more illustrious or important persons, were buried in wooden chambers beneath barrows. The unburnt corpse was laid on a four-wheeled waggon or cart, or the dismantled parts of one were placed near it. The male corpse was equipped with an iron sword and spears, and pottery and various horse-trappings were laid nearby. Female skeletons were adorned with brooches, bracelets and anklets, often of gold, and with beads of stone and amber and were accompanied by drinking vessels of bronze and silver.

La Tène

By the mid-fifth century BC the centre of power and wealth had moved north-wards and westwards to the Rhineland and the adjacent areas of present-day France, and the so-called La Tène culture came into being, named after a great deposit of weapons and other objects found together with some skeletal remains in a small bay in the south-eastern part of Lake Neuchâtel in Switzerland. The major part of the deposit dates to the second century BC and it is thus a late mani-festation of the culture to which it gives its name. The objects are believed to have been placed in the lake as some form of votive offerings; the presence of a small platform such as could have been used in the process being one of the factors that suggested this inference. The practice of depositing offerings in pools and lakes was a Celtic custom and La Tène has become the type-site of the European Celts. A comparable site was discovered some forty years ago at Llyn Cerrig Bach in Anglesey, Wales.

These two type-sites, Hallstatt and La Tène, form the basis on which the European Iron Age has been classified.*

During the La Tène period iron became common as the material for implements and weapons, bronze being used chiefly for ornamental purposes. The fact that an expansion and a burgeoning of the older culture was responsible rather than any influx of new immigrants is demonstrated in a number of ways, most notably in the continuation of the practice of rich burials, although now the

---

* Hallstatt is subdivided into 1 and 2 in the French system and into C and D in the German; La Tène is subdivided into 1, 2 and 3 in the French system and A–D in the German.

bodies were placed on two-wheeled carts or chariots. Some of the earliest La Tène objects were found in princely graves in the middle Rhineland. As before, the corpses were accompanied by rich ornaments, by drinking vessels and by swords. This culture reached far beyond the areas penetrated by Hallstatt influence and its contacts with the Mediterranean world were more widespread and sustained, as the contents of the chariot graves show. It is to these foreign contacts that one of the basic characteristics of the La Tène culture must be ascribed, namely its distinctive art style, which T. G. E. Powell (1966, 185) called 'the first conscious art style to be created in Europe north of the Alps'.

In addition to its Hallstatt inheritance, La Tène borrowed Eastern, Greek and Etruscan forms and ideas, with special emphasis on plant forms, and it imprinted what might almost be called a trademark upon them. The resultant style was curvilinear and abstract, repetitive yet varied, and above all, essentially decorative. At the height of its expansion, La Tène influence had spread over a wide area and could be found from France to south Russia and Asia Minor, disseminated by the Celts. Although by this time it had absorbed many extraneous influences and had promoted many regional developments, there was sufficient unity overall in the culture for affinities to be recognized between examples widely separated in a spatial sense. This unity is all the more remarkable when it is realized that there was no political unity to hold the Celts together even at the peak of their power. In addition to material culture, it is probable that they shared a common ancestral language, and it was no doubt these elements that first brought them to the notice of the classical civilizations on their southern borders.

The Celts

From the close of the sixth century BC, mention of a barbarian people corresponding to the Celts occurs in the works of historians and ethnographers, first from Greek sources and later from Roman. While many of the accounts best known today are late, they rely to a great extent on older sources and so take us back several centuries before the date at which they were written. Even Julius Caesar, whose descriptions might be expected to have relied on contemporary if not actual first-hand experience, often took his information from older authors. From about the mid-fourth century BC the accounts must be reasonably accurate, as, owing to their incursions beyond the Alps into the civilized world of the south and south-east, the Celts had by then literally entered upon the stage of history. T. G. E. Powell (1958, 52) has put forward the interesting hypothesis that the name *Keltoi*, which was used by the Greeks when speaking of a barbarian people to the north of them, was actually that of the dominant or royal tribe of the Hallstatt waggon-grave people and that it gradually became adopted by the inhabitants of the North Alpine cultural and linguistic province and its extensions.

The name *Keltoi* has generally been equated with the Celts as a whole, though David Greene (1964, 14) pointed out that:

> we cannot even be sure that Celtic-speaking peoples are meant when classical writers use the names *Keltoi* or *Galatae*, for these ethnic names were used with looseness – indeed, we do not know what *Keltoi* or *Galatae* meant originally but there is no evidence that they are Celtic words or that any Celtic-speaking peoples ever called themselves by those names.

Nevertheless, the balance of probability must lie in favour of the equation of these names with the Celts, and the genesis of the latter, as they were to become known to the classical world, may be attributed to the Hallstatt people with a reasonable degree of assurance. Later, as already noted, the centre of power shifted farther west to the Rhineland and the Marne area of France, where we find the beginnings of La Tène culture. To most archaeologists this latter is the true expression of the Celts, particularly in their artistic manifestations, so much so that La Tène has come to be synonymous with the archaeology of the Celts as a whole.

Language

No study of the Celts can afford to neglect the linguistic element, especially where Ireland is concerned. In linguistic terms 'Celtic' refers to a branch of the Indo-European family of languages that originated in the area between the Baltic and the Black Sea. This group is ancestral to most European languages of the present day as well as to a majority of those of north India and Persia. Linked to its spread in the third millennium BC was the exploitation of metal ores and the development of trade in these valuable commodities. The Indo-Europeans probably also had a common code of religious beliefs and a common semi-barbaric social organization consisting of the three elements of overlord, learned man and freeman, a structure that was to be exemplified much later in Irish society.

The ancestral language of the Indo-Europeans is purely theoretical in the sense that no factual record of it exists. From it, languages and groups of languages such as Celtic, Germanic, Italic, Greek, and so on, developed in due time. Except for Greek, these languages are also based on theory; no record of them exists. Linguists are divided as to the date at which Celtic became differentiated from the parent group. It has been proposed that it was a distinct element by 2000 BC and as such may have been spoken by the Late Neolithic/Bronze Age people as far west as Armorica, Iberia, and even Britain and Ireland, brought perhaps by the same influences that were responsible for the introduction of Beaker ware.

According to Myles Dillon (Dillon and Chadwick 1967, 2): 'it is better to regard as already Celtic whatever can be dated to the beginning of the second millennium BC'. This is no new view, for it was first expressed by Abercromby in his great work on Bronze Age pottery published in 1912, and by Hubert in 1934, but linguists nowadays favour a more conservative approach (Greene 1983) and do not usually propose a more precise date than some time in the first half of the first millennium BC at the earliest.

Nevertheless, the fact remains that there was an influx of new ideas, if not actually new peoples, at the beginning of Bronze Age times. It is only relatively recently that proof has been obtained that the Mycenaeans spoke a branch of Indo-European about the mid-second millennium BC, namely Greek. As far as Ireland is concerned, bearing in mind the so-far negative evidence for any large-scale invasion or immigration in Iron Age times, there may be something in the theory that, linguistically speaking, the Celtic roots of this country are very deep indeed.

The next stage in the evolution of Celtic, or 'Common Celtic' as it is usually called, was its separation into dialects, for three of which there is tangible evidence, namely, Gaulish spoken in Gaul, Brythonic spoken in Britain and Gaelic or Irish in Ireland. In early historic times Brythonic was to develop into Welsh, Breton and Cornish, and Gaelic into Irish, Scots Gaelic and Manx; there was no development of Gaulish owing to the Roman conquest of that territory. Early factual records of these three dialects survive, mainly in the shape of commemorative inscriptions. Archaeologically, the speakers of these dialects can be identified as the iron-using peoples of La Tène. The La Tène culture is well documented in Gaul and Britain, and the Roman conquests provided convenient demarcation lines at the younger ends of the time-scale, but since Ireland was very much a peripheral area, to judge by the comparative absence of any large body of material remains, one is forced to ask how and when the Celtic language became established here.

One of the most noteworthy and most publicized features differentiating the Gaelic – or so-called Goidelic – dialect from other known Celtic ones is the use of a k-sound, derived from an older q-sound, as compared to a p-sound in the others. The predominance of the q-form of Celtic in Ireland over the p-form in Gaul and Britain (though it must be said that no form is exclusive to either area) is taken by some authorities as implying that Gaelic is the older and may have become established before the development of Gaulish and Brythonic. This theory does not altogether take into account the occurrence of traces of q-Celtic in Gallo-Iberian and in Gaulish. Another possibility sometimes proposed is that Gaelic or Goidelic evolved separately in Ireland. Either proposal involves early separation of Goidelic from the parent branch and early development of the Celtic language in Ireland. The more conservative approach prefers to place

Goidelic on a level with the other dialects and to confine speculation to the factual evidence provided by inscriptions, place-names, words incorporated into other languages, and so on. Brythonic is known from Roman inscriptions and so also is Gaulish. Some light has been thrown on the language spoken in Ireland in the centuries before Christ by the Greek geographer, Ptolemy, who, about AD 150, gave an account of the British Isles and mentioned the names of nine 'cities' on or near the Irish coast. Scarcely any are unassailably identifiable with actual sites, though some of the names are linguistically Celtic. One of the supposedly identifiable 'cities' is *Isamnion* which has been equated with Emain Macha near Armagh.

Ogam

The earliest testimony of the earliest known form of Irish comes from ogam inscriptions. In the view of many linguistic scholars, the earliest of the inscriptions date to about the fourth century AD or a little before but in the opinion of James Carney 'the earliest possible date for its invention is not 400 AD as is widely assumed today. It is rather some time within the first century before Christ' (Carney 1975, 57).

Ogam is a cipher based on the Latin alphabet, and while it has been assumed that it was invented in Ireland after the knowledge of that alphabet and language had been introduced here by the earliest converts to Christianity, there are some who hold that the perfected cipher was introduced to Ireland from the European mainland where it had been invented and developed. Carney suggests that its place of origin may have been 'an area where Romans, Celts and Germans were in contact'; that it was 'brought into being by political or military necessity' and that: 'Its purpose could be to send messages, probably on wood, which if inter-

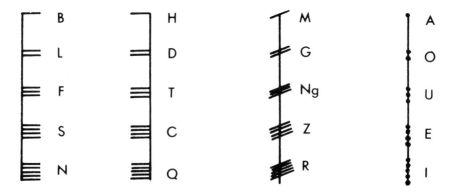

129 The Ogam cipher (after J. Carney)

cepted, could not be read or interpreted' (Carney 1975, 63). Ogam inscriptions on wood or other perishable materials have not survived on the Continent and there are no known inscriptions on stone monuments there either. A European mainland invention of the cipher must therefore for the time being remain questionable.

Some three hundred inscriptions have survived in Ireland, mainly in the south. There are 125 in Co. Kerry, eighty-five in Co. Cork and forty-seven in Co. Waterford; Co. Kilkenny has twelve and Mayo and Kildare have eight each. No other Irish county has more than four while many have only one or two. The largest number outside of Ireland is in Pembrokeshire in Wales where there are fifteen; ogam stones are found also in Scotland and in the Isle of Man. The letters used are represented by lines or by dots, up to five in number, cut or marked to left, right, on, or across, a central stem-line and are usually read from the bottom upwards. In the case of commemorative stones the edge or arris of the slab usually served in lieu of a drawn stem-line. The inscriptions are in very early Irish and David Greene makes the point that the language in them may already have been archaic and confined to the learned classes (Greene 1966, 10), whereas the language of the common people was already in the form now known as Old Irish.

130 Keel townland, Co. Kerry, ogam stone

R. A. S. Macalister has recorded all the inscriptions known up to 1945, and the numbers found since then are not great. In the introduction to his published *corpus* (Macalister 1945) he sets out the various formulae in which the inscriptions are written. These range from single personal names in the genitive case, e.g. 'stone of so-and-so', or names with the word *anm* prefixed, that is, 'name of' or 'soul of', to those where the father's name is also given and in some instances also, the name of the eponymous ancestor or ancestress. Sometimes too the person commemorated is said to be 'nephew of' or 'servant of' or 'grandson of', but the inscriptions are maddeningly uninformative about the doings of the persons named. There is no verb, adverb or adjective in any inscription. A typical one, from Co. Cork (now preserved in University College, Cork), runs in transliteration: GRILAGNI MAQI SCILAGNI – Grilagnos son of Scilagnos.

Early Irish literature

The earliest surviving manuscripts written more or less completely in Irish date from the twelfth century AD, but since much of the material had been copied and recopied many times from older manuscripts the content is older than the twelfth century. The eighth and succeeding centuries were the golden age of Irish literature, both prose and poetry being represented; much of the latter was incorporated in the prose texts. A great diversity of subject matter is present, but for convenience it is customarily divided into mythological tales, heroic tales, stories of kings, stories of the Fianna and romantic stories. One of the interesting facets of the literature, both prose and poetry, is that it was not conceived as written literature but was a setting-down of material already preserved in oral form. Thus, impressive as many of the stories are in the form now familiar to us, they are only imperfect renderings of what was essentially an oral medium and an oral art which was for hearing, not reading. The earliest written records of the vernacular literature, therefore, dating to about the seventh century, were preceded by an oral tradition which, given the professional training of its exponents, the *filid* or learned men, had preserved the material more or less intact for centuries. One may ask what length of time is envisaged for this process? In general, scholars concede a span of about three hundred years so that material contained in the twelfth century Book of Leinster, for example, may originally have been compiled in the fourth century or earlier.

Kenneth Jackson (1964, 52) interestingly illustrated the mechanics of this chain of reasoning in the case of the best known of the heroic tales, *Táin Bó Cuailgne*, popularly translated as 'The Cattle Raid of Cooley'. The earliest extant version of this story appears in a manuscript of about AD 1100 which had been compiled by conflating two different ninth-century versions. These in turn are thought to have been derived from a story known in the first half of the eighth century and which had already been recorded in writing in the mid-seventh century. Before this again a further three or more centuries of existence in oral form can be presumed, so that a saga like the *Táin* could, in theory at least, have been current in the fourth century or earlier, though not necessarily in the exact form recorded in the manuscripts.

Many scholars, however, believe that the Ulidian cycle of stories, to which the *Táin* belongs, does not reflect Irish society in the fourth century AD but that of a much earlier time – around or even before the first century AD. In preliterate days, Irish society was structured according to nobles, a learned class and freemen. The learned class was charged with the preservation in oral form from one generation to the next of a considerable body of material in which the tales, poems, genealogies, eulogies, and even the laws of society were enshrined. The laws were first written down in the seventh century or late sixth and in the eighth they were codified. D. A. Binchy (1954, 53) has pointed out that 'the pattern of society outlined in these ancient tracts goes back far behind the eighth century'. The structure outlined in the law tracts is basically the same as that of the continental Celts of nearly a millennium earlier; more striking still is its similarity to Hindu law, which shares a common Indo-European inheritance with Irish law. The law tracts are therefore an indication of the longevity of oral tradition as fostered and preserved by the learned class, and there is nothing inherently improbable in proposing a first-century or earlier date for the sagas also.

The Irish learned class, the *aes dána*, comprising poets, storytellers, lawyers, historians, wise men, and many other grades, had its counterpart in the *druides* of Gaul. Later, the word *druid* came to have a more restricted meaning than the one it enjoyed in Celtic Gaul where it embraced a wide variety of functions apart from its religious one. The same applied in Ireland originally although by the time the earliest references occur, the name *druid* was more or less interchangeable with *fili*, meaning wise man or seer. Another word held in common in Ireland and Gaul was *bard*, meaning 'the learned man in his function as the praiser of great men' (Greene 1954, 22). The Irish aristocratic privileged learned class preserved its records and promulgated its lore in oral form in the same manner as did its Gaulish counterpart. Julius Caesar expressly mentions that only oral learning was taught in the Gaulish schools. While Roman rule put an end to the Celtic way of life on the Continent, in Ireland this learned class continued until the end of the seventeenth century, when the last of the old order of Irish chieftains dispersed and with them went the patronage essential for survival.

Just as the Irish law tracts mirror many aspects of the society of Continental Gaul as revealed by the classical writers, so are the Irish heroic tales regarded as bearing witness to an earlier age when a type of warrior society existed in Ireland comparable to that of Gaul in the third and fourth centuries BC. Particular importance is attached to practices such as fighting from war-chariots, to boasting and duelling before battle, to feasting and to the 'champion's portion', and so on, all practices attributed by the classical writers to the Celts. Unfortunately we have no knowledge of the heroic literature of Gaul and have to rely on the above sources. It is instructive to reflect, however, that these characteristics are not confined to Celtic epic literature but are well-nigh universal, being found, to take but two examples, in Greek heroic literature of a thousand years earlier and in Teutonic literature of several centuries later. One must question therefore how much actuality is presented in individual exploits and events, certainly as far as Ireland is concerned. In view of the fact that so few material remains of the sort of society outlined in the sagas have been discovered, a doubt must remain as far as the archaeologist is concerned. As we shall see below, the tribal or kingly capitals mentioned in the sagas and chronicles, such as Emain Macha, the capital of the *Ulaid*, Dún Ailinne, the capital of the *Laigin*, and others, are complex structures containing the material remains of many periods from the Neolithic onwards. Very little material has been found that is consonant with the rich aristocratic warlike peoples portrayed in the heroic literature as occupying these sites, and, in fact, doubt has recently been cast on the authenticity of no less an item than the sword which figures so prominently in the exploits around which the sagas are centred. J. P. Mallory (1982, 107) asserts that 'the majority of datable motifs used to describe the swords in the tales fits best with the Viking period'.

The chariot, which is frequently mentioned in the literature, is one of the items advanced as evidence for a warrior society in Iron Age Ireland. It is equated with the Continental chariot associated with battles and princely burials, depicted on stelae and on coins, and frequently mentioned in the classical accounts. The chariot in one form or another is known in Britain, and although its use in Gaul had died out long before the Roman conquest, it continued to be used in Scotland as late as the third century AD. The chariot or cart burials found in Britain have already been mentioned, and indeed they continue to be discovered in East Yorkshire in the course of gravel digging; in Ireland chariots are portrayed on several of the High Crosses dating from the eighth century AD upwards, but factual remains in the shape of spoked wheels, poles, fittings, etc., are meagre in the extreme.

Various studies of the subject (Harbison 1971a; Greene 1972) draw similar conclusions about the Irish 'chariot', though that of Greene is based mainly on the evidence afforded by linguistic and literary considerations. The Old Irish was *carpat*, a word also used by the Gauls, later to be borrowed by the Romans as *carpentum*. Greene makes the point that this is the only word in the vocabulary of chariotry to be found in another Celtic dialect besides Irish and that the rest of the vocabulary evolved in Ireland. This factor among others led him to regard the Irish 'chariot' as a largely indigenous vehicle. He pictures it as consisting of a two-wheeled cart in which two could sit, one behind the other; the wheels were shod with iron tyres and the two horses were harnessed to a centre-pole by a yoke attached thereto. Harbison visualizes it as being similar in some ways to the two-wheeled carts in use in rural Ireland up to fairly recently, having large wheels and solid sides. The vehicle known from Continental representations on stelae, etc., was low-slung with arcaded sides and seems more built for speed than endurance and solidity. Both authors conclude that the so-called Irish chariot was used more for the transport of persons engaged in peaceful pursuits than in those of war.

In Greene's study (1972, 64) he assumes that the wheels 'had spokes, though no word for these is attested, because it was possible to see through them. A rough idea of their size . . . would suggest wheels larger than the three-foot diameter given by the Llyn Cerrig Bach tyre.' In his study of prehistoric block-wheels, A. T. Lucas gives diameters of the surviving Irish ones as about 1m, that is, a little larger than the Welsh example cited. While the Irish wheels are not spoked, they have lunate openings, one on either side of the axle-hole, large enough to see through. A pair of block-wheels of alder, found in a peat bog at Doogarymore, Co. Roscommon, in the late 1960s, provided radiocarbon dates. One wheel was intact and was dated to 2400 ± 35 BP and a surviving fragment of the second was dated to 2315 ± 35 BP. Lucas says of the wheels (1972, 31): 'While it cannot be assumed that a workaday vehicle of the period would necessarily have been equipped with wheels less well finished, the concern with appearance which the wheels so obviously manifest may denote that the vehicle to which they belonged was a symbol of social status or used for ceremonial purposes.' While no identifiable part of the vehicle to which the wheels belonged had survived, have we in these examples direct evidence of the *carpat* and was it a sort of multi-purpose box-cart with block wheels rather than the light elegant vehicle of Britain and the Continent?

An interesting anomaly remarked upon by David Greene is the lack of mention in the sagas of horse-riding. He adduces this as proof of the archaic nature of the literature, since horse-riding would certainly have been known and practised at the time the tales were written down. Against this must be set the fact that while the archaeological evidence for wheeled transport is very meagre there is abundant evidence for horse-bits and for the unique horse-trappings known as pendants. Barry Raftery has shown that these together 'constitute more than one quarter of the known metal objects referred to as of La Tène type from Ireland' (Raftery 1984, 56). They are fairly well dispersed, at least throughout the northern two-thirds of the country, and he says there are grounds for dating the earliest horse-bits to the second century BC or earlier. Therefore if, as Greene has suggested, archaism is the reason for the lack of mention in the sagas of the practice of horse-riding, it follows that the tales must relate to the period before it was adopted.

The archaeological evidence

Both phases of the European Iron Age are represented in Britain. From about the eighth century BC, elements characteristic of a North Alpine culture were becoming evident in the structure of farms and field systems and in pottery, bronze harness-fittings and waggon parts. True Hallstatt-type weapons of bronze and iron and military trappings began to appear from the end of the seventh century, perhaps the product of adventurers rather than of settlers or colonists, because evidence of elements connected with a settled domestic way of life were as yet absent.

131 Doogarymore, Co. Roscommon, block-wheel

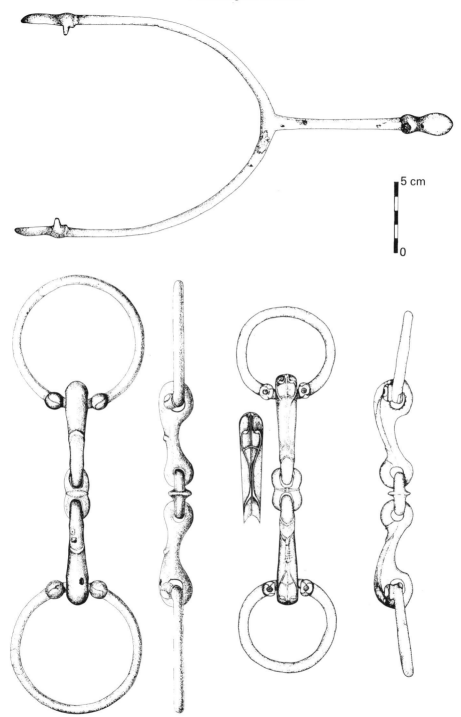

132 Three-link bronze horsebits; pendant (after B. Raftery)

La Tène influences are discernible in Britain from the latter part of the fifth century BC. The Arras culture of East Yorkshire with its square-ditched barrows and cart- or chariot-burials is an intrusive element dating to La Tène 1 with origins in the Champagne region of northern France. Some centuries later another continental link can be traced in the Belgae, a tribe recorded by Julius Caesar as occupying the north-eastern part of what was then Gaul. He mentions their initial incursions as raiders in the second half of the second century BC and their subsequent settlement in the south-eastern part of England. Caesar himself invaded in 55 and 54 BC but it was almost a hundred years before the Roman conquest proper took place.

The picture in Ireland is obscure by comparison. The Hallstatt phase of Europe and Britain is represented by a small number of objects only, and while they are more likely to be due to contact with the wider spheres of Hallstatt influence in Britain and Western Europe, it cannot be ruled out that adventurers or settlers from Britain and the Rhineland may not have been at least partly responsible. The trade routes established during the Bronze Age were no doubt still in operation, and the first knowledge of iron metallurgy must have come along one or more of them.

The La Tène phase is similarly, though more abundantly, represented, again by more or less portable objects, a few of which may have reached Ireland within a short time of the inception of that culture on the Continent, but the bulk of the material categorized as of La Tène type and art style is late by European standards, that is, first-century BC and first- and second-century AD, and is an insular Irish response to influences already widespread in Britain and Western Europe. The La Tène Iron Age is in fact represented in Ireland more by an art style than by a material culture; the princely tombs, the great cemeteries, the 'chariot-graves' and the distinctive pottery of Continental La Tène and its British counterparts are lacking, at least on the basis of such evidence as is available up to the present.

In Ireland, associations with the La Tène culture mainly lie in objects of gold, bronze, stone and bone, decorated in styles broadly linked with those current on the Continent and in Britain in the first three or four centuries before Christ. Slavish copying was never a feature of the Irish La Tène style; on the contrary, the artefacts are often a continuation in type from Late Bronze Age times but with the new-style motifs added. The Irish La Tène was not only insular but was also archaic to a degree as it continued to develop long after foreign exemplars had become extinct or obsolete. This is but one of the many reasons why it is difficult to provide a chronological framework for the Iron Age in Ireland. All too many of the objects are chance finds and too many of the sites attributed to the period are either peculiar to Ireland or are unproductive of diagnostic finds, so that attempts to define or delimit the period are beset with difficulties. At present, the chronology in so far as it exists at all is largely founded on art styles – not the most secure undertaking at best, but when applied to the kind of insular art found in Ireland it is doubly hazardous.

Unlike some other art styles, notably Greek art of the same period, La Tène or Early Celtic art is relatively uncomplicated, consisting of varied arrangements of curvilinear patterns. Not a whole lot of progressive development is possible, nor is it in fact attempted, so that differences in treatment of a particular design may merely reflect preferences or grades of prowess of individual craftsmen rather than chronological or typological progression. When to this inherent characteristic of the art style is added the fact that one finds La Tène-type motifs on seventh- and eighth-century Christian objects, one realizes that consideration of art style alone is insufficient for the positive identification of particular phases of Iron Age activity.

All one can say on present evidence – and this is very inadequate – is that the gradual transformation from a society based of necessity on the use of bronze for tools and weapons because it knew no other to one that was aware of the new metal, iron, but not yet accustomed to or practised in its use took place some time before the middle of the first millennium BC. We do not know precisely when iron began to replace bronze in Ireland in those spheres in which it was undeniably superior, but to judge by the available archaeological evidence the process must have begun about the middle of the first millennium BC. The fact that bronze continued to be used has caused some scholars to prolong the so-called 'Dowris Phase' of the LBA well beyond reasonable limits. The writer prefers to treat the prolongation as part of the customary and normal overlap between the demise of the old and the birth of the new, that is, a period of gradual and patchy transformation, and to bring within its scope monuments such as certain hillforts and crannogs, groups of burial tumuli and a few other sites, each in its own way a response to the environmental, social and technological changes that swept westward from continental Europe in the course of the first millennium BC.

Technology

It is probable that the slow spread of the use of iron was due to the difficulty of extracting the metal from its ores for, as is now realized, the smelting of iron is a more difficult process than is the case with copper; also, until the smith had learnt how to harden it, it was not superior to a good bronze. On the other hand, to make a good bronze two substances were needed, copper and tin, and while copper ores were available in Ireland, the necessary tin had to be obtained outside the country and transported across the sea. Iron ores such as limonite (bog ore) and haematite were readily available in Ireland as was also the timber for the making of charcoal fuel, so that no expensive imported additive was required. It must have been considerations such as these, as well as appreciation of its properties in relation to tools and weapons, that spurred on the native smiths not only to learn the techniques of iron smelting but also to learn how to harden the resultant metal during the subsequent process of forging.

The mines were open-cast and the rock had to be pounded and cleaned before being smelted. The same type of small bowl furnace used during the Bronze Age could be, and was, used for smelting iron. It consisted of a small pit scooped in the ground, about 30cm in diameter and 20 to 30cm in depth. Clay was usually plastered on to the sides and bottom. Fixed on one edge was a funnel-like piece of clay about 20cm in length and up to 15cm in maximum outside diameter. Lengthwise through it a funnel-shaped hole was made; the outer opening had a large diameter, up to 10cm, while the inner end which slanted downward into the pit or bowl was only about 2–3cm in diameter. A forced draught was directed through this opening when the furnace was charged. Fragments of these blast-holes or tuyères, though frequently found on excavations, have not always been recognized for what they are. The pieces that remain are the parts that were nearest the furnace and which were converted into a pottery-like substance by the heat.

In order to make the smelt, wood charcoal was charged into the pit and set alight. Layers of soft ore such as limonite were spread over the burning fuel and when the furnace was fully charged, a clay dome was built over the top, leaving a small hole at the centre for the escape of the gases. There was an essential difference in technique between bronze and iron smelting that had to be learnt by the ironworkers and carefully followed in practice. In copper or bronze working the smelted copper particles melted as they were produced and ran down through the fuel to form, when cool, a cake of metal in the bottom of the furnace bowl. When producing iron, however, the smelting temperature had to be tightly controlled between 1100° and 1200°C so as to *prevent* the iron particles from melting. If the iron did melt it absorbed carbon from the charcoal as it ran down through the fuel. This resulted in a hemispherical cake of iron/carbon alloy which was non-malleable and therefore useless to the smith since he had no means of removing the carbon again in order to restore malleability. Consequently, the result of his labour had to be discarded, and it was thus that at least some of the objects called 'furnace bottoms', common on Iron Age and later sites, were formed: they can be regarded as smelting failures.

The aim in smelting iron is to produce a sponge-like mass or bloom of iron particles which must not be allowed to melt. The air supply must be carefully controlled or the necessary saturation of carbon monoxide which is formed by the partial combustion of charcoal with air from the tuyère will not be maintained and the smelt will fail.

Fluxes such as lime or limestone do not seem to have been used in primitive ironworking and in experiments which the writer has carried out (O'Kelly 1961) their use did not improve the result. A continuous forced draught had to be maintained throughout and for this we used two sets of bellows, the blow-pipes of which were inserted loosely into the open end of the tuyère; we worked the bellows alternately in rhythm. The time taken to complete a smelt would vary for one reason or another but would rarely be less than four to six hours and a single charge of the furnace did not often produce more than about a half-kilo of usable iron. In order to remove the bloom of smelted iron, the dome had to be broken and for this reason it is not found intact on ancient sites. Indeed, since the bloom often became attached to the inside of the tuyère and to the inside of the furnace itself because of the residue of slag, the whole furnace was usually broken up in the process of extracting the red hot bloom. The bloom was then hammered on a stone anvil so as to weld the iron particles together and to knock away the slag and other waste surviving from the ore. After a succession of re-heatings and hammerings the piece of iron was ready for final forging into a knife blade or other desired object. Unlike copper, iron could not be cast in a crucible.

In finishing an object such as a blade it was laid red hot on an anvil dusted with finely ground charcoal and hammered. The surface of the hot metal absorbed enough carbon to become 'case hardened', that is, the outer layer of the metal became an iron/carbon alloy and therefore much harder than the body of the piece. Such case-hardening enabled the blade to be sharpened to a lasting cutting edge.

The smelting of iron ore by the method described above is a difficult technological process which is very unlikely to have been discovered by accident. If the technique was not imported and disseminated by immigrant practitioners it seems to us that the only way it could have been discovered was by smiths already well-trained in copper and tin smelting who, having seen iron products for themselves, experimented consciously with iron ores using their knowledge and skill. Once the difficult iron smelting and hardening techniques had been mastered they appear to have been practised on virtually every site of the maturer phases of the Iron Age and of the Early Christian period, to judge by the numbers of furnace bottoms, slag and furnace dross that are familiar from sites both in Ireland and in Britain. By a lucky chance, while we were pursuing our experiments in iron smelting, the excavation of some Iron Age huts at Kestor in Devon (Fox 1954, 40) produced a bowl furnace with a forging or heating pit nearby, very similar to what had been envisaged by us.

The artefacts

Hallstatt influence

From about the sixth century BC or earlier, influences from iron-using communities on the Continent began to manifest themselves in certain of the bronze artefacts, notably in the swords at first and chiefly in the northern two-thirds of Ireland. The so-called 'fish-tail' or 'eared' swords (Eogan's Class 5) derived from a mature stage of the Hallstatt culture of central Germany and Bohemia have been mentioned in an earlier chapter (p. 167). While a few may have been imported, in general they express an insular response to the sword fashions then current both on the Continent and in Britain. These Irish Hallstatt C-type weapons derive from the short Gündlingen type, though they are classed as short only because of the formidable length of the other type of sword then fashionable in Europe, that of Mindelheim. These average 85cm in length when complete.

A model in wood of the Irish Gündlingen-type sword was recovered from a boggy field in Cappagh townland, Co. Kerry (NMI 1960, 24). It was made in one piece but the point is missing. The present length is 34.5cm. The pommel was cut in one with the rest of the sword and since this component is almost always missing from finds of metal swords, its shape is of special interest. In cross-section it is in the shape of a truncated cone while in plan it is oval. J. D. Cowen, who has published a valuable study of bronze Hallstatt-type swords, remarks (1967, 393, n. 2) that 'this is the first decisive evidence to become available for the shape of the pommels of Gündlingen swords and proves that some at all events . . . did have simplified versions of the distinctive Mindelheim hat-form'.

In the past, the occurrence of these Hallstatt C-type weapons, particularly in Ulster, added strength to the theory of the invasion of this part of Ireland by a warrior aristocracy, and perusal of the heroic tales celebrating the exploits of the mighty Ulster champions did little to counteract the idea. Unfortunately nothing can be found in the archaeological record to substantiate it, since the majority of the weapons are unassociated. Cowen, reviewing both British and Irish examples, is of the opinion that the earliest appearances of Hallstatt C swords 'were due to trade, to the operations of travelling swordsmiths, or maybe to princely gifts and exchanges; that thereafter the imported varieties were quickly copied by local swordsmiths, with modifications of their own which led to the development of purely insular varieties' (*ibid.*, 422).

A curious fact concerning them is that well over half of the known total of Irish examples was found in or near rivers, lakes and marshy places, the courses of the rivers Bann and Shannon and tributaries particularly. The explanation offered has been that the weapons and other items of martial equipment were deliberately deposited in watery places in deference to some religious ritual. The same phenomenon has been noted in Britain and elsewhere. Over ninety metal objects were found in 1943 in a bog at Llyn Cerrig Bach in Anglesey, Wales, and it appeared that a series of deposits or offerings had been made over a period of time in what was then a lake. This took place in the two centuries before the coming of the Romans. The Rivers Shannon and Bann have been mentioned above as focal points for sword and other finds but we must also question to what extent the distributional pattern may have been distorted because of drainage or dredging in modern or relatively modern times. The dredging of the bed of the River Shannon, for example, was completed in the mid-1930s and of 617 archaeological objects recovered, five hundred were stone implements such as axes, chisels and so on, and fifty were stone line-sinkers. The prestigious metal items among the remainder, though very much in the minority, have naturally excited the most interest.

None of the scabbards or scabbard plates of the Hallstatt C swords have survived but a small number of the characteristic chapes are known, all but two being of the distinctive winged type (Eogan 1965, 174–6). The wing tips were very vulnerable to damage, as can be seen from the extant specimens, most of which are incomplete in some way. A complete specimen in NMI measures 16.2cm from tip to tip. While superficially the chapes might seem to constitute a clumsy attachment to the end of the scabbard, it has been suggested that the swordsman could hook one of the wings behind his thigh – or if on horseback, beneath his foot – to expedite the withdrawal of the sword from the scabbard. Spears must also have been common, but in the absence of any specific characteristics that would distinguish them from types in use earlier, examples in use concurrently with the Hallstatt-type swords cannot be isolated.

Cauldrons and situlae (buckets) of sheet bronze continued to be imported and to be made. A portion of a wooden cauldron or container of some sort, carved in one piece from poplar, was found in 1933 at Altarte Glebe, near Clones, Co. Monaghan. It was equipped with lugs cut from the solid which contained movable handles of yew. Except for the fact that the lugs are situated on the shoulder and not on the rim, it closely resembles the Late Bronze Age cauldrons. An interesting feature is the incised ornament below the rim, consisting of concentric patterns connected by tangential bands, the whole punctuated by dots (Mahr 1934). Incidentally, this was the first archaeological object in Ireland to be associated with pollen analysis.

A few items of ornament display Hallstatt influence: a small number of brooches of safety-pin type, a bronze bracelet with knobbed terminals, and a few 'swan's neck' pins. The knobbed penannular bracelet was found in a hoard at Kilmurry, Co. Kerry, with two plain bracelets, a socketed bag-shaped axe and a leaf-shaped spearhead. The bracelet can be paralleled in Alsace. The 'swan's neck' pins indicate a break with the previously dominant disc-headed form of Irish dress pin. An iron 'swan's neck' pin was found in the Rathtinaun crannog in Co. Sligo.

Tools and implements possibly underwent little change during this period as it had yet to be demonstrated how much longer-lasting an iron tool was than one of bronze which could so easily be made by the casting process. There are a few examples of iron objects copying bronze ones, two iron socketed axes, for instance, one from Toome and one from the Lough Mourne crannog, both in Co. Antrim. The artificers were obviously attempting to create in iron an object for which bronze was a more suitable medium. Clearly in these cases the different potentials of the two metals had not been grasped. Shaft-hole axes made from

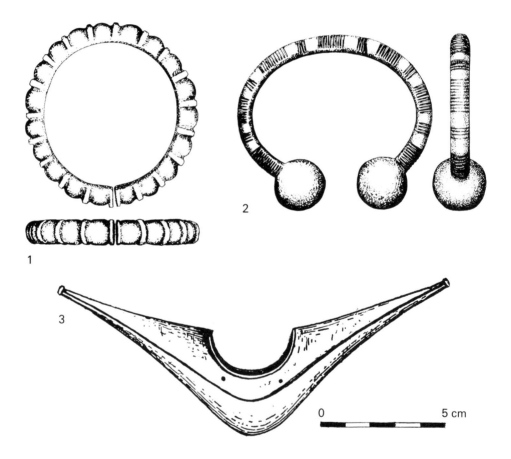

133 Hallstatt influence. Bronze bracelets: 1 and 2 Co. Antrim (after B. Raftery); 3 Bronze winged scabbard chape (Ireland, no locality) (after G. Coffey)

several sheets of iron are also known, one of them from Rathtinaun. A cauldron from Drumlane, Co. Cavan, was constructed from a number of sheets of iron riveted together in the manner of bronze vessels and it has been suggested that this may be another bronze/iron transitional piece.

One of the most attractive items linked with Hallstatt influence is a hollow bronze shaft, 29cm in length, at the end of which is a pair of solid bronze hooks. On the shaft itself two water-birds (swans?) with three of their young sail serenely along in line astern and are confronted by two smaller stockier birds, perhaps crows or ravens. Diametrically opposite each bird on the shaft is a free-moving ring (Powell 1966, 172). This object was found in 1829 at Dunaverney near Ballymoney, Co. Antrim, and is now in the British Museum. It has variously been interpreted as a flesh-hook for extracting meat from a vessel; a steelyard, that is to say, a mechanism or lever to which weights could be attached for the purpose of weighing; and the mount of a goad for horses. T. G. E. Powell (*ibid.*, fig. 170) illustrates somewhat similar stylized birds swimming up one of the legs of a ritual stand found in a grave in the Hallstatt cemetery itself. E. C. R. Armstrong (1924, 117) illustrates another 'flesh hook', also from the north of Ireland, but without the birds or rings.

La Tène influence

Artefacts that can be attributed to the final centuries of the first millennium BC and the opening ones of the Christian era are more numerous and more diverse in type. In addition to bronze, materials such as iron, gold, bone, stone, wood, jet, and so on are represented, and the ornament is different from the rather rigid geometrical motifs employed in the first half of the millennium. Unfortunately, once again the vast majority are without provenance, and just as unfortunate is the fact that in the past many of them fell at one stage or other into the hands of dealers and collectors who had little time for such a seemingly unimportant detail as exact provenance; moreover the dealers, and indeed a great many of the collectors also, had no time at all for the unimpressive and unattractive objects of iron. This must go a good way toward explaining the scarcity of the latter in our museums and collections today. To give but one example of what must have been all too common even in relatively recent times, Sir Cyril Fox tells how an iron wheel-tyre discovered at Llyn Cerrig Bach was thrown back into the bog again as of no interest.

The wholesale destruction that took place at Lisnacrogher, Co. Antrim, towards the end of the last century did untold damage to a deposit that rivalled in many ways the finds at Llyn Cerrig Bach and, even in its depleted form today, remains the major complex of material displaying La Tène influences in Ireland. Estyn Evans (1966, 48) quotes the late Professor Macalister as stating that when

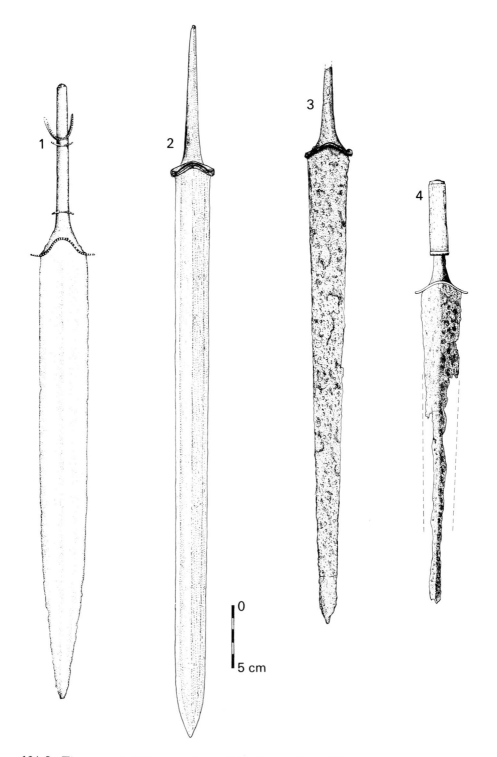

134 La Tène swords: 1 Lisnacrogher, 2 Ballinderry, 3 Dún Ailinne, 4 Lough Gur (after B. Raftery)

this site is mentioned every scholar must feel that a periodical Act of Humiliation should be performed in the shrine of Irish archaeology!

According to W. F. Wakeman, an assiduous and painstaking antiquarian who visited Lisnacrogher in 1883, the site was at the edge of a nearby drained lough, and he identified it at once as a crannog by its resemblance to Lagore crannog, which he knew well, and Ballinderry crannog. He noted a good deal of 'basket-like work' and timbers. The site had become revealed through the activities of turf cutters the previous year and many finds had already been made and speedily dispersed. As the turf cutting proceeded season by season, at least until 1889, so did the finds continue to be made until no trace of the site or its contents was left (Wakeman 1883–4; 1889; 1890–1). Wakeman described and illustrated a good many of the artefacts, among them the most prestigious items, the scabbard plates. It has been suggested that Lisnacrogher was not a crannog-type structure but a place of votive offerings, and it has also been alleged that the attribution of some of the finds, including the scabbard plates, to the site is dubious; that dealers gave the Lisnacrogher provenance to their wares in order to get a better price. If Wakeman's account had been other than virtually contemporary with the discoveries and if the man himself had been other than who and what he was, there might be firmer grounds for agreeing with the latter proposition. Wakeman was a schooled observer and a skilled antiquarian and there is no reason to doubt his accuracy. In the absence of evidence to the contrary it is only fair to assume that the site must have been devoted to metal working, perhaps highly specialized. Apart from iron swords and bronze scabbard plates, Barry Raftery notes that no less than seventeen spearbutts of the knobbed type were recovered. These were presumably fitted on the end of the spearshafts, and in a few cases traces of the wooden shaft remain. A few iron swords were found but except for one fairly complete example with a broad leaf-shaped blade and central mid-rib, they are represented mainly by their characteristic bell-shaped bronze hilt-guard mounts. Wakeman (1890–1, 542) illustrates one which had, he says, been 'somewhat recently found'.

The iron swords of the period are short, averaging 37cm to 44cm in length. The longest and best-preserved example is from Ballinderry and is 57.9cm in total length. According to Barry Raftery (1984, 62), up to the time of writing he could locate at most twenty-two specimens of La Tène type or affinities, either in complete or fragmentary form. There were a few others which could belong also, but corrosion made it difficult to be more certain. The distinctive bronze hilt-guard mounts when present offer one of the best indications.

An iron sword discovered in the thatch of a derelict cottage in Cashel townland, Co. Sligo, is of La Tène type (Rynne 1960), another came from the River Shannon at Killaloe and the most recent find is from the River Corrib (Rynne 1983–4). The excavations at Dún Ailinne, Co. Kildare, produced an example of

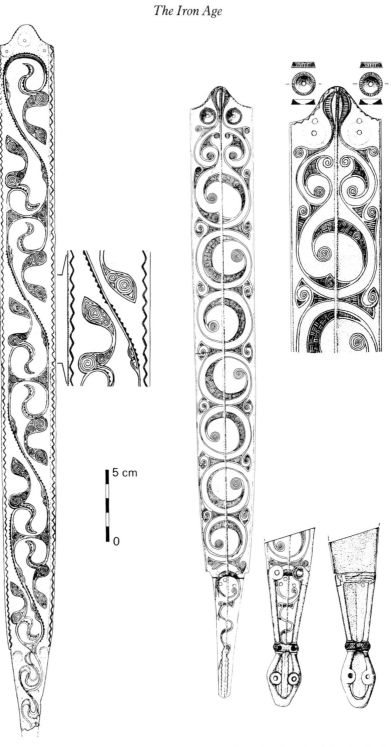

135 Bronze scabbard plates and chapes, Lisnacrogher, Co. Antrim (after B. Raftery)

the very short variety, the edges of the blade converging towards the point so as to give a triangular shape (B. Raftery 1984, 65). In some swords the organic grip survives, usually of animal bone (as in an example found at Lough Gur) or horn. The hilt plates rarely survive, and the pommels were even more vulnerable to destruction. A wooden sword of La Tène type found in Ballykilmurry Bog, Co. Wicklow, has a sub-conical pommel with rounded base. A half-cylindrical piece projects from one face of the blade just below centre point.

The bronze scabbard plates are among the most remarkable items of the period because of the quality of the engraved decoration. Of those that survive, a substantially complete scabbard, undecorated, came from Lisnacrogher together with three single decorated plates. Three other decorated plates came from Toome, Co. Antrim, and one from the River Bann (MMA 1977, pl. 17). They consist of slightly curved pieces of sheet bronze, each scabbard originally having two plates. The edges of one plate would have overlapped that of the other and both were squeezed together. A chape was fixed to the tip or tongue of the scabbard and of six typical chapes of openwork type which survive, three are still attached to their scabbards. The decoration on the scabbard plates was executed by means of a graver, a pointed metal tool held in the hand. Depending on the type of point, whether round-nosed, sharp, and so on, and also on the type of arm-movements used in the execution, different effects were produced. The process is interestingly explained and illustrated, with particular reference to the Lisnacrogher type, in Lowery *et al.* 1971. The ornament can be summed up as consisting of a series of flowing S-curves joined so as to give a continuous wave-like motion. All the patterns are abstract and curvilinear and were obviously the product of a highly skilled school of smiths in this north-eastern part of Ireland.

Items of personal adornment such as ring-headed pins with inlaid studs, a penannular neckring, bracelets and rings, all of bronze, also came from Lisnacrogher. Wakeman (1890–1, 673) records and illustrates two vessels made of sheets of iron riveted together, but of these no trace now exists. The absence of horse-trappings, such as bridle bits and associated objects, is notable.

Barry Raftery has produced two volumes (Raftery 1983; 1984) which catalogue and illustrate all the Irish artefacts of La Tène type, and he provides a detailed and informative commentary on them. These sources show that horse-bits and related trappings form the largest single group of La Tène-type bronzes in Ireland. It is all the more singular therefore that they were not represented at a site as productive as Lisnacrogher, and it lends added weight to the theory that a specialized workshop was present. The anomaly may also be due in part to the fact that two different periods of time are in question; perhaps the use of horse trappings became common only when the Ulster weapon-centre or centres were in decline or obsolete.

Of 135 recorded examples of Irish horse-bits (Raftery 1984, 15ff.) the great majority are of the three-link type. Some fine examples are known with raised ornament and red 'enamel' studs, the nature of the decoration being perfectly adapted to their slender shape. The objects most commonly found in association with them are the Y-shaped artefacts known as pendants, ninety-six of which have been recorded. They have no definite parallels outside Ireland and their purpose is unknown. Possibly they were suspended below the bridle.

In contrast, the evidence for wheeled or horse-drawn transport is very scant.

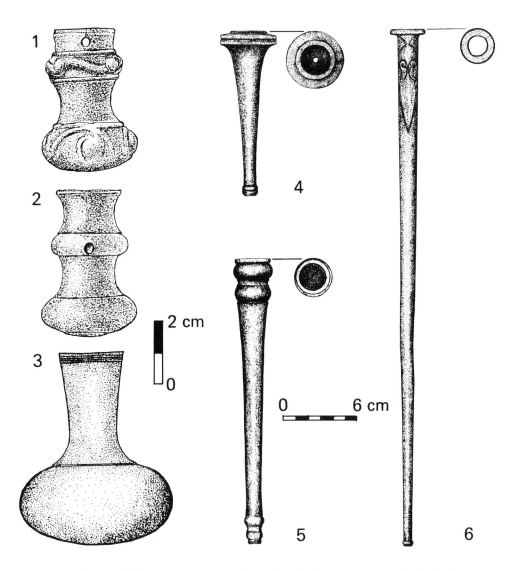

136 Spearbutts: 1–2 Lisnacrogher type, 3 doorknob, 4 conical, 5 and 6 tubular (after B. Raftery)

Mention has already been made of prehistoric block-wheels and of the references to chariots or carts in the early Irish literature (p. 254). Barry Raftery (1984, 57–63) notes the existence of bronze terrets (i.e. rings through which driving reins were passed), some wooden horse-yokes, and, from Lough Gur, two hollow bronze mounts which may have fitted on the ends of yokes.

The use of the spear is documented more by the survival of the terminals or butts of the spearshafts than by the functional part of the weapons themselves, that is to say, the actual spearhead, though a fine example is known from Lisnacrogher. Few spearheads are known for which an unequivocal Early Iron Age date can be claimed but the butts, on the other hand, after bridle-bits and pendants, constitute the single largest assemblage, to the number of over sixty (Raftery 1984, 110). They can be divided into knobbed types and into tubular and conical examples. The latter two are indigenous to Ireland but the knobbed ones are well known in Britain. There are two types of knobbed butts, the Lisnacrogher type and the doorknob type. These bronze butts are believed to have acted as terminals into which the spearshafts fitted. Two butts of the Lisnacrogher type were attached to sizeable lengths of shaft when found (B. Raftery 1982, 75). On the other hand, it has been pointed out (Raftery 1984, 119) that in the doorknob variety particularly, the orifice of the socket can sometimes be little more than 1cm in diameter, so the usefulness of such a slender shaft must be questioned except in matters of display or ceremonial. In all cases, however, the butts are striking and varied in shape and decoration.

Another item of equipment which might be expected to be represented in some quantity if the society of the period in question was as martial as is sometimes presumed is the shield, but in fact only a single example is known, found in Clonoura townland in Littleton Bog, Co. Tipperary. It is of rectangular shape, made of alderwood and covered in leather (NMI 1962, 152). On the front there is a raised boss made separately and this accommodates and protects the grip at the back, made of oak. A separate piece of leather is stitched on over the boss. The shield measures 57cm by 35cm. The shields of Late Bronze Age type made from organic materials have already been mentioned and possibly this practice continued in succeeding centuries, accounting for their poor survival rate. The bronze umbo or boss of a shield found on Lambay Island off the Dublin coast is of possible first- or second-century AD date but the associated finds are exotic in the present context.

To turn for a moment to what could be regarded as some of the more civilized accoutrements of the society of the period, the find of four bronze trumpets from a bog at Loughnashade, Co. Armagh, may be mentioned. The site is only a short distance from Navan Fort, which is identified with the kingly capital of the *Ulaid*, the people of Ulster. Only one now survives, a splendid specimen 186.5cm measured along the convex edge of the slender curved tube. The two edges are sealed from behind by a strip of bronze fastened to them by over six hundred rivets. The mouth or bell of the trumpet is decorated in repoussé technique. A trumpet from Ardbrin crannog in Co. Down contains no less than 1,094 rivets (Raftery 1984, 134–6). Several wooden specimens survive of which one at least, from a bog at Kilfaddy, near Clogher, Co. Tyrone, may be of Iron Age date (Raftery 1984, 136). The Loughnashade trumpet resembles one depicted on the famous 'Dying Gaul' masterpiece in the Capitoline Museum in Rome, a copy of a second-century BC bronze cast at Pergamon (now Bergama in Turkey) to celebrate the victory of the kings of Pergamon over the Gauls or Galatians. The Gaul is sinking into death accompanied by his weapons and horn, and around his throat is a torc.

Also relying on the technique of repoussé for overall effect as well as on the simplicity and elegance of the designs are a number of bronze discs from 24cm to 30cm in diameter, each with a sunken saucer-shaped hollow placed off-centre. Their function is unknown and they are unique to Ireland. Two of the seven known were found at Monasterevin, Co. Kildare. While different from one another in each case, the general lay-out of the designs resembles that on a crescentic plaque from Llyn Cerrig Bach, and also that on an object nearer home, the so-called Petrie Crown, so named because it was in the possession of the famous antiquary, George Petrie (1789–1866). Unfortunately it has no

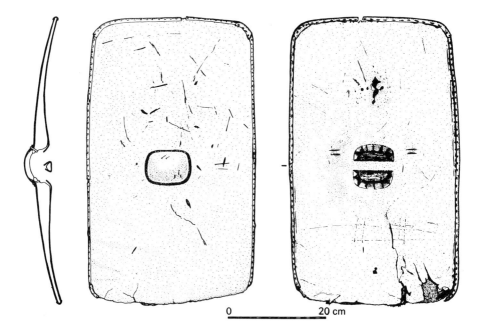

137 Clonoura, Co. Tipperary, leather-covered wooden shield (after B. Raftery)

provenance. The technique employed to achieve the ornament on the 'Crown' is the same as that used on the Cork helmet-horns and the Bann disc and is therefore, like them, presumed to be the product of Irish workmanship.

The Bann disc (Jope and Wilson 1957), found at Camus near Coleraine, Co. Derry, in 1939, is a good deal smaller than the Monasterevin examples and unrelated to them. It is only 10.5cm in diameter, is slightly concavo-convex, and there are three equally spaced holes in the circumference, one containing a bronze ring. The design is one of very fine sweeping trumpet curves ending in stylized birds' heads. The Petrie Crown is a more complex, though incomplete, piece. In its present form a frieze of sheet bronze supports an upright disc with a horn behind it. A second disc is present but the horn is missing. The same type of low-relief ornament is present as on the Bann disc. This complex object is fully described in MMA 1977, 89. The third piece, the Cork horns (O'Kelly 1961a), was found in made ground near the River Lee in Cork city in 1909. The object consists of three tall cones which are now separate pieces, but a strip of the mounting flange of one side-horn is held loosely by a single rivet to the centre horn. This piece of the flange must have become detached from the side-horn after they were found because, according to contemporary accounts, two of the horns were joined together when the discovery was made. It appears that the three were originally attached to some perishable material to form a helmet. They

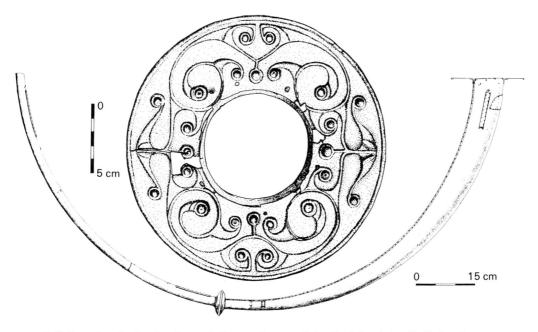

138 Loughnashade, Co. Armagh, bronze horn and detail of disc (after B. Raftery)

are now in the Cork Public Museum. The ornament has much in common with that on the Crown and on the Bann disc but the birds are absent. Close examination (O'Kelly 1961a) showed that the ornament was achieved by etching or tooling away the surface of the surrounding metal so as to leave the design in very low relief.

The same spare flowing design was used on one of the brooches of safety-pin type from Navan Fort. Here the central feature would have contained a stud, possibly of red enamel. There are five of these Navan-style brooches, two from the fort itself, and they differ from other Irish examples by virtue of their open-work bows displaying trumpet and lentoid boss ornament. In the majority of fibulae the bow is solid and is either rod-like or of elongated leaf-shape. The catch-plate is in the shape of a stylized bird's head or in that of a zoomorph of some kind. Since only about two dozen Irish fibulae of La Tène type are known

139 The 'Petrie Crown'

it must be presumed that the dress pin with head and straight shank continued in use together with ring-headed pins. These had a circular ring at the head and a straight shank, the whole normally cast in one piece. There is an S-bend in some of the shanks near the head, and there are numerous other variants.

Finally, two important hoards may be mentioned, one from the north of Ireland about which there was and still is a certain amount of controversy, and the other from the west. The so-called Broighter hoard constitutes the richest col-

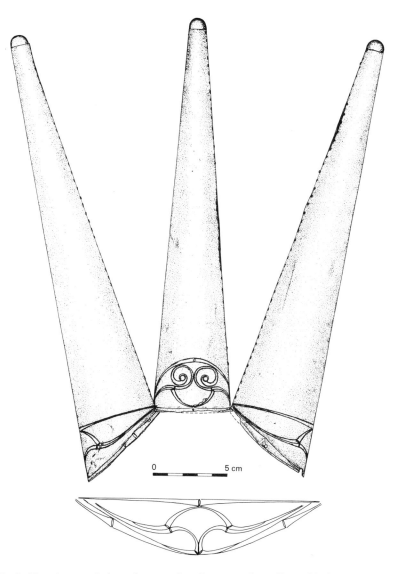

140 Cork City, bronze helmet horns; also diagram of motif on side horn (not to scale) (after B. Raftery)

275

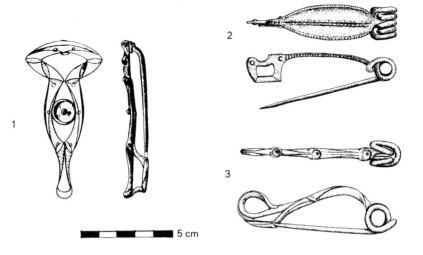

5 cm

141 Safety-pin brooches: 1 Navan type, 2 leaf-bow type, 3 rod-bow type (after B. Raftery)

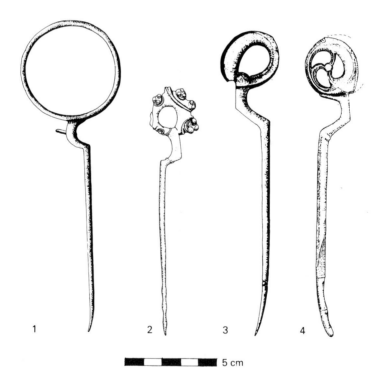

5 cm

142 Ring-headed pins: 1 Co. Antrim, 2–4 no provenance (after B. Raftery)

276

lection of gold objects of Iron Age date to be found in Ireland. The objects were discovered in 1896 when some land at Broighter, near Limavady, Co. Derry, near the shore of Lough Foyle, was being ploughed. The hoard consisted of a model boat with oars, mast and other attachments (Lucas 1973, fig. 34), a bowl, two chain necklaces, two rod-twisted neck torcs and a hollow torc or collar ornamented in repoussé work. The two chains were inside the collar and unfortunately most of the objects had been damaged by the plough. When news of the discovery became known the Royal Irish Academy claimed it as treasure trove but by this time it was already in the hands of a dealer from whom the British Museum subsequently purchased it. A tug-of-war then ensued between the two institutions for custody of the famous hoard. After a lengthy parliamentary enquiry and a lawsuit it was declared to be treasure trove, that is, the circumstances of the find had shown that it had been deliberately concealed by the owner with a view to eventual retrieval. Since the owner was unknown, according to law it was now properly vested in the Crown. At this time the whole of Ireland was part of the United Kingdom and the Crown was represented by King Edward VII who ordered the objects to be given to the Royal Irish Academy. This body placed them with its own collection of antiquities in NMI where they

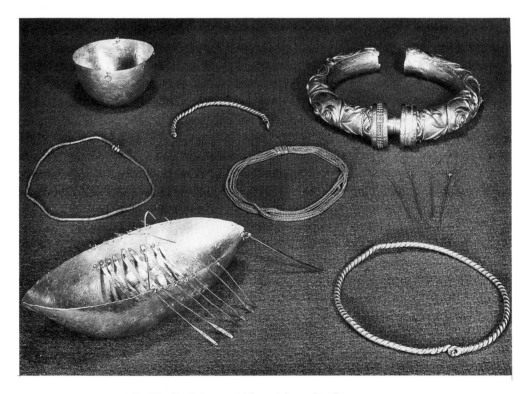

143 The Broighter gold hoard from Co. Derry

remain today. The trustees of the British Museum argued that the find-place had formerly been part of Lough Foyle and that the objects had not been concealed in any way but cast into the waters as a votive deposit. Had this been the case it would have meant that the owner had abandoned the objects and by law the finders, and subsequently the purchasers, would have been entitled to them. The find-place of the hoard is interestingly discussed by Richard Warner (1982, 31) and the find itself and the lawsuit by E. C. R. Armstrong (1933). In addition, Barry Raftery (1984, 183) provides some background information about the discovery that has not previously been available.

The hoard is controversial to this day. The gold collar has been claimed as an import from north-western Europe and the model boat and other items as of Indian origin. As Warner convincingly shows, however (1982, 29), 'there is not the slightest reason to doubt that the hoard represents a genuine associated ancient deposit'. The splendid hollow gold collar with buffer terminals and repoussé ornament is related to types well known in Britain (notably at Snettisham in Norfolk) and in Europe and is a masterpiece of craftsmanship. It is made from two plates of thin gold soldered together into tubular form. The repoussé ornament of trumpet patterns, lentoid bosses and flowing tendrils was executed while the metal was still flat. The two buffers at the ends of the tubes contain an intricate locking device. By contrast, in a gold torc found in a bog at Clonmacnoise, Co. Offaly, the buffers at the front were fused together and a box-

144 The Broighter gold collar or torc

like element diametrically opposite allowed sufficient movement for one of the tubes to be freed from the buffer by the removal of a pin. This torc is an early type, well known in Gaulish contexts, so much so that it is widely regarded as an import (RIA 1983, 101–2; MMA 1977, pl. 14). Raftery dates it to the end of the fourth or beginning of the third century BC and says that: 'It therefore represents the earliest certain evidence of a La Tène presence in the country' (B. Raftery 1984, 178). The two chain or wire necklaces in the Broighter hoard are also believed to be non-native, so close are they to Mediterranean parallels.

The second hoard to be mentioned above was found in 1954 in the townland of Somerset, Co. Galway (J. Raftery 1960; NMI 1961, 93; RIA 1983, 102–4). Ten items were recovered, one of gold, the others of bronze, though sadly, other items of bronze and inevitably ones of iron are known to have been discarded or dispersed. At present the hoard consists of a gold ribbon torc, five bronze mounts, a bronze fibula, a bronze cup-handle, an oval cake of bronze and a rod-shaped ingot of bronze. The torc was tightly coiled and was fitted into one of the mounts. This was of a shallow cylindrical lid-like shape with repoussé ornament, and over it was placed a plain 'lid', somewhat larger. Inside the circle of the torc lay an openwork mount with a hemispherical boss of red enamel in the centre. The 'box' or container was clearly an improvisation and if the two 'lids' belong to the same object some other component must have been present originally. There are two other openwork mounts in the hoard but the decorative centre of one of them, or so it is presumed, was cut away in antiquity leaving a void. In addition to the five Somerset mounts, five others are known, some of them of openwork design, as in a beautiful example from Cornalaragh, Co. Monaghan (MMA 1977, pl. 19).

The gold torc is of open ribbon-twist but the terminals, rectangular in cross-section, are not everted as are those of otherwise similar torcs attributed to a much earlier time (Eogan 1983, 91). A twisted ribbon torc was found with the Clonmacnoise buffer torc, again in an Early Iron Age context, and again differing from other examples in having large pear-shaped terminals (MMA 1977, pl. 15). It can be seen therefore that a gap of about a millennium exists between the La Tène-type torcs and those of the Bronze Age (p. 182). In his study of ribbon torcs, Eogan (1983, 92) says that: 'As there is no positive evidence for the use of ribbon torcs during the final stages of the Bronze Age, those Irish torcs with Iron Age associations then appear to represent borrowing from La Tène cultures outside Ireland.'

The Somerset fibula comes into the category of the Navan-type brooches already mentioned. In addition to the central setting for enamel, there was a circular enamelled disc at each of the three extremities. The bronze cup handle is paralleled by the handle of the beautifully made Keshcarrigan cup or bowl from a tributary of the Shannon in Co. Leitrim (MMA 1977, pl. 20). There is a single zigzag line of decoration on the rim of the bowl but the handle takes the shape of a bird's head. The Somerset bowl would have had a swelling body and everted neck, judging from the contour of the surviving handle. This is cast in the shape of a stylized bird's head, long-necked and long-billed (J. Raftery 1960, 3).

In addition to objects of metal and wood of Iron Age date, there are beads of amber, glass, bone and stone, as well as bracelets of jet and glass. The beads are not easily pinned down to a particular period unless provenanced. The Iron Age glass beads derive mainly from burials or burial mounds rather than occupation sites. However, examples are known from Navan Fort, Dún Ailinne and the secondary phase at Carn H, Loughcrew. Many of the beads are paralleled in Early Christian sites and for this reason a secure context is essential before a bead can be accepted as a chronological indicator.

Small blue glass beads which can be as little as a few millimetres in diameter are among the commonest, being found with Iron Age burials at Knowth, Co. Meath; Oranbeg and Grannagh, both in Co. Galway and at Loughey, Co. Down, among others (p. 334). White or colourless beads are also common and like the blue examples are not confined to the Iron Age. O'Neill Hencken, who found both types at Lagore, raised the question as to whether the colourless ones might not in fact have been blue originally (Hencken 1950, 135). Another Iron Age bead found also in later contexts is one of clear glass with yellow spirals, the so-called 'Meare spiral' type after the lakeside village of that name in Somerset in Britain. Eight of these were among a total of 152 beads retrieved in 1850 from a presumed burial site at Loughey near Donaghadee, Co. Down (Jope and Wilson 1957a). Two similar ones were among a group of ten glass beads from Grannagh but they were present also at Early Historic sites such as Garryduff I, Co. Cork (O'Kelly 1962) and Lagore (Hencken 1950). A blue bead with little groups of tiny 'eyes' contained within circles is among the Grannagh beads and is also found at Kiltierney, Co. Fermanagh (B. Raftery 1984, fig. 100). The latter site produced a knobbed or globular bead in blue with yellow spirals and a cable bead in herringbone pattern. This is another type known both in Iron Age and later contexts. The process of manufacture is described in O'Kelly 1962, 75–6 and in Warner and Meighan 1981, 55. Dumb-bell beads, not perforated, vary in colour and have been found with material of Iron Age date at Knowth, Loughcrew, Grannagh and Kiltierney and also in Early Christian-period sites. They are regarded as toggles. A clear green example was found in the northern tomb at Dowth, Co. Meath, with secondary occupation material (O'Kelly and O'Kelly 1983, 180), and another similar example is on record as having been found at the close of the last century in one of the two tumuli, either K or L, close to the Newgrange mound (O'Kelly *et al.* 1978, 286).

Four pear-shaped bone beads with V-perforations at the narrow end, now in the Ulster Museum, are also said to have been 'found in a grave at Newgrange'

(Flanagan 1960, 61; O'Kelly *et al.* 1978, 286). They are possibly from the same source as the dumb-bell bead. Similar beads are known from Grannagh and Knowth. What appears to have been an anklet consisting of twelve bone beads was found near the foot of a female skeleton at Carrowbeg North, Co. Galway. These various Iron Age burial sites will be described in more detail below (p. 329).

Another interesting facet of the art of the period is the survival of a small number of human and animal representations, the best known among the latter being two tiny figurines of boars only about 8cm in length (MMA 1977, pl. 18). Wild boars are a well known Celtic motif and this, in fact, is almost the sole reason for the inclusion of the Irish examples in the Iron Age repertoire, as they have no provenance. On the other hand, a sculpture in the round in yew wood, 114cm in height, of a human figure found in a bog at Ralaghan, Co. Cavan (RIA 1983, 26), is accepted as early – perhaps Late Bronze Age/Iron Age. The arms were not represented but the face, the reproductive organs and the lower limbs are naturalistically carved. An anthropoid sword-hilt (MMA 1977, pl. 16) was fished from the sea in Ballyshannon Bay, Co. Donegal, early this century. It would have formed part of a triangular iron sword and it is of a type well known in Britain and France (Clarke and Hawkes 1955). The human figure forming the hilt is of 'barbarous' Gaulish type and it is believed that the object was a direct import.

Carn H, Loughcrew, has been mentioned previously in connection with glass beads. A substantial amount of Iron Age material was found in this passage tomb by Eugene Conwell when it was first investigated in the 1860s. The tomb is cruciform in shape. As well as the normal passage tomb finds such as human bones, both burnt and unburnt, and stone and chalk balls, bone pins, and so on, he also found objects of glass, amber, bronze and iron. The find which occasioned the most interest, however, and which remains of great importance today was that of thousands of what Conwell called 'bone implements' (Conwell 1873, 52). He counted 4,071 plain fragments which had at one time been polished but many of which by then were in poor condition: 108 nearly perfect in shape, i.e. about 9–11cm in length; fourteen fragments were pierced at one end; 500 were ornamented with rows of parallel transverse lines; ninety-one were engraved by compass in curvilinear designs and there were thirteen objects which he referred to as combs. Among the ornamented flakes there was only one non-abstract representation, that of an antlered stag, and even this, made up as it is at present of three fragments, is incomplete. Quite a considerable literature exists concerning the bone flakes (see Crawford 1925, 28, for list of references published up to then) and since Crawford's time they have appeared in all studies of Irish La Tène-type art. The most recent examination and evaluation appears in Raftery 1984, 251ff.

He has succeeded in tracing 4,350 pieces, including fourteen or possibly fifteen combs, eleven perforated flakes and 138 decorated ones. He estimates that the number of complete flakes represented by the fragments must have been in the order of between 500 and 600. All were made from bones of cattle, were highly polished and carefully shaped either to an oval or ovoid form, to a parallel-sided one, or, as Conwell depicted them, with one straight edge and one convex. The ends were rounded or sometimes pointed to needle sharpness. He found the average length to agree with Conwell's estimate though large variation occurs.

The bulk of the decoration was executed by compass and when free-hand designs were attempted the standard was not very high. Raftery (*ibid.*, fig. 126) presents a 'pattern book' of the art motifs in most general use and then goes on to demonstrate analogies for them in other Irish material. Among the latter are the Somerset-type openwork mounts, including that of Cornalaragh, the Broighter collar, and a small group of enigmatic objects which have not been mentioned above, known variously as 'castanets' or, more prosaically, 'spoons' (Lucas 1973, 46). Only six have been found in Ireland but they are more common in Britain. They are, or should be, in pairs and are of cast bronze. Each pair consists of an oval concave plate pointed at one end and there is a rounded handle-like attachment at the other. The concave part of one disc of the pair is ornamented with a cross running from top to bottom and from side to side of the plate and there is a small circle at the crossing of the lines. The other disc of the pair has a small perforation midway on one long side. The 'handles' bear the most decoration and it occurs on both sides. The designs were first outlined by compass and then deepened and worked over. Raftery attributes the 'spoons' to the same type of workshop that inspired the designs on the Loughcrew flakes.

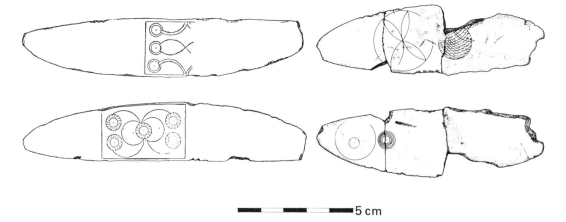

145 Loughcrew, Co. Meath, bone flakes (after B. Raftery)

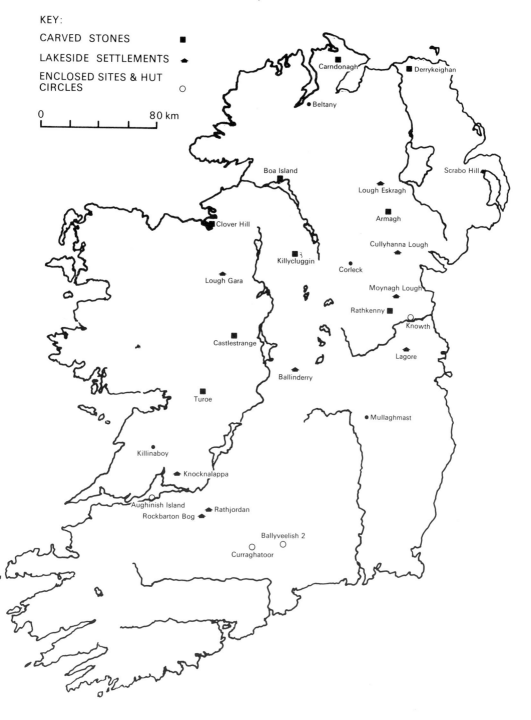

146 Carved stones; lakeside settlements; enclosed sites; hut circles

Carved stones

There is a small number of carved standing stones or pillar stones which display ornament comparable to that on the more portable artefacts of the Irish Iron Age, and in addition there are carved heads, busts and figures in relief. All are found in the northern half of the country with the exception of one rather doubtful pillar stone in Co. Kildare. They are seen as manifestations of pagan Celtic religious beliefs, superstitions and customs and, if this is so, they form almost the only material evidence thereof, since the sanctuaries, shrines and cult sites with which one would expect them to have been associated have not been identified. None of the pillar stones is connected with archaeological remains and the heads and human figures are located in ancient graveyards and churches, or are built into walls, or have been found in the ground, or have no known find-place. There is thus no dating help available from association, and stylistic criteria have to be invoked. In the process, comparisons have been made with prototypes far removed geographically, and sometimes stylistically, from the Irish objects. Terence Powell has remarked (1966, 236) that: 'In studies of Celtic art the relation of one piece to another seems often to be deduced on too prosaic a consideration of style, little credit being given to the difference in powers of possibly contemporary artists.' In many of the examples considered below this holds good; their individuality is very clear and is only to be expected from the insular type of society proposed for Ireland during the period in question, that is, the centuries immediately preceding and succeeding the birth of Christ. Stylistic considerations are even less effective in determining chronological parameters in the case of the human representations, and in some of the thirty or so examples examined by Etienne Rynne (1972) local traditions of stone carving of fairly recent date must be suspected.

Pillar stones

Four, or at most five, carved pillar stones survive in which La Tène influence is clear. They are decorated in abstract curvilinear patterns familiar from the metal and other artefacts of the period though their exact chronological position is not an agreed one. The examples are from Turoe, Co. Galway; Castlestrange, Co. Roscommon; Killycluggin, Co. Cavan; Mullaghmast, Co. Kildare; and in the 1970s another decorated stone was found on the gable-end of a church at Derrykeighan, Co. Antrim (Waterman 1975).

The Turoe stone is the best known and the best executed. It is a roughly cylindrical boulder of granite, 1.68m high, the rounded top and sides covered with a running pattern of spirals, curves, trumpets, triskeles and circles,

147 The Turoe stone, Co. Galway

asymmetrically disposed. The pattern was skilfully executed in relief by picking back the surface of the boulder on two levels so as to leave the ornament proud of the surface. So complex is the whole composition that the positive or relief elements and the negative or background ones combine to provide a very lively, flowing design in three planes. The design continues downward for more than half the height of the stone and terminates in a broad incised step pattern. The stone now stands on the lawn in front of Turoe House in Loughrea in Co. Galway but according to George Coffey (1904, 260), before it was moved in the 1850s it stood near the Rath of Feerwore in the same townland 'some distance to the west of the fort, towards the bottom of the slope on which the fort is placed'. This location has since been confirmed by John Waddell from information garnered in the locality (personal communication).

Michael Duignan (1976, 204) has demonstrated that the ornament is organized on a quadripartite basis, consisting of two triangular compositions (on north and south faces) and two scutiform or hemispherical ones on the other two faces. In addition, he isolates the various motifs employed and convincingly shows that their contexts lie in insular La Tène-derived art.

The curvilinear design is terminated at base by an incised step pattern which is illustrated in developed form by John Waddell (1982, 25). He shows that three different designs are represented in the step motif and that they bear no relationship to the curvilinear design above them. In stressing the insular nature of the Turoe ornament as a whole he says: 'It seems clear that the Turoe artist had a repertoire of both curvilinear and rectilinear designs, part of an artistic heritage which was mainly a distinctively insular expression of a wider European phenomenon' (*ibid.*).

This stone has been studied extensively by many scholars since George Coffey first brought it to notice at the beginning of this century. Both phallic and omphalic symbolism has been claimed for it and comparisons have been made with stelae in Brittany, notably one from Kermaria, Pont-l'Abbé, in Finistère. The latter, however, is less than half the size of the Turoe stone, being more in the nature of a baetyl stone. It is quadrangular in shape, tapering towards the top, and the design centres around four separate cartouches, one of which contains a swastika. The whole impression created by it is at variance with that of the Irish stone, and the detailed study of the Breton stone recently carried out by John Waddell reinforces this opinion. He says that: 'In fact, other than an occasional generalised similarity of shape, and the use of stone, it seems clear that the Irish, Breton and indeed Rhenish pillars have very little in common' (Waddell 1982, 26). One cannot help feeling that had the Turoe stone been a portable object it would have had to fight hard to sustain its claim to an Irish origin.

The Castlestrange stone is also of granite but is oval rather than cylindrical. Its maximum dimensions are 90 by 68 by 60cm and it lies on one of its slightly less-curved surfaces which is not carved. The ornament is not executed in relief but it nevertheless resembles that of Turoe, the whole exposed surface being covered with open spirals linked by flowing curves; there is no border. The stone was moved from its original (unknown) position to a site beside the avenue of the now derelict Castlestrange demesne.

The Killycluggin stone was deliberately broken into several parts, two of which survive, and these are now in NMI. The lower portion of the stone was the first to be discovered, in the 1920s (Macalister 1922). It is roughly cylindrical and about the same height as the Turoe stone. The ornament consists of incised spirals joined by curves in the manner familiar from La Tène ornament. The spirals, in contrast to the open, loose ones of Turoe and Castlestrange, are closely coiled, multiple ones, resembling those found in passage grave art. The second fragment was found some thirty years later at the other end of the same field and was considered by its finder, S. P. Ó Ríordáin (1952, 68), to have constituted the top of the stone. The fragment is dome-shaped, 80cm in height, and on it are carved a series of incised parallel lines about 8cm apart which curve over the top of the stone. They are terminated by an incised line which encircles the fragment; a similar encircling line occurs on the bottom fragment. Some further ornament can be seen near the fractured base of the dome-shaped piece and it is possible

148 The Killycluggin stone, Co. Cavan

that a third fragment may have originally been present. When the first fragment of the stone was brought to Macalister's notice in 1921 he observed that its upper fractured surface was then more or less flush with ground level and from this he deduced that it was part of a stele or pillar stone that had been deliberately smashed. Excavation carried out in 1974 before its removal to NMI bears this out (B. Raftery 1978). Raftery found that a pit, 80cm in depth, had been dug to receive the fractured stump. This act of destruction has variously been attributed to farmers anxious to clear obstructions from their land; or, as Professor Macalister surmised, the deed 'may not impossibly have been the work of people who lived so early that Iron Age paganism was not yet forgotten, and when it would seem both desirable and laudable to destroy pagan monuments' (Macalister 1922, 114).

It is interesting to note that the area about Killycluggin is said to be the Magh Slécht where the chief Celtic idol of Ireland, Crom Dubh, was set up, surrounded by twelve lesser gods – a stone circle with central pillar stone? Macalister records the finding of a burial cist beside the fragment and adds that there was a small stone circle nearby. A pit which Barry Raftery considered could conceivably represent the one-time cist was found during the excavation. He also noted that on the summit of the hillock above the then position of the stone was a small circle of free-standing stones, and he did not rule out the possibility that the pillar stone when whole and entire stood on or near the summit.

The Mullaghmast stone is odd man out on several counts. It is of limestone and is four-sided and comes from the eastern and southern part of the country rather than from the west where the other three are located. It is carved in panels, some in relief and some incised. The design is not unitary and none of the separate elements is as free and flowing as in the other examples. It measures at present 90cm in height by 40cm in width and is approximately square in section. At one time it was built into the wall of a castle and pieces had been broken off, probably to adapt it to its position. Various typical La Tène motifs are represented such as spirals, trumpets, a triskele, etc., but there is no attempt to unite or unify them. It is generally considered to be later than the other stelae, perhaps considerably later. It is now in NMI.

The Derrykeighan stone is of rectangular shape and section. The decoration on the first face to be noticed is very well organized, consisting of an open symmetrical design of flowing trumpet curves with voids, reminiscent of those on the Turoe and Mullaghmast stones (Waterman 1975; Raftery 1984, pl. 106). The other face has only recently been exposed.

Various authorities have looked to the Continent for the counterparts of the Irish pillar stones, not an easy task on account of their uncompromising abstraction as opposed to the tendency towards human symbolism in the Gaulish stones. For a stone-carving tradition one need not look outside Ireland where, from

Neolithic times onward, an impressive series of carving on both free-standing and earthfast boulders and on rock outcrops has been recorded. Just as the Entrance Stone at Newgrange remains one of the finest examples of Neolithic sculpture, so must Turoe take a similar place in the Early Iron Age.

Other decorated stones

Apart from the pillar stones, there are few other decorated stones for which an Iron Age date is claimed. Confined to the northern part of the country are quern stones of 'beehive' shape. Seamas Caulfield (1977) has noted decoration on some of them consisting of curvilinear motifs, radial and concentric grooves, and so on, which are in keeping with the decorative motifs current in the centuries immediately before and after the birth of Christ.

Two stone monuments have been singled out as portraying motifs of La Tène type, Clover Hill, Co. Sligo, and Rathkenny, Co. Meath. The former is a long oval pit lined with slabs and sunk into the ground. Three of the slabs are ornamented. The motifs are of a curvilinear type dissimilar to that found in passage grave art, but there are some dot-and-circle motifs on one slab. It appears likely that only this carving is ancient. The other decorated surfaces, while superficially similar to La Tène-type ornament, do not seem to ring true and may be medieval at the earliest.

The Rathkenny 'dolmen' (so-called) is also doubtful. There are only two stones, an orthostat and another large one leaning against it. There are designs on the underside of the latter and on the inner face of the standing stone. Cupmarks, circles, arcs and dot-and-circles are mainly represented; and other designs which have been claimed as displaying La Tène influence (J. Raftery 1937–40) are not definitive enough to warrant an Iron Age attribution. Very similar markings of an equally ill-defined character are present in the megalithic art at Newgrange and Dowth but in general the Rathkenny motifs appear closer to rock art than to anything else.

Human representations

A study undertaken by Etienne Rynne (1972) has listed more than thirty sculptures representing the human figure and allegedly of pagan Celtic significance. The majority are heads and busts and are in the northern half of the country. About half are associated with church sites but in fact, exact provenance is wanting in almost all cases. In addition, local traditions of stone carving of fairly recent times must be suspected in some instances. It is proposed to discuss only the most prominent figures.

A group of six sculptures was reputedly found on Cathedral Hill, Armagh city, during restoration work on the cathedral in the last century and some, at least, can be considered to be of pre-Christian date. They consist of a bust, a figure in relief, a head and three animal figures which appear to represent boars and which could well be medieval in date. The best known sculpture is the bust, the 'Tanderagee idol', so-called because it was said to have been at one time in the grounds of Ballymore rectory at Tanderagee, Co. Down, having been brought there, so it was said, from its find-place in a bog at Newry. Rynne, however, claims that it can be provenanced to Cathedral Hill on stylistic grounds and because of its known history.

The bust is a compelling piece of sculpture, about 60cm in height with disproportionately large head and strongly delineated face. Two knobs protrude at the front of the head, one at each side, and have been variously interpreted as vestigial horns emerging from the head or as horns belonging to a cap or helmet. The left arm extends straight downward and the right stretches diagonally across the chest while the hand grasps the cuff of the other arm. The whole effect is barbaric and menacing and this figure must be one of the least doubtful of the allegedly pagan sculptures extant in Ireland. Most commentators liken the Tanderagee bust to a Janus statue from Holzgerlingen in Württemberg in Germany by virtue of the carving and posture of the right arm (the only one portrayed in the Janus) but since it is rather timidly pressed against the waist of the figure, it is difficult to believe that this pose carries the same message as the expansive gesture of the Tanderagee idol.

The second Armagh figure is the so-called 'sun god' or 'radiate figure', a male effigy rather crudely delineated in relief, emphasis being placed on the head and arms. The face is set in an oval frame from which lines radiate outwards on all sides from about chin level upwards, and this has led to its being classed as a radiate figure or deity akin to classical models (Ross 1967, 380). The legs are separated and the feet splay outward. The figure may well be of pagan Celtic origin, though Roman influence must be suspected. A similar outlining of the face appears on a head from Camlyball in Co. Armagh, and the radiate lines appear on the third sculpture from Cathedral Hill, usually referred to as the 'bearded head'. In this case, however, the 'rays' spring from the forehead only and sweep back over the head itself, a reminder that an Irish context might be as legitimate as the North British one envisaged by Ross and others, because it realistically depicts the artificially stiffened hair mentioned in the *Táin* and known also from Gaul. Diodorus Siculus stated that the Gauls drew their hair 'back from the forehead to the crown and to the nape of the neck, with the result that their appearance resembled that of Satyrs or of Pans, for the hair is so thickened by this treatment that it differs in no way from a horse's mane. Some shave off the beard, while others cultivate a short beard' (Tierney 1960, 249). Such a beard is depicted in the Armagh head.

149 The Tanderagee figure, Co. Armagh

The supposed find-place of these sculptures is interesting because Armagh Cathedral was reputedly built on the traditional site of St Patrick's principal church and the site had formerly been a pagan cult centre. Indeed, according to the tradition, Patrick had chosen it for that very reason. There is no substantiating evidence for this or for the supposition that the sculptures are connected with a pagan cult.

There are two interesting carvings in the ancient graveyard of Caldragh on Boa Island in Lower Lough Erne in the north-west of Ireland. One is a double human effigy, often referred to as the Boa Island Janus, and the other is known as the Lustymore idol since it was discovered on the neighbouring island of that name. The find-places in both cases are associated with Christian rather than pagan worship, that is, with a pre-Reformation church and a monastery respectively. Both stones were a good deal damaged when found and they have since been set up adjoining one another on modern pillars on the island.

The Janus effigy portrays two almost identical figures back to back. They terminate at a point just below the waist but since damage is clearly indicated, more may have been present originally. There is some evidence that there was a tenon on the base of the stone and that it 'could have been fitted on to another stone' (Lowry-Corry 1933, 201). The stone is c.73cm in height, 45cm wide on the two broader surfaces and 30cm on the two narrow ones. Françoise Henry (1940, 7) said of the double effigy: 'the faces are triangular, with stereotyped features, terrifying in their inhumanity'. In the writer's opinion, however, they appear benign, particularly the north-east effigy (Lowry-Corry 1933) which looks almost jovial. While such judgements are necessarily subjective, it would be hard to deny that the double effigy is less menacing than the Tanderagee figure.

On account of its Janus structure, the Boa Island effigy also has been compared to the Holzgerlingen statue already mentioned, but nearer home, a carving on a pillar stone at Carndonagh, Co. Donegal, portrays a figure much closer in appearance. In this latter the head is disproportionately large, the eyes are strongly outlined and the crossed arms are meagre and straplike as in the Boa figures. It is clear, however, that in this case an ecclesiastic is portrayed because the figure holds a bell and a book, and a crozier lies at his feet. If the lower part of this figure were missing would it be recognized as Christian, particularly as, on an adjacent surface of the stone, a curious horned figure holding two discs and a hammer is carved?

The so-called Lustymore idol is about 70cm in height and the head and upper part of the body are clearly seen. It has been said that the lower limbs are also represented, in a squatting position, and for this reason the figure has been likened to a Sheela-na-gig, a type of explicit female fertility figure peculiar to Ireland and of uncertain date. Rynne failed to find any certain evidence for legs or hips (1972, 86).

It is difficult to state unequivocally that the two Boa Island figures are pagan, much less Celtic. While the crossed arms of one and the squatting posture of the other can invoke pagan menhirs and Gaulish statues, they can equally invoke Christian associations, as we have seen. Furthermore, the Lower Lough Erne area is rich in Christian remains, including sculpture. At White Island eight statues have been unearthed, the majority portraying clerics. In the churchyard of Killadeas on the eastern shore of the lake there are other sculptures, including a fine slab portraying on one side an ecclesiastic, stepping out with bell and crozier. On another side there is a head in relief and a panel of interlace. It is clear that the head was carved before the ecclesiastic was sculpted on the adjoining surface and also that the stone was trimmed at yet another period because both head and cleric were damaged thereby. A long period of occupation of this site, of the White Island one, and perhaps of those on the other islands also is probable.

Apart from the Tanderagee figure, one of the best known sculptures to which a pagan Iron Age date is generally assigned is the three-faced head from Corleck in Co. Cavan. At least two other heads are extant from the area (Rynne 1972, 84–5) and wooden figures have also been found, such as that from Ralaghan (p. 281) though the latter may be earlier than any of the stone sculptures. Only a single massive head is represented in the Corleck figure, and the three faces are

150 West face of Janus figure, Boa Island,
Lower Lough Erne

151 Three-faced head from Corleck,
Co. Cavan

293

evenly distributed around the block of sandstone. The total height is *c.*32cm. The faces are not identical but are nonetheless very similar, the mouths shown as narrow slits and the expression on each face remote and withdrawn. A hole in the bottom of the figure is taken to indicate that it was originally affixed by means of a dowel to some other stone or object.

Three-faced heads are known from Gaul, particularly in the Marne region and in the area of the Côte d'Or, but in Britain and Ireland the Corleck head is unique. It has been compared with one or two other pieces both here and in Britain (Ross 1967, 75; Rynne 1972, 84) but the correspondence lies more in the number of faces than in the style or iconography. A date in the first century AD is the one generally accepted. There are a number of other stone busts and heads in NMI but while one can pick out individual points of resemblance to other figures both here and abroad, there is not sufficient dating evidence or unequivocal resemblance. Stuart Piggott has summed up the difficulty as follows: 'What seems mainly brought out by iconographic and epigraphic studies is the enormous diversity and parochiality that the aspects of the Celtic deities could assume, and the impossibility of trying to reduce to a system a scheme where no system need have existed, and where inconsistencies were irrelevant . . .' (1968, 87).

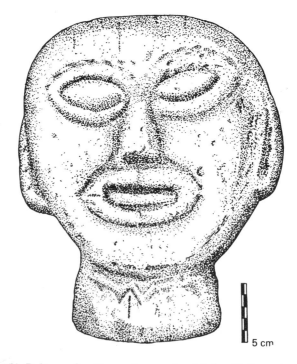

152 Beltany, Co. Donegal, stone head (after E. Rynne)

One other head deserves mention. It came reputedly from the stone circle known as the Beltany Ring at Raphoe in Co. Donegal, or its immediate vicinity. Its main interest lies in the shallow picked grooves which encircle the neck so as to hint at a collar or necklet or torc. Rynne has pointed out (1967, 147) that the T-shaped or tau-cross at Killinaboy near Corofin in Co. Clare, which shows two opposed faces, chin to chin, on the transom, has a ridged feature in the space between them, i.e. the neck. This is not dissimilar in some respects to the 'collar' on the Beltany figure because the same inverted V-nicks appear in both. Rynne has convincingly compared the Killinaboy cross to the tau-croziers of the Early Christian Period in Ireland (*ibid.*) and consequently, the necklet on the Beltany sculpture can scarcely be sufficient on its own to affirm a pagan Celtic origin.

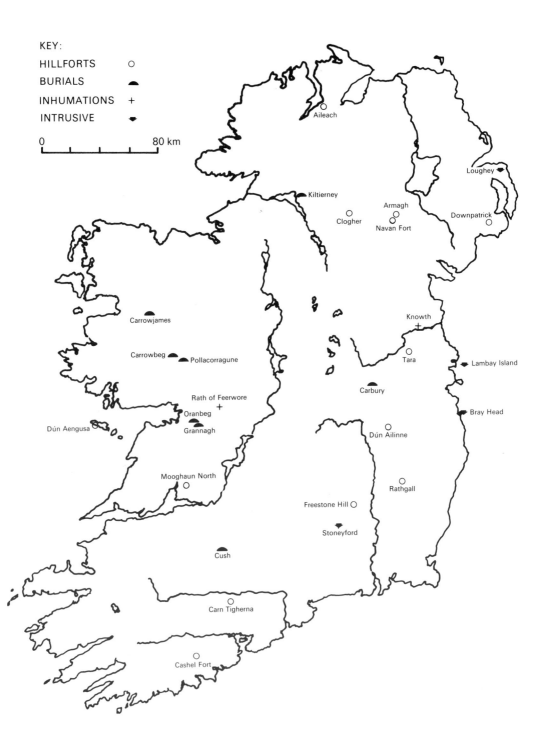

KEY:

HILLFORTS ○

BURILS ◗

INHUMATIONS +

INTRUSIVE ◄

0 ————————— 80 km

Aileach

Loughey

Kiltierney

Armagh
Clogher
Navan Fort

Downpatrick

Knowth +

Carrowjames

Carrowbeg ◗ Pollacorragune

Tara

Lambay Island

Rath of Feerwore +

Carbury

Oranbeg ◗
Grannagh

Dún Aengusa

Bray Head

Dún Ailinne

Mooghaun North

Rathgall

Freestone Hill ○

Stoneyford

Cush

Carn Tigherna

Cashel Fort

153 Hillforts; Early Iron Age burials

296

11
Later prehistoric settlement

It has already been stressed that the divisions into which the various periods or 'ages' are separated are both artificial and arbitrary, and occasionally idiosyncratic. They mostly represent a convenient method of ordering a collection of material, much of which is inadequate in quantity and quality. The LBA, while rich in artefacts, is extremely poor in identifiable field remains. There is no clear dividing line between the phasing out of the so-called Bronze Age and the initiation of the succeeding Early Iron Age (EIA), nor is there any clear definition of the term itself. Does it mean the period when iron was being worked or when influences from iron-using communities elsewhere had begun to make themselves felt? There are hints that iron was being worked in Ireland before the middle of the first millennium BC and in the latter part of the millennium there is clear evidence for contact with iron-using communities outside Ireland, but these new influences are unevenly distributed and they are mainly recognizable in the northern two-thirds of the country.

Barry Raftery (1984, 4) has summarized the problem as follows:

> The collection of artifacts which we refer to as La Tène do not in themselves provide us with an 'Iron Age'. They are, however, indicative of something new in the country . . . a significant La Tène presence here even if the precise nature of that presence, or the means of its introduction, remain to be defined.

He also highlights another aspect of the problem, namely the fact that La Tène material is virtually absent from the southern part of Ireland and that 'an entire "Iron Age" assemblage, devoid of La Tène influences, awaits full recognition' (*ibid.*).

Were it not for radiocarbon dating much of the prehistory of the millennium would be a closed book due to the virtual absence of links between the remains in the ground and the collections of unassociated artefacts recovered from lakes and rivers, from hoards, from destroyed sites and from the dealers and antiquarians. Many of the monuments that were traditionally attributed to the later part of the millennium, to the 'Iron Age' proper, are now known, due to radiocarbon dating, to have had much earlier beginnings. The change from Dowris to Hallstatt and La Tène which can be detected in the technology of the artefacts is not generally discernible in the settlement and burial remains. On the contrary, such changes as occur can be attributed to the type of indigenous regional development that takes place in any normal progressive society undisturbed by any large intrusive influx of population. Until many more sites are securely dated by radiocarbon and dendrochronology the lack of any firm chronological indicators for the settlements and burials of the final stages of the Bronze Age and for the Early Iron Age must be accepted.

Lake settlements

A type of lake or lakeside settlement which radiocarbon dating has shown to have had its beginnings in the first half of the first millennium BC is the crannog, a term derived from *crann*, the Irish word for a tree, this being a reference to the amount of timber used in their construction. Lake and lakeside dwellings are known from all over the world and they were built in the manner that best suited the terrain and the environment. Many hundreds are known in Ireland, mainly west and north-west of the central plain, though in fact any small lake provided a suitable location. They most frequently come to light when through one cause or another the water level is lowered. Lough Gara in Co. Sligo was drained in the 1950s and the remains of over three hundred crannog-type sites were revealed, two of which were excavated. When the surrounding water has been lowered or drained away, the crannogs appear as mounds in marshy or boggy areas, and attention has been drawn to them as a rule because of the finding of quantities of animal bones and sometimes of pottery and other artefacts.

Traditionally they are associated with the Early Christian period and in function they were defensive, or at any rate, separated from the mainland, though occasionally traces of a causeway have been found. They were single homesteads and, judging by some of the excavated examples, were occupied by a wealthy class. They are frequently mentioned in the annals and other early historic sources. One such is the crannog at Lagore, Co. Meath, excavated in the 1930s (Hencken 1950), which was claimed as the residence of the kings of South Brega in the mid-seventh century AD. The crannog proper is an artificial island constructed by driving piles into the mud of the lake and building it up with layers of peat, brushwood, stone, branches and other available material until it rose above the water level. Wood was not exclusively employed; the materials nearest to hand were those commonly used. In the classic examples such as those at Lagore and at Ballinderry, Co. Offaly, the island was encircled by a stout palisade which was generally strongest at the side most accessible from the mainland.

The Late Bronze Age settlements, whether lake or lakeside, though frequently constructed in a similar manner, are lacking the defensive element. This is clearly seen at Ballinderry II in Co. Offaly. What was once a natural island, but is now a tongue of land protruding into the lough, was first occupied for a short time over an area about 45m long by 27m wide. This was in the nature of a lakeside settlement rather than an artificial island or crannog. At one end of the area the foundation planks of what may have been a house, 11.5m square, were found (Hencken 1942). The planks were of oak, mortised together to form a framework for the base and for the uprights forming the sides and end walls. The latter had probably been of wattle construction plastered with mud. At the other end of the area were the bases of nine circular structures built also of wattles and also originally plastered with mud. They varied in diameter between 1 and 2m and it was thought at the time that they may have been used for storing grain. Similar features found later at Rathtinaun in Lough Gara, Co. Sligo, were shown to have served the purpose of fire-baskets, that is, hearths sunk in the ground.

The house occupants had used flat-bottomed coarse ware not unlike the Late Neolithic ware of the same shape. In fact, one of the difficulties in regard to these coarse domestic wares is that when found by themselves, that is, unassociated with other datable objects, one cannot easily distinguish pots of Neolithic date from those of the Late Bronze or Iron Ages. While this late coarse ware, as at Ballinderry, is probably descended from the Neolithic coarse ware, some allow

154 Craggaunowen, Co. Clare, conjectural model (full scale) of a crannog

299

for the possibility that it was introduced into Ireland at the end of the LBA (Hawkes and Smith 1957, 159; Eogan 1965, 21). If this is admitted as a possibility the pottery may foreshadow the beginning of the Iron Age, if indeed it does not actually belong to this period, as has been argued for similar pottery from another site to be discussed below, Knocknalappa.

The inhabitants of Ballinderry II kept cattle, pigs, and sheep/goat and these must have been grazed on the land around the lake. Their meat was eaten, and occasionally a red deer killed in the hunt provided some venison. The bones of all these animals were found on or near the site. Cereal crops were grown and stone saddle querns and grain rubbers were used to grind the grain, more probably for use as porridge than as flour for the making of bread. Bone and stone spindle-whorls (the fly-wheel weights of hand-turned spindles) show that the sheep's wool was spun into thread, and this was probably woven into cloth, though there is no direct evidence of the presence of a loom. Some fragments of leather may indicate that this material was also used for garments and two bronze awls may have been used as perforators to facilitate sewing the pieces together. Two bronze pins are likely to have been used for fastening the clothing. Ornaments worn by the womenfolk were amber beads and bracelets and armlets or anklets made of shale and lignite (fossil wood), though some were large enough to fit the men also. Various objects were made from yew, ash and hazel wood, which included a bowl, pins and various fragmentary objects, the purpose of which could not be determined.

The occupation was brought to an end by a rise in the level of the lake. During this high-water period the buildings decayed or were swept away and the whole area of the settlement became covered by a layer of chalk mud. It was reoccupied in the Early Christian Period at a date attributed by the excavator to the eighth century AD. The new settlement was of crannog construction consisting of a stout outer palisade protecting a permanent settlement.

Another site excavated in the 1930s was one that came to be known as Knocknalappa crannog after the townland in Co. Clare in which it lay (J. Raftery 1942). On a slight natural rise on the floor of Rossroe Lough, near Newmarket-on-Fergus, an artificial island, oval in shape and measuring 40m by 20m, was raised above the lake level to provide an area for a habitation. On the primary marl of the lake-bed was spread a thick layer of artificially deposited peat, on this was placed a layer of stones, and over this a layer of marl. All was held in place by timber piles driven into the primary marl around the edge of the artificial platform. While there were objects of a domestic nature – pottery, animal bones, etc. – there was no evidence that houses or huts or hearths had been built. Sherds of five or six pottery vessels were found, one of which was capable of being restored. It had a slightly everted neck above a swelling body narrowing downward to a flat base. The pot is 22cm high, 16cm in diameter at the rim and 10cm at base. This large vessel, dull grey-black in colour, is similar to some of the pots from the early phase of Ballinderry II. Other objects consisted of a fragment of a lignite armlet and some amber beads.

This site had been brought to attention in the first instance by the finding on the foreshore of a bronze sword of Eogan's Class 4, a socketed bronze gouge and a stone axe. The two bronze items clearly belonged to the Dowris Phase but the excavator argued that the pottery already showed strong Iron Age influences in its profile (J. Raftery 1942, 60). The foreshore finds cannot, however, be shown to be directly connected with the crannog. According to Raftery, the crannog was never used, and the likelihood was that the finds incorporated in its structure came from a disused site, possibly on the nearby lake shore, and were part of the fill utilized in the building up of the crannog. On the other hand, it is also possible that occupation of a very temporary and discontinuous nature took place from time to time by which the resources of the lake and surrounding terrain could be seasonally exploited.

Something of this nature was proposed by the excavators of a crannog-type structure at Rathjordan, Co. Limerick, in the same townland as the ring-barrows mentioned earlier (p. 206). The field in which it was situated had produced a large number of stone axes and, during the 1940s, when excavations were in progress at Lough Gur, a few kilometres to the west, it was decided to investigate (Ó Ríordáin and Lucas 1946–7). The field was originally a marsh with pools of open water. Brushwood anchored by stakes into the underlying clay was laid down over a total area *c.* 11m in diameter. A layer of timber had been laid over this and stones heaped on top to cover an area about 8m in diameter. There were profuse amounts of charcoal and the stones showed considerable evidence of fire. A small amount of animal bone, mainly ox, was recovered, but there was little or no other evidence of occupation. After a lapse of time, peat encroached on the perimeter and two hearths were built. Embedded in a clay foundation beneath one of them was a single sherd of cord-ornamented pottery of Bronze Age type. The excavators concluded that: 'to whatever point in Bronze Age times we date the sherd the crannog must appreciably pre-date it to allow for the growth of the intervening layer of peat' (*ibid.*, 74). They proposed that the site was a temporary one analogous to those from Rockbarton Bog in the same neighbourhood which produced spreads of ash and contained pottery of EBA type (Mitchell and Ó Ríordáin 1942). The latter sites were of a more flimsy nature than the Rathjordan one but it was felt that all served a temporary and seasonal purpose such as fowling, fishing, gathering fruit and so on.

Excavations in the 1950s at Crannog 61 at Rathtinaun in Lough Gara, Co. Sligo, revealed a small LBA settlement lying on a foundation of peat and brushwood held in place on the marl by wooden piles. At that time the surrounding area was a phragmites swamp. No house plan was recovered, but the lowermost level produced typical bronzes, a small penannular gold ring and coarse flat-rimmed ware. There were several hearths including one set in a basket of woven twigs plastered with clay.

This occupation layer was inundated by the lake, and a thin spread of sand separated it from the next level, also LBA but with a few artefacts of iron, including a crudely made shaft-hole axe forged from three pieces. Again there were no house foundations, but further fire-baskets were found. The same bucket-shaped ware as before was present and also many fragments of clay moulds and of wooden dishes. Close to the site a hoard of amber, bronze, gold and tin ornaments was discovered. These included a pair of tweezers, an ornamented pin, three gold-plated penannular rings made of lead, other rings of various sizes in bronze and tin, an amber necklace of thirty-one beads and two polished boar's tusks (Eogan 1964, 347). Eogan attributes these objects to the Dowris Phase, but it must be stressed that they are not associated stratigraphically with the crannog. Samples obtained from the hazel twigs forming the fire-baskets gave ^{14}C determinations of 2150 ± 130 BP and 2070 ± 130 BP among others, suggesting that an LBA culture lasted on in certain parts of the country at least to the third or second century BC (J. Raftery 1963, 109–10; 1972, 2–3). The radiocarbon measurements, taken as a whole, made little distinction between this occupation level and the earlier one (*Radiocarbon* 1961, 34–5).

Barry Raftery, on the other hand, casts doubts on the accuracy of the radiocarbon dates and feels that they are scarcely in keeping with the archaeological evidence which shows bronze and iron artefacts in use simultaneously in the second level. He states (1984, 11–12): 'It seems more likely that the relevant levels are anything up to half a millennium older than the dates suggest.' While this may seem to be an example of special pleading, the fact is that radiocarbon dates in the second half of the first millennium BC present problems. The calibration curves for this particular time-span often show several dates for each 'raw' (radiocarbon) measurement.

In due course the settlement was again inundated, and at about AD 200, according to the excavator, the site was occupied and rebuilt on at least two subsequent occasions (Lucas 1958, 11). The material from this phase, which included textiles, objects of wood, bronze and iron, bone combs, glass beads, rotary querns, etc., resembles that from Lagore and similar sites and it has been argued that 'the reoccupation of the Rathtinaun site as a *piled* crannog took place in what is now conventionally called the Early Christian period and is later than 500 AD' (Lynn 1983, 54). These uncertainties can be resolved only by a definitive publication of the results.

Another settlement that deserves mention is in Lough Eskragh, Co. Tyrone. In the 1950s an artificial lowering of the water level revealed three areas of wooden piling, all close to the eastern shoreline (Collins and Seaby 1960). Site A consisted of two discontinuous areas of piling, while another better-defined one to the north-west was clearly of crannog construction. Two dug-out canoes of oak were found in the mud nearby. They were up to 8m in length and 78cm in maximum beam. One contained a two-piece vessel of alderwood and part of another. Portions of saddle querns were recovered from the lake bed.

Site B was smaller and fragments of clay moulds for casting leaf-shaped bronze swords were concentrated in the occupation area, but no artefacts of a domestic nature were recovered. It was believed to be the site of a bronze-worker's smithy. A bag-shaped bronze socketed axe was picked up from the modern lakeshore. Worked flints which may show occupation of the lake shore at an earlier era were also found. Site C consisted of two low mounds surrounded by rings of piles and some burnt clay or daub from wattlework.

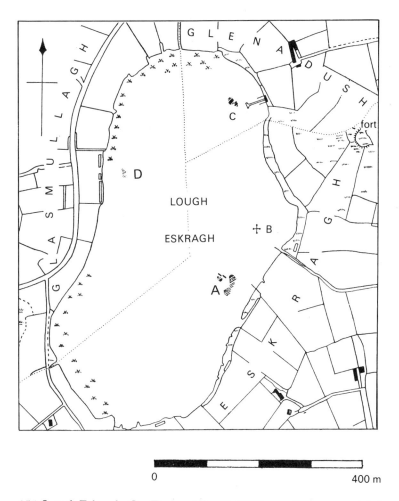

155 Lough Eskragh, Co. Tyrone (after B. Williams; Crown copyright)

Twenty years later the water level was again low and the opportunity was taken to obtain samples for dendrochronological and radiocarbon measurement. A limited excavation was also carried out as by this time one of the sites was already destroyed and the 'smithy' site was threatened. The subsequent investigations (Williams 1978) produced the best evidence to date for LBA lake or lakeside settlement. The two discontinuous areas of piling in Site A were found to be one unit containing almost six hundred birch and ash piles, and there were a number of whole and fragmentary saddle querns scattered on the lake bed among them. One of the piles was radiocarbon-dated to 2475 ± 45 BP. The crannog-like structure nearby was shown to be of a domestic nature, as two complete coarse pottery vessels were recovered. One was bucket-shaped, reminiscent of the sheet bronze situlae of the Dowris Phase, and was 32.4cm high and 16.7cm in diameter at the flat base, with a bulging body and pronounced shoulder narrowing to an internally bevelled rim, 29cm in diameter. The other vessel, also flat-based, was 11.2cm in diameter at bottom, had a slightly rounded body 17.2cm high with internally bevelled rim, 17.2cm in diameter. In each vessel the coarse outer surface with its many angular grits was coated with a buff-coloured slip. The second vessel may have been used as a kettle.

A two-piece bucket of alderwood was also found, 27.2cm high, 22.3cm in rim diameter and 24.3cm at base. The dish-like bottom fitted into the cylindrical body and was caulked with a black resinous substance. A fragment of a jet ring and a stone axe were also recovered, as well as more saddle querns. The pottery is similar to that found at the early phase of Ballinderry II and the jet bracelet is paralleled by six lignite examples found at the latter site. The wood vessel can probably be linked with the two found previously in the canoe, and the canoes in turn were probably used by the crannog dwellers. An oak plank from this site gave a ^{14}C date of 2690 ± 45 BP.

Site B, the metal-working site, was excavated and found to consist of a lake platform 10.5m in diameter, situated on a rise in the lake floor near the margin and not on an artificially constructed island which, strictly speaking, is regarded as the true crannog of Early Christian times. A foundation of brushwood was laid with horizontal birch timbers embedded in and lying upon it, their purpose being to consolidate the layer. One of these timbers gave a ^{14}C date of 3105 ± 80 BP. Only two artefacts were found in this layer, a fragment of a sword mould and a broken saddle quern. The next layer was of twigs and pebbles covering the entire area. Numerous fragments of burnt daub, some of which bore impressions of wattlework, were scattered around the perimeter of the area. This was defined by piles and enclosed a space of about 9m diameter. The burnt daub can be interpreted as the remains of an enclosing fence that was later destroyed by fire. Almost all the finds occurred at this level – fragments of clay moulds for socketed axes and for swords, crucibles, a bronze ring and the remains of eight saddle querns. A deposit of fine yellow sand overlay the site after occupation had ceased.

Site C had been almost totally destroyed by the time of the second investigation, but two piles remained and one was radiocarbon-dated to 2360 ± 45 BP. A linear group of piles was observed at the western margin of the lake, but conditions did not allow of investigation. Saddle querns were again present. An overall total of thirty-six querns, either whole or fragmentary, was found during the two investigations. Two phases were envisaged: (1) the construction of the metal-working site in the earlier part of the Bronze Age; (2) the construction of the other sites in or about the first half of the first millennium BC (calendar years).

The findings at L. Eskragh are similar to those from a crannog in Lough Tay in Scotland (Dixon 1984) where underwater excavation was commenced in 1980. There were at least three phases in the Oakbank crannog and these were radiocarbon-dated by means of samples from the piles and stakes. The earliest piles driven into the lake bed were dated to 2545 ± 55 BP and the final occupation was dated to 2360 ± 60 BP. Owing to the excellent preservation of organic remains it was established that the inhabitants were primarily farmers, raising cattle and sheep and cultivating cereals. From dung found in the crannog it was inferred that some animals at least were kept on the settlement. There were no signs of warlike activity.

A site at Cullyhanna Lough near Crossmaglen, Co. Armagh, became visible in the 1950s when the water level was lowered as a result of drainage. A ring of posts projected above the gradually shelving lake bottom on the northern side. It was about 17m in maximum diameter and two small mounds which had been built up of stones and clay could be detected. Traces of occupation remained in

156 Cullyhanna Lough, Co. Armagh, conjectural reconstruction
(after H. W. M. Hodges; Crown copyright)

these and in one case consisted of the foundation of a circular hut with central fireplace. The latter rested on a raft or platform of timbers. No substantial timber structures were found in either of the two mounds apart from the remains of a wicker-work fence to the west of the hearth. The excavator (Hodges 1958) suggested that the site was used as an open-air hunting camp or cooking place. There was a complete lack of datable small finds, but examination of the posts of the surrounding palisade showed them to consist of oak timbers which had been sharpened with a fairly heavy axe. Not unnaturally, it was assumed that the axe was an iron one and that the structure dated to the EIA or later. However, a decade or so after the excavation, low water levels enabled samples to be taken from one of the palisade posts and ^{14}C dates of 3475 ± 75 BP and 3305 ± 50 BP were obtained (Hillam 1976). Tree-ring dating established the age of the timbers at 1526 BC.

One of the most recent investigations of a lakeside settlement was commenced in 1980 as a result of land reclamation in what was formerly Moynagh Lough in Co. Meath. Beneath a typical palisaded crannog of the Early Christian Period, traces of occupation from Mesolithic times onwards were discovered. The earliest occupation was centred on two knolls which rose above the former surface of the lough (Bradley 1982–3; 1984). A platform of twigs, stones and brushwood was constructed, and evidence of occupation in the form of a layer of charcoal-flecked mud together with over one hundred fragments of chert and flint, many of them worked blades, was found. In time, the lake water rose and the Mesolithic level was covered by a layer of naturally formed mud. A sample of charcoal from the Mesolithic occupation has been radiocarbon-dated to 5270 ± 60 BP (Bradley 1984, 86).

When the accumulation of lake mud had almost reached the top of the knolls the area was again occupied. Finds of hearths, a tanged-and-barbed arrowhead and some sherds of decorated ware of EBA type were uncovered. One of the charcoal spreads has been radiocarbon-dated to 3460 ± 35 BP. On the southern part of the site, evidence of LBA activity was found on mud which had accumulated after the site was abandoned in the EBA. Finds consisted of a bronze leaf-shaped socketed spearhead, a fragment of a jet bracelet and a jet bead. Pottery with internally bevelled rim was similar to that found at Ballinderry II and Knocknalappa. The socketed spearhead would place this occupation in the Dowris Phase of the LBA. Subsequently, in Early Christian times, the substantial crannog already mentioned was constructed.

Enclosed sites

Another type of site for which early beginnings have been claimed is the ringfort, essentially, like the crannog, a phenomenon of Early Christian and later periods.

Indeed, ringforts continued to be constructed down to the seventeenth century of the present era (O'Kelly 1970, 53). The term 'ringfort', like many archaeological terms, is a misnomer. In its loosest context it merely means the stackyard enclosure of a farming family within which was the dwelling house or houses and the animal shelters. A few sites have been excavated which come within this loose category. Carrigillihy has already been mentioned (p. 219) and another interesting site is that at Aughinish Island on the Shannon estuary. Nevertheless, the strict use of the term ringfort, like that of crannog, is perhaps best reserved for structures of the Early Christian Period, such as Garranes and Garryduff, both in Co. Cork, and numerous others throughout the whole of Ireland.

At Aughinish, two stone-built enclosures of similar construction, *c.*35m in diameter and close together, were excavated in the 1970s. There was an interior and an exterior stone facing and a rubble core, and no trace of a ditch. There were indications of a house in each enclosure. Site 1 was built on the bedrock, and traces of an occupation layer underlay the internal wall collapse, producing coarse pottery, saddle querns, a few bronze artefacts and a heavily corroded horse-bit of possible Hallstatt-C type. The pottery was similar to that known from other first millennium BC contexts in Ireland, and one of the bronze artefacts, a chisel, was of Dowris type (Kelly 1974, 21).

The Site 2 house was better defined, circular in shape and about 8m in diameter. It also produced coarse pottery. There were some pits and entrance features but further details await publication of the excavation report.

Barry Raftery, commenting on the Aughinish finds, says: 'The presence . . . of an iron horse-bit might indicate that the same Hallstatt horizon which was present at Rathtinaun Phase 2 could also be present here. The horse-bit may have been an import, but the Aughinish Island people were clearly on the threshold of an iron using era' (Raftery 1976a, 192).

The absence of La Tène-type finds at this and other sites previously mentioned is noticeable. The only site of ringfort type for which this phase has been claimed is the Rath of Feerwore in the townland of Turoe, Co. Galway. Because of a tradition that the Turoe Stone originally stood beside the rath or ringfort (p. 286), excavation was undertaken in 1938 (J. Raftery 1944). Three phases of occupation were recognized but only the final one was of ringfort construction, that is, the site was enclosed by a bank faced with dry stone masonry. There was no evidence to show that the pillar stone was connected with this phase. An iron fibula of rod-bow type, an iron axehead with rectangular socket, and some other finds, were associated with the earliest habitation layer, but it is now generally accepted that this stratum pre-dates the earthen enclosure bank. It is possibly of first-century BC date and may be related to a phase of Iron Age activity in the vicinity of the pillar stone, provided that the tradition relating to the latter is correct.

An interesting example of the modification of an existing monument so as to adapt it to a ringfort-type settlement is found at Knowth, Co. Meath. Two deep concentric ditches were dug into the main mound (Site 1), one of them around the base of the mound inside the perimeter kerb and the other around the summit. The date at which the trenches were dug has not been established, but it is suggested that 'during the early centuries A.D. a group of people, or probably a prominent family, took over the main mound at Knowth and transformed it into a well-protected site' (Eogan 1977a, 70).

An enclosure of a somewhat different type, though possibly for similar purposes to the ringfort-type examples, was recently excavated at Ballyveelish 2, Co. Tipperary. This was one of three dissimilar sites excavated in the townland – Site 3 has already been discussed (p. 208). Site 2 consisted of a sub-rectangular enclosure with an entrance on the east side. It was delimited by a shallow ditch (Doody unpublished). The excavation had to be confined to a 30m-wide corridor since it was carried out as part of the archaeological exploration of the proposed natural gas pipeline from Cork to Dublin and as a consequence the overall dimensions could not be accurately determined, as more than half of the site lay outside the corridor. Its size has been estimated at 47m N–S by 25m E–W. The interior had suffered considerable disturbance and the occupation horizon, if such had existed, had been removed, and possibly the uppermost layers of the ditch fill also. The ditch as found was 1.8m wide at the mouth and *c.*1m in maximum depth. There was no evidence of a bank but this could have been removed in the past. There was (and still is) a natural spring within the enclosure, just inside the entrance.

The accumulation in the ditch suggested that after its initial digging it was allowed to silt up, and domestic refuse accumulated. Finds consisted of charcoal, animal bones (cattle, pig and sheep), objects of bone and stone, a lignite bracelet and 246 sherds of pottery, most of them in weathered condition. Of forty-seven recognizable sherds, there were twenty rims, six shoulders, eighteen body sherds and three base sherds. About ninety-five per cent represented domestic flat-based ware consisting of tubby jars and bowls similar to the functional pottery of Class II from Lough Gur. Some charred grains of barley were also discovered. Two radiocarbon dates were obtained from wood charcoal from the upper fill of the ditch at north and south sides of the entrance respectively: 2550 ± 130 BP and 2770 ± 60 BP.

Hut circles

Unenclosed dwellings, generally in groups, are usually referred to (often with no very good reason) as hut circles. One such group is that on Scrabo Hill at the head of Strangford Lough in Co. Down (Owens 1970, 9; 1971, 11). There was evidence of extensive settlement including several groups of hut circles. The excavation of one of the huts in the late 1960s, together with earlier finds, showed the area to have been occupied during the second half of the first millennium BC. The excavation revealed a circular structure *c.*10m in diameter, with the remains of a shallow wall-trench. Postholes supported the roof but others formed part of a smaller structure within the circle. Intense burning was found in a pit and the majority of the pottery, which was coarse, with little or no decoration, was found here. The walls would have been of timber and vegetable matter supported by an outer ring of stones. A radiocarbon date of 2305 ± 70 BP was obtained for charcoal from the wall-slot. A comment on the archaeological evidence (*Radiocarbon* 1971, 451–2) suggests that '[the] site was occupied at transition between Bronze and Iron ages. Comparable dates from Navan (Fort), Co. Armagh and Lough Gara, Co. Sligo'.

Three circular huts, unmarked on the surface, came to light at Curraghatoor, Co. Tipperary, during the investigation of the natural gas pipeline above-mentioned. All three were close together but only one contained a hearth. This hut was 6.5m in diameter and had been constructed of vertical timbers, possibly supporting wattle walls, and a thatched roof. Charcoal from a pit within the hut gave a radiocarbon date of 2840 ± 35 BP (Doody unpublished). A few sherds of pottery found in the hut were of coarse domestic ware. Evidence for the cultivation of cereals was provided by the finding of spikelets of emmer wheat in one of the perimeter postholes of Hut 1.

In a completely different context from Curraghatoor, other evidence of cereal cultivation during the LBA/EIA transition was obtained during the excavation of Grave 26 in the Carrowmore megalithic cemetery in Co. Sligo (p. 108) (Burenhult 1980, 33ff.; 1984, 60). During secondary use of the monument, three cultivation furrows had been dug within the boulder circle together with a number of pits. One of these contained carbonized grains of naked and hulled barley as well as some of rye (Hjelmqvist *in* Burenhult 1980, 37, 130–2). A radiocarbon date of 2480 ± 55 BP was obtained from a sample of grain.

Hillforts

The type of monument which more than any other is traditionally believed to have had its origins in the Celtic Iron Age is the hillfort, but increased excavation is tending to show that the picture is by no means so clearcut. The monuments are frequently of very large size and spectacularly situated, and some of them are mentioned in Early Irish literature, but the truth is that by comparison with, for instance, British examples, or with the ubiquitous Irish ringfort or the crannog, the type is only marginally represented in this country. Barry Raftery (1976, 354) has mentioned a figure of about sixty, but this includes inland promontory forts as well. It excludes, however, the coastal promontory forts and the stone-built *cashels* or ringforts of the south and west which are also sited in commanding situations.

The name 'hillfort' is an unfortunate one as far as Ireland is concerned because enough of the enclosed hilltop-type settlements have not been excavated to allow of a more exact definition of the hillfort proper. The very name implies a defensive structure, but in Ireland this has yet to be proven. The tendency has been to equate them with their namesakes in Britain, where they consist of defensive and defendable sites numbered at well over a thousand, and where a considerable proportion have been excavated and the full results published.

From superficial evidence the Irish sites are either single-ramparted or have two or more, but in the latter case, without excavation it is impossible to know whether or not the multiple ramparts were erected as part of a unitary defensive system, or in the case of the single rampart, whether it is other than a fairly modern enclosure device. In general, though not invariably, the ramparts tend to follow the contour of the hill, and the areas enclosed by them can vary enormously from one site to another. The ditch or fosse can be outside or inside the bank, and the few excavated examples show a certain amount of diversity. Large-scale excavations of a small number of sites within the past two decades have posed more questions than solutions to the problem of Irish hillforts. This is compounded by the fact that only one, that at Freestone Hill, Co. Kilkenny, has been published in full and then only at second-hand by Barry Raftery (1969) who undertook the task of interpreting the field notes and other data after the demise of Dr G. Bersu, the excavator. It is proposed to deal only with these and with a few others where small-scale exploration took place. In the absence of a significant amount of excavation it is impossible to place the hillforts or the many other similar sites such as the hill-enclosures and cliff-top enclosures – Mooghaun in Co. Clare, Carn Tigherna and Cashel Fort, both in Co. Cork, Dun Aengus on the Aran Islands, the Grianán of Aileach in Donegal, and numerous others – in any meaningful perspective or chronological sequence. Hillfort studies in Ireland are still in an embryonic stage, and a different picture from the one now prevalent may well emerge in the not too distant future. Past experience dictates that for the present it is best to avoid undue theorizing on the subject.

Freestone Hill, Co. Kilkenny

Like most of the hilltop sites there is an extensive view on all sides from the top. A bank and an external ditch, now dilapidated, surround the summit, enclosing an area of about 2ha. The bank was of earth and rubble and faced originally with stone; the fosse was deeply cut into the bedrock. On the summit there was a cemetery mound (or multiple cist cairn) 23m in diameter, which contained fifteen certain burial deposits, and there was another burial just outside its perimeter. Both inhumation and cremation were represented. The burial cairn probably dates to the latter part of the EBA. The remains of at least five Food Vessels, all except one of Bowl type, and a plano-convex flint knife were among the artefacts recovered (B. Raftery 1969).

The main focus of habitation overlay the remains of the burial cairn, which had been denuded to build an oval stone enclosure, 36m by 30m; only the lowest courses of the wall survived. It was badly preserved but there appeared to be an inturned entrance on the south-east. A circular stone wall within this enclosure proved to be modern. A black habitation layer 20–40cm thick filled the oval enclosure, three-quarters of which was excavated. The finds were numerous and

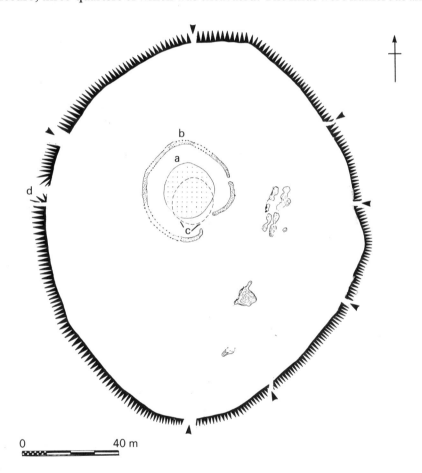

157 Freestone Hill hillfort, Co. Kilkenny, showing surrounding enclosure, the excavated sections of which are shown by arrows. Point d indicates position of entrance. In centre: (a) cairn (b) Iron Age enclosure (c) modern enclosure (after G. Bersu and B. Raftery)

were interpreted as being roughly contemporaneous, though the duration of the occupation, which was of a domestic nature, could not be ascertained. There were at least seven hearths within the enclosure but no trace of structures came to light. Finds, mainly of pottery, also came from areas excavated on other parts of the hill, e.g. adjacent to the outer enclosing bank and from the fill of the ditch.

It was unfortunate but unavoidable under the circumstances in which the publication of the excavation results was undertaken that at the outset a Roman coin, a memorial issue of Constantine II, dated *c*.AD 337–40, found near the centre of the oval enclosure, was taken as providing a central date for the habitation layer. This coloured the interpretation of the finds. Raftery's own subsequent excavations at the Rathgall hillfort in Co. Wicklow later prompted him to doubt this deduction. Pottery identical with some of that of Freestone Hill, containing minute perforations beneath the rim, was found at Rathgall in association with clay mould fragments of LBA date, and caused Raftery to conclude that 'inevitably the question arises as to whether the wares from Freestone Hill, identical with those from Rathgall, represent remarkable cultural continuity over a period of nearly a millennium or whether the pottery from the Kilkenny site derives from an earlier Late Bronze Age settlement on the hilltop which was undetected by the excavator and which became mixed with objects from later levels . . . the likelihood of a Late Bronze Age date for the Freestone Hill pottery becomes now a distinct possibility' (B. Raftery 1976a, 194).

Apart from the sherds containing minute perforations 7mm to 10mm below the rim, the pottery found at Freestone Hill is fairly uniform, representing coarse, flat-bottomed undecorated pots, bucket- or barrel-shaped with flat rims. Artefacts of bronze, iron, glass, bone and stone are also represented. Among the latter were over fifty whetstones. The iron objects were heavily corroded but needles, nails and blades could be recognized. There was a portion of a glass bracelet and beads of blue and green glass. Among the bronze objects were portions of two bracelets, decorated with dots, concentric circles and linear devices which are regarded as of sub-Roman style. The most interesting artefact was a tinned bronze mount consisting of a disc with lightly engraved ornament of circles and trumpet-ended curves surrounded by an openwork border. It was in the same horizon as the Roman coin and various artefacts of Roman inspiration and can possibly be allotted a central date in the mid-fourth century AD (B. Raftery 1970, 209, n. 40).

The ditch and bank surrounding the hillfort had been examined at a number of points. Raftery interpreted the excavated sections as indicating a roughly quarried ditch, the material from which had been transported uphill and packed behind a stone rampart-wall of modest dimensions. In places, traces of pre-existing occupation debris were found beneath the rampart.

Rathgall, Co. Wicklow

Before excavations commenced in 1969 four concentric enclosures were visible on the hilltop, but the innermost one proved to be of medieval date and was built of granite stones. The outermost rampart or bank, which was badly destroyed or absent in places, enclosed an area of about 7ha. About 50m or so inside this were two closely spaced ramparts, 10–12m apart, and apparently conceived as a single defensive element (B. Raftery 1976, 339ff.).

The focus of the settlement was a circular house, 15m in diameter, built of timber uprights set in a bedding trench. A boundary ditch of V-shaped profile, 35m in diameter, surrounded the house foundation. No hearth was definitely associated with the house but at least nine were found, some within the enclosure and some elsewhere. Not all were of a domestic nature: some were connected with a bronze-working industry. A pit near the centre of the house was almost filled by a large boulder set in dense black carbonized organic material, and beneath the boulder was a small penannular gold ring and a scatter of burnt human bone, the whole representing a carefully made deposit. Coarse potsherds formed the major part of the finds over the entire area within the enclosure ditch – over 5,000 of them – and represented flat-based bucket-shaped pots, some with pin-pricks below the rim as noted at Freestone Hill. Several bowls were also represented and, though ornament was uncommon, zigzags, hatched triangles and, in a few cases, cordons were present.

As well, blue glass beads, part of a lignite bracelet and stone objects of a domestic nature such as hones, spindle whorls and a complete saddle quern were found. The most interesting find was a small tinned strap-tag or strap-end (Raftery 1970) found in the layer of domestic refuse which covered the area in question. It is so far without parallel in Ireland, though objects of this type were common in Europe from late La Tène times until well into the first millennium AD (*ibid.*, 202). It invites comparison with the tinned bronze mount found at Freestone Hill, also in an apparent coarse ware context, but Raftery rejects this context in both cases as being due to interference with the stratigraphy. Of Rathgall he says (Raftery 1976a, 194): 'At a late stage in the first season's work . . . Late Bronze Age clay mould fragments began to appear and the apparent association of coarse pottery with the bronze strap-tag came to be regarded as questionable since the layer which contained these objects proved to have been disturbed by rabbit activity.'

The greatest concentration of clay mould fragments came from a habitation layer east of the V-shaped ditch of the enclosure and was associated with the foundations of a large timber structure, apparently a workshop or smithy connected with the manufacture of bronze artefacts such as swords, possibly spears, and

158 The Rathgall hillfort, Co. Wicklow

socketed implements. A bronze socketed gouge was among the objects found and also lignite, stone, glass, amber and gold. Coarse pottery was also present in abundance (Raftery 1971, 297).Among the four gold objects was a composite bead or pendant of gold and glass which testified to the technical expertise of the Rathgall artisans.

Evidence of primitive iron-working was found in a pit which had been dug into the fill of the V-shaped enclosure-ditch when it had become completely silted-up. A large quantity of slag was scattered about, between fourteen and sixteen kilos in weight. During the fourth season of excavation, to the east of the V-shaped enclosure-ditch and partly under the granite wall of the medieval 'cashel', a burial enclosure was discovered (p. 210).

In the fullest account of the excavations to be published to date, the excavator sums up as follows (Raftery 1976, 347):

> Apart from the probably early evidence of iron-working on the site indications of a fully developed Iron Age culture at Rathgall are so far

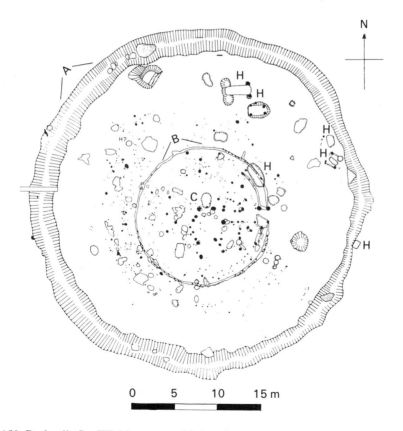

159 Rathgall, Co. Wicklow, central habitation complex: A boundary ditch, B bedding trench, C ritual(?) pit, H hearths (after B. Raftery)

meagre in the extreme. The main defensive ramparts could conceivably be Iron Age in date but this has not yet been tested by excavation. In view of the great paucity of Iron Age finds after four years' excavation it must be admitted that this becomes increasingly unlikely.

A series of radiocarbon dates relating to the different phases of this complex site have been obtained (Raftery 1973a, 29; *Radiocarbon* 1980, 1028) but comment on them must await the definitive excavation report.

Dún Ailinne, Co. Kildare

This, the third of the excavated hilltop sites, is also situated in the southern half of Ireland, that is, south of the Dublin–Galway line. It is documented in early Irish sources under the name *Ailinn* and was the chief seat of the kings of *Laigin*,

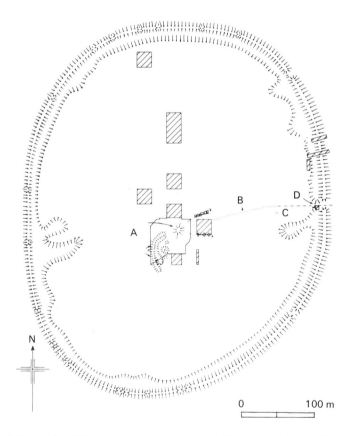

160 Dún Ailinne, Co. Kildare, general site plan: A Features visible before excavation, B Projected course of 'roadway', C Visible part of roadway, D Original entrance (after B. Wailes)

the people of Leinster. The hill itself goes by the name of Knockaulin, which is the townland name. Excavations took place from 1968 to 1974.

A bank and interior ditch surround the hilltop, enclosing an area of *c*.14ha. The original entrance was on the east. The interior had been divided up and placed under cultivation in the more recent past, and this disturbance of the stratification was evident from the way in which artefacts of different periods and phases tended to be mixed together. The only ancient feature visible before excavations began was an almost imperceptible low mound on the summit.

The fullest account of the excavations, an interim report prepared after the first five seasons' work (Wailes 1976, 319ff.), postulated seven phases of Iron Age activity, but in effect these can be condensed to three main phases followed by two final ones, as the reports prepared after the 1973 and 1974 seasons make clear (Wailes 1971–6). Each of the three main phases was marked by the construction of circular palisade trenches in the same general area but not on the same foundations. There were no indications of residential or domestic use nor could the excavator find any evidence of a hiatus between the phases. On the contrary, he says (Wailes 1971–6, 354) that 'the dismantling of each phase indicates that the ground was being cleared for the next phase'. These conclusions are, however, premature until such time as the final report appears.

The Phase 1 enclosure was 22m in diameter and those of the succeeding phases were 35m and 45m respectively in overall maximum diameter. There were three closely spaced rings in the Phase 2 structure, broken at the eastern side by an entrance, and two linear palisade trenches which flanked the entrance ran down the slope of the hill towards the main entrance to the site. The excavator suggested that, in the absence of postholes in the interior of this enclosure such as would have supported a roof, 'the evidence points to a "raked" timber structure around an open space' (Wailes 1976, 325). It was also found that the outermost of the palisade trenches of this phase had sliced through a large pit, almost but not quite destroying a Linkardstown-type pot.

In the Phase 3 structure there were two concentric palisade trenches and a complex entrance. The iron La Tène-type sword previously mentioned (p. 269) was found deep in the fill of one of the trenches though, according to a personal communication from the excavator, there is a doubt as to whether the weapon was in the primary or the secondary fill. At the centre of the enclosed area there was a feature tentatively identified as a 'hut', though no trace of occupation was recorded. While the palisades of the Phase 3 structure were still standing, a series of large posts was erected concentric with them. In due course the palisades were dismantled but the circle of posts was left standing for some time. Finally, the large posts, each up to 50cm thick, were removed, and during this phase intense burning took place which affected the floor of the 'hut' also.

In the final stages, a layer of redeposited glacial till and some flat slabs were laid down, and lastly a large area became covered by a layer of burnt material consisting of blackened earth and burnt stones with a considerable content of animal bones. This formed the low mound detected before excavations began, and it was interpreted as having lasted for a few years during which periodic activities took place and no continual use.

A series of radiocarbon dates has been published (*Radiocarbon* 1973a, 399–400) relating to the palisade trenches and to the subsequent levels, but it is premature to comment on them at this stage. On present evidence the Phase 3 palisade trenches are later than Phase 2, a picture not unlike that found at Navan Fort (to be discussed below). In regard to finds, an interim report on the first two seasons' excavations (Wailes 1970, 88) mentioned that 'numerous small finds of

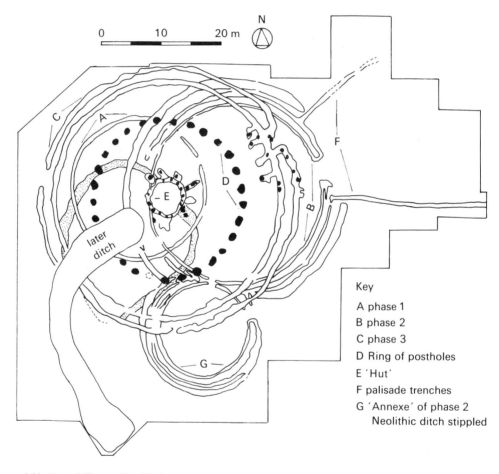

161 Dún Ailinne, Co. Kildare, central area: simplified plan of the three main Iron Age phases (after B. Wailes)

stone, bone, iron, bronze and glass' had come from the Iron Age levels. Most of the iron finds were heavily corroded, and in addition to the iron sword, there were portions of knife blades, nails and rings. There were some fragmentary bronze fibulae, glass beads, portions of blue glass bracelets and a number of whetstones. Two of the fibulae or brooches came from the Phase 3 trenches and are of Romano-British type dating to the period spanning the birth of Christ (C. F. C. Hawkes 1982, 65).

Navan Fort, Co. Armagh

This hilltop site, excavated between 1961 and 1972, is another 'kingly capital', identified with *Emain Macha*, the one-time capital of Ulster. The name 'Navan' is a corruption of *Emain*. Because of certain similarities in the ritual use presumed for both sites, Dún Ailinne has been bracketed with it. The low hill on which the fort is situated is only a few kilometres west of Armagh city. There are extensive views on all sides. At the foot of the hill is Loughnashade, the find-place of the famous bronze trumpets mentioned earlier (p. 271). A bank and inner ditch surround the hill, enclosing an area of *c*.7ha. Crowning the hill is a large mound, Site B, traditionally associated with the ancient seat or dwelling of the *Ulaid*, the people of Ulster whose kingdom, together with those of Tara in Co. Meath and Cruachu in Connacht, was one of the ancient 'Fifths' or five divisions of Ireland. The heroic saga, *Táin Bó Cuailgne*, concerns the disagreements between the kingdoms of *Ulaid* and the *Connachta*. The final overthrow of *Emain Macha* is variously dated by the medieval Irish chroniclers to between AD 337 and 450.

Excavation* showed evidence of occupation on the hill as early as Neolithic times but, apart from scatters of flint and potsherds, the remains had been removed by ploughing before the beginning of the main period of settlement in the seventh century BC. The principal visible remains on the summit were the substantial grass-grown mound, Site B, and nearby, a ploughed-out ring-ditch, Site A, of uncertain date. Excavation showed that the ring-ditch cut through part of a settlement which contained a series of three concentric ring-slots, possibly representing round houses.

There were two main periods of use in Site B, the first perhaps representing domestic activity; the second main period of use was certainly ceremonial. The first period of use was represented by a succession of ring-slots which may well have been the foundation trenches of circular houses of planks or wattle,

---

* Owing to the untimely death of the excavator, Mr D. M. Waterman, the definitive report is being prepared by a colleague, Mr C. J. Lynn of the Historic Monuments and Buildings Branch, Dept of the Environment (NI). The best description so far published of the excavations is by Selkirk and Waterman 1970.

*c.*10–14m in diameter. There were nine of these in all and structural remains or 'annexes' associated with some of the later ones could be interpreted as farmyards or stockades, but it must be stressed that a domestic interpretation for this period of activity is by no means certain (C. J. Lynn, pers. comm.). The enclosure ditch was not maintained throughout this time and some of the later ring-slots encroached on it. At a still later stage the lay-out was altered and three further circular structures were erected on a different spot.

Many small finds were recovered. There were several hundred sherds of coarse bucket-shaped flat-rimmed pots; artefacts of glass, lignite and bronze were also recovered, e.g. glass beads, a ring-headed pin, a bronze socketed sickle, a tiny bronze socketed axe and the wing of a Hallstatt C-type scabbard chape. There was no evidence of iron-working but some small iron artefacts were found. The assemblage as a whole showed cultural continuity from LBA to EIA times.*

The second main period of use began with the erection over the remains of the ring-slots of a massive circular structure consisting of widely spaced timber uprights, 3–5m apart and linked by horizontal planks laid out so as to fit within the primary LBA enclosure-ditch which by this time was almost silted up. Within the space enclosed by the outer ring there were four other concentric rings of oak posts about 3m apart, and the posts of each ring were an average distance of 1.5m from one another. At the centre a great posthole was found with a large ramp leading to it, and it has been suggested that it must have contained an exceptionally tall, and possibly non-structural, post. The entrance-way through the rings of posts was on the west side, on the axis of the ramp. It is not known if the structure as a whole was roofed but details of the construction suggest that it was. There was evidence for some 275 posts in all. Dendrochronological examination of samples of the timbers, carried out in the Palaeoecology Centre of Queen's University, Belfast, has established that all the timbers were cut down at the same time, i.e. *c.* 100 BC (in calendrical years), and it appears that very little, if any, time had elapsed between the end of the first main period of use of the site and the second, or ritual period.

Perhaps as little as a decade or so after its erection (Mallory 1985) the interior of the multi-ring structure was filled with a cairn of stones approximately 2.8m in height at the centre. When the oak posts of the structure rotted away they left voids in the cairn filling, showing that the posts were standing when the cairn material was inserted. There were no small finds that would have assisted in the interpretation of these two stages. The next stage in what was apparently a continuous process was the burning of the outer wall. This would seem to have

---

* This information and that contained in succeeding paragraphs has been provided by courtesy of Mr C. J. Lynn in advance of his publication.

been a deliberate act as the remains of brushwood which could have served as kindling material was found in the form of charred twigs around the perimeter. There were no traces of burning on top of or within the cairn.

The latter was covered over fairly soon with a mound of redeposited turves. It had a thickness of 2.5m at the centre and a fairly flat top, and it sloped down at the sides so as to cover the line of the Period I enclosure-ditch. The entire mound, including cairn material, measured 5m in height and 50m in diameter at the time of the excavation. It must be remembered, however, that these turves would have suffered a certain amount of shrinkage in the course of time and the sides would have slipped and spread outwards; therefore the original Site B mound would probably have been greater in height and smaller in diameter.

In a summing-up of the extraordinary sequence of events that led to the creation of the mound as we know it today, C. J. Lynn writes:

> The . . . timber building was apparently not used for occupation. Its regular, almost geometric lay-out, and its size suggest that it was erected as a communal effort under the supervision of a technically competent

162 Navan Fort (*Emain Macha*), Co. Armagh: surrounding hedge roughly coincides with bank/ditch; Site B under excavation, Site A above and to the right

person or group. The presence of a structurally unnecessary and probably free-standing post at centre suggests that it was used for a ritual or ceremonial purpose in the Early Iron Age. Indeed the construction of the building, its use, the immediate insertion of the cairn, the burning and the addition of the sod mound may well have been planned from the start as part of a single almost continuous series of ritual acts.

It is of great significance that timbers from 'The Dorsey' in South Armagh, a series of cross-dykes and an earthwork, traditionally the southern frontier of the kingdom centred on Navan Fort, were shown to be of identical dendrochronological date as those from Site B (allowing for the absence of sapwood) (Lynn 1982). We must, therefore, take seriously the proposition that the same group or community was responsible for the erection of both monuments.

Navan Fort has attracted attention over a considerable period of time, as has another famous northern site, that of Lisnacrogher, and unfortunately, one of the reasons is the same in each case, namely, destruction by the hand of man. This was noted at Navan Fort even in the last century and is still relevant today because of the huge commercial quarry development on the eastern side of the hill.

163 Navan Fort, Co. Armagh, Site B: surface of cairn after removal of turf mound. Radial divisions visible on surface

Clogher, Co. Tyrone

This site consists of a complex of earthworks in Clogher demesne on Castle Hill to the south of the town of Clogher. The shoulder of the hill or drumlin is surrounded by the remains of a prominent bank, parts of which are still fairly well preserved. It encloses an area, quadrilateral in shape, of about 2ha in extent. The north end of the enclosure contains several parallel banks, but excavation showed that they had not been erected as a single defensive system but over a period of time. The summit is now crowned by a ringfort with an entrance on the east. Immediately south of the ringfort is a roughly triangular mound, 15m in diameter, with steep sides and a flat top which is likely to be the 'inauguration mound' of the chiefs of Airgialla, a powerful federation of tribes in mid-Ulster which came into prominence, according to the medieval historians, from about the fifth century AD onwards. As with the other hillforts mentioned above, with the exception of Freestone Hill, the Clogher excavations await publication and one must rely on short interim reports (Warner 1969; 1971; 1972; 1972a; 1973; 1974; 1975–6).

Evidence of occupation and utilization of the hill from Neolithic times

164 Navan Fort, Co. Armagh, Site B: south-west quadrant showing ring-slots. Ranging rods at top of picture mark large postholes of outer slot of 40m-diameter timber building

through both EBA and LBA and into both early and later stages of the Iron Age
was documented in the artefactual evidence, though, prior to the Iron Age levels,
this mostly took the form of scattered finds or fragmentary remains of structures.
A sample of charcoal antedating the 'inauguration mound' and probably belonging to a scatter of prehistoric remains was radiocarbon-dated to 3045 ± 75 BP.
The next phase relates to a 'habitation' platform with hearths, small postholes
and stakeholes associated with flat-based coarse ware and a ^{14}C date of 2630 ±
45 BP was obtained. The 'platform' was cut by ploughmarks. In the next phase
there were large pits with associated club-rim coarse ware, and these appeared to
be bounded by a drystone 'cashel'-like wall. There seem to have been horizontal
timbers lying transversely through the wall at the height of the second course, a
feature so far unique in Ireland (R. B. Warner, pers. comm.).

The exact chronological position of the bank enclosing the hill in relation to
these internal features is not clear but the excavator proposed that it could be

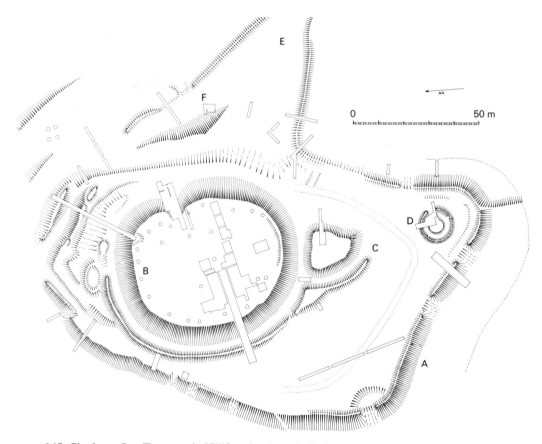

165 Clogher, Co. Tyrone. A Hillfort bank and ditch, B Ringfort, C 'Inauguration
mound', D Ringbarrow, E 'Doorway', F Furnaces (after R. Warner; Crown copyright)

connected with the last phase mentioned above. Excavation showed that the bank was thrown up from material taken from a shallow external ditch of U-section. A bronze spiral finger- or toe-ring was found low in the fill. The ditch was destroyed in the east by the construction of an extensive platform for iron smelting. The furnaces had been dug into the filled-up ditch. At least two were present, one of simple bowl type which had been used several times; the other was partly stone-built. An annular iron brooch was associated with them. Charcoal from the bowl furnace produced a radiocarbon date of 1555 ± 45 BP. The surrounding bank and ditch, that is, the hillfort proper, is tentatively dated by the excavator to the early centuries of the Christian era.

On the summit the remains of a circular enclosure were found, 50m in internal diameter. It was delimited by a broad flat-bottomed ring-ditch inside which was a palisade and on the outside a low bank capped by another palisade. Postholes representing wooden structures were found within the enclosure. It produced both insular and imported objects. Native artefacts included a 'mottled bead', a multi-spiral bronze ring and the debris of zoomorphic penannular brooch-manufacture. The latter, in typological terms at least, suggests a date of fifth/sixth century AD. Sherds of imported amphorae were also present.

A ringfort, c.70m across internally, was constructed over the area occupied by the ring-ditch, and its bank partly overlay the partially silted-up ring-ditch, sealing material of that particular phase. Imported E-ware which included sherds of jars and bowls was found beneath and against the ringfort bank, and other artefacts included penannular brooches, a hand-pin and a hoard of iron objects among which were a double-edged axe, a small sickle and a pair of shears. In the 1975 season, excavation of the entrance showed evidence of roadways and wooden gateposts. The earliest phase was associated with E-ware, 'thus confirming the building of the ringfort during the period of importation of this class of pottery' (Warner 1975–6, 18). The evidence suggests the abandonment of the ringfort about 800 AD, and ^{14}C dates from samples of charcoal from the occupation levels of the ringfort tend to support the sixth- to eighth-century occupation date proposed by the excavator.

Other excavated sites

The Rath of the Synods on the Hill of Tara in Co. Meath is a structure of ringfort-type which derives its name from a tradition that synods of the early Irish Church were held there at various times by Saints Patrick, Ruadhán and Adamnán (the latter the biographer of St Colmcille of Iona at the close of the seventh century). It was excavated by S. P. Ó Ríordáin in 1952–3 but like its immediate neighbours, Ráth na Ríogh (see below) and the Mound of the Hostages (p. 105), remains unpublished owing to his death in 1957. In the 1950s, Ó Ríordáin was

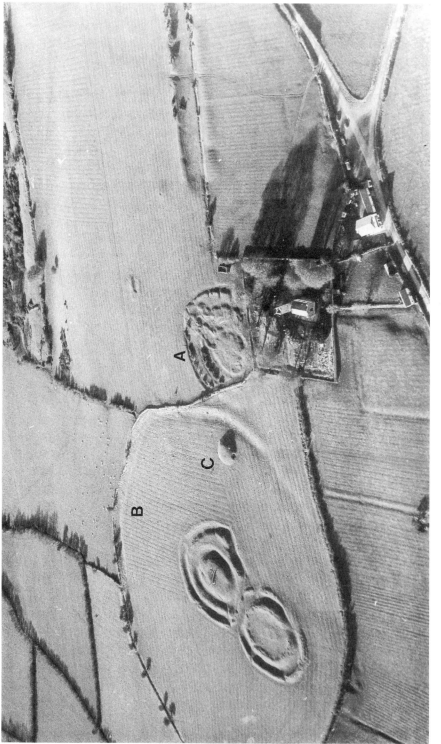

166 Hill of Tara, Co. Meath: A Rath of the Synods, B Ráth na Ríogh, C Mound of the Hostages

about to embark on a campaign of excavations on the Hill of Tara and he chose the Rath of the Synods as an initial trial excavation because, although it had been grievously damaged at the end of the last century by a group known as the British Israelites, he felt it would enable him to get the feel of the terrain before under-taking untouched sites.

R. A. S. Macalister who endeavoured to piece together the history of the earlier 'diggings' at the Rath of the Synods explains that the members of the group believed the Ark of the Covenant to be buried there, and since the site was then in private ownership, they persuaded the proprietor to allow them to dig it up. He speaks unflatteringly of them as 'certain people who held a doctrine known as "British Israel" – an abortion begotten of unscholarly ignorance of the nature of the Biblical historical record, upon unbridled national bumptiousness' (Macalister 1931, 32). Elsewhere (*ibid.*, 39) he says: 'Had the "Ark of the Covenant" dreamers even done so much as to record what they actually did find, much might have been forgiven them.' From eye-witness reports he gathered that Roman coins of Constantine the Great and a bracelet, perhaps of gold, were among the finds, together with human and animal bones.

In a brief note, Ó Ríordáin (1985, 25–6) describes the site as a central space surrounded by three concentric banks, rock-cut fosses and palisade trenches, built during four successive phases, the overall diameter being about 80m. Between the outermost bank and the middle one there was a flat-topped burial mound containing both burnt and unburnt human remains. A succession of wooden houses had occupied the central space, and Roman-type finds such as a lock, a seal, fragments of glass and pottery were identified and dated the site to the first to third century AD.

Immediately to the south is another of the 'kingly' sites, Ráth na Ríogh, the Rath of the Kings, said to have been built by Cormac Mac Airt who supposedly lived in the fourth century AD. It consists of a great oval enclosure about 290m by 240m surrounded by a deep fosse and the slight remains of an outer bank. The Mound of the Hostages, a Neolithic passage grave (p. 105), lies just within the enclosure at the north and in fact the ditch and bank of Ráth na Ríogh bend out-ward to accommodate it. More or less centrally placed within the enclosure are two earthworks known as the Forradh (Royal Seat) and Teach Chormaic (Cormac's House). A trial section was cut through the bank and ditch of Ráth na Ríogh by Ó Ríordáin in 1953. The ditch was found to be over 3m in depth and the material removed from it would have been sufficient to build a substantial surrounding bank. Inside the fosse he found 'a trench which would have held a great wooden palisade' (Ó Ríordáin 1985, 9). Barry Raftery has since examined the drawings and has deduced that the proposed palisade trench post-dated the silting-up of the fosse (Raftery 1972, 42–3). If true, this would imply that Ráth na Ríogh is yet another multi-period monument.

Just as some hillforts and enclosures have been singled out by tradition as centres of secular pagan power and associated with various powerful dynasties, there are two sites in the north-east of Ireland which are related to the coming of Christianity to Ireland in the fifth century. These are Armagh and Downpatrick. Armagh, which has been mentioned previously in connection with pagan Celtic carvings (p. 289), was reputedly chosen by St Patrick for his principal church, and the hill itself, with whatever structure or structures were on it, was said to have been given him by the local chieftain. Today, the Cathedral Church of St Patrick crowns the hill and the city clusters on its flanks, the streets and houses near the top following the line of the old rampart.

Rescue excavation carried out in 1968 uncovered a substantial ditch dating from before 1660 ± 80 BP (Gaskell Brown and Harper 1984). It was found that an outer bank had been deliberately pushed back into the ditch some time after this date and the ditch used in part as a dump for debris from an Early Christian Period metal workshop. Numerous finds relating to the latter were recovered. The ditch was almost full by 1430 ± 85 BP. When calibrated these dates are not inconsistent with the substance of the Patrician legend. Within the enclosure fragmentary remains of various structures dating from the fifth century onwards were traced and showed that the hill or 'city' had been continuously occupied up to the present day.

The second site with Patrician associations is Downpatrick, where the saint supposedly built one of his earliest churches and where he is reputed to be buried. Like Armagh, the Cathedral Church of Down is situated on the summit within an enclosure. A limited excavation confined to the south-western slope of the hill was undertaken in the 1950s (Proudfoot 1954; 1956). He found indications that the hill had been occupied in Neolithic times, though little factual evidence remained apart from potsherds and stone axes. In the early part of the first millennium BC activity recommenced with an open settlement, but the main period of activity on the hill appears to belong to a considerably later time. Excavations taking place on the hill at present are tending to emphasize the medieval character of the site.

Unconnected with the Proudfoot excavations, though very close to them, two finds of gold objects were made. The find-places were close together but the discoveries took place at two different times, in 1954 and in 1956, when a new graveyard was being opened west of the cathedral. The hoards were similar and had been carefully deposited. There were fourteen gold penannular bracelets in all and a fragment of another one together with a neck-ring (Proudfoot 1955; 1957). On stylistic grounds they can be dated to about the seventh century BC. Proudfoot suggests that the gold was hidden 'while the site was occupied during the transitional period from bronze to iron age' (Proudfoot 1955, 31).

12

Iron Age burial

There is at present no certain record of the burial traditions prevailing in Ireland in Early Iron Age times until the final centuries of the first millennium BC when objects of adornment such as beads, brooches, bracelets and occasional personal possessions are sometimes found with the remains. Were it not for these, on the basis of the evidence at present available from the published record, it would be impossible to determine to which particular part of the millennium they related. There is a considerable gap between these and the few examples mentioned earlier (p. 210) for the first part of the millennium, i.e. the LBA. This is due either to the failure to recognize a characteristic burial tradition which could be presumed to have lasted unchanged throughout the 'hiatus' or else to the fact that no such single distinctive type existed. The problem is not peculiar to Ireland but is found in Britain also if one excepts the square-ditched barrows and cart burials of eastern Yorkshire and the extensive cremation cemeteries of the south-east.

Burial mounds

Barrow mounds are a type of monument in which burials of both Bronze Age and Iron Age tradition are represented, and some of the better documented examples have been mentioned earlier (p. 205). Unfortunately, these are 'old' excavations, e.g. Cush, Carrowjames, Pollacorragune, Carrowbeg North, and so on, carried out in the 1930s and 1940s in pre-radiocarbon days and at a time when the distinction between the later part of the Bronze Age and the EIA appeared to be a lot more clear-cut than it is now believed to be.

Tumulus I of the group of three at Cush, Co. Limerick, can be dated securely enough to the later part of the Early Bronze Age but Tumulus II and possibly no. III are probably Early Iron Age in date. Each mound was about 2m in height and 13.7m and 16.46m respectively in diameter with enclosing fosse. On the old ground surface beneath the mound of no. II there were spreads of charcoal mixed with fragments of cremated bone. The excavator (S. P. Ó Ríordáin) assumed that this represented the site of a cremation fire. A pit was found in one of the spreads, filled with cremated bone and charcoal, and near the top was a small ornamented bone plaque of La Tène type which had been subjected to heat (Ó Ríordáin 1940, 155–6). It was compared to the ornamented bone flakes found at Loughcrew (p. 281) but Barry Raftery (1984, 248–50) says that it bears a closer resemblance to a plaque from Mentrim Lough crannog in Co. Meath. He believes the objects in question were gaming pieces. On the evidence of association, and because both of the tumuli at Cush are similar to one another, an Iron Age date is likely for them.

At Pollacorragune near Tuam, Co. Galway, we have seen that Mound I, a round stone-covered barrow, contained a primary burial of Bronze Age date, while immediately below the surface of the mound there was indirect evidence of a secondary interment in the shape of a scatter of tiny blue glass beads. The latter have been found elsewhere in association with Iron Age burials. Mound II was about 220m SE of the first. Both mounds were sited on an esker and the irregular nature of the second mound raises the question as to whether it was not, in fact, merely part of the natural gravel ridge. There were some scatters of charcoal, and four extended burials were found in shallow irregular trenches dug into the gravel. Some fragments of iron were recovered (Riley 1936) and an Iron Age or possibly later date is presumed.

A long period of use has been postulated for the Carrowjames cemetery (J. Raftery 1940–1) and some of the tumuli have already been described. The excavator considered that Tumulus 8 was the most important monument in the cemetery from the point of view of finds and of the number of burials it contained. The mound was practically invisible before excavation though the surrounding ditch was well defined. The overall diameter, including external

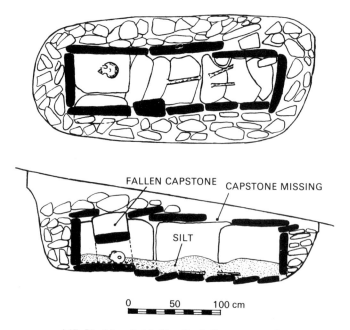

167 Hoddersfield, Co. Cork, long stone cist

330

bank, was 15.5m. Apart from a few patches of charcoal and cremated bone in the ditch, there were twenty-five cremations, all in small irregular pits, and nine of them were accompanied by grave goods. These consisted of glass beads and small objects of bronze such as rings, beads and studs (*ibid.*, 33–7).

The burial mound at Grannagh, near Ardrahan in Co. Galway, was first excavated in 1916 by R. A. S. Macalister and later, in 1969, by Etienne Rynne. Fragments of cremated bone were 'strewn on the ground in handfuls . . . no attempt having been made to protect them with urns, with stones or in any other way' (Macalister 1917, 509). Glass beads and part of a bone pin were found and when the monument was re-excavated in 1969, further pockets of cremated bone were recovered, mainly from the fosse. Finds included three fragmentary bronze La Tène-type fibulae of rod-bow type, glass beads of various kinds including one of dumb-bell shape, bone beads and pins and some items of iron (Rynne 1969). The glass beads, ten in all, some associated with cremation deposits and others unstratified within the mound, are of considerable interest (p. 280). Barry Raftery illustrates and comments on some of them (1984, 201–2; fig. 100) and a fuller illustrated account comes from C. F. C. Hawkes (1982, 59–61; figs. 8 and 9). The latter authority is in agreement with the excavator in dating the cremation burials to the first century BC and perhaps continuing on into the next century. On the other hand, Raftery, in a discussion of the Grannagh finds (1981, 195–6), inclines to the later rather than to the earlier date. In his 1984 volume (p. 201) he suggests 'A putative Roman context for burial activity at the Grannagh monument . . . further enhanced by Macalister's early discovery there of two fragmentary beads of bluish-green glass which, according to Guido, may well be made of re-used Roman bottle glass'.

A small ring-barrow similar to Grannagh and in the same area was excavated by Etienne Rynne at Oranbeg in 1970. The primary burial remains were fragmentary but a small cremation deposit in the fosse was accompanied by over eighty tiny beads, mostly of yellow paste, and since some of them were fused together, it was apparent that they had been subjected to intense heat, perhaps in the cremation pyre (Rynne 1970). Some fragmentary bronze objects were also recovered. The similarity of Oranbeg to the Grannagh monument indicates a similar date.

Three burial sites were excavated at Carbury, Co. Kildare, in the 1930s (Willmot 1938). Two of them, Sites A and B, were in the nature of enclosures with a bank and an irregular interior ditch which presumably acted as a quarry for the enclosure bank. There appeared to have been no mound. In the central 'platform' of Site A there was a small pocket of cremated bone, and nearby was a fragment of fused blue glass. A secondary cremation was found in the fosse. The small finds included flints, a few sherds of pottery, a handled jet spoon, an iron file and an unfinished spindle whorl. The sherds may possibly be medieval or even recent (B. Raftery 1981, 186). Raftery compares the jet spoon to silver communion spoons of late Roman times but he feels, nevertheless, that while this may have some bearing on the date of Site A, the evidence is too flimsy for definitive assumptions.

Site B was somewhat similar, though larger. There were four cremations and fifteen extended inhumations. None of the cremations was central to the enclosure. If such a burial was originally present, it could have been disturbed by the subsequent ones. The excavator proposed that the site had been used over a period of time because some inhumations were disturbed by later ones. Two iron rings were found with one of the cremations and a pair of iron shears with one of the inhumations. These two finds, however, do little more than establish that the secondary burials in Site B were post-Bronze Age in date.

There was no dating evidence for Site C, a small mound less than 200m from Site B. Near the apparent centre was a cremation placed in a shallow hollow in the bedrock. Its situation at the very summit of the hill led the excavator to suggest that since it occupied the best position, it might perhaps be the earliest burial (Willmot 1938, 140).

The two mounds excavated at Carrowbeg North in Co. Galway (Willmot 1938–9) contained primary Bronze Age cremations, as mentioned earlier (p. 207). In addition, four secondary interments, three extended and one flexed, were found in the surrounding fosse of Mound I. The flexed burial was that of a female. Near the shoulder there was a bronze locket-like object which had traces of woven cloth still adhering to it. B. Raftery (1984, 206) remarks that 'this is the only piece of textile from Ireland for which an Iron Age date may be argued'. Near one of the ankles were twelve bone beads. The mound was later raised by the addition of a capping of earth in which was some cremated bone.

A similar raising or heightening of a mound was carried out in the Archdall deerpark at Kiltierney, Co. Fermanagh. The monument in this case was a 'carn', so-called, which reputedly covered a passage tomb. This has been mentioned previously (p. 144). The Kiltierney deerpark and surrounds are – or were – extremely rich in archaeological remains and obviously constituted an important cemetery. The passage grave mound was explored several times in the course of the past hundred years and when another brief excavation was carried out in 1969 by Laurence Flanagan, the site was already sadly dilapidated, though the two decorated orthostats were still lying on top of the mound and the fosse and the encircling ring of small mounds noted in 1942 by Oliver Davies were still present (Davies 1946). About half of the mounds were examined, either in the last century, or by Davies, or by Flanagan.

The 1969 excavation has not been published but in a brief note (Flanagan 1969) it was stated that no evidence of a central chamber had been discovered in the large mound. It was confirmed that it had been heightened. The excavation revealed a scatter of finds which included a leaf-shaped arrowhead, a sherd of Food Vessel and a sherd of Carrowkeel ware. In addition, there were Early Iron Age cremation burials, and the associated finds included a bronze safety pin fibula and some decorated glass beads. The cremations were in pits similar to those found at Grannagh, and there is a general resemblance between the finds from both sites. The finds are discussed by C. F. C. Hawkes (1982, 63–4) and by B. Raftery (1984, 155–6). The bronze fibula is a unique specimen and comes within the leaf-bow category. The four glass beads, which include a dumb-bell example, resemble some of the Grannagh beads, and a date spanning the birth of Christ was assigned on stylistic grounds as well as on those of associated context.

Since these accounts were published, the site came under threat and in 1983 it was decided to excavate those of the small mounds in the surrounding ring which had not previously been investigated.* It was shown that the ring of small mounds lay on the outer edge of the fosse which surrounded the cairn and that it formed a reasonable circle. The central cairn or mound was 20m in diameter and 1.8m in height. The surrounding small mounds were *c*.3m in diameter and about 1m in height. They were about 4.5m apart from centre to centre and were built of material dug from the fosse. A cremation was found beneath one of them, accompanied by an iron fibula together with fragments of a bronze artefact, or artefacts. A first-century AD date was proposed for the fibula. It appeared that the fosse, the ring of small mounds or barrows and the adaptation of the Neolithic cairn all comprised a unitary feature.

Inhumation

While inhumation burials, usually extended, either in simple pits or in long cists, are known from the Bronze Age, this practice is more commonly associated with the Iron Age and later. In cases where cremation and inhumation occur as secondary interments in the same mound, e.g. Site B at Carbury, the cremations appear to be the earlier (Willmot 1938, 136), but by and large, the evidence on the matter is not nearly as definite as one would wish. A small number of inhumations for which a date within the Iron Age is 'reasonably probable' are listed by Barry Raftery (1981, 191–4). These include the inhumed burials found in secondary positions in the immediate vicinity of Site 1 at Knowth, Co. Meath, in the passage-grave cemetery. Up to and including 1972, twenty burials were exca-

---

* This was carried out by the officers of the Historic Monuments and Buildings Branch of the Dept of the Environment (NI), and Claire Foley has kindly provided a summary of the results in advance of publication.

vated and have been published (Eogan 1968; 1974) but at least half a dozen others have been excavated since then. None of the twenty published burials was protected, the bodies being laid mostly in flexed positions in pits dug in the subsoil. One was a double burial of two men aged about thirty and the associated grave goods included bone dice, bone 'gaming pieces' and a number of smooth stone pebbles which may also have been used in the same pursuit. Many of the Knowth remains did not constitute formal burials, that is, some were fragmentary and others consisted of the skull only. At least eight were accompanied by gravegoods such as blue glass beads, bone beads, bronze rings and some curious conical stone objects which again may be gaming pieces.

In the Rath of Feerwore in the townland of Turoe, Co. Galway (p. 307), the disturbed inhumation of a female was found in the NW quadrant, and it appears to have been contained in a long stone cist without grave goods (J. Raftery 1944a). The excavator assigned the burial to the latest Iron Age phase of activity at the site. A cist burial containing a cremation is also said to have been associated with the ringfort, though no trace remained at the time of the excavation. It was allegedly found in the bank of the ringfort but John Waddell (1974–5, 10) says that while there is no firm evidence to date the cist to the Bronze Age, it probably pre-dated the construction of the ringfort.

Long stone cists

While some long stone cists are known from Bronze Age contexts, found mainly in tumuli or cairns (Waddell 1970, 94–6), it was at one time customary to regard the majority as constituting another manifestation of the later stages of the Iron Age. Over forty years ago, J. Raftery (1941) listed upwards of eighty examples, most of which were grouped in cemeteries. Grave goods were markedly absent except in cases where pottery was present and Bronze Age influence was to be suspected. Many more have been excavated since that time but the almost completely negative evidence as regards grave goods has been maintained. Long stone cists usually contain a single skeleton. The sides and floor are lined with stone slabs and similar ones are laid over the top. Normal dimensions are about 2m in length and about 50cm in maximum width. The fact that they are usually orientated E–W, or approximately so, lends weight to the proposition that they are later than the EIA proper and were a response to influences emanating from the Roman world if not from Christianity itself. That the custom of inhumation gradually superseded that of cremation from the beginning of the first millennium AD is evident, and even if the exact role of the long cist in this process remains problematical, inhumation is only one of the factors which reflected the Romanizing influences that were reaching Ireland at this time.

Intrusive burials

In contrast to the native or insular types of EIA burial, none of which show any very specific foreign or intrusive elements beyond those which can be explained by reason of Ireland's contacts with Britain and beyond, there are a few examples where more specific extraneous influences were responsible. A few instances may be cited.

At Bray Head on the coast south of Dublin Bay, a cemetery of inhumations in long stone cists was reported in 1835. The find was mentioned by Samuel Lewis in the first volume of his *Topographical Dictionary of Ireland* published in 1837, and from the point of view of contemporaneity at least, some weight must be given to his account. He said (*ibid.*, 223) that the find was made in sand near the sea and that 'several human skeletons of large dimensions were discovered, lying regularly east and west, with a stone at the head and another at the feet of each'. Several coins of the Emperor 'Adrian' were allegedly found at the same time. On the evidence of the coins, the second century AD is indicated, but whether they can be firmly associated with the interments is not entirely clear. Somewhat later accounts mentioned that the coins, attributed to Trajan and Hadrian, had been placed on the breast or beside each skeleton.

Another early discovery was the so-called 'Loughey' find, made about the year AD 1850, which is now dispersed between the British Museum and the Ashmolean Museum, Oxford – and in addition, there are the inevitable 'missing' pieces. The location of the site of Loughey itself is unknown but research (Jope and Wilson 1957a) points to the coast of Co. Down near Donaghadee as the likely find area. The objects were in a pit and the finder made no mention of human bones, cremated or otherwise, or of pottery. Possibly he had eyes for nothing but the 'treasure'. This consisted of glass armlets and over 150 glass beads, as well as miscellaneous bronzes, including a brooch of simple Nauheim-derivative type which was current in Britain in the first century AD. It is said that the missing finds had included a brass coin, amber beads and several more glass armlets. The finds are fully discussed and illustrated in Jope and Wilson (*ibid.*), and the burial (probably a cremation) with which they were associated was almost certainly that of a female. A southern English origin, dating probably to the first century AD, has been argued on the basis of the finds.

La Tène-type and Roman or Romano-British finds from burials on Lambay Island, Co. Dublin, have been extensively researched by Etienne Rynne (1976). The most important are the burials on the western side of the island which were discovered in 1927 during harbour works. R. A. S. Macalister reported on the discovery shortly afterwards but by then everything had been dispersed and he could only endeavour to piece together whatever first-hand information was available on the spot (Macalister 1929). At least two crouched burials in pits had been recognized. One was presumed to have been that of a warrior because of the nature of the associated finds, i.e. a shield (only the boss of which remained) and an iron sword. A female or females are presumed to have been interred also. There were five fibulae of Roman type, possibly an iron mirror, and numerous fragments of sheet bronze, which have since been reconstructed to form two decorative discs or plaques, as well as rings of bronze and shale, a beaded bronze collar or torc and a glass bracelet or anklet. Earlier finds included an iron sword (now lost) and an incomplete gold band (now in NMI).

Etienne Rynne assigns dates within the second half of the first century AD to these finds which are clearly exotic in type, of Gallo-Roman and British origin, and the question remains as to how they and those who owned them came to be interred on Lambay. The island is less than 5km from the coast of north Co. Dublin yet it is not one from which ready access can be gained to Dublin Bay, and therefore casual trade links do not provide an easy explanation. In fact, R. B. Warner (1976, 278) makes the point that the island was described by Ptolemy as 'uninhabited'. A suggestion which has gained much currency is that the cemetery was that of a group of 'refugees (Brigantian and other central British and north Welsh) fleeing from the Roman advance into, and subjugation of, central Britain in the 70s' (*ibid.*, 279).

Another 'old' burial was one 'found in a rath and protected with stones in a field . . . near Stoneyford, Co. Kilkenny', the meagre details of which are preserved in manuscript in the Royal Irish Academy, Dublin (Bateson 1973, 72–3). The discovery of the burial was made either in 1832 or in 1852, it is not clear which. A green glass urn about 25cm in height contained cremated human bones and there was also another vessel (a glass phial or bottle) and a bronze disc-mirror. The urn is now missing. This is clearly a Roman interment and Barry Raftery claims that it is the only genuine one of Roman type from Ireland. One of the curious features about it is that it is situated so far inland, where the casual Romano-British trader or voyager would not be expected to penetrate. On the other hand, it is close to a major river crossing and, as Richard Warner has pointed out (1976, 274) in reference to the finds: 'The fact of the existence of such fragile material must surely imply the presence of a strong and secure Roman community.' The coastal areas may not, therefore, have had a monopoly of Roman incursions, a point well discussed by Warner (*ibid.*). In this context it must be remembered that gold and other ornaments of Romano-British type and twenty-five Roman coins of gold, silver and bronze, dating from the first to the fourth century AD, were discovered at Newgrange, a site about 14km from the coast (Carson and O'Kelly 1977). Most were found during the 1962–75 excavations and the most plausible explanation of their presence is that they were

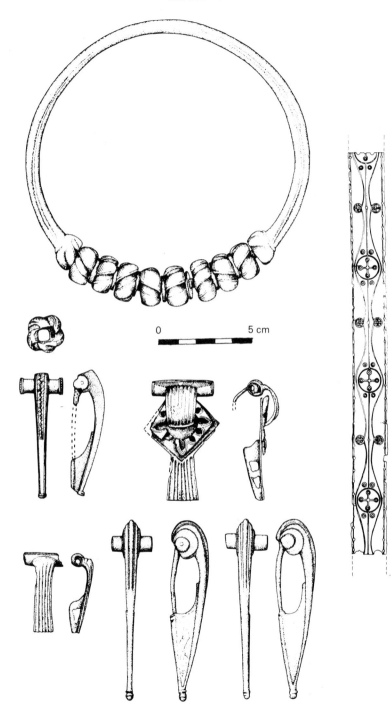

168 Lambay, Co. Dublin, beaded bronze collar, gold band and fibulae (after B. Raftery)

votive offerings. Whether this is true or not it does testify to a Roman or Romano-British presence, however fleeting, during the period or periods in question.

By and large the volume of Roman finds which has come to light up to the present is not great, being in the minority of cases confined to coins of first- and second- and fourth- and fifth-century date. These are the periods when contacts between Ireland and Roman Britain seem to have been closest. In the early centuries there were influxes of refugees fleeing from the Roman advance and when the Empire fell into decline in the fourth century the Irish in common with other 'barbarians' were not slow to take advantage of the changed circumstances. Booty was brought back to Ireland, some of it in the form of slaves, and in one raiding party was no less a captive than the young Patrick who was later to bring Christianity to Ireland.

In Britain the Roman occupation provides a closely datable horizon between the end of the Iron Age and the beginning of the Anglo-Saxon Period. In Ireland the absence of such a stratum makes it difficult to date the final phase of the Iron Age, particularly when one can find La Tène motifs surviving to a very late period, often with very little change of form. While it is accepted that AD 432 is the traditional date for the advent of Christianity in Ireland, the old ways continued and overlapped with the beginning of the Christian Period. It must be said that circumstances made the blending of old and new easier. The coming of Christianity ought to have initiated Ireland's entry into the larger European world, but at this very time Europe itself suffered the barbarian invasions and England fell to the Saxons. The Christian communities of Ireland became cut off from Europe for about a century and a half, and we have, therefore, little or no

169 Newgrange, Co. Meath, disc brooches of cast bronze, front surfaces gilded, of Romano-British type

knowledge of the process by which the insular pre-literate society which obtained in Ireland in the pagan Iron Age developed into the strong civilization of the Early Christian Period which was to earn her the title of 'The Island of Saints and Scholars'.

Appendix A
Radiocarbon dating

Until the method of dating organic materials by the radioactive carbon content was propounded in 1949 by Willard P. Libby of Chicago, archaeologists had to rely largely on relative chronologies and typologies. The radiocarbon dating method is based on the fact that carbon in all living matter, plant and animal, is ultimately derived from carbon dioxide (CO_2) in the atmosphere or in water. A small amount of this carbon consists of the radioactive isotope ^{14}C which is constantly produced in the atmosphere out of nitrogen, by nuclear reactions with neutrons in the so-called cosmic radiation.

Half-life

When life ceases, no more incorporation of ^{14}C takes place, and it begins to decay at a known rate. The half-life is the fixed length of time taken for half of a radioactive substance to decay into a non-radioactive one, the other half remaining. By international convention the half-life is still estimated at 5568 ± 30 years even though this figure has, in fact, been revised upwards.

It was originally assumed that the ratio of ^{14}C to ^{12}C (carbon) in the atmosphere had remained constant through time and that therefore the concentration of ^{14}C in the sample at death was always a known factor. This, together with the measurement of ^{14}C remaining in the sample submitted for analysis, enabled the age to be determined. It is now clear that there have been fluctuations in the concentration of ^{14}C in the atmosphere and this has led to complications. The basic principles on which the method are based, however, remain unchanged. Charcoal, wood, peat, human and animal bone and shell are the types of material usually sampled and at present the method is effective up to about 70,000 years ago.

Standard deviation

Owing to statistical problems involved in the measurement of the radioactivity remaining in the sample, the radiocarbon laboratories present ^{14}C dates with a plus/minus factor attached, known as the standard deviation. A date of 4000 ± 60 BP, for instance, implies that there is a 66 per cent chance that the date lies between 4060 and 3940, but there is a 95 per cent chance that the date may lie between twice the amount of the standard deviation (2 sigma), that is, 4120 and 3880. When quoting ^{14}C dates the standard deviation and the laboratory name and sample number must also be included. The date of the sample is expressed in radiocarbon years BP (before present time) and by international agreement 'present time' is taken as AD 1950.

Calibration

In the early stages of the radiocarbon 'revolution' it was believed that dates expressed in radiocarbon years were the same as solar or calendar ones. In the 1960s a series of wood samples of which the solar or calendar date had been established by tree-ring analysis (see p. 343) were submitted for radiometric determination and it was found that as a rule there was little or no parity between them, particularly for dates earlier than the second millennium BC. The tendency was for the ^{14}C dates to be too young (recent). A calibration table or curve based on tree-ring (dendrochronologic) sequence is therefore necessary in order to obtain the approximate equivalent in calendar years.

As a very rough-and-ready rule of thumb it may be said that uncalibrated dates in the first half of the third millennium BP are too recent by 100–200 years; in the fourth millennium BP by 200–500+ years; and in the fifth millennium BP by 500–800 years (Burgess 1980, 18).

Uncalibrated radiocarbon dates

According to the British convention and one that has been widely used in Ireland also, uncalibrated radiocarbon dates tend to be expressed in lower case 'bp', 'bc' and 'ad', upper case symbols being used for calibrated or calendar dates. This conflicts with international convention, whereby all raw radiocarbon dates are expressed as BP, and CAL.BC/CAL.AD represents the date ranges of calibrated radiocarbon dates (see Appendix D). Now that a calibration curve of radiocarbon dates spanning the last seven millennia is available (Pearson *et al.* 1986) it is possible to convert raw radiocarbon dates into an estimate of real age, and 'all such dates in the last seven millennia should therefore be calibrated' (Baillie 1985, 19).

Appendix B
Dendrochronology (tree-ring analysis)

It is a matter of common observation that the cross-section of a tree trunk is made up of a series of rings, known as growth rings. In a temperate climate, one ring of cells is laid down every year, each distinctive in shape, the newest ring being immediately under the bark. The rings vary according to the climate prevailing in the particular area in any particular year but the number of rings determines the age of the tree.

The theory underlying the building up of a master tree-ring chronology is as follows: a series of growth rings from a tree of known age (for instance, a living tree) are correlated with a dead tree overlapping it in age (for example, historic timbers found in old buildings, etc.). The central rings (the oldest ones) of the tree of known date must be such as to match the outer ones (the youngest ones) of the dead tree. In turn, the central rings of the latter must correlate with the inner ones of a still older but partly contemporary specimen, and so on, backwards in time.

The usefulness of dendrochronology as a precise dating method is enormous as also is its contribution towards the calibration of radiocarbon dates. When samples of wood of which the calendar date has been ascertained through tree-ring analysis are radiocarbon-dated, the two sets of dates can be plotted and a calibration table or curve established. The method was pioneered in America. The Californian bristlecone pine is a tree known to be capable of surviving for

170 Diagram of overlapping tree-rings starting from a tree of known age (no. 1) (after S. De Laet)

thousands of years, and it was possible to build up a master chronology extending beyond 8,000 years ago. When samples of known dendrochronological age were submitted for radiocarbon analysis, discrepancies were found between the respective dates and these tended to increase the farther back in time they were.

There is no comparable long-lived species in Europe and the oak is the most useful substitute. On this basis a dendrochronology project was initiated in the Palaeoecology Centre at Queen's University Belfast at the end of the 1960s. Oak is particularly suitable in Ireland as it is the only native timber commonly available from both historic and archaeologic contexts and, in addition, sub-fossil oak is present in peat deposits. One of the problems, however, is the much shorter growth pattern compared with the American species; consequently, many more overlapping specimens are required to make a continuous sequence. The account of how this was achieved between the years 1975 and 1985 is given in Baillie 1985.

The team of workers at the Belfast Centre has now succeeded in building up a master chronology for the past 7,000 years and in providing a calibration curve or graph for the relevant radiocarbon dates. Precisely dated samples of Irish oaks for all periods back to 5000 BC were submitted to the Belfast Radiocarbon Laboratory for measurement. The radiocarbon dates when plotted against the dendro or calendar ones gave a calibration curve from which the true age of the ^{14}C samples could be read. The results were presented in the summer of 1985 at the 12th International Radiocarbon Conference held at Trondheim in Norway (Pearson *et al.* 1986).

The calibration of radiocarbon dates in Appendix D is based on this curve (Copyright Pearson *et al.* 1985, Radiocarbon Research Unit, Palaeoecology Centre, Queen's University, Belfast).

Appendix C
Pollen analysis

Pollen grains of trees, shrubs, grasses and flowers are well-nigh indestructible, particularly when they are incorporated in peat, lake sediments and similar anaerobic (oxygen-free) deposits and in acid soils. As the pollen of each species is different, by identifying the pollen grains under a high-powered microscope, the tree and plant associations which grew in the general area of the particular deposit can be established. The number of grains of each species in a sample is counted and the relative abundance or otherwise of the various groups for a sequence of samples enables the vegetational history of that location to be reconstructed. Since the environment can vary enormously between one location and another in close proximity, only broad vegetational changes are valid over large areas. However, while there is a variation in the vegetational sequence from one area to another, it is possible to construct local pollen assemblage zones for sample sites.

Various methods are used for taking the samples and the results are presented in pollen diagrams in the form of graphs or histograms. The technique is mainly used today in environmental studies. A series of samples taken from a particular location, such as a site being excavated, or its immediate vicinity, can document the ecological background.

The application of radiocarbon dating to organic material from pollen cores (samples) has in recent years given rise to the possibility of independent dating of the pollen assemblage zones determined by pollen analysis.

Appendix D
Calibration of radiocarbon dates
After Pearson *et al.* 1986; multiplication factor (MF) not applied;
95% outer probability range given

Site	Lab. no.	Radiocarbon date BP	Calibrated range (2 sigma) calendar years BC/AD
Annaghmare, Co. Armagh	UB-241	4395 ± 55	3320–2900 BC
Ardcrony, Co. Tipperary	GrN-9708	4675 ± 35	3630–3350 BC
Armagh, Castle Street	UB-283	1660 ± 80	AD 130–600
	UB-285	1430 ± 85	AD 430–760
Ashley Park, Co. Tipperary	GrN-11036	4765 ± 40	3670–3370 BC
Ballintruer More, Co. Wicklow	GrN-10469	4800 ± 70	3770–3370 BC
Ballyferriter, Co. Kerry	BM-2227A	5190 ± 110	4330–3720 BC
	BM-2228A	5620 ± 80	4710–4340 BC
Ballyglass, Ma.13, Co. Mayo	SI-1450	4680 ± 95	3690–3120 BC
	SI-1452	4480 ± 90	3490–2910 BC
Ma.14	SI-1460	4055 ± 130	2910–2190 BC
	SI-1461	4390 ± 100	3350–2700 BC
	SI-1463	4270 ± 90	3100–2610 BC
Ballykeel, Co. Armagh	UB-239	3350 ± 45	1860–1520 BC
Ballymacaldrack, Co. Antrim	UB-2029	4940 ± 50	3940–3640 BC
	UB-2030	5150 ± 90	4230–3720 BC
	UB-2045	4630 ± 130	3690–2920 BC

Site	Lab. no.	Radiocarbon date BP	Calibrated range (2 sigma) calendar years BC/AD
Ballynagilly, Co. Tyrone	UB-201	5165 ± 50	4210–3820 BC
	UB-555	4050 ± 50	2870–2460 BC
	UB-556	3860 ± 50	2490–2130 BC
	UB-557	3780 ± 70	2450–1980 BC
Ballyscullion, Co. Antrim	UB-116	5530 ± 60	4500–4240 BC
	UB-296	5815 ± 90	4940–4460 BC
Ballyveelish 2, Co. Tipperary	GrN-11445	2550 ± 130	980–390 BC
	GrN-11658	2770 ± 60	1130–810 BC
Ballyveelish 3	GrN-11656	2810 ± 90	1260–810 BC
	GrN-11657	3580 ± 50	2120–1770 BC
	GrN-11659	3485 ± 40	1940–1680 BC
Beaghmore, Co. Tyrone	UB-11	3485 ± 55	1970–1670 BC
	UB-163	2725 ± 55	1000–800 BC
Behy, Co. Mayo	UB-153F	3890 ± 110	2850–1980 BC
	UB-158F	3930 ± 105	2860–2130 BC
Behy/Glenulra, Co. Mayo	SI-1464	4460 ± 115	3500–2780 BC
Belderg Beg, Co. Mayo	SI-1470	4220 ± 95	3030–2500 BC
	SI-1471	3220 ± 85	1730–1310 BC
	SI-1473	3170 ± 85	1670–1220 BC
Carnanbane, Co. Derry	UB-534	4930 ± 80	3950–3530 BC
Carnkenny, Co. Tyrone	UB-599	2815 ± 50	1130–850 BC
Carrigillihy, Co. Cork	GrN-12916	3100 ± 50	1510–1220 BC
	GrN-12917	2810 ± 50	1130–840 BC

Site	Lab. no.	Radiocarbon date BP	Calibrated range (2 sigma) calendar years BC/AD
Carrowmore 4, Co. Sligo	LU-1840	5750 ± 85	4840–4370 BC
Carrowmore 7	LU-1441	5240 ± 80	4230–3970 BC
Carrowmore 27	LU-1698	5040 ± 60	3990–3700 BC
	LU-1808	5000 ± 65	3970–3650 BC
	LU-1810	4940 ± 85	3960–3530 BC
Carrowmore 26 (secondary)	LU-1584	2480 ± 55	800–400 BC
Cashelkeelty, Co. Kerry	UB-2413	5845 ± 100	4940–4470 BC
Clogher, Co. Tyrone	UB-837	3045 ± 75	1510–1020 BC
	UB-839	2630 ± 45	900–780 BC
	UB-844	1555 ± 45	AD 400–610
Coney Island, Co. Tyrone	UB-43	3350 ± 80	1880–1420 BC
Cullyhanna Lough, Co. Armagh	UB-341	3475 ± 75	2030–1540 BC
	UB-688	3305 ± 50	1740–1450 BC
Curraghatoor, Co. Tipperary	GrN-11660	2840 ± 35	1130–910 BC
Doogarymore, Co. Roscommon	GrN-5990	2315 ± 35	400–260 BC
	GrN-5991	2400 ± 35	760–390 BC
Dundrum, Co. Down	UB-412	4775 ± 140	3940–3120 BC
	UB-413	4565 ± 135	3640–2910 BC
Garrett Island, Lough Gur	D-39	4090 ± 140	3020–2190 BC
Goodland, Co. Antrim	D-46	4150 ± 200	3330–2140 BC
	UB-320E	4575 ± 135	3640–2910 BC

Site	Lab. no.	Radiocarbon date BP	Calibrated range (2 sigma) calendar years BC/AD
Island, Co. Cork	D-49	3110 ± 140	1730–990 BC
	GrN-10631	3050 ± 35	1410–1160 BC
	GrN-10632	3090 ± 30	1510–1270 BC
Kilgreany A, Co. Waterford	BM-135	4580 ± 150	3690–2900 BC
Killeens I, Co. Cork	C-877	3506 ± 230	2490–1310 BC
	GrN-11438	3115 ± 35	1510–1280 BC
Knocknarea, Co. Sligo	LU-1947	4250 ± 75	3030–2610 BC
Knowth, Site 8, Co. Meath	BM-1076	4852 ± 71	3780–3380 BC
Knowth, Site 16	BM-1078	4399 ± 67	3330–2790 BC
Langdale Pikes, Westmorland	BM-281	4680 ± 135	3780–2940 BC
	BM-676	4474 ± 52	3350–2920 BC
Lough Eskragh, Site A, Co. Tyrone	UB-965	2475 ± 45	790–400 BC
	UB-1472	2690 ± 45	960–800 BC
Lough Eskragh, Site B	UB-948	3105 ± 80	1520–1150 BC
Lough Eskragh, Site C	UB-950	2360 ± 45	750–290 BC
Lough Gur, Circle L, Co. Limerick	D-40	4410 ± 240	3690–2460 BC
	D-41	4690 ± 240	3980–2710 BC
Meadowlands, Co. Down	UB-471	3575 ± 70	2130–1750 BC
	UB-472	3795 ± 75	2460–1980 BC
	UB-473	3265 ± 80	1750–1400 BC
Milmorane, Co. Cork	D-68	4040 ± 150	3000–2130 BC
Moneen, Co. Cork	GrN-10629	3960 ± 60	2850–2280 BC
	GrN-11904	3755 ± 30	2310–2040 BC

Site	Lab. no.	Radiocarbon date BP	Calibrated range (2 sigma) calendar years BC/AD
Monknewtown, Co. Meath	UB-728	3810 ± 45	2450–2040 BC
	UB-734	3465 ± 80	2030–1530 BC
Mount Gabriel, Co. Cork	BM-2336	3130 ± 80	1610–1160 BC
	VRI-66	3450 ± 120	2120–1460 BC
Moynagh Lough, Co. Meath	GrN-11442	3460 ± 35	1890–1680 BC
	GrN-11443	5272 ± 60	4320–3970 BC
Newgrange (passage grave), Co. Meath	GrN-5462C	4425 ± 45	3320–2910 BC
	GrN-5463	4415 ± 40	3320–2910 BC
Newgrange (turf mound)	GrN-9057	4480 ± 60	3360–2920 BC
Newgrange (multiple arc)	GrN-6342	3885 ± 35	2490–2190 BC
	GrN-6344	4050 ± 40	2860–2460 BC
	UB-2394	3875 ± 90	2850–2040 BC
Oakbank crannog, L. Tay, Perthshire	GU-1323	2545 ± 55	830–410 BC
	GU-1463	2360 ± 60	760–260 BC
Rathtinaun, Lough Gara, Co. Sligo	D-53	2070 ± 130	390 BC–AD 210
	D-59	2150 ± 130	510 BC–AD 120
Rockmarshall, Co. Louth	I-5323	5470 ± 110	4530–4010 BC
Scrabo, Co. Down	UB-414E	2305 ± 70	750–190 BC
Shanballyedmond, Co. Tipperary	GrN-11431	4930 ± 60	3940–3540 BC
	GrN-11432	3475 ± 40	1930–1680 BC
Sutton, Co. Dublin	I-5067	5250 ± 110	4340–3790 BC
Townleyhall II, Co. Louth	BM-170	4680 ± 150	3780–2920 BC

Site	Lab. no.	Radiocarbon date BP	Calibrated range (2 sigma) calendar years BC/AD
Tully, Co. Fermanagh	UB-2115	4960 ± 85	3970–3540 BC
	UB-2119	4890 ± 65	3890–3520 BC
	UB-2120	4785 ± 85	3780–3360 BC

Bibliography

Abbreviations

JCHAS   *Journal of the Cork Historical and Archaeological Society*
JGAHS   *Journal of the Galway Archaeological and Historical Society*
JKAHS   *Journal of the Kerry Archaeological and Historical Society*
JRSAI   *Journal of the Royal Society of Antiquaries of Ireland*
PPS   *Proceedings of the Prehistoric Society*
PRIA   *Proceedings of the Royal Irish Academy*
UJA   *Ulster Journal of Archaeology*

Abercromby, J. 1912. *A Study of the Bronze Age Pottery of Great Britain and Ireland and its associated grave-goods*, Oxford.

Addyman, P. V. 1965. Coney Island, Lough Neagh: Prehistoric settlement, Anglo-Norman castle and Elizabethan native fortress. *UJA* 28, 78–101.

Anati, E. G. 1962. Dos nuevos rocas prehistoricas grabadas. *Ampurias* 24, 35–56.

1963. New petroglyphs at Derrynablaha, Co. Kerry. *JCHAS* 68, 1–15.

ApSimon, A. 1969. An Early Neolithic house in Co. Tyrone. *JRSAI* 99, 165–8.

1969a. The Earlier Bronze Age in the North of Ireland. *UJA* 32, 28–72.

1971. Ballynagilly. *Current Archaeology* 24, 11–13.

1976. Ballynagilly and the beginning and end of the Irish Neolithic. In *Acculturation and Continuity in Atlantic Europe*, fourth Atlantic Colloquium, Ghent, 1975, edited by S. J. de Laet, Brugge, 15–30.

Armstrong, E. C. R. 1917. The great Clare Find of 1854. *JRSAI* 47, 21–36.

1922. Some Irish Bronze Age finds. *PRIA* 36C, 134–49.

1924. The Early Iron Age, or Hallstatt Period in Ireland. *JRSAI* 54, 1–14.

1933. *Catalogue of Irish Gold Ornaments in the Collection of the Royal Irish Academy*, Stationery Office, Dublin.

Baillie, M. G. L. 1985. Irish dendrochronology and radiocarbon calibration. *UJA* 48, 11–23.

Barber, J. 1973. The orientation of the recumbent-stone circles of the south-west of Ireland. *JKAHS* 6, 26–39.

Barfield, L. H. 1969. Two Italian halberds and the question of the earliest European halberds. *Origini* 3, Rome, 67–83.

Barfield, L. and Hodder, M. 1981. Birmingham's Bronze Age. *Current Archaeology* 78, 198–200.

Bateson, J. D. 1973. Roman material from Ireland: a reconsideration. *PRIA* 73C, 21–97.

Bengtsson, H. and Bergh, S. 1984. The hut sites at Knocknarea North, Co. Sligo. In Burenhult 1984, 216–318.

Binchy, D. A. 1954. Secular institutions. In *Early Irish Society*, edited by M. Dillon, Dublin, 52–65.

Binchy, E. 1967. Irish razors and razor-knives of the Middle Bronze Age. In *North Munster Studies, essays in commemoration of Monsignor M. Moloney*, edited by E. Rynne, Limerick, 43–60.

Bradley, J. 1982–3. Excavations at Moynagh Lough, Co. Meath, 1980–1. *Ríocht na Midhe* 7, 12–32.

1984. Excavations at Moynagh Lough, 1982–3. *Ríocht na Midhe* 7, 86–93.

Brannon, N. F. 1984. An examination of a bronze cauldron from Raffrey Bog, Co. Down. *Journal of Irish Archaeology* 2, 51–7.

Bremer, W. 1926. A founder's hoard of the Copper Age at Carrickshedoge, Nash, Co. Wexford. *JRSAI* 56, 88–91.

Brindley, A., Lanting, J. N. and Mook, W. G. 1983. Radiocarbon dates from the Neolithic burials at Ballintruer More, Co. Wicklow, and Ardcrony, Co. Tipperary. *Journal of Irish Archaeology* 1, 1–9.

Burenhult, G. 1980. *The Archaeological Excavations at Carrowmore, Co. Sligo, Ireland, 1977–79*. Theses and papers in North European Archaeology 9, Institute of Archaeology, University of Stockholm.

1984. *The Archaeology of Carrowmore, Co. Sligo*. Theses and papers in North European Archaeology 14, Institute of Archaeology, University of Stockholm.

Burgess, C. B. 1969. Chronology and terminology in the British Bronze Age. *Antiquaries Journal* 49, 22–9.

1974. The Bronze Age. In *British Prehistory, a New Outline*, edited by C. Renfrew, London, 165–232.

1980. *The Age of Stonehenge*, London.

Butler, J. J. and van der Waals, J. D. 1966. Bell Beakers and early metal-working in the Netherlands. *Palaeohistoria* 12, 41–139.

Carney, J. 1975. The invention of the Ogom cipher. *Ériu* 26, 53–65.

Carson, R. A. G. and O'Kelly, C. 1977. A catalogue of the Roman coins from Newgrange, Co. Meath, and notes on the coins and related finds. *PRIA* 77C, 35–55.

Case, H. J. 1961. Irish Neolithic pottery: distribution and sequence. *PPS* 27, 174–233.

1969. Settlement patterns in the North Irish Neolithic. *UJA* 32, 3–26.

1973. A ritual site in north-east Ireland. In *Megalithic Graves and Ritual*, third Atlantic Colloquium, Moesgård, 1969, edited by G. Daniel and P. Kjaerum, Copenhagen, 173–96.

Case, H. J., Dimblebey, G. W., Mitchell, G. F., Morrison, H. E. S. and Proudfoot, V. B. 1969. Land use in Goodland townland, Co. Antrim, from Neolithic times until today. *JRSAI* 99, 39–53.

Caspari, W. A. 1983. Identification of seeds. In O'Kelly, M. J. *et al.*, 1983, 57.

Caulfield, S. 1973. Belderg Beg, Co. Mayo. In *Excavations 1973*, edited by T. G. Delaney, Ulster Museum, Belfast, 17–18.

1977. The beehive quern in Ireland. *JRSAI* 107, 104–38.

1978. Neolithic fields: the Irish evidence. In *Early Land Allotment in the British Isles*, BAR British Series 48, edited by H. C. Bowen and P. J. Fowler, Oxford, 137–43.

1983. The Neolithic settlement of North Connaught. In *Landscape Archaeology in Ireland*, BAR British Series 116, edited by T. Reeves-Smyth and F. Hamond, Oxford, 195–215.

Champion, T. 1971. The end of the Irish Bronze Age. *North Munster Antiquarian Journal* 14, 17–24.

Childe, V. G. 1949. *Prehistoric Communities of the British Isles*, London (First edition 1940).

Clark, J. G. D. 1965. Traffic in stone axe and adze blades. *The Economic History Review*, second series 18, 1–28.

Clarke, D. L. 1970. *The Beaker Pottery of Great Britain and Ireland*, I and II, Cambridge.

Clarke, R. R. and Hawkes, C. F. C. 1955. An iron anthropoid sword from Shouldham, Norfolk, with related Continental and British weapons. *PPS* 21, 198–227.

Cleary, R. M. 1983. Newgrange: the ceramic assemblage. In O'Kelly, M. J. *et al.*, 1983, 58–117.

1985. A Bronze Age cist grave at Pound, Portmagee, Co. Kerry. *JKAHS* 18, 215–23.

Coffey, G. 1904. Some monuments of the La Tène Period recently discovered in Ireland. *PRIA* 24C, 257–66.

1913. *The Bronze Age in Ireland*, Dublin.

Coghlan, H. H. and Case, H. J. 1957. Early metallurgy of copper in Ireland and Britain. *PPS* 23, 91–123.

Coghlan, H. H. and Raftery, J. 1961. Irish prehistoric casting moulds. *Sibrium* 6, Varese, 223–44.

Coles, J. M. 1962. European Bronze Age shields. *PPS* 28, 156–90.

1963. Irish Bronze Age horns and their relations with North Europe. *PPS* 29, 326–56.

1967. Some Irish horns of the Late Bronze Age. *JRSAI* 97, 113–17.

1971. Bronze Age spearheads with gold decoration. *Antiquaries Journal* 51, 94–5.

1971a. Dowris and the Late Bronze Age of Ireland: a footnote. *JRSAI* 101, 164–5.

1973. *Archaeology by Experiment*, London.

Collins, A. E. P. 1952. Excavations in the sandhills of Dundrum, Co. Down. *UJA* 15, 2–26.

1954. The excavation of a double horned cairn at Audleystown, Co. Down. *UJA* 17, 7–56.

1956. A stone circle on Castle Mahon Mountain, Co. Down. *UJA* 19, 1–10.

1957. Excavations at two standing stones in Co. Down. *UJA* 20, 37–42.

1957a. Excavations at the Giant's Ring, Ballynahatty, Co. Down. *UJA* 20, 44–50.

1959. Further investigations in the Dundrum sandhills. *UJA* 22, 5–20.

1959a. Further work at Audleystown long cairn, Co. Down. *UJA* 22, 21–7.

1965. Ballykeel dolmen and cairn, Co. Armagh. *UJA* 28, 47–70.

1976. Dooey's Cairn, Ballymacaldrack, Co. Antrim. *UJA* 39, 1–7.

1981. The flint javelin heads of Ireland. In *Irish Antiquity, essays and studies presented to M. J. O'Kelly*, edited by D. Ó Corráin, Cork, 111–33.

355

1983. Excavations at Mount Sandel, Lower site, Coleraine, Co. Londonderry. *UJA* 46, 1–22.

Collins, A. E. P. and Seaby, W. A. 1960. Structures and small finds discovered at Lough Eskragh, Co. Tyrone. *UJA* 23, 25–37.

Collins, A. E. P. and Waterman, D. M. 1955. *Millin Bay, a Late Neolithic Cairn in Co. Down*, Archaeological Research Publication (N. Ireland), no. 4, HMSO, Belfast.

Collins, A. E. P. and Wilson, B. C. S. 1964. The excavation of a court cairn at Ballymacdermot, Co. Armagh, *UJA* 27, 3–22.

Conwell, E. A. 1873. *The Discovery of the Tomb of Ollamh Fodhla*, Dublin.

Corcoran, J. W. X. P. 1969. The Cotswold-Severn group. In *Megalithic Enquiries in the west of Britain: a Liverpool Symposium*, Liverpool, 13–104.

Cowen, J. D. 1967. The Hallstatt sword of bronze: on the Continent and in Britain. *PPS* 33, 377–454.

Crawford, H. S. 1924. The Dowris hoard. In Armstrong 1924, 14.

1925. The engraved bone objects found at Lough Crew, Co. Meath, in 1865. *JRSAI* 55, 15–29.

Cremin-Madden, A. 1969. The Beaker wedge tomb at Moytirra, Co. Sligo. *JRSAI* 99, 151–9.

Daniel, G. 1950. *The Prehistoric Chamber Tombs of England and Wales*, Cambridge.

1972. The origin of the megalithic tombs of the British Isles. In *Die Anfänge des Neolithikums vom Orient bis Nordeuropa*, edited by H. Schwabidessen, Cologne and Vienna, 233–47.

Daniells, M. J. and Williams, B. B. 1977. Excavations at Kiltierney Deerpark, Co. Fermanagh. *UJA* 40, 32–41.

Davies, O. 1938. Castledamph stone circle. *JRSAI* 68, 106–12.

1946. The cairn in Castle Archdale Deer-Park. *UJA* 9, 53–7.

Davies, O. and Radford, C. A. R. 1935–6. Excavation of the horned cairn of Clady Halliday. *Proceedings of the Belfast Natural History and Philosophical Society*, 76–85.

Deady, J. and Doran, E. 1972. Prehistoric copper mines, Mount Gabriel, Co. Cork. *JCHAS* 77, 25–7.

De Valera, R. 1960. The court cairns of Ireland. *PRIA* 60C, 9–140.

1965. Transeptal court cairns. *JRSAI* 95, 5–37.

1985. Excavation of the Mound of the Hostages. In Ó Ríordáin 1985, 27–8.

De Valera, R. and Ó Nualláin, S. 1961. *Survey of the Megalithic Tombs of Ireland I, Co. Clare*, Stationery Office, Dublin.

1964. *Survey of the Megalithic Tombs of Ireland II, Co. Mayo*, Stationery Office, Dublin.

1972. *Survey of the Megalithic Tombs of Ireland III, Counties Galway, Roscommon, Leitrim, Longford, Westmeath, Laoighis, Offaly, Kildare, Cavan*, Stationery Office, Dublin.

1982. *Survey of the Megalithic Tombs of Ireland IV, Counties Cork, Kerry, Limerick, Tipperary*, Stationery Office, Dublin.

Devoy, R. J. 1983. Quaternary shorelines in Ireland: an assessment of their implications for isostatic land movement and relative sea-level changes. In *Shorelines and Isostasy*,

[Academic Press,] edited by D. E. Smith and A. G. Dawson, London, 227–54.

Dillon, M. and Chadwick, N. K. 1967. *The Celtic Realms*, London.

Dixon, N. 1984. Oakbank Crannog. *Current Archaeology* 90, 217–20.

Doody, M. Unpublished. A Late Bronze Age enclosure at Ballyveelish 2, Co. Tipperary.
Unpublished. An Early Bronze Age cist burial at Ballyveelish 3, Co. Tipperary.
Unpublished. Three prehistoric huts at Curraghatoor, Co. Tipperary (Department of Archaeology, University College, Cork).

Duignan, M. V. 1976. The Turoe Stone: its place in insular La Tène art. In *Celtic Art in Ancient Europe: Five Protohistoric Centuries*, edited by P.-M. Duval and C. F. C. Hawkes, London, 201–17.

Eogan, G. 1962. Some observations on the Middle Bronze Age in Ireland. *JRSAI* 92, 45–60.
1963. A Neolithic habitation site and megalithic tomb at Townleyhall townland, Co. Louth. *JRSAI* 93, 37–81.
1964. The Later Bronze Age in the light of recent research. *PPS* 30, 268–351.
1964a. The excavation of a stone alignment and circle at Cholwichtown, Lee Moor, Devonshire. *PPS* 30, 25–38.
1965. *Catalogue of Irish Bronze Swords*, Stationery Office, Dublin.
1967. Knowth, Co. Meath, excavations. *Antiquity* 41, 302–4.
1967a. The associated finds of gold bar torcs. *JRSAI* 97, 129–75.
1968. Excavations at Knowth, Co. Meath. *PRIA* 66C, 299–400.
1969. Lock-rings of the Late Bronze Age. *PRIA* 67C, 93–148.
1972. 'Sleeve-fasteners' of the Late Bronze Age. In *Prehistoric Man in Wales and the West, essays in honour of Lily F. Chitty*, edited by F. Lynch and C. Burgess, Bath, 189–209.
1974. Pins of the Irish Late Bronze Age. *JRSAI* 104, 74–119.
1974a. Report on the excavations of some passage graves, unprotected inhumation burials and a settlement site at Knowth, Co. Meath. *PRIA* 74C, 11–112.
1977. Two decorated stones from Knowth, Co. Meath. *Antiquity* 51, 48–9.
1977a. The Iron Age–Early Christian settlement at Knowth, Co. Meath. In *Ancient Europe and the Mediterranean, studies presented in honour of Hugh Hencken*, edited by V. Markotic, England, 69–76.
1981. Gold discs of the Irish Late Bronze Age. In *Irish Antiquity, essays and studies presented to M. J. O'Kelly*, edited by D. Ó Corráin, Cork, 147–62.
1983. Ribbon torcs in Britain and Ireland. In *From the Stone Age to the Forty-five, studies presented to R. B. K. Stevenson*, edited by A. O'Connor and D. V. Clarke, Edinburgh, 87–126.
1983a. *Hoards of the Irish Later Bronze Age*, University College, Dublin.
1984. *Excavations at Knowth I*, Royal Irish Academy, Dublin.

Evans, E. E. 1935. Excavations at Aghnaskeagh, Co. Louth: Cairn A. *Co. Louth Archaeological Journal* 8, 235–55.
1938. Doey's Cairn, Dunloy, Co. Antrim. *UJA* 1, 59–78.
1939. Excavations at Carnanbane, Co. Londonderry: a double horned cairn. *PRIA* 45C, 1–12.

1953. *Lyles Hill, a Late Neolithic Site in Co. Antrim*, Archaeological Research Publication (N. Ireland), no. 2, HMSO, Belfast.

1966. *Prehistoric and Early Christian Ireland, a Guide*, London.

Evans, E. E. and Davies, O. 1933–4. Excavation of a chambered horned cairn at Ballyalton, Co. Down. *Proceedings of the Belfast Natural History and Philosophical Society*, 79–104.

Fahy, E. M. 1954. Bronze Age cemetery at Ballyenahan North, Co. Cork. *JCHAS* 59, 42–9.

1959. A recumbent-stone circle at Drombeg, Co. Cork. *JCHAS* 64, 1–27.

1961. A stone circle, hut and dolmen at Bohonagh, Co. Cork. *JCHAS* 66, 93–104.

1962. A recumbent-stone circle at Reenascreena South, Co. Cork. *JCHAS* 67, 59–69.

Flanagan, L. N. W. 1960. Bone beads and ring from Newgrange, Co. Meath. *UJA* 23, 61–2.

1969. Kiltierney, Co. Fermanagh. In *Excavations 1969*, edited by T. G. Delaney, Ulster Museum, Belfast.

Fox, A. 1954. Excavations at Kestor. *Trans. of the Devonshire Association for the Advancement of Science, Literature and Art* 86, 21–62.

Gaskell Brown, C. and Harper, A. E. T. 1984. Excavations on Cathedral Hill, Armagh, 1968. *UJA* 47, 109–61.

Giot, P.-R. 1960. *Brittany*, London.

Goddard, I. C. 1974. On Chronology. *Irish Archaeological Research Forum I*, Part 1, edited by B. G. Scott and D. E. Walshe, Queen's University, Belfast, 39–51.

Göransson, H. 1984. Pollen analytical investigations in the Sligo area. In Burenhult 1984, 154–93.

Greene, D. 1954. Early Irish literature. In *Early Irish Society*, edited by M. Dillon, Dublin, 22–35.

1964. The Celtic language. In *The Celts*, edited by J. Raftery, Cork, 9–21.

1966. *The Irish Language*, Cork.

1972. The chariot as described in Irish literature. In *The Iron Age in the Irish Sea Province*, CBA Research Report 9, edited by C. Thomas, London, 59–73.

1983. The coming of the Celts: the linguistic viewpoint. In *Proceedings of the sixth International Congress of Celtic Studies*, Galway, 1979, edited by G. Mac Eoin, Galway, 131–7.

Groenman-van Waateringe, W. 1983. The early agricultural utilization of the Irish landscape: the last word on the elm decline? In *Landscape Archaeology in Ireland*, BAR British Series 116, edited by T. Reeves-Smyth and F. Hamond, Oxford, 217–32.

1984. Pollen and seed analyses. In Eogan 1984, 325–9.

Groenman-van Waateringe, W. and Butler, J. J. 1976. The Ballynoe stone circle: excavations by A. E. van Giffen, 1937–8. *Palaeohistoria* 18, 73–110.

Groenman-van Waateringe, W. and Pals, J. P. 1982. Pollen and seed analyses. In O'Kelly 1982, 219–23.

Grogan, E. and Eogan, G. Forthcoming in *PRIA*. Lough Gur excavations by Seán P. Ó Ríordáin: further Neolithic and Beaker habitations on Knockadoon.

Harbison, P. 1968. Catalogue of Irish Early Bronze Age associated finds containing copper or bronze. *PRIA* 67C, 35–91.

1969. *The Daggers and the Halberds of the Early Bronze Age in Ireland*, Munich.

1969a. *The Axes of the Early Bronze Age in Ireland*, Munich.

1971. Hartmann's gold analyses: a comment. *JRSAI* 101, 159–60.

1971a. The old Irish 'chariot'. *Antiquity* 45, 171–7.

1973. The Earlier Bronze Age in Ireland. *JRSAI* 103, 93–152.

Hartmann, A. 1970. *Prähistorische Goldfunde aus Europa: Studien zu der Anfängen der Metallurgie* 3, Berlin.

1979. Irish and British gold types and their West European counterparts. In *The Origins of Metallurgy in Atlantic Europe*, fifth Atlantic Colloquium. Dublin, 1978, edited by M. Ryan, Dublin, 215–28.

Hartnett, P. J. 1951. A Neolithic burial from Martinstown, Kiltale, Co. Meath. *JRSAI* 81, 1–5.

1957. Excavation of a passage grave at Fourknocks, Co. Meath. *PRIA* 58C, 197–277.

Hartnett, P. J. and Prendergast, E. M. 1953. Bronze Age burials, Co. Wexford. *JRSAI* 83, 46–57.

Hawkes, C. F. C. 1940. *The Prehistoric Foundations of Europe to the Mycenaean Age*, London.

1982. The wearing of the brooch: Early Iron Age dress among the Irish. In *Studies on Early Ireland, essays in honour of M. V. Duignan*, edited by B. G. Scott, Belfast, 51–73.

Hawkes, C. F. C. and Smith, M. A. 1957. On some buckets and cauldrons of the Bronze and Early Iron Ages. *Antiquaries Journal* 37, 131–98.

Hawkes, J. 1941. Excavation of a megalithic tomb at Harristown, Co. Waterford. *JRSAI* 71, 130–47.

Heggie, D. 1981. *Megalithic Science*, London.

Hencken, H. O'N. 1935. A cairn at Poulawack, Co. Clare. *JRSAI* 65, 191–222.

1939. A long cairn at Creevykeel, Co. Sligo. *JRSAI* 69, 53–98.

1942. Ballinderry crannog, no. 2. *PRIA* 47C, 1–76.

1950. Lagore crannog: an Irish royal residence of the 7th to 10th centuries AD. *PRIA* 53C, 1–247.

Hencken, H. O'N. and Movius, H. L. 1934. The cemetery-cairn of Knockast. *PRIA* 41C, 232–84.

Henry, F. 1940. *Irish Art in the Early Christian Period*, London.

Herity, M. 1970. The prehistoric peoples of Kerry: a programme of investigation. *JKAHS* 3, 4–14.

1981. A Bronze Age farmstead at Glenree, Co. Mayo. *Popular Archaeology* 2, 36–7.

Herring, I. J. 1938. The forecourt, Hanging Thorn Cairn, Ballyutoag, Co. Antrim. *Proceedings of the Belfast Natural History and Philosophical Society*, 43–9.

Hillam, J. 1976. The dating of Cullyhanna hunting lodge. In *Irish Archaeological Research Forum* III, Part 1, edited by B. G. Scott and D. E. Walshe, Queen's University, Belfast, 17–20.

Hjelmqvist, H. 1980. An Irish cereal find from the transition between Bronze and Iron Age. In Burenhult 1980, 130–2.

Hodges, H. W. M. 1958. A hunting camp at Cullyhanna Lough near Newtown Hamilton, Co. Armagh. *UJA* 21, 7–13.

Holmes, P. 1979. The manufacturing technology of the Irish Bronze Age horns. In *The Origins of Metallurgy in Atlantic Europe*, fifth Atlantic Colloquium, Dublin, 1978, edited by M. Ryan, Dublin, 165–88.

Hubert, H. 1934. *The Rise of the Celts*, London.

Hunt, J. 1967. Prehistoric burials at Cahirguillamore, Co. Limerick. *North Munster Studies, essays in commemoration of Monsignor Michael Moloney*, edited by E. Rynne, Limerick, 20–42.

Iversen, J. 1941. Landnam i Danmarks Stenalder: land occupation in Denmark's Stone Age. *Danmarks Geologiske Undersøgelse*, Series II, 66, 1–68.

Jackson, J. S. 1968. Bronze Age copper mines on Mount Gabriel, west Co. Cork, Ireland. *Archaeologia Austriaca* 43, Vienna, 92–114.

1979. Metallic ores in Irish Prehistory: copper and tin. In *The Origins of Metallurgy in Atlantic Europe*, fifth Atlantic Colloquium, Dublin, 1978, edited by M. Ryan. Dublin, 107–25.

1984. The age of primitive copper mines on Mount Gabriel, west Co. Cork. *Journal of Irish Archaeology* 2, 41–50.

Jackson, K. H. 1964. *The Oldest Irish Tradition: a Window on the Iron Age*, Cambridge.

Jessen, K. 1949. Studies in Late Quaternary deposits and flora-history of Ireland. *PRIA* 52B, 85–290.

Jope, E. M. 1952. Porcellanite axes from factories in north-east Ireland: Tievebulliagh and Rathlin. *UJA* 15, 31–60.

Jope, E. M. and Wilson, B. C. S. 1957. The decorated cast bronze disc from the River Bann, near Coleraine. *UJA* 20, 95–102.

1957a. A burial group of the first century AD near Donaghadee, Co. Down. *UJA* 20, 73–95.

Jovanovič, B. 1979. The technology of primary copper mining in South-west Europe. *PPS* 45, 103–10.

Kavanagh, R. M. 1973. The Encrusted Urn in Ireland. *PRIA* 73C, 507–617.

1976. Collared and Cordoned Cinerary Urns in Ireland. *PRIA* 76C, 293–403.

1977. Pygmy Cups in Ireland. *JRSAI* 107, 61–95.

Kelly, E. 1974. Aughinish Island, Sites 1 and 2. In *Excavations 1974*, edited by T. G. Delaney, Ulster Museum, Belfast, 21.

Kilbride-Jones, H. E. 1950. The excavation of a composite Early Iron Age monument with 'henge' features at Lugg, Co. Dublin. *PRIA* 53C, 311–32.

1954. The excavation of an unrecorded megalithic tomb on Kilmashogue Mountain, Co. Dublin. *PRIA* 56C, 461–79.

Kitchin, F. T. 1983. The Carrowmore megalithic cemetery, Co. Sligo. *PPS* 49, 151–75.

Knowles, W. J. 1906. Stone axe factories near Cushendall. *JRSAI* 36, 383–94.

Lanting, J. N. and van der Waals, J. D. 1972. British Beakers as seen from the Continent. *Helinium* 12, 20–46.

Leask, H. G. 1937. The Long Stone, Punchestown, Co. Kildare. *JRSAI* 67, 250–2.

Leask, H. G. and Price, L. 1936. The Labbacallee megalith, Co. Cork. *PRIA* 43C,

77–101.

Lehane, D. 1983. Newgrange: the flint work. In O'Kelly *et al.* 1983, 118–67.

Le Roux, C.-T. 1981. Circonscription de Bretagne: Morbihan. *Gallia Préhistoire* 24, 420–2.

1983. Circonscription de Bretagne: Morbihan. *Gallia Préhistoire* 26, 332–3.

Lewis, S. 1837. *A Topographical Dictionary of Ireland* I, London.

L'Helgouach, J. 1965. *Les Sépultures Mégalithiques en Armorique*, Rennes.

Liversage, G. D. 1958. An island site at Lough Gur. *JRSAI* 88, 67–81.

1960. A Neolithic site at Townleyhall, Co. Louth. *JRSAI* 90, 49–60.

1968. Excavations at Dalkey Island, Co. Dublin, 1956–59. *PRIA* 66C, 53–233.

Longworth, I. H. 1961. The origins and development of the primary series in the Collared Urn tradition in England and Wales. *PPS* 27, 263–306.

Lowery, P. R., Savage, R. D. A. and Wilkins, R. L. 1971. Scriber, graver, scorper, tracer: notes on experiments in bronzeworking technique. *PPS* 37, Part 1, 167–82.

Lowry-Corry, D. 1933. The stones carved with human effigies on Boa Island and on Lustymore Island, in Lower Lough Erne. *PRIA* 41C, 200–4.

Lucas, A. T. 1958. *COWA Survey 1 (Republic of Ireland)*, Council for Old World Archaeology, Cambridge, Mass., 10–12.

1965. Washing and bathing in ancient Ireland. *JRSAI* 95, 65–114.

1972. Prehistoric block-wheels from Doogarymore, Co. Roscommon, and Timahoe East, Co. Kildare. *JRSAI* 102, 19–48.

1973. *Treasures of Ireland, Irish Pagan and Early Christian Art*, Dublin.

Lynch, A. 1976. The stone alignments of Cork and Kerry, unpublished MA thesis, National University of Ireland.

1981. *Man and Environment in South-west Ireland*, BAR British Series 85, Oxford.

1981a. Astronomical alignment or megalithic muddle? In *Irish Antiquity, essays and studies presented to M. J. O'Kelly*, edited by D. Ó Corráin, Cork, 21–7.

1982. Astronomy and stone alignments in SW Ireland. In *Archaeoastronomy in the Old World*, edited by D. Heggie, Cambridge, 205–13.

Lynch, F. M. 1969. The megalithic tombs of North Wales. In *Megalithic Enquiries in the West of Britain: A Liverpool Symposium*, Liverpool, 107–48.

1979. Ring-cairns in Britain and Ireland: their design and purpose. *UJA* 42, 1–19.

Lynn, C. J. 1973–4. The excavation of a ring-cairn in Carnkenny townland, Co. Tyrone. *UJA* 36 and 37, 17–31.

1982. The Dorsey and other linear earthworks. In *Studies on Early Ireland, essays in honour of M. V. Duignan*, edited by B. G. Scott, Belfast, 121–8.

1983. Some 'Early' ring-forts and crannogs. *Journal of Irish Archaeology* 1, 47–58.

Macalister, R. A. S. 1917. A report on some excavations recently conducted in Co. Galway. *PRIA* 33C, 505–10.

1922. On a stone with La Tène decoration recently discovered in Co. Cavan. *JRSAI* 52, 113–16.

1929. On some antiquities discovered upon Lambay. *PRIA* 38C, 240–6.

1931. *Tara, A Pagan Sanctuary of Ancient Ireland*, London.

1945. *Corpus Inscriptionum Insularum Celticarum I*, Stationery Office, Dublin.

Macalister, R. A. S., Armstrong, E. C. R. and Praeger, R. Ll. 1912. Bronze Age cairns on Carrowkeel Mountain, Co. Sligo. *PRIA* 29C, 311–47.

1913. A Bronze Age interment near Naas. *PRIA* 30C, 351–60.

MacKie, E. 1973. Duntreath. *Current Archaeology* 36, 6–7.

Mahr, A. 1934. A wooden cauldron from Altarte, Co. Monaghan. *PRIA* 42C, 11–29.

Mallory, J. P. 1982. The sword of the Ulster Cycle. In *Studies on Early Ireland, essays in honour of M. V. Duignan*, edited by B. G. Scott, Belfast, 99–114.

1985. *Navan Fort: the Ancient Capital of Ulster*, Ulster Archaeological Society, Belfast.

Mallory, J. P. and Hartwell, B. 1984. Donegore. *Current Archaeology* 92, 271–5.

Manning, C. 1985. A Neolithic burial mound at Ashleypark, Co. Tipperary. *PRIA* 85C, 61–100.

Manning, C. and Eogan, G. 1979. A find of gold torcs from Coolmanagh, Co. Carlow. *JRSAI* 109, 20–7.

Maryon, H. 1938. The technical methods of the Irish smiths in the Bronze and Early Iron Ages. *PRIA* 44C, 181–228.

May, A. McL. 1953. Neolithic habitation site, stone circles and alignments at Beaghmore, Co. Tyrone. *JRSAI* 83, 174–97.

Mitchell, G. F. 1947. An early kitchen-midden in Co. Louth. *Co. Louth Archaeological Journal* 11, 169–74.

1949. Further early kitchen-middens in Co. Louth. *Co. Louth Archaeological Journal* 12, 14–20.

1951. Studies in Irish Quaternary deposits, no. 7. *PRIA* 53B, 111–206.

1955. The Mesolithic site at Toome Bay, Co. Londonderry. *UJA* 18, 1–16.

1956. An early kitchen-midden at Sutton, Co. Dublin. *JRSAI* 86, 1–26.

1957. The Pleistocene Epoch. In *A View of Ireland*, British Association for the Advancement of Science, Dublin, 32–8.

1958. Radiocarbon dates and pollen zones in Ireland. *JRSAI* 88, 49–56.

1965. Littleton Bog, Tipperary: an Irish vegetational record. *Geological Society of America, Inc.*, special paper 84, 1–16.

1965a. Littleton Bog, Tipperary: an Irish agricultural record. *JRSAI* 95, 121–32.

1969. Pleistocene mammals in Ireland. *Bulletin of the Mammal Society* 31, 21–5.

1970. Some chronological implications of the Irish Mesolithic. *UJA* 33, 3–14.

1971. The Larnian culture: a minimal view. *PPS* 37, 274–83.

1972. Further excavation of the early kitchen-midden at Sutton, Co. Dublin. *JRSAI* 102, 151–9.

Mitchell, F. [G. F.] 1976. *The Irish Landscape*, London.

Mitchell, G. F. and Ó Ríordáin, S. P. 1942. Early Bronze Age pottery from Rockbarton Bog, Co. Limerick. *PRIA* 48C, 255–72.

Mitchell, G. F. and Sieveking, G. de G. 1972. Flint flake, probably of Palaeolithic Age, from Mell townland, near Drogheda, Co. Louth. *JRSAI* 102, 174–7.

MMA 1977. *Treasures of Early Irish Art, 1500 BC to 1500 AD*, The Metropolitan Museum of Art, New York.

Mogey, J. M. and Thompson, G. B. 1956. Excavation of two ring-barrows in

Mullaghmore townland, Co. Down. *UJA* 19, 11–28.

Movius, H. L. 1935. Kilgreany Cave, Co. Waterford. *JRSAI* 65, 254–96.

1942. *The Irish Stone Age*, Cambridge.

1953. Curran Point, Larne, Co. Antrim: the type-site of the Irish Mesolithic. *PRIA* 56C, 1–195.

Murphy, B. 1977. A handaxe from Dún Aenghus, Inishmore, Aran Islands, Co. Galway. *PRIA* 77C, 257–9.

NMI 1960. National Museum of Ireland, archaeological acquisitions in the year 1958. *JRSAI* 90, 1–40.

1961. National Museum of Ireland, archaeological acquisitions in the year 1959. *JRSAI* 91, 43–107.

1962. National Museum of Ireland, archaeological acquisitions in the year 1960. *JRSAI* 92, 139–73.

1973. National Museum of Ireland, archaeological acquisitions in the year 1970. *JRSAI* 103, 177–213.

O'Brien, W. 1986. Primitive ore exploitation in south-west Ireland, unpublished PhD thesis, National University of Ireland.

Ó Drisceóil, D. 1980. Fulachta Fiadha: A Study, unpublished MA thesis, National University of Ireland.

O'Kelly, C. 1973. Passage-grave art in the Boyne valley, Ireland. *PPS* 39, 354–82.

1978. *Illustrated Guide to Newgrange and the other Boyne Monuments*, Cork.

O'Kelly, M. J. 1944. Excavation of a cist-grave at Bealick, Macroom, Co. Cork. *JCHAS* 49, 116–21.

1949. An example of passage-grave art from Co. Cork. *JCHAS* 54, 8–10.

1950. Two burials at Labbamolaga, Co. Cork. *JCHAS* 55, 15–20.

1951. An Early Bronze Age ring-fort at Carrigillihy, Co. Cork. *JCHAS* 56, 69–86.

1952. Excavation of a cairn at Moneen, Co. Cork. *PRIA* 54C, 121–59.

1954. Excavations and experiments in Irish cooking-places. *JRSAI* 84, 105–55.

1958. A horned-cairn at Shanballyedmond, Co. Tipperary. *JCHAS* 63, 37–72.

1958a. A wedge-shaped gallery grave at Island, Co. Cork. *JRSAI* 88, 1–23.

1958b. A new group of rock-scribings in Co. Kerry. *JCHAS* 63, 1–4.

1960. A wedge-shaped gallery grave at Baurnadomeeny, Co. Tipperary. *JCHAS* 65, 85–115.

1961. The ancient Irish method of smelting iron. *Bericht über den V Internationalen Kongress für vor- und Frühgeschichte, Hamburg, 1958*, 459–61.

1961a. The Cork Horns, the Petrie Crown and the Bann Disc. *JCHAS* 66, 1–12.

1962. Two ring-forts at Garryduff, Co. Cork. *PRIA* 63C, 17–125.

1967. Two examples of megalithic art from the Newgrange area. *JRSAI* 97, 45–6.

1968. Surface-collected flints from two sites in the Boyne valley, Co. Meath. *JCHAS* 73, 114–19.

1969. Radiocarbon dates for the Newgrange passage-grave, Co. Meath. *Antiquity* 43, 140.

1969a. A stone mould for axeheads from Doonour, Bantry, Co. Cork. *JRSAI* 99, 117–24.

1970. Problems of Irish ring-forts. In *The Irish Sea Province in Archaeology and History*, Cambrian Archaeological Association, edited by D. Moore, Cardiff, 50–4.

1972. Further radiocarbon dates from Newgrange, Co. Meath. *Antiquity* 46, 226–7.

1981. The megalithic tombs of Ireland. In *Antiquity and Man, essays in honour of Glyn Daniel*, edited by J. D. Evans, B. Cunliffe and C. Renfrew, London, 177–90.

1982. *Newgrange, Archaeology, Art and Legend*, London.

O'Kelly, M. J. and C. 1981. *Illustrated Guide to Lough Gur, Co. Limerick*, Cork (first edition 1978).

1983. The tumulus of Dowth, Co. Meath. *PRIA* 83C, 135–90.

O'Kelly, M. J., Cleary, R. M. and Lehane, D. 1983. *Newgrange, Co. Meath, Ireland: the Late Neolithic/Beaker Period Settlement*, BAR International Series 190, edited by C. O'Kelly, Oxford.

O'Kelly, M. J., Lynch, F. M. and O'Kelly, C. 1978. Three passage-graves at Newgrange, Co. Meath. *PRIA* 78C, 249–352.

O'Kelly, M. J. and Shee, E. A. 1974. Bronze Age burials at Coolnahane and Ballinvoher, Co. Cork. *JCHAS* 80, 71–85.

O'Kelly, M. J. and Shell, C. A. 1979. Stone objects and a bronze axe from Newgrange, Co. Meath. In *The Origins of Metallurgy in Atlantic Europe*, fifth Atlantic Colloquium, Dublin, 1978, edited by M. Ryan, Dublin, 127–44.

Ó Nualláin, S. 1972. A Neolithic house at Ballyglass, near Ballycastle, Co. Mayo. *JRSAI* 102, 49–57.

1972a. Ballyglass, Co. Mayo. In *Excavations 1972*, edited by T. G. Delaney, Ulster Museum, Belfast, 20–2.

1975. The stone circle complex of Cork and Kerry. *JRSAI* 105, 83–131.

1976. The central court-tombs of the north-west of Ireland. *JRSAI* 106, 92–117.

1978. Boulder-burials. *PRIA* 78C, 75–114.

1979. The megalithic tombs of Ireland. *Expedition* 21, no. 3, University of Pennsylvania, 6–15.

1983. Irish portal tombs: topography, siting and distribution. *JRSAI* 113, 75–105.

1984. A survey of stone circles in Cork and Kerry. *PRIA* 84C, 1–77.

Ó Ríordáin, A. B. 1967. A Cordoned Urn burial at Laheen, Co. Donegal. *JRSAI* 97, 39–44.

1969. Prehistoric burials at the Bishop's Bush, Knockmant, Co. Westmeath. *JRSAI* 99, 125–31.

Ó Ríordáin, S. P. 1936. Excavations at Lissard, Co. Limerick and other sites in the locality. *JRSAI* 66, 173–85.

1937. The halberd in Bronze Age Europe: a study in prehistoric origins, evolution, distribution and chronology. *Archaeologia* 86, 195–321.

1939. Excavation of a stone circle and cairn at Kealkil, Co. Cork. *JCHAS* 44, 46–9.

1940. Excavations at Cush, Co. Limerick. *PRIA* 45C, 83–181.

1947. Excavation of a barrow at Rathjordan, Co. Limerick. *JCHAS* 52, 1–4.

1948. Further barrows at Rathjordan, Co. Limerick. *JCHAS* 53, 19–31.

1951. Lough Gur excavations: the great stone circle (B) in Grange townland. *PRIA* 54C, 37–74.

1952. Fragment of the Killycluggin Stone. *JRSAI* 82, 68.

1954. Lough Gur excavations: Neolithic and Bronze Age houses on Knockadoon. *PRIA* 56C, 297–459.

1955. A burial with faience beads at Tara, 1955. *PPS* 21, 163–73.

1985. *Tara, the Monuments on the Hill*, revised edition, Dundalk (first edition 1954).

Ó Ríordáin, S. P. and De Valera, R. 1952. Excavation of a megalithic tomb at Bally-edmonduff, Co. Dublin. *PRIA* 55C, 61–81.

Ó Ríordáin, S. P. and Lucas, A. T. 1946–7. Excavation of a small crannog at Rathjordan, Co. Limerick. *North Munster Antiquarian Journal* 5, 68–77.

Ó Ríordáin, S. P. and Ó Danachair, C. 1947. Lough Gur excavations: Site J, Knockadoon. *JRSAI* 77, 39–52.

Ó Ríordáin, S. P. and Ó hIceadha, G. 1955. Lough Gur excavations: the megalithic tomb. *JRSAI* 85, 34–50.

Österholm, I. and S. 1984. The kitchen middens along the coast of Ballysadare Bay. In Burenhult 1984, 326–45.

Owens, M. 1970. Early Iron Age hut circle, Scrabo townland, Co. Down. In *Excavations 1970*, edited by T. G. Delaney, Ulster Museum, Belfast, 9.

1971. Scrabo hut circle. In *Excavations 1971*, edited by T. G. Delaney, Ulster Museum, Belfast, 11.

Patrick, J. 1974. Midwinter sunrise at Newgrange, Co. Meath. *Nature* 249, 517–19.

Pearson, G. W., Pilcher, J. R., Baillie, M. G. L., Corbett, D. M. and Qua, F. 1986. High-precision 14C measurement of Irish Oaks to show the natural 14C variations from AD 1840–5210 BC. *Radiocarbon* 28, 911–34.

Piggott, S. 1965. *Ancient Europe from the Beginnings of Agriculture to Classical Antiquity*, Edinburgh.

1968. *The Druids*, London.

Piggott, S. and Powell, T. G. E. 1948–9. The excavation of three Neolithic chambered tombs in Galloway, 1949. *Proceedings of the Society of Antiquaries of Scotland* 83, 103–61.

Pilcher, J. R. 1969. Archaeology, palaeoecology, and 14C dating of the Beaghmore stone circle site. *UJA* 32, 73–91.

1975. Finds at Beaghmore stone circles, 1971 and 1972. *UJA* 38, 83–4.

Pilcher, J. R., Smith, A. G., Pearson, G. W. and Crowder, A. 1971. Land clearance in the Irish Neolithic: new evidence and interpretation. *American Association for the Advancement of Science* 172, 560–2.

Pollock, A. J. and Waterman, D. M. 1964. A Bronze Age habitation site at Downpatrick. *UJA* 27, 31–58.

Powell, T. G. E. 1938. Excavation of a megalithic tomb at Ballynamona Lower, Co. Waterford. *JRSAI* 68, 260–71.

1941. The excavation of a megalithic tomb at Carriglong, Co. Waterford. *JCHAS* 46, 55–62.

1958. *The Celts*, London.

1963. The chambered cairn at Dyffryn Ardudwy. *Antiquity* 37, 19–24.

1966. *Prehistoric Art*, London.

1973–4. The Sintra Collar and the Shannongrove Gorget: aspects of Late Bronze Age goldwork in the west of Europe. *North Munster Antiquarian Journal* 16, 3–13.

Prendergast, E. M. 1959. Prehistoric burial at Rath, Co. Wicklow. *JRSAI* 89, 17–29.

Proudfoot, V. B. 1954. Excavations at the Cathedral Hill, Downpatrick, Co. Down, preliminary report on excavations in 1953. *UJA* 17, 97–102.

1955. *The Downpatrick Gold Find*, Archaeological Research Publications (N. Ireland) no. 3, HMSO, Belfast.

1956. Excavations at the Cathedral Hill, Downpatrick, Co. Down: preliminary report on excavations in 1954. *UJA* 19, 57–72.

1957. A second gold find from Downpatrick. *UJA* 20, 70–2.

Radiocarbon 1961. Dublin Radiocarbon dates I, vol. 3, 32–8.

1968. British Museum Natural Radiocarbon Measurements V, vol. 10, 1–7.

1970. Belfast Radiocarbon dates I, vol. 12, 285–90.

1971. Belfast Radiocarbon dates IV, vol. 13, 450–67.

1973. Belfast Radiocarbon dates V, vol. 15, 212–28.

1973a. Smithsonian Institution Radiocarbon Measurements VIII, vol. 15, 388–424.

1974. Belfast Radiocarbon dates VII, vol. 16, 269–93.

1980. Dublin Radiocarbon dates III, vol. 22, 1028–30.

Raftery, B. 1969. Freestone Hill, Co. Kilkenny: an Iron Age hillfort and Bronze Age cairn (Excavation by G. Bersu 1948–9). *PRIA* 68C, 1–108.

1970. A decorated strap-end from Rathgall, Co. Wicklow. *JRSAI* 100, 200–11.

1971. Rathgall, Co. Wicklow: 1970 excavations. *Antiquity* 45, 296–8.

1972. Irish hillforts. In *The Iron Age in the Irish Sea Province*, CBA Research Report 9, edited by C. Thomas, London, 37–58.

1973. Rathgall: a Late Bronze Age burial in Ireland. *Antiquity* 47, 293–5.

1973a. Rathgall hillfort. In *Excavations 1973*, edited by T. G. Delaney, Ulster Museum, Belfast, 28–9.

1974. A prehistoric burial mound at Baunogenasraid, Co. Carlow. *PRIA* 74C, 277–312.

1974a. Rathgall. In *Excavations 1974*, edited by T. G. Delaney, Ulster Museum, Belfast, 28–9.

1976. Rathgall and Irish hillfort problems. In *Hillforts, Later Prehistoric Earthworks in Britain and Ireland*, edited by D. W. Harding, London, 339–57.

1976a. Dowris, Hallstatt and La Tène in Ireland: problems of the transition from bronze to iron. In *Acculturation and Continuity in Atlantic Europe*, fourth Atlantic Colloquium, Ghent, 1975, edited by S. J. de Laet, Brugge, 189–97.

1978. Excavations at Killycluggin, Co. Cavan. *UJA* 41, 49–54.

1981. Iron Age burials in Ireland. In *Irish Antiquity, essays and studies presented to M. J. O'Kelly*, edited by D. Ó Corráin, Cork, 171–204.

1982. Knobbed spearbutts of the Irish Iron Age. In *Studies on Early Ireland, essays in honour of M. V. Duignan*, edited by B. G. Scott, Belfast, 75–92.

1982a. Two recently discovered bronze shields from the Shannon Basin. *JRSAI* 112, 5–17.

1983. *A Catalogue of Irish Iron Age Antiquities*, Marburg.

1984. *La Tène in Ireland: Problems of Origin and Chronology*, Marburg.

Raftery, J. 1937–40. Early Iron Age decoration on the dolmen at Rathkenny, Co. Meath. *Co. Louth Archaeological Journal* 9, 258–61.

1938–9. The tumulus cemetery of Carrowjames, Co. Mayo, Part 1. *JGAHS* 18, 157–67.

1940–1. The tumulus cemetery of Carrowjames, Co. Mayo, Part 2, Carrowjames II. *JGAHS* 19, 16–88.

1941. Long stone cists of the Early Iron Age. *PRIA* 46C, 299–315.

1942. Knocknalappa crannog, Co. Clare. *North Munster Antiquarian Journal* 3, 53–72.

1944. A Neolithic burial in Co. Carlow. *JRSAI* 74, 61–2.

1944a. The Turoe Stone and the Rath of Feerwore. *JRSAI* 74, 23–52.

1960. A hoard of the Early Iron Age. *JRSAI* 90, 2–5.

1960a. *A Brief Guide to the Collection of Irish Antiquities, National Museum of Ireland*, Stationery Office, Dublin.

1961. The Derrinboy hoard, Co. Offaly. *JRSAI* 91, 55–8.

1963. A matter of time. *JRSAI* 93, 101–14.

1967. The Gorteenreagh hoard. In *North Munster Studies, essays in commemoration of Monsignor Michael Moloney*, edited by E. Rynne, Limerick, 61–71.

1971. Irish prehistoric gold objects: new light on the source of the metal. *JRSAI* 101, 101–5.

1972. Iron Age and Irish Sea: problems for research. In *The Iron Age in the Irish Sea Province*, CBA Research Report 9, edited by C. Thomas, London, 1–10.

1973. A Neolithic burial mound at Ballintruer More, Co. Wicklow. *JRSAI* 103, 214–19.

RIA 1983. *Treasures of Ireland, Irish Art 2000 BC–1500 AD*, Royal Irish Academy, Dublin.

Riley, F. T. 1936. Excavations in the townland of Pollacorragune, Tuam, Co. Galway. *JGAHS* 17, 44–64.

Ross, A. 1967. *Pagan Celtic Britain*, London.

Ryan, M. 1980. An Early Mesolithic site in the Irish midlands. *Antiquity* 54, 46–7.

1981. Poulawack, Co. Clare: the affinities of the central burial structure. In *Irish Antiquity, essays and studies presented to M. J. O'Kelly*, edited by D. Ó Corráin, Cork, 135–46.

Rynne, E. 1960. La Tène sword from near Lough Gara. *JRSAI* 90, 12–13.

1966. Bronze Age cemetery at Scarawalsh, Co. Wexford. *JRSAI* 96, 39–46.

1967. The Tau-cross at Killinaboy: Pagan or Christian? In *North Munster Studies, essays in commemoration of Monsignor Michael Moloney*, edited by E. Rynne, Limerick, 146–65.

1969. Grannagh, near Ardrahan, Co. Galway. In *Excavations 1969*, edited by T. G. Delaney, Ulster Museum, Belfast, 9.

1970. Oranbeg, Co. Galway. In *Excavations 1970*, edited by T. G. Delaney, Ulster Museum, Belfast, 10.

1972. Celtic stone idols in Ireland. In *The Iron Age in the Irish Sea Province*, CBA Research Report 9, edited by C. Thomas, London, 79–98.

1976. The La Tène and Roman finds from Lambay, Co. Dublin: a re-assessment. Colloquium on Hiberno-Roman relations and material remains. *PRIA* 76C, 231–44.

1983–4. Military and civilian swords from the River Corrib. *JGAHS* 39, 5–26.

Scott, B. G. 1976. The occurrence of platinum as a trace element in Irish gold: comments on Hartmann's gold analyses. *Irish Archaeological Research Forum* 3, Part 2, edited by B. G. Scott and D. E. Walshe, Queen's University, Belfast, 21–4.

Scott, B. G. and Francis, P. J. 1981. Native copper in north-east Ulster: a contributory factor in the establishment of the earliest Irish metalworking? In *Irish Antiquity, essays and studies presented to M. J. O'Kelly*, edited by D. Ó Corráin, Cork, 28–41.

Selkirk, A. and W. and Waterman, D. M. 1970. Navan Fort. *Current Archaeology* 22, 304–8.

Shee, E. A. 1968. Some examples of rock-art from Co. Cork. *JCHAS* 73, 144–51.

1972. Three decorated stones from Loughcrew, Co. Meath. *JRSAI* 102, 224–33.

Shee Twohig, E. A. 1981. *The Megalithic Art of Western Europe*, Oxford.

Shee, E. A. and Evans, D. M. 1965. A standing stone in the townland of Newgrange, Co. Meath. *JCHAS* 70, 124–30.

Shee, E. A. and O'Kelly, M. J. 1971. The Derrynablaha 'shield' again. *JCHAS* 76, 72–6.

Sheridan, A. 1983. A reconsideration of the origins of Irish metallurgy. *Journal of Irish Archaeology* 1, 11–19.

Forthcoming in *UJA* 49. Porcellanite artifacts: a new survey.

Simpson, D. D. A. and Thawley, J. E. 1972. Single grave art in Britain. *Scottish Archaeological Forum* 4, 81–104.

Singh, G. and Smith, A. G. 1966. The post-glacial marine transgression in Northern Ireland – conclusions from estuarine and 'raised beach' deposits: a contrast. *Palaeobotanist* 15, 230–4.

Smith, A. G. 1975. Neolithic and Bronze Age landscape changes in Northern Ireland. In *The Effect of Man on the Landscape: the Highland Zone*, CBA Research Report 11, edited by J. G. Evans, S. Limbrey and H. Cleere, London, 64–74.

Smith, A. G. and Collins, A. E. P. 1971. The stratigraphy, palynology and archaeology of diatomite deposits at Newferry, Co. Antrim, N. Ireland. *UJA* 34, 3–25.

Smith, A. G., Pilcher, J. R. and Pearson, G. W. 1971. New radiocarbon dates from Ireland. *Antiquity* 45, 97–102.

Smith, A. G., Gaskell Brown, C., Goddard, I. C., Goddard, A., Pearson, G. W. and Dresser, P. Q. 1981. Archaeology and environmental history of a barrow at Pubble, Loughermore townland, Co. Londonderry. *PRIA* 81C, 29–66.

Smith, I. F. and Simpson, D. D. A. 1966. Excavation of a round barrow on Overton Hill, N. Wiltshire. *PPS* 32, 122–55.

Somerville, B. T. 1930. Five stone circles in west Cork. *JCHAS* 35, 70–85.

Sweetman, P. D. 1971. An earthen enclosure at Monknewtown, Slane: preliminary report. *JRSAI* 101, 135–40.

1976. An earthen enclosure at Monknewtown, Slane, Co. Meath. *PRIA* 76C, 25–73.

1985. A late Neolithic/Early Bronze Age pit circle at Newgrange, Co. Meath. *PRIA* 85C, 195–221.

Taylor, J. J. 1968. Early Bronze Age gold neck-rings in Western Europe. *PPS* 34, 259–65.

1970. Lunulae reconsidered. *PPS* 36, 38–81.

Thom, A. 1967. *Megalithic Sites in Britain*, Oxford.

Tierney, J. J. 1960. The Celtic ethnography of Posidonius. *PRIA* 60C, 189–275.

Timoney, M. A. 1984. Earthen burial sites on the Carrowmore peninsula, Co. Sligo. In Burenhult 1984, 319–25.

Tratman, E. K. 1928. Report on excavations in Ireland in 1928. *University of Bristol Spelaeological Society* 3, 109–53.

Waddell, J. 1970. Irish Bronze Age cists: a survey. *JRSAI* 100, 91–139.

1974–5. The Bronze Age burials of Co. Galway. *JGAHS* 34, 6–20.

1976. Cultural interaction in the insular Early Bronze Age: some ceramic evidence. In *Acculturation and Continuity in Atlantic Europe*, fourth Atlantic Colloquium, Ghent, 1975, edited by S. J. de Laet, Brugge, 284–95.

1978. The invasion hypothesis in Irish prehistory. *Antiquity* 52, 121–8.

1982. From Kermaria to Turoe? In *Studies on Early Ireland, essays in honour of M. V. Duignan*, edited by B. G. Scott, Belfast, 21–8.

Wailes, B. 1970. Excavations at Dún Ailinne, Co. Kildare: 1968–9 interim report. *JRSAI* 100, 79–90.

1971–6. Knockaulin: excavations at Dún Ailinne. *Journal of the Co. Kildare Archaeological Society* 15, 234–41; 345–58.

1976. Dún Ailinne: an interim report. In *Hillforts, Later Prehistoric Earthworks in Britain and Ireland*, edited by D. W. Harding, London, 319–38.

Wainwright, G. J. 1969. A review of henge monuments in the light of recent research. *PPS* 35, 112–33.

Wakeman, W. F. 1883–4. The *trouvaille* from Lisnacroghera, near Broughshane, Co. Antrim. *JRSAI* 16, 375–408.

1889. On the crannog and antiquities of Lisnacroghera, near Broughshane, Co. Antrim. *JRSAI* 19, 96–106.

1890–1. On the crannog and antiquities of Lisnacroghera, near Broughshane, Co. Antrim. *JRSAI* 21, 242–5; 637–75.

Wallace, P. F. 1977. A prehistoric burial cairn at Ardcrony, Nenagh, Co. Tipperary. *North Munster Antiquarian Journal* 19, 3–20.

Walshe, P. T. 1941. The excavation of a burial cairn on Baltinglass Hill, Co. Wicklow. *PRIA* 56C, 221–36.

Warner, R. B. 1969. Clogher Hill Fort, Co. Tyrone. In *Excavations 1969*, edited by T. G. Delaney, Ulster Museum, Belfast, 3.

1971. Clogher Demesne. In *Excavations 1971*, ed. Delaney, 23–4.

1972. Clogher Demesne. In *Excavations 1972*, ed. Delaney, 27–8.

1972a. The excavations at Clogher and their context. *Clogher Record* 8, 5–12.

1973. Clogher Demesne. In *Excavations 1973*, ed. Delaney, 25.

1974. Clogher Demesne. In *Excavations 1974*, ed. Delaney, 27.

1975–6. Clogher Demesne. In *Excavations 1975–6*, ed. Delaney, 18.

1976. Some observations on the context and importation of exotic material in Ireland, from the first century BC to the second century AD. Colloquium on Hiberno-Roman relations and material remains. *PRIA* 76C, 267–92.

1982. The Broighter hoard: a reappraisal, and the iconography of the collar. In *Studies on Early Ireland, essays in honour of M. V. Duignan*, edited by B. G. Scott, Belfast, 29–38.

Warner, R. and Meighan, I. G. 1981. Dating Irish glass beads by chemical analysis. In *Irish Antiquity, essays and studies presented to M. J. O'Kelly*, edited by D. Ó Corráin, Cork, 52–66.

Warren, W. P. 1979. The stratigraphical position of the Gortian Interglacial deposits. *The Geological Survey of Ireland Bulletin* 2, no. 4, 315–32.

Waterman, D. M. 1964. The stone circle, cairn and alignment at Drumskinny, Co. Fermanagh. *UJA* 27, 23–30.

1965. The court cairn at Annaghmare, Co. Armagh. *UJA* 28, 3–46.

1968. Cordoned Urn burials and ring-ditch at Urbalreagh, Co. Antrim. *UJA* 31, 25–32.

1975. The Derrykeighan Stone. *UJA* 38, cover illustration.

1978. The excavation of a court cairn at Tully, Co. Fermanagh. *UJA* 41, 3–14.

Wijngaarden-Bakker, L. H. van 1974. The animal remains from the Beaker settlement at Newgrange, Co. Meath: first report. *PRIA* 74C, 313–83.

1986. The animal remains from the Beaker settlement at Newgrange, Co. Meath: final report. *PRIA* 86C, 17–111.

Williams, B. B. 1978. Excavations at Lough Eskragh, Co. Tyrone. *UJA* 41, 37–48.

Willmot, G. F. 1938. Three burial sites at Carbury, Co. Kildare. *JRSAI* 68, 130–42.

1938–9. Two Bronze Age burials at Carrowbeg North, Belclare, Co. Galway. *JGAHS* 18, 121–40.

Windle, B. C. A. 1912. Megalithic remains surrounding Lough Gur, Co. Limerick. *PRIA* 30C, 283–306.

Woodman, P. C. 1974. The chronological position of the latest phases of the Larnian. *PRIA* 74C, 237–58.

1976. The Irish Mesolithic/Neolithic transition. In *Acculturation and Continuity in Atlantic Europe*, fourth Atlantic Colloquium, Ghent, 1975, edited by S. J. de Laet, Brugge, 296–307.

1977. Recent excavations at Newferry, Co. Antrim. *PPS* 43, 155–99.

1978. *The Mesolithic in Ireland*, BAR British Series 58, Oxford.

1981. A Mesolithic camp in Ireland. *Scientific American* 245, 120–32.

1985. *Excavations at Mount Sandel 1973–77, Co. Londonderry*, Northern Ireland monographs: no. 2. Department of the Environment for Northern Ireland, HMSO, Belfast.

Woodman, P. C., Duggan, M. A. and McCarthy, A. 1984. Excavations at Ferriter's Cove: preliminary report. *JKAHS* 17, 5–19.

Wright, W. B. and Muff, H. B. 1904. The pre-glacial raised beach of the south coast of Ireland. *Scientific Proceedings of the Royal Dublin Society* 10, 250–308.

Index

References to figures are italicized